HANDBOOKS

D1132453

WALT DISNEY WORLD® & ORLANDO

LAURA REILEY

© DISNEY

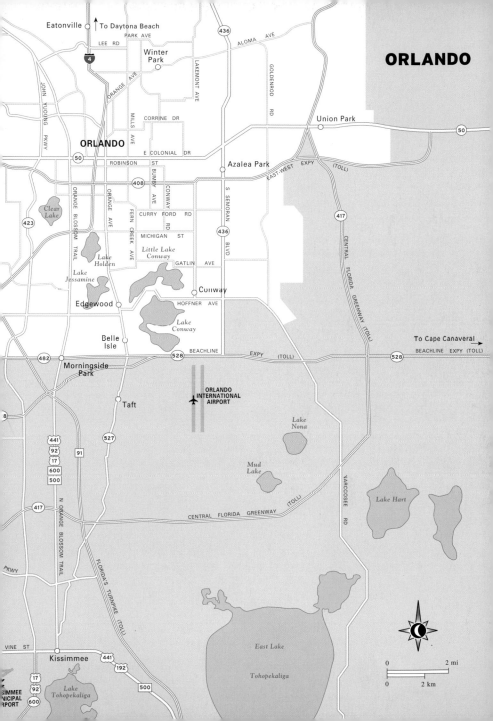

DISCOVER WALT DISNEY WORLD & ORLANDO

Orlando, much like Las Vegas, draws people in with the lure of fantasy, magic, and fun – but with fewer vices or ladies in feathered headdresses.

Walt Disney World Resort features a brand of magic and fun that is by and large wholesome as well as ever-changing, as theme parks add, revise, and try to outdo the competition. What holds it all together and gives it a sense of continuity is the destination's ongoing flair at appealing to many different kinds of people.

There is no Disney "type." Nuclear families come from all corners of the globe to visit Disney World and Orlando's other tourist attractions, but they are just part of the story. People come to Orlando on business and for pleasure. People come with children and without. People come as children and in their golden years. Some people come grudgingly; others visit every chance they get.

it's a small world at the Magic Kingdom® Park

© DISNEY

In Vegas, what happens there, stays there, usually subdued in a fog of excess. But what happens in Orlando is the content of scrapbooks, the subject of family holiday photo cards, fodder for countless "what I did on my summer vacation" essays, and maybe most important of all, the stuff of oft-recounted family memories.

By way of evidence, or maybe in the name of my own "what I did on my summer vacation" essay, I submit my own first experience at Disney's Animal Kingdom. I had a single day and a half-baked plan to go with myself (a devoted riding-the-rides theme-park veteran), my daughter (ditto, only younger), my mother (no thanks on the rides), her brother (69, no rides, a die-hard aesthete), and my other uncle (79, maybe rides, if they're tame, also a fairly highbrow guy). Everyone in our party is ambulatory, but at different paces and with different levels of enthusiasm for theme parks.

Expedition Everest in Disney's Animal Kingdom®

© DISNEY

I'm the most type-A, so I consult the park map: I'll definitely run to Expedition Everest and get our FASTPASS so we get an assigned time and bypass the major lines, while everyone else enjoys the Flights of Wonder live bird show. We reconvene and return to slowly circle The Tree of Life and take in the 3-D Pixar movie *It's Tough to Be a Bug!* We're all charmed, the older contingent taken by surprise by the squirts of water and other special effects.

It's time for Everest. Only one of our party balks, choosing to sit on a bench in the lovely Tibetan section of Asia. After our pulses return to normal, we grab a quick order of french fries (all right, not the best choice) so we can slide in line at Kilimanjaro Safaris. The line's fairly long, but there's a lot to see in the queue. We all board and the five of us have a tremendous time – it's gorgeous and exciting, with a story line that allows you to suspend disbelief and, for a while, almost believe you're in Africa. We even consult the species chart overhead and check off animals along the way.

Some of them are flagging, I can tell. They're muttering; they're getting mutinous. All we need to do is sit for a bit at Safari Barbecue

SeaWorld animal trainer Eric Lang and his first mate, Clyde the sea lion.
COURTESY OF SEA WORLD ORLANDO

to regroup and refuel, and they're back with me. But it's getting hot – and Kali River Rapids is the answer (at least for some of us). We split up: The ladies go to Kali; the gentlemen view the animals on the nearby Maharajah Jungle Trek.

We need to sit down, get out of the sun. It's time for the new puppets-and-black-light show, *Finding Nemo*. The line is long, but it will be spectacular and we must endure. We make it, and the show is worth every bit of shuffling and huffing.

As the older three in our contingent shop and enjoy a cold drink, the two youngest zip to DinoLand U.S.A. for a few guilty-pleasure, midway-style rides. Afterward, we all find each other and together marvel at the afternoon Mickey's Jammin' Jungle Parade – a good way to end the day. We take the tram back to our car, still talking about the huge African animal puppets.

What makes Walt Disney World Resort and Orlando the number one tourist attraction in the world is their ability to entertain very different people, with very different tastes and needs, simultaneously. Babies, teenagers, singles, seniors, those who speak no

Gatorland, Kissimmee

COURTESY OF GATORLAND

English, the preternaturally childlike and the nearly humorless – Orlando's attractions can leave just about anyone smiling, wide-eyed, and whooping.

Disney sets the tone for all other theme parks and visitor attractions in Orlando. At each of Orlando's attractions – not just the four Disney parks, but Universal Orlando Resort, SeaWorld Orlando, the water parks, "old-school" attractions such as Gatorland or Cypress Gardens, the dozens of smaller, half-day attractions along International Drive, or even the cultural allures of Downtown Orlando – fun has been calibrated to appeal to the differently abled and the differently interested. What started as a black and white mouse introduced at the Colony Theater in New York on November 18, 1928, has become a whole industry devoted to re-discovering the unfulfilled dreams of generations of visitors. As the sage Cinderella once said, "A dream is a wish your heart makes." Orlando offers the opportunity to make that wish come true.

gingerbread men at Mickey's Very Merry Christmas Parade at the Magic Kingdom® Park

© DISNEY

Contents

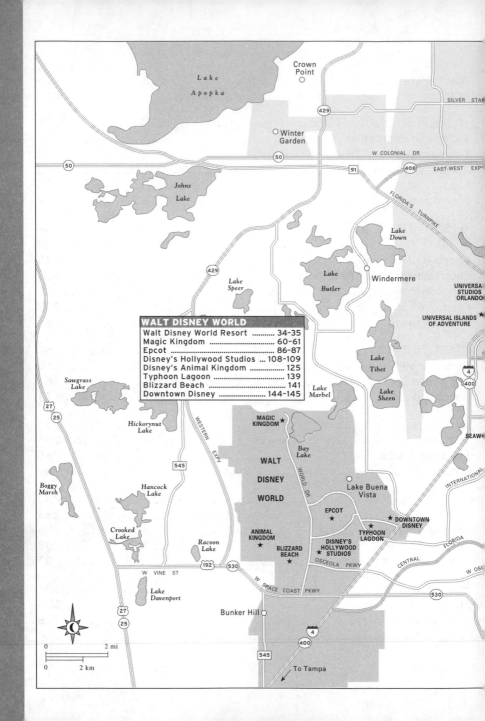

Crown
Point

Lake
Apopka

SILVER STA

O Winter
Garden

W COLONIAL DR

50

91

408

EAST-WEST EXP

FLORIDA'S TURNPIKE

Johns
Lake

Lake
Down

429

Lake
Speer

Lake
Butler

Windermere

UNIVERSA
STUDIOS
ORLANDO

UNIVERSAL ISLANDS
OF ADVENTURE

Lake
Tibet

4
400

Sawgrass
Lake

Lake
Marbel

Lake
Sheen

27
25

Hickorynut
Lake

WESTERN EXPY

MAGIC
KINGDOM ★

Bay
Lake

WALT

545

DISNEY

Boggy
Marsh

Hancock
Lake

WORLD

WORLD DR

Lake Buena
Vista

SEAW

INTERNATIONAL

EPCOT
★

★ DOWNTOWN
DISNEY

Crooked
Lake

Racoon
Lake

ANIMAL
KINGDOM
★

BLIZZARD
BEACH
★

DISNEY'S
HOLLYWOOD
STUDIOS
★

TYPHOON
LAGOON

OSCEOLA PKWY

FLORIDA

192

530

W VINE ST

W SPACE COAST PKWY

CENTRAL

W OSC

530

27
25

Lake
Davenport

Bunker Hill O

4
400

0   2 mi

545

0   2 km

To Tampa

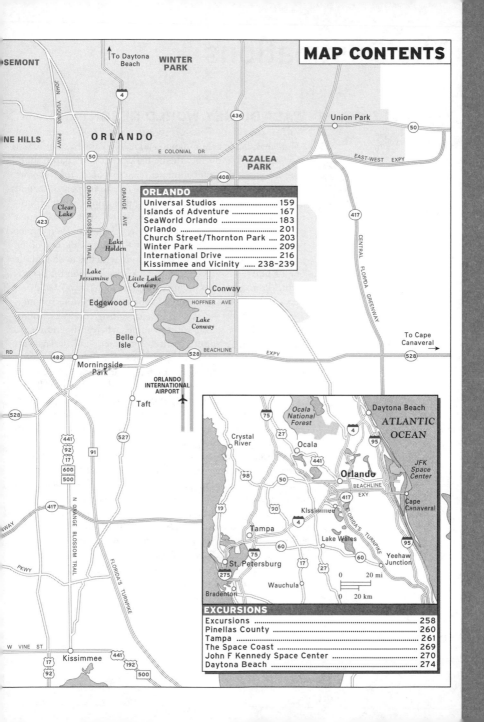

MAP CONTENTS

The Destinations

© DISNEY

WALT DISNEY WORLD RESORT

Walt Disney World Resort is spread across 27,000 acres, about 43 square miles, half in Orlando and half in Lake Buena Vista. It encompasses four distinct theme parks, two water parks, shopping and entertainment complexes, 22 resort hotels (plus another 10 that aren't Disney owned, but are on the property), six golf courses, a sports complex, and many other things. For the uninitiated, who have a vague notion that Walt Disney World is that park with the castle in the middle, thorough investigation cannot be undertaken on a single day. **Magic Kingdom,** the first of the parks, is divided into seven themed lands, with lots to do for little ones. **Epcot,** what used to be EPCOT, an acronym for Experimental Prototype Community of Tomorrow, has two "worlds"— Future World, which is mostly about science and technology, and World Showcase, pavilions representing countries around the world. Epcot appeals most to adults, whereas the third park, **Disney's Hollywood Studios,** lures teens and tweens with its movie-themed rides and attractions. The fourth and newest park, **Disney's Animal Kingdom,** is not a zoo but rather an animal-themed assemblage of exhibits and thrill rides. All four parks tend to host a festive afternoon parade, an evening celebration (many with fireworks), and special events throughout the year. Costumed Disney characters mill around at all four parks for photo ops and autograph signing.

Typhoon Lagoon and **Blizzard Beach** are the two themed water parks, each requiring separate entry. **Downtown Disney** is a shopping and dining complex with an adult nightclub area called Pleasure Island, a huge virtual-reality and video arcade called DisneyQuest, and a theater in which Cirque du Soleil performs La Nouba. The **Wide World of Sports** complex hosts sports events such as the Atlanta Braves spring training, the Richard Petty Driving Experience enables you to drive a real race car, and fifteen miles south The Nature Conservancy oversees **Disney Wilderness Preserve.**

© 2007 UNIVERSAL ORLANDO.
ALL RIGHTS RESERVED.

UNIVERSAL ORLANDO RESORT

Universal Orlando Resort began with an idea: Build a working film and TV studio that is also a theme park in which guests are immersed in the world of the movies, dynamic rides, attractions, 3-D movies, and exhibits celebrating cinema. In 1999, there sprung a second park, **Islands of Adventure,** three resort hotels, and a dining and nightlife complex called **CityWalk.** The tagline for Universal Studios Florida is "Ride the Movies;" for Islands of Adventure, it's "Live the Adventure." The distinction is a little blurry, but what you need to know is that Islands of Adventure has some of the most hair-raising, sweaty-palmed thrill rides in all of Orlando, cases in point being Incredible Hulk Coaster and The Amazing Adventures of Spider-Man. And whereas Disney's Hollywood Studios focuses a little more on nostalgic old films, the efforts at Universal Studios are more inspired by popular films, divided into six themed areas within the park. Islands of Adventure draws from classic comics and comic book heroes.

SEAWORLD ORLANDO

COURTESY OF SEAWORLD ORLANDO

It's not an amusement park, but it's certainly no aquarium or zoo. SeaWorld Orlando is a celebration of sea life, with a special emphasis on those amazingly smart marine mammals. Shamu and friends are put through their paces in a variety of shows that are constantly evolving. The current killer whale show, Believe, and the dolphin show, Blue Horizons, are offered several times daily along with other live shows that make up the core of the park's attractions. There are a couple of thrill rides, but the park's real strengths are the animal shows and educational walk-throughs of animal environments.

Just across the road is its more upscale sibling, **Discovery Cove.** Limited to 1,000 guests per day by reservation, the lush Caribbean resort allows visitors to swim with a dolphin, snorkel along a saltwater coral reef, frolic among stingrays, or just loll on a chaise lounge on a sandy beach.

COURTESY OF ORLANDO/ORANGE COUNTY CONVENTION & VISITORS BUREAU, INC.

DOWNTOWN ORLANDO AND WINTER PARK

For a stiff shot of culture, head to Downtown Orlando. Yes, Orlando has one, about 20 minutes northeast of all the tourist sprawl. The Downtown Orlando area and the nearby historic town of Winter Park are home to many of the area's top **museums:** See Tiffany stained glass at the Charles Hosmer Morse Museum of American Art; the work of folk artist Earl Cunningham and others at the Mennello Museum of American Art; a great permanent collection of American art, including works by Georgia O'Keefe and Ansel Adams, at the Orlando Museum of Art; or a thoughtfully curated show at the Cornell Fine Arts Museum, considered one of the country's top college art museums. Kids are entertained at the hands-on **Orlando Science Center** or the 50 acres of botanical gardens at the nearby **Harry P. Leu Gardens,** while sports fans might want to catch an NBA's Orlando Magic game at the arena.

INTERNATIONAL DRIVE

Often shortened to I-Drive, this is the most intensive tourist strip of the greater Orlando area, running southwest of downtown roughly parallel to I-4 and linking SeaWorld Orlando and Universal Orlando Resort with the Orange County Convention Center and the two monster **outlet malls.** For visitors splitting their time between the various theme parks, I-Drive is an ideal and centralized place to stay, offering midpriced and luxury high-rise hotels along its length. Some of the area's nicer restaurants crowd along I-Drive with many of the half-day tourist attractions **(Wonder Works, Ripley's Believe It or Not!, SkyVenture, Skull Kingdom).** The downside is grueling, bumper-to-bumper traffic during rush hour. It is less crowded on its southern end near the convention center, unless there's a huge convention going on.

COURTESY OF GATORLAND

COURTESY OF KENNEDY SPACE CENTER

KISSIMMEE AND VICINITY

Kissimmee wins Central Florida's "hardest city to pronounce" award. The city is 18 miles due south of Orlando and just east of Walt Disney World Resort. Its roots are firmly planted in cattle ranching, and a rough-and-tumble cowboy image lingers. Folks go to see the rodeo, do a little bass fishing, ride an airboat through gator-studded waters, or tramp around on the beautiful Florida Trail. Through Kissimmee, the U.S. Highway 192, or Irlo Bronson Memorial Highway, is the jackpot for budget-minded Disney visitors. Moderately priced motels, family restaurants and fast food, and a staggering number of minigolf emporiums dot its length.

Between Kissimmee and Walt Disney World Resort lies the town of **Celebration.** Clusters of eerily perfect Victorian homes align on neat streets of the Disney Corporation's prototypical community of the future. It's not exactly what Mr. Disney had in mind with EPCOT—but it's close.

EXCURSIONS

After the hot and humid, crowded and frenetic theme parks, it can be a relief to get out of town for part of your vacation. An hour to the west are the beaches and natural allures of the **Tampa Bay** area. It's an excellent vacation destination, especially for families, home to Busch Gardens and the Florida Aquarium. There's a magical confluence of warm weather, affordable accommodations, professional sports, kids' attractions, and strangely posh shopping that seems to suit every taste. One hour northeast and you'll hit the Birthplace of Speed in **Daytona Beach,** a must for any racing fan. Head 45 minutes due east to blast off the **Space Coast,** home of the Kennedy Space Center and the Astronaut Hall of Fame.

Planning Your Trip

For the 50 million people who visit Orlando each year, there are nearly as many travel strategies. Some pore over books, maps, and websites all year and chart their plan of attack down to the minute, orchestrating a delicate mélange of theme parks and Orlando's secondary allures. Others buy their tickets, book a room, and just show up. A fair amount of your particular planning strategy depends on the stakes involved. For those planning a once-in-a-lifetime, pull-out-all-the-stops family vacation in Orlando, it pays to do your homework: There are discounts through package deals, the diligent will find coupons for many attractions, and pre-mapping your course can cut down the time spent standing around peering down at park maps and bickering. The stakes are lower for Florida residents, with easy access to Orlando, or for repeat visitors. Get a general idea of your objectives, arrange your hotels and park tickets in advance (keep in mind that Florida residents get steep discounts on annual passes), and then see where your fancy takes you. There's always something new to explore.

Resources abound for the most written-about tourist destination in the world—choose one that fits your sensibilities. But as with all things, being informed and having reasonable expectations enriches the experience. The ready availability of planning tools (books, the convention and visitors bureau, Disney's own website, travel agents) makes this a snap.

WHEN TO GO

Walt Disney World Resort itself gives the following information on park attendance:

Lowest Attendance: January (except New Year's Day) until just before Presidents' week in February; the week after Labor Day until just before Thanksgiving week; the week after Thanksgiving until the week before Christmas.

Moderate Attendance: After Presidents' week in February through early March; late April through early June (except Memorial Day weekend); the first part of Thanksgiving week.

Highest Attendance: Presidents' week in February; mid-March through late April ("spring break"); Memorial Day weekend; mid-June through Labor Day; Thanksgiving Day and weekend; Christmas week through New Year's Day.

If you're flexible, consider visiting during off-season. The lines are shorter, the prices lower, and the weather tends to be better. Late fall and very early spring don't suffer from the same heat, humidity, and thunderstorms of other parts of the year. January and February are lovely months in Central Florida, with daytime temperatures in the low 70s. September and October are significantly hotter, with daytime temperatures in the mid-80s to low 90s; is also Florida's hurricane season, which means frequent afternoon thunderstorms.

Going during off-season also comes with the advantage of lower hotel rates; at a Disney resort hotel, the difference between peak and off-season can mean as much as a $100 difference per night for a room. The inexpensive hotels and motels that line U.S. Highway 192 in Kissimmee also compete for off-season guests, posting incredible bargains on their marquees. Airline rates reflect the same savings; there's often a difference of up to $100 between traveling at the end of January (off-season) versus mid-March (peak).

However, during January and February the water parks close for refurbishment and it's when many of the theme park rides are overhauled or upgraded. (Visit www.disneyworld. disney.go.com for operational updates for each park). Also, each of the theme parks closes several of its restaurants during the slowest times to cut down on costs, which may mean that the remaining open restaurants are really busy.

All the theme parks stay open the longest during the summer (sometimes until nearly midnight), so you get more bang for your buck then, versus 6 or 7 P.M. in January and February. If you have stamina and aim to spend lots of time at each park, the summer might be right for you.

If you want to avoid the crowds, plan accordingly, but bear in mind that convention traffic can drastically affect crowd levels at most attractions; check www.orlandoinfo.com for a list of conventions. Also, events such as Mickey's Not-So-Scary Halloween Party or Gay Days draw huge numbers to the parks, so it's also worth checking Disney's annual calendar of events.

WHAT TO TAKE

Florida is casual, with all the good and bad that that entails. You must wear shoes and shirts at all of the theme parks, and Disney cast members will look askance if your shirt is emblazoned with a foul or risqué slogan. Beyond that, comfort is the only guiding principle. Footwear is the most important choice, as you will hoof it miles and miles at every theme park. Flip-flops are not ideal because they can fling off into the stratosphere on intense rides. Sandals are OK if they have backs. Sneakers or running shoes are good, but at Animal Kingdom, SeaWorld Orlando, and a couple of other parks you are likely to get wet repeatedly. If you don't like the squish of wet sneakers, bring an extra pair of shoes to change into.

From about March through November, Florida can be hot. Pack accordingly. However, you also need to bring a sweater or sweatshirt because everything is overly air-conditioned, from movie theaters to restaurants. If you want to bring something dressy for evenings out, a twin set and slacks are fine for women; for men a breezy collar knit and chinos will do. In all of Orlando, only the Victoria and Albert's restaurant requires a jacket for men. If you're in Orlando for a convention or on business—and you aim to tour theme parks or Orlando's other famous sights—pack appropriate nonbusiness attire and footwear. Navigating Magic Kingdom in a suit is a recipe for heatstroke.

At the water parks, you will obviously need a bathing suit, one without a metal belt, rivets, or any metal or plastic decorations that might scratch the ride surfaces. The plunge at the bottom of each flume will cause extreme bathing suit wedgies. Beyond being uncomfortable, repeated wedgies can stretch out your suit. Wear an old one.

Bring sunscreen, a rain poncho, multiple cell phones or walkie-talkies for keeping track of everyone, a hat for each traveler, sunglasses, and a waterproof camera. If you plan on venturing into nature, either at the beach or in one of Central Florida's forests, bring beach toys, bug spray, and a good day pack. All of the parks frown on bringing food in from outside, but many security checkers don't raise any red flag if your bag is stocked with a few sandwiches or snacks.

WHERE TO STAY

With more hotel rooms than New York City, Orlando's accommodations offerings are vast and, thus, daunting. There are 500 hotels, 26,000 vacation homes, 16,000 vacation-rental units, and a fair number of campgrounds. And these numbers are always on the rise: By 2011, resorts and condo-hotel developments by Inter-Continental, Four Seasons, Sonesta, Mona Lisa, and Waldorf-Astoria will be added to the mix.

Visitors must make their decisions on the basis of price and where, geographically, they plan on spending the most time. Walt Disney World Resort boasts more than 20,000 rooms in various themed hotels at nearly every price point, from no-frills, motel-like accommodations to massive luxury/golf/spa hotels. If you plan on spending the bulk of your time at Magic Kingdom, Epcot, Disney's Hollywood Studios, or Disney's Animal Kingdom, Disney offers a number of perks and incentives to visitors that make it worthwhile to consider staying on the property. If you aim to spend a lot of time at Downtown Disney and Pleasure Island, you may want to investigate the large, non-Disney-owned high-rise hotels along Lake Buena Vista Hotel Plaza at the northern entrance of Walt Disney World. On the other hand, U.S. Highway 192 in Kissimmee is the closest area to Walt Disney World Resort and Lake Buena Vista, the length of it dotted with inexpensive motels and hotels. If you plan on spending long days at Disney's parks and just need a bed to cradle your fall at night, Kissimmee's offerings will keep your overall vacation cost down.

If, on the other hand, your travel plans include spending a great deal of time at Universal Orlando Resort or SeaWorld Orlando, you may prefer one of the many large high-rise luxury hotels along International Drive. More expensive than hotels in Kissimmee, they have the advantage of being closer to these parks and to many half-day and second-tier attractions and a real wealth of the area's nicer restaurants. Although traffic can be fierce along I-Drive, the I-Ride Trolley obviates the need to drive everywhere. Universal has three of its own hotel properties, and like Disney, it provides incentives to park-goers to stay there.

You don't care about the theme parks, but you want to explore the cultural allures of Orlando? Downtown Orlando has several large luxury hotels (Sheraton Orlando Downtown Hotel, Grand Bohemian Hotel-Orlando) and the lovely adjacent city of Winter Park has a few more affordable midsize hotels and a couple of charming inns.

There are 176 golf courses within an hour of downtown Orlando, with world-class courses designed by golf legends such as Arnold Palmer, Jack Nicklaus, and Tom Watson, as well as golf academies for beginners or those determined to improve their games. If golf is at the top of your agenda, the Ritz-Carlton Orlando, Grande Lakes; Hyatt Regency Grand Cypress; Orlando World Center Marriott Resort and Convention Center; Omni Orlando Resort at ChampionsGate; and Ginn Reunion Resort are worth investigating.

No matter where you stay, hotels are likely to have swimming pools, many will include a continental breakfast, and a number offer discounts or free stays for children. Be sure to ask when calling for reservations. All over Orlando you'll run into people trying to talk you into time-share or vacation club properties. Proceed with extreme caution—these are seldom fiscally prudent.

WHAT IT WILL COST

Let's just play a little game. For the sake of argument, let's say you're a family of four, with one 11-year-old and one six-year-old. You decide you're going to Orlando for six days during spring break. You're going to Walt Disney World Resort for two of those days, but you want to hustle through and see all four parks in that time. That's $132 each for three tickets, $110 for the six-year-old's, plus $45 per ticket for the Park Hopper option so you can move between parks. Oh, and $10 parking each day. Then, you want to go to Universal for two days. When you look at prices online, you realize it's smarter to do the Four-Park Orlando Flex Ticket, which gives you unlimited admission for up to 14 consecutive days to Universal Studios, Universal's Islands of Adventure, SeaWorld, and Wet 'n Wild, for $189.95 adults, $155.95 children (plus three days of $10 parking). So now you've got two days at Disney, one day at the two Universal parks, another day at SeaWorld Orlando, a fifth day at Wet 'n Wild, but your six-year-old has his heart set on seeing Gatorland. So, your sixth day will cost $19.95 each for three of you, $12.95 for the young gator lover. You've heard good things about the Gaylord Palms Resort and it is five minutes from Walt Disney World Resort, so you spring for the $279 per night for a double queen room during March. The room doesn't come with breakfast, but you eat cereal, milk, coffee, and so on in the room each morning ($40 for the week). For lunch, you eat at the theme parks each day ($35 per day). For dinner, you have two cheapies ($40 total) at fast-food restaurants because the kids are tired, but another night you get the urge to go to the Pirate's Dinner Adventure, which will set you back $51.95 for each of the two adults and $31.95 for each of the kids. The day that you go to Walt Disney World Resort, you surprise your family with the much-coveted character dinner at Magic Kingdom's Cinderella's Royal Table, $50 adults, $30 kids. The other two nights you eat at the very nice buffet at the hotel ($100 each night for the whole family). For the rental car, you've gotten a week's rental on a midsize Pontiac from Avis for $217.79.

Now, I don't know where you live, so I can't guess about your airfare. But once you hit the ground in Orlando, this six-day vacation, at a very bare minimum, is going to set you back $4,114.19.

There are ways to make it cheaper. Go off-season for better hotel rates (this means September–November, January, or February). Buy a package deal on hotel and park tickets either at Walt Disney World Resort or Universal Orlando Resort. For SeaWorld, Orlando Marriott and Renaissance Hotels and Resorts allow kids nine and under to stay free with a minimum two-night stay and offer free park tickets with a paid adult ticket. In the off-season, haggle with

the hotel reservationist and don't settle for the printed "rack rates." Ask for corporate rates, AAA rates, or free breakfasts.

Limit the number of big-ticket park days. Honestly, several days in a row of slogging through crowded Disney parks isn't that fun—mix it up and spend one day playing minigolf on International Drive or taking a Boggy Creek Airboat ride in Kissimmee. Or visit Wonder Works on International Drive one morning and go to the big movie theater at Downtown Disney that afternoon.

Camp. It's fun, really. One of the single coolest places to stay at Walt Disney World is Disney's Fort Wilderness Resort and Campground, where you can get a spot for as little as $41 per night, with nice bathrooms and a nightly campfire and marshmallow roast with Disney characters and a Disney movie. If you are a large group staying for multiple days, the most economical thing to do is rent a vacation home in the greater Kissimmee area for a week. Then you can make meals at home, spread out a bit more, and accommodate different bedtimes and schedules.

Many of the websites listed in the *Resources* section offer discounts and inexpensive package deals—do not, I repeat, *do not* type in the words "Discount Disney tickets" on Google. What you'll find are sites that lure you in to pitch you a time-share property.

Explore Walt Disney World and Orlando

THE BEST OF DISNEY WORLD AND ORLANDO

You parachute into Orlando with 72 hours until you are airlifted to safety. Actually, this is many people's experience with Orlando—either vacation schedules are tight, you're touring as part of a several-day convention, or you want to say you've been there with the least possible wallet gouging.

Day 1

Many people, being linear thinkers, believe it's wisest to start at the beginning: Disney's **Magic Kingdom.** Each Disney park has an iconic symbol—Epcot has that big golf ball–looking geosphere, Disney's Hollywood Studios has the Sorcerer Mickey Hat, Disney's Animal Kingdom has The Tree of Life, but Magic Kingdom trumps them all. Cinderella Castle is synonymous with Disney, so you may need the social currency of having visited Magic Kingdom. Start your visit this way, but not if it's on a Monday or Tuesday when all the other vacationers seem to be starting their visit this way. Once at the park, do not attempt to do everything—like the universe itself, the parks keep expanding. There's always more and there's always something new. Be choosy: Of the dark rides, choose Pirates of the Caribbean and The Haunted Mansion over The Many Adventures of Winnie the Pooh and Snow White's Scary Adventures. After each passive attraction, choose something active such as exploring the Swiss Family Treehouse or Tom Sawyer Island. Go light on lunch—maybe try the kicky Southwest chicken salad at Pecos Bill Tall Tale Inn and Café, so you're ravenous by day's end. Depart the park at 6 P.M. or so before the hordes, and head to the Grand Floridian for dinner at the lush Mediterranean **Citricos** (make a reservation far in advance, and opt for the hotel's 1900 Park Fare instead if you have young children in your entourage). Linger over a glass of wine and gorgeously executed French-Med while you watch Magic Kingdom's evening fireworks spectacular

out the wide windows. It's late, so speed to your hotel, the nearby **Gaylord Palms Resort** if you're feeling flush, or **Disney's Fort Wilderness Resort and Campground** if you have a sense of adventure and an urge to economize.

Day 2

The next day you arise to find that a gorgeous, but slightly warm, Florida day greets you. Today you're going Old School, heading east of Disney to Kissimmee's **Gatorland,** which started life as a roadside attraction in 1949, well before the Mouse's appearance. A fire in 2006 caused some renovations and improvements at the park, but it's still all "Real Florida" camp, 110 acres covered with alligators, crocodiles, and the wading birds that seem to live symbiotically with them. It's a cheap day, so splurge on the Adventure Tour, whereby you get to go behind the fence and toss huge meat chunks into the mouths of a crowd of gators. Nothing is between you and them except a park employee with a stick.

Continuing in this vein, your next stop is **Boggy Creek Airboat and Swamp Buggy Rides,** for which you don a set of hearing protectors and head out into the wetlands on an airboat to point and gape at bald eagles, countless lurking gators, great egrets, and diamondback terrapins. It's loud, it's fast, and it's over in 30 minutes, at which point you can add on a swamp buggy tour through a working cattle ranch.

Feeling suitably tough and cowboyish, you need to end Day 2 with the granddaddy of Central Florida's dinner shows. **Medieval Times Dinner and Tournament** is like a theme park meets mediocre banquet food (which, incidentally, you eat with your hands medieval-style). Doesn't sound appealing? It's a hoot, set in a huge arena with horses and knights, who joust, sword fight, and fling around maces and bolas. The story line features King Alfonso and Princess Esperanza, but mostly it's an opportunity to heckle while waving a chicken leg in the air.

Day 3

Day 3 means some tough decisions. Still itching to ride the rides? Get a one-day, two-park pass at Universal Orlando and spend a half day each at **Islands of Adventure** and **Universal Studios,** culminating in dinner at Universal's **CityWalk,** or head to **Emeril's Restaurant Orlando** if you're in the mood for something fancy by way of Louisiana. The wine list alone exerts a powerful come-hither force on the average foodie.

If your itch for theme parks has been scratched, you can spend your third day discovering that Orlando is indeed a real place. It has a downtown and lovely neighborhoods where people live non-theme-park lives, about 15 minutes northeast of the tourist area. Arrayed around downtown's Loch Haven Park, you'll find the **Orlando Museum of Art,** the **Mennello Museum of American Art,** the **Orlando Repertory Theatre,** the **Orlando-UCF Shakespeare Festival,** and the **Orlando Science Center.** Five minutes away is **Harry P. Leu Gardens,** 50 acres of botanical gardens harboring 2,000 species varying from camellias to cacti. Follow your personal cultural leanings, and then end the day with a meal at one of Winter Park's many upscale restaurants—maybe a plate of chicken with mushroom fricassee, asparagus, and fava beans at **Luma on Park.**

DISNEY FOR KIDS

Children are different—meaning, from other more evolved life forms such as adults or dolphins, but also from each other. The very young need naps, downtime, and snacks nearly every 10 minutes. Elementary school–age kids like a little more action and variety, have a little more stamina, and need snacks nearly every 10 minutes. Teens and tweens appreciate a bit more independence (that's why you bought them the cell phone, after all) and rely more heavily on emotions such as ennui, except in the face of thrill rides. And they, too, need snacks nearly every 10 minutes.

Preschool-Age Children and Toddlers

Do not be overambitious when scheduling an Orlando visit with very young children. Preschool-age children and toddlers will find loads of thrills, but they need time to decompress and regroup. Thus, where you stay is the most important choice you make. If your aim is to spend time at the Walt Disney World Resort, stay in a resort property so you can whisk them

What park will your child like best?

© DISNEY

home after lunch for a nap. Then, before dinnertime, head back to the park. Many theme park veterans think that the resort properties themselves offer enough fun on-site—pools, themed restaurants, playgrounds, and kids' programs that at least one day should be spent entirely at the hotel property. For instance, at **Disney's Animal Kingdom Lodge,** kids can watch African animals on a 33-acre savanna right outside their window, frolic in the wading pool, hang out in Simba's Clubhouse while parents are out to dinner, or play on the Hakuna Matata playground. Guests also have access to an early-morning tour of Kilimanjaro Safaris at Disney's Animal Kingdom, which is offered only to resort guests.

Children under the age of six will find the most to do and see at **Disney's Animal Kingdom, Magic Kingdom,** and **SeaWorld Orlando.** Universal's parks and Disney's Hollywood Studios have too many vexing height limitations and scary rides; Epcot is educational, but it really requires reading skills to be adequately appreciated.

Take advantage of child-swap options at the parks. This means that Parent A can ride the ride while Parent B stays with progeny on the ground. Parent A disembarks, retrieves progeny, and Parent B zaps to the head of the line to ride the ride.

Elementary School–Age Children

School-age kids are cheap dates. They will like **Disney's Animal Kingdom** ($56 ages 3–9) and they will like **Gatorland** ($12.95 ages 3–12) just as much. They will enjoy a character meal at Magic Kingdom's **Crystal Palace** ($15) and they will enjoy exploring the world's largest **McDonald's** playroom ($3 or so) just as much. Do some of the superspendy theme parks, but feel comfortable heading out to Kissimmee's **Boggy Creek Airboat** rides ($15.95 for kids) for a day. When they get home, eavesdrop and see what they brag about: Was it zooming by a mama gator and her 12 striped young, or was it riding in the little boat and viewing Peter Pan's Flight? Sometimes the unmediated, less-sanitized experience gets the nod. School-age kids may prefer an afternoon of **minigolfing** at the mega courses on Kissimmee's U.S. Highway 192 to being herded through the **Shrek 4-D** queue at Universal Studios. Plan accordingly. To assure everybody's equanimity, add a "wide leash" day after a crowded day at a theme park.

When it comes to souvenirs, give each child a total expenditure budget before the trip starts. Allow them to shop throughout each day, but they must make their purchases in the last 20 minutes of a theme park visit (this might entail backtracking for somebody, but it prevents buyer's remorse and also somebody's having to schlep the goods all day long). If they elect to buy an autograph book and character-autograph pen, take pictures of each greeting and slap that developed shot on each page adjacent to the character's scrawl for a quick and dirty ad hoc scrapbook.

Tweens and Teens

With a greater interest in thrill rides, generally speaking, this group will gravitate toward, in descending order: **Universal's Islands of Adventure, Disney's Hollywood Studios, Universal Studios,** all three water parks (**Blizzard Beach, Typhoon Lagoon,** and **Wet 'n Wild**), **Disney's Animal Kingdom,** and **SeaWorld Orlando.** Having done a fair amount of fieldwork on the subject, I would say that Magic Kingdom and Epcot reliably cause teens and tweens to exhibit boredom, eye rolling, and the mocking of elders.

Parents of teens often praise the efforts of **Disney Cruises.** Planning a family vacation with the stranger inhabiting the body of your former elementary schooler can be tricky. Disney Cruises seems to strike the right balance of family togetherness and independent activity. Children's activities are divided by age, with lots of options specifically for teens, and because you're at sea, your teen is less likely to have a driving infraction, a brush with the law, or a curfew snafu.

Orlando's theme parks are a relatively safe place to give your teen some freedom. With tools such as cell phones and walkie-talkies, families can split up for an hour or two, allowing the older kids to head to the monster rides while parents accompany the little ones on, shudder, "it's a small world."

DISNEY FOR THE KID AT HEART

As with children, there are different kinds of adults. My husband wouldn't set foot in a theme park. Me, I like to ride the rides and wave my arms in the air like I just don't care, occasionally whooping and squealing. If you squint, we both seem like adults.

The Thrill Seeker

Disney's Animal Kingdom's **Expedition Everest** is my top choice. It's new, the theming is outrageously detailed with authentic Nepalese doodads all over, and the ride itself won't give you whiplash or cause incontinence. There are no inversions but lots of drama. Universal Orlando Resort has two of the top five attractions: **Incredible Hulk Coaster** in Islands of Adventure and **Men in Black Alien Attack** in Universal Studios. The former is the archetypal gut-lurching coaster with an amazing blastoff and seven inversions. At 54 inches, the height requirement alone makes this one of the most "adult" attractions in Orlando. The latter is a makes-you-feel-like-a-kid-again deal, a dark ride in which you zap aliens with your laser gun in the streets of New York. The ride's ending depends on your team's score. The award for Single Priciest Attraction goes to Discovery Cove, SeaWorld Orlando's superexclusive, superluxurious, reservations-only, 30-acre Caribbean-theme water park. Its **Dolphin Encounter** is thrilling, though, if you are comfortable ponying up the dough. (You're in the water with this beautiful creature. You can pet him, talk to him, kiss him, and then you grab hold of a dorsal fin and as a couple you go zooming across a lagoon, kicking up a wake on either side.) At any age, the nightly fireworks extravaganza held above Cinderella Castle at Magic Kingdom, called **Wishes Nighttime Spectacular,** is a grand finale to any Orlando visit. Like the best Fourth of July display you've ever seen, it's souped up further with music, a vague story line, and Tinker Bell flying above it all.

And after a day of gut-lurching thrill rides, there's nothing like a little fine dining to settle the nerves and convince yourself that you don't in fact suffer from arrested development. The Grand Floridian's Provence-meets-Tuscany **Citricos** is a worthwhile reservation to procure, as is the stunning, seafood-heavy **Todd English's bluezoo** at the Walt Disney World Dolphin. Allow a little time for digestion before dashing over to the adult revelry at the many music clubs of Universal's **CityWalk.**

The Nature Lover

The adult who could take or leave the theme parks, but who would rather spend some relaxing time tramping about in nature, might focus the bulk of his or her Orlando visit in or around Kissimmee. Hire a guide and spend a morning stalking bass on **Lake Tohopekaliga** (just call it Lake Toho) or an afternoon taking a guided ecosafari at **Forever Florida,** a 4,700-acre working cattle ranch and wildlife preserve in St. Cloud. For a quiet afternoon of contemplation in a lovely setting, the **Historic Bok Sanctuary** in Lake Wales is hard to beat, with gardens designed by Frederick Law Olmsted Jr., of Central Park fame, and a marble-and-coquina bell tower that hosts bell recitals

at 1 P.M. and 3 P.M. daily, such that sweet tones ring out across the Lake Wales Ridge.

Historic Bok Sanctuary's on-site Carillon Café is a lovely venue for a sophisticated lunch salad or sandwich; for dinner consider taking in one of the area's more cerebral dinner shows, such as **Capone's Dinner and Show** on U.S. Highway 192 in Kissimmee. It's one-stop-shopping for a dinner and an evening activity. On the other hand, grabbing a quick bite somewhere before taking in the **Silver Spurs Rodeo** (in February and October) is a guaranteed memory maker.

The Art Buff

Art buffs will adopt a different tack entirely. Downtown Orlando and nearby Winter Park are awash in wonderful special-interest museums, most on an intimate scale. A delightful day could be spent lingering for an hour in Winter Park at the **Albin Polasek Museum and Sculpture Gardens,** listed on the National Register of Historic Places and showcasing 200 pieces of the Czech sculptor's work as well as a hodgepodge of stuff he collected during his lifetime. After that, zip over to the **Charles Hosmer Morse Museum of American Art** to view the amazing leaded-glass windows of Louis Comfort Tiffany and a

Disney's attractions appeal to kids of all ages.

© DISNEY

gorgeous array of American decorative art from the mid-19th century to the early 20th century. After that, have lunch at one of the lovely cafés on Park Avenue in Winter Park. Refreshed, spend a little time in Eatonville at the **Zora Neale Hurston National Museum of Fine Arts.** The celebrated African American writer was from Eatonville; this one-room museum showcases the work of African American artists and other artists of African descent. End your visit with **Winter Park's Scenic Boat Tour,** a local tradition for 50 years. The one-hour narrated tour glides you through the canals and lakes that wind through the backyards of Winter Park's most affluent residents and the campus of Rollins College.

For dinner sans young ones, enjoy the oh-so-adult pleasures of a leisurely meal at **Hue Restaurant** in Thornton Park or the nearby **Midnight Blue,** after which amble over to Church Street Station and see what bars or music venues suit your mood.

RAINY-DAY DISNEY

"The sun did not shine. It was too wet to play. So we sat in the house all that cold, cold wet day." Except for the "cold, cold" part, this Dr. Seuss rhyme sounds a little like Central Florida in the storm season—every afternoon given over to an impressive deluge or, at the very least, some ominous gloom. But you don't need that rascally Cat, or even Thing One or Thing Two, to help you while away a wet afternoon in Orlando. (*The Cat in the Hat* trivia: The book contains 236 different words, of which 54 occur exactly once and 33 occur twice.)

Magic Kingdom

Magic Kingdom is a fairly indoor-oriented park, with lots of ride-throughs of lands populated by animatronic figures. The problem is that crowds flock instantly to the indoor rides during a rainstorm, yielding punishingly long lines. **Peter Pan's Flight, The Many Adventures of Winnie the Pooh, "it's a small world,"** and **Pirates of the Caribbean** all get long lines in inclement weather. Many of the lesser rides are shielded from the elements by an overhang, so choose these instead if you want to ride out the weather. If rains coincide with mealtimes, everybody gets the brilliant idea of taking a chow break at the same time—lines instantly double or triple (character meals, if they're not already at capacity, are immediately booked). If your aim is to persevere and slosh through moistened theme parks, bring rain ponchos or even big plastic bags to keep yourself dry. Disney-issue ponchos are very cheap and available at most retail shops in the parks, but until 2007 were all a uniform yellow—meaning everybody instantly looks the same and family members had a hard time keeping track of each other. Now, these few-buck ponchos (essentially disposable after one wearing) are clear plastic. Outdoor attractions will shut down in a driving rain or any hint of electrical storm, but many attractions persevere in a light rain. Attractions that are very likely to close during rain include Astro Orbiter and Tomorrowland Indy Speedway, The Magic Carpets of Aladdin, and Tom Sawyer Island. Be aware that lightning is a real danger in Florida, killing or injuring a number of people each year. At the first sign of an electrical storm, take shelter under a roof or overhang. Monorails, trams, and buses still function during storms. Parades and fireworks continue as planned in a very light rain.

Epcot

Of the theme parks, Epcot's Future World has the greatest number of indoor entertainments—in fact, every attraction is contained in a covered pavilion; the park's other half, World Showcase Pavilions, is much more outdoors, so save that for when the rains have passed.

Future World attractions such as **Innoventions West** and **Innoventions East** are your best bet, because you can go at your own pace, the rain allowing you to really take your time and explore in the way a sunny day doesn't encourage. Slow down and follow your bliss through all the interactive technology exhibits. Pavilions that contain multiple attractions (such as **Wonders of Life,** which is open only during high season, or **Imagination!**) are better than single-attraction pavilions (Test Track) because you can spend more time in lines waiting out the weather.

If you do find yourself in the World Showcase area when rains begin, head for long, sit-down films such as *American Adventure* or *Impressions de France* versus shorter or stand-up films such as *O Canada!*

Test Track may close in a heavy rain, but most attractions at Epcot stay open.

Disney's Hollywood Studios

Some of this park's central draws are outdoor shows that will shut down in a heavy rain or at the first sight of lightning: Indiana Jones Epic Stunt Spectacular!, The Disney's Hollywood Studios Backlot Tour, and Lights, Motors, Action! Extreme Stunt Show are all inclined to close in Florida's frequent thunderstorms. Rock 'n Roller Coaster Starring Aerosmith is also apt to grind to a halt in heavy rain.

Set your sights instead on the longer, indoor movie-oriented shows such as **Muppet Vision 3-D** or **The Great Movie Ride.** These provide seating and a substantial break from sloshing around outdoors (although heavy air-conditioning may be aversive if you've gotten very wet outdoors). If you're visiting the park with younger children, head to **Animation Courtyard** at the threat of rain—both Voyage of the Little Mermaid and Playhouse Disney-Live on Stage! will entertain the troops indoors and they're right near each other.

Animal Kingdom

This is the single worst of the four parks in the rain, so if your aim is to see Animal Kingdom during a day with a rainy forecast, consider buying Park Hopper tickets so you can resort to another park and Plan B with the threat of a deluge. Animal Kingdom's biggest asset is its vast size and meandering landscaped walkways between attractions. Almost nothing here is full indoors (with the exception of the Dinosaur ride): Expedition Everest will close in the rain, the animals take shelter in the rain (yielding a very boring Kilimanjaro Safari ride, which will keep running in moderate rain), and rides such as Primeval Whirl and TriceraTop Spin tend to close if rains get heavy.

Not surprisingly, people swarm to the shows in inclement weather, making **Finding Nemo - The Musical** and the **Festival of the Lion King** a mob scene. Likewise, **Rainforest Café** is inundated with folks trying to stay dry.

Universal Orlando and SeaWorld

There's no such thing as a "rain check" at Universal Orlando. It rains nearly every afternoon here in the summer, so when you anticipate rain, head for the indoor shows and ride it out. Nonetheless, covered parking and covered walkways make much of this complex workable in the rain. Crowds also seem to thin quite a bit during days with inclement weather—if you don't mind getting a little wet, you may benefit from shorter lines.

Universal Studios is better than Islands of Adventure on a rainy day, with a significant number of indoor attractions. Aim for longer indoor attractions such as **Revenge of the Mummy** versus short ones such as Shrek 4-D. Attractions such as Fear Factor Live, Jaws, and outdoor shows such as The Blues Brothers get called on account of rain.

At Islands of Adventure, you must walk from attraction to attraction so pick up a $6 poncho (available in most shops). Coasters and thrill rides such as Incredible Hulk Coaster, Dueling Dragons, and Dr. Doom's Fearfall will keep

© DISNEY

Pirates of the Caribbean at DisneyQuest®

running during a moderate rain, but be advised that the raindrops feel like needles and it can actually hurt a bit. In case of an electrical storm, all of these rides close down. Indoor attractions such as The **Amazing Adventures of Spider-Man** or **Poseidon's Fury** may be a better spot from which to wait out the weather.

CityWalk also provides respite from bad weather, with restaurants connected by overhangs and a huge multiplex for a rainy-day flick.

At SeaWorld, nearly a third of the attractions are indoors, and many others are shielded from the elements by canopies and roofs—head for these in case of rain, or be content to pick up ponchos from one of the concession stands. In general, rides and tours are closed during Florida's frequent summer afternoon thunderstorms.

Outdoor shows will be canceled in the case of lightning or very heavy rain. Indoor walkthroughs are more forgiving ways to spend a little time; **Penguin Encounter** and **Shark Encounter** are especially inviting (and after seeing Sharks, you can get a snack at its restaurant, Sharks Under Water). Thrill rides such as Kraken and Journey to Atlantis are quick to close at the threat of lightning or very heavy rains. Also, Dine with Shamu and the evening luau will be canceled in a driving rain or elec-

trical storm. At SeaWorld's sister park, Discovery Cove, dolphin encounters will be canceled in bad weather.

More Disney Attractions

Obviously, if your objective is to get wet at one of the water parks, a little rain isn't going to kill your buzz. Blizzard Beach, Typhoon Lagoon, and Wet 'n Wild will close during electrical storms; get your hand stamped so you can return to the parks once the deluge has passed.

Downtown Disney is an obvious destination on a foul-weather day—everything is indoors and you can mostly stay dry zipping from one shop to another. DisneyQuest (a huge gaming arcade) will entertain the troops for hours, the AMC 24 Theatres show all the first-run blockbusters you can name, and shops such as the Virgin Megastore can easily pass the time.

Disney's Wide World of Sports is a little tricky—outdoor events will be canceled, but sporting events held in the Milk House field house are unaffected (call for details). **Disney Wilderness Preserve** is a very dreary and muddy undertaking on a bad-weather day.

Some of the more luxury-oriented **Disney Resorts** offer amazing amenities to their guests—which can in large measure be enjoyed by nonguests. At Animal Kingdom Lodge, tell the guard at the gate that you want to take a look around or dine in one of the on-site restaurants. Then wander the grounds, viewing the animals on the savanna (they tend to take shelter in a driving rain), check out the amazing lobby, dine, shop, and more. Disney's Grand Floridian, Disney's Contemporary, Disney's Polynesian Resort, and Disney's BoardWalk Inn all make for fun wandering on a rainy day.

Orlando

If the weather forecast is really bleak, skip the parks altogether: **Downtown Orlando** has a concentration of excellent small museums. Kids may prefer a morning noodling through the interactive exhibits at the Orange County Regional History Center or the Orlando Science Center, whereas adults may want to take in a matinee performance of the much celebrated Orlando Ballet or wander the lush Tiffany glass collection at the Charles Hosmer Morse Museum of American Art before grabbing a little lunch on sophisticated Park Avenue in Winter Park. Dating to the turn of the 20th century, when it was a winter playground to New England's wealthy, Winter Park is one of the few places in Central Florida to have a palpable sense of history.

International Drive will also entertain the troops on a wet day: Wonder Works, Ripley's Believe It or Not!, Skull Kingdom, or Titanic—The Experience are geared toward a half day of pleasant investigation for families. I-Drive is also a shopper's paradise, with Prime Outlets Orlando at its north end and Orlando Premium Outlets at its south end, with close to 350 stores between them.

On I-Drive, sprawling, lively restaurants such as Bahama Breeze or Ming Court are almost like the dining equivalent of a theme park (huge menus, lots to see, entertainment in the case of the former). In **Kissimmee,** a "dinner show" such as Medieval Times Dinner and Tournament or Arabian Nights Dinner Attraction have enough drama and pageantry to entertain people who've been cooped up all day because of inclement weather.

Excursions

If your weather forecast is truly grim, perhaps it's wiser to cut bait entirely and just get out of town. Weather patterns can be very different an hour to the west in **Tampa** or an hour to the east in **Daytona Beach** or the **Space Coast.** If the weather is dismal all over, the Space Coast and its Kennedy Space Center are your best bets—just about everything runs as planned at the visitors' complex, and the bus tour drops you off under an overhang.

BE OUR GUEST. . . AGAIN

If you find yourself in Orlando with any regularity, consider buying season tickets at Walt Disney World Resort or the other theme parks. It doesn't take too many visits to make this a prudent choice: For instance, a one-day both-park ticket to Universal is $85, whereas the annual passes start at $129.95. For longer visits, a park-hopper or multipark ticket makes the most sense.

Day 1

For thrill-seekers, the most recent Walt Disney World news was the April 2006 opening of **Expedition Everest** in Disney's Animal Kingdom's Asia section. It's a scale model of Mt. Everest, with a Himalayan village, a runaway coaster, and a ticked-off Yeti.

Make Animal Kingdom your first stop of the day and FASTPASS Expedition Everest as soon as the park opens. Relax afterward at the

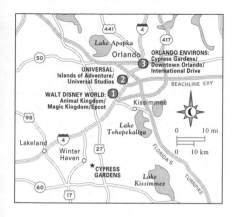

second day at one of Orlando's other theme parks.

At Universal Orlando's Islands of Adventure, hit the whimsical **High in the Sky Seuss Trolley Train Ride** to give little kids a bird's-eye view of Seuss Landing. Afterward, stop off at the nearby Caro-Seuss-el for a spin. And while it's not new, **Poseidon's Fury** has recently added a new story line and effects. Head to CityWalk for lunch at the latest in the **Bubba Gump Shrimp Co.** chain and return later to dance the night away at the **The Red Coconut Club.**

If your visit falls in summer, incorporate one of two shows into your evening plans. The all-ages, **Universal 360: A Cinesphere Spectacular** originally made its debut in summer 2006 at Universal Studios. The evening show with movie clips, lasers, and pyrotechnics will be returning summers, from June 30 to August 18. At Universal Orlando Resort, the big news is the arrival of the cerulean-hued yet bald **Blue Man Group,** launching in June 2007, which will permanently occupy a newly created live performance venue accessible from both Universal CityWalk and Universal Studios.

Alternatively, head to SeaWorld Orlando to check out the new, evocatively themed **Believe** show of killer whales and the newish **Shamu Express** family coaster. Spend lunch at the park's top restaurant, **Sharks UnderWater Grill,** which offers a new family option—adults dine while their progeny are engaged by American Camping Association instructors.

SeaWorld Orlando tends to close earlier than other theme parks, so for some evening activity, stop off for a Guinness at **Lucky Leprechaun Irish Pub** or hum a few bars at **Howl at the Moon,** both on International Drive.

new show **Finding Nemo - the Musical,** a black-light spectacular with original music and big puppets in the newly enclosed Theater in the Wild. Stop for lunch at the new Asian-themed Yak and Yeti (which Landry's Restaurants plans to open in September 2007), before park-hopping over to Magic Kingdom by bus or car. Rumor has it that the classic **Space Mountain** ride will soon undergo a major update so be sure to FASTPASS it while it's still up and running. The **Monsters, Inc. Laugh Floor Comedy Club** opened in spring 2007 and can entertain you while you wait. The interactive comedy show is hosted by Mike Wazowski; audience members can text-message in their favorite jokes.

Afterward, head over to Epcot where Nemo makes another appearance at **The Seas with Nemo and Friends,** where animated Nemo characters are projected onto a six-million-gallon saltwater aquarium. Finish off your day at Downtown Disney, in the new **World of Disney** store, with its interactive pirate-themed Adventure Room and the Bibbidi Bobbidi Boutique, a little-girl beauty salon in the store's Princess Room. End with dinner at Marketplace's latest addition, **T-Rex: A Prehistoric Family Adventure, A Place to Eat, Shop, Explore and Discover.**

Day 2

Take a break from the mouse and spend your

Day 3

Spend today exploring Orlando and environs. Get up bright and early to devote half the day to one of Central Florida's oldest, most-overlooked attractions. **Cypress Gardens** in Winter Haven has been pulled back from the brink of death and refurbished. The old-timey theme park has water-ski shows, beautiful landscaping, and mild thrill rides—with sparser crowds and a prevailing feeling of nostalgia, it's a different day at the park than the mouse-dominated ones a bit to the north.

Leave Cypress Gardens, heading north on Highway 29 and then northeast on I-4 to Downtown Orlando (one hour). In the greater downtown area just east of Lake Eola Park, you'll find the neighborhood of Thornton Park and worthy lunch spots such as Dexter's of Thornton Park or Doc's Restaurant.

Fortified, spend the late afternoon exploring the **Orlando Science Center,** which has hosted such exhibits as the fabulous (and controversial) Our Body: The Universe Within. The center is open until 6 P.M. weekdays and 9 P.M. on weekends so you'll have time to linger.

For dinner, head back southwest along I-4 to the International Drive area. Try a glass of cabernet at **The Grape** wine bar before enjoying an Islands-inflected steak at **Tommy Bahama's Tropical Café;** both are at the Pointe Orlando shopping center. After dinner, it's off to Destiny Nightclub, the new hot spot on Universal Boulevard. Or stay put in Orlando and spend the evening downtown enjoying the nightly live music and 21 beers on tap at the Orlando Brewing Co.—hey, it's healthy; its own beers are certified organic.

Accommodations

As part of Walt Disney World Resort's 2006 "Year of a Million Dreams," a newly tricked-out suite in Cinderella Castle is now available for overnight rental. Stay here or book accommodations at **Disney's All-Star Music Resort,** which recently converted 400 of its guest rooms to 192 family suites that each sleeps up to six people. You can also stay at the new villas at **Disney's Animal Kingdom Lodge** and enjoy African-inspired amenities and views of an expanded savanna inhabited by African animals.

WALT DISNEY WORLD RESORT

© DISNEY

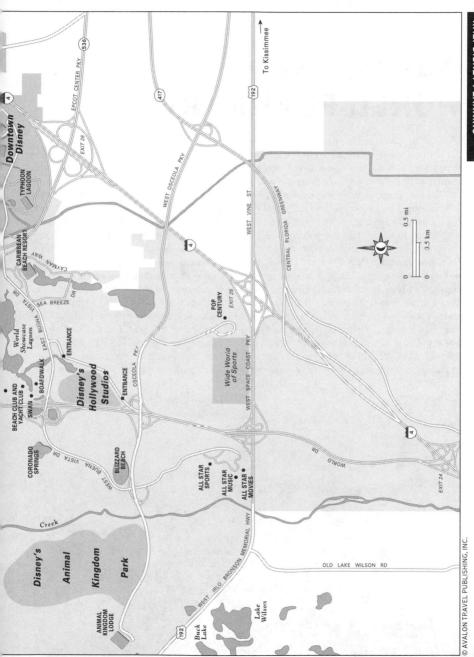

© AVALON TRAVEL PUBLISHING, INC.

WALT DISNEY WORLD PLANNING

Walt Disney World Resort is the single most popular tourist destination in the world. More than 16 million visitors visit Magic Kingdom annually, 10 million go to Epcot, nearly nine million tour Disney's Hollywood Studios, and a little more than eight million explore Disney's Animal Kingdom. Who visits Walt Disney World Resort? The vast majority are the American nuclear family on an annual vacation. But consider this: Orlando is now the number two convention destination in the country. This means that conventioneers go to Walt Disney World. These include singles and couples traveling without children, repeat visitors, sports groups, retirees, gays and lesbians, honeymooners, ironic hipsters, and those with mobility issues. Certainly, this presents certain challenges for the parks and this is what they do best: There is always something for everyone, and there is always something new.

Wander through the Disney's Hollywood Studios attraction Walt Disney: One Man's Dream, and you'll see interview clips of the man responsible for more than 100 feature-length films. He's got an aw-shucks humility as he talks about just wanting a clean, wholesome place to take his daughters for some family entertainment, someplace that was actually fun for a couple of generations simultaneously. Whatever you may think of Disney the Man, the resort has maintained its status as the benchmark against which all other theme parks are judged. Disney parks are clean, Disney "cast members" are cheery and helpful, and Disney attractions aim to be more moral and educational—and fun.

Each park is a strategically designed mélange

© DISNEY

of thrill rides, sweet animatronic tear-jerkers, educational exhibits, Disney character meet-and-greets, funny 3-D movies, restaurants, and shops. There is always a new attraction being erected while elsewhere an older favorite is being retired. "Hidden Mickeys" and a wealth of subtle details continue to thrill the longtime Disney aficionados, while attractions combining cutting-edge technology with 21st-century film and television tempt the Disney novice.

HISTORY

If you take the tour at Wakulla Springs, about 15 miles south of Tallahassee on Florida's Panhandle, someone invariably mentions Walt Disney. It seems Mr. Disney once went to pay a call on local landowner Edward Ball. He had a theme park project in mind for which he needed some wide-open land. Mr. Ball kept Disney waiting all day, only to send one of his minions at day's end to inform Disney that Mr. Ball "didn't do business with carnies." Central Florida owes Edward Ball a debt of gratitude

for his shortsightedness. Disney's vision for a second theme park, one to match the one he opened in Anaheim, California, in 1955, was executed here instead. Magic Kingdom opened in 1971 and Central Florida has never been the same.

Disney died before ground was broken on the park in 1967. But upon touring Magic Kingdom at its opening, Disney's widow told people she felt confident that Walt would have approved. On that 43 square miles of virgin land, about the size of Boston, construction has just kept going: After Magic Kingdom came Epcot in 1982, Disney's Hollywood Studios in 1989, and Disney's Animal Kingdom in 1998. Oh, and then came two water parks, Typhoon Lagoon in 1989 and Blizzard Beach in 1995, and Downtown Disney in 1997, dozens of hotels, six golf courses, two spas, and Disney's Wide World of Sports. The thing is, Lillian Disney would probably say the same thing were she to tour the Disney empire today. Walt would have approved.

Planning Your Trip

WHICH PARK IS FOR YOU?

Many visitors start with Magic Kingdom because it is synonymous with Walt Disney World Resort. It was the first, and it has the iconic castle. Not everyone will like Magic Kingdom best, however. It's always dangerous to generalize, but here goes: Families with preschool- and early elementary school-age kids will find the most to do in Magic Kingdom; adults traveling without children may prefer Epcot; teenagers will be the most excited with the offerings at Disney's Hollywood Studios. Disney's Animal Kingdom is appealing to all ages, assuming you like animals and don't mind doing a bit of walking.

The water parks are slam-dunks, so to speak, for teens and tweens; sports aficionados of any age will enjoy Disney's Wide World of Sports. Downtown Disney is appropriate for all ages with its crowd-pleasing array of shops and

brand-name restaurants, whereas Pleasure Island is a strictly-adults playground. And for something entirely un-Disney, visitors who prefer the outdoors can explore Disney Wilderness Preserve 15 miles south of Walt Disney World Resort.

WHEN TO GO

From October to May the average daytime low temperature is in the low 70s, the high in the mid-80s. From June to September the average daytime low temperature is in the upper 80s, the high in the mid-90s. This means it is very hot and very humid all summer. Still, summer vacation has the highest visitation numbers at the parks, along with the December holiday season and the traditional spring break vacation period (March and April, especially around Easter weekend). The best travel times are February or September through November if you want

EXTRA MAGIC HOURS

Every day one of the Disney theme parks opens an hour early or stays open up to three hours after regular park closing, so Disney Resort guests can revel in easy access to select attractions without all the unwashed masses gumming up the works. There's tricky math, though: on Extra Magic Hours days, certain parks become especially alluring. Extra Magic Hours at Magic Kingdom, for instance, seem to get park-goers in a twitter, so lines may be every bit as long right from the get-go. Morning "extra" hours tend to be a little busier, evening hours less so (because, technically, it's close to child abuse to ask a six-year-old who has walked in the hot sun all day to stay up to 11 P.M. to take in a few bonus rides).

The current Extra Magic Hour schedule is as follows: At Magic Kingdom it's Thursday mornings and Sunday evenings; at Epcot it's Tuesday mornings and Friday evenings; at Disney's Hollywood Studios it's Saturday mornings and evening hours vary; and at Animal Kingdom it's Monday mornings and Wednesday evenings. The days do change, so check the website for up-to-date Extra Magic Hours and for those of the water parks.

Not all attractions run during Extra Magic Hours. Check the Disney website for a list of attractions that run for these extra hours and the restaurants that open early or close late. Even if you are a resort guest, you need a Park Hopper Option on your Magic Your Way base ticket to zap from one park over to another that has extended hours.

closed), and the parks close down several of their restaurants to reduce food costs. If you are traveling during this time and have your heart set on particular attractions, check the operational updates section of the disneyworld. disney.go.com website. Huge conventions and trade shows may also affect the parks' business. Visit www.orlandoinfo.com for a list of events going on during your visit.

Special Events

Each of the four Disney parks hosts an annual array of events and a short list of Walt Disney World Resort–wide special events. Each mid-January, Walt Disney World Resort hosts a marathon and half marathon on one weekend, allowing some intrepid folks to complete the **Goofy's Race-and-a-Half Challenge,** running both events for a combined 39.3 miles. The first week in June the parks open their doors for **Gay Days,** in which more than 100,000 gays and lesbians convene from all over the country for a week of fun. Then during Labor Day weekend the parks host the **Tom Joyner Family Reunion** event, a largely African American celebration with celebrity entertainers such as Aretha Franklin, Sinbad, and LL Cool J. The beginning of December brings **Mousefest,** an annual get-together of Disney fans from all over, which then runs smack into the December holiday season at the parks—which all four parks celebrate with great zeal. All four parks decorate lavishly, with additional events throughout the month.

At Magic Kingdom there's a nightly tree-lighting ceremony on Main Street U.S.A., and the afternoon parade is called the **Very Merry Christmas Parade** for the month. **Mickey's 'Twas the Night Before Christmas** is performed at the Galaxy Palace Theater and there's a hard-ticket event (that means it's a dated ticket, separate from admission to the park) called **Mickey's Very Merry Christmas Party.**

At Epcot, **international holiday storytellers** are ensconced in each pavilion around World Showcase during the day. Storytellers tell the indigenous holiday tales from their own country (in the Germany pavilion, for

to avoid crowds, but remember that September and October are smack-dab in the middle of Florida's hurricane season. During these months afternoon thunderstorms are common.

One thing to bear in mind, though, is that in January and February rides and attractions get serviced and refurbished (and are thus

example, a storyteller tells the tale of St. Nikolaus Eve on December 6). Then at 6 P.M. the park stages a tree-lighting ceremony with Mickey at the World Showcase Plaza Tree Stage and a **Candlelight Processional** with a nightly reading of the Christmas story by a celebrity narrator.

During the winter holidays at Disney's Hollywood Studios, the park is illuminated with five million Christmas lights strung on more than 350 miles of wire for the annual **Osborne Family Spectacle of Lights.** At Disney's Animal Kingdom, the daily parade is renamed **Mickey's Jingle Jungle Expeditions.**

TICKETS

Walt Disney World Resort changed its ticket pricing structure in 2005. In all likelihood, the ticket pricing will have changed again by the time this book goes to print. The Magic Your Way Disney World Tickets system is essentially a base ticket, to which you add days, parks, or other options. First, choose the number of days you want on a base ticket, which allows you to enter one theme park each day. Then decide which option you want to add, paying only for those features you want, such as the ability to visit multiple Disney theme parks each day or to visit Disney water parks, Downtown Disney, Pleasure Island, and so on.

Disney accepts American Express, Visa, MasterCard, Discover, Diners Club, and The Disney Credit Card. Travelers checks and cash are also accepted. Disney Resort IDs can serve as a charge card.

Base Tickets

The base ticket includes admission to *one* of the four Walt Disney World theme parks (Magic Kingdom, Epcot, Disney's Hollywood Studios, or Disney's Animal Kingdom), one park per day (in other words, no park hopping), and expires 14 days after the first use. Admission to the water parks, Pleasure Island, DisneyQuest, or Disney's Wide World of Sports complex is not included. Ticket prices do not include tax (6 percent in Florida, but it's rumored to be going up soon).

Park Hopper

This option allows you to come and go as you please through all four Disney theme parks on the same day or every day for each day of your pass. The extra cost to the base-price ticket is $45.

Water Park Fun and More

The Water Park option entitles guests to a specific number of visits to a choice of entertainment and recreation venues. Choices include Disney's Blizzard Beach water park, Disney's Typhoon Lagoon water park, DisneyQuest, Downtown Disney Pleasure Island, or Disney's Wide World of Sports complex. The extra cost to the base-price ticket is $50 (this includes 3–6 visits to these attractions, depending on the number of base ticket days you buy).

No Expiration

Disney base tickets expire 14 days after their first use. If you don't want them to expire, adding the No Expiration option means you are free to come back to Walt Disney World and take advantage of unused tickets at any time. The extra cost to the base-price ticket starts at $10 for a 2–3 day base ticket and goes up to $155 for the 10-day ticket.

Annual Passes

Annual passes ($434 ages 10 and up, $382 ages 3–9, younger than three free) allow unlimited entry into the four theme parks for one year from the purchase date.

Premium annual passes ($559 ages 10 and up, $493 ages 3–9, younger than three free) include admission for 365 days from the purchase date to the theme parks, Pleasure Island, Disney's water parks, DisneyQuest, and Disney's Wide World of Sports complex, as well as parking.

Florida residents get a discount on annual passes:

- Regular annual passes: $339 ages 10 and up, $298 ages 3–9

- Premium annual passes: $445 ages 10 and up, $394 ages 3–9

DISNEY TICKET OPTIONS

TICKET	1-DAY	2-DAY	3-DAY	4-DAY	5-DAY
Base Ticket					
Ages 10 and up	$67	$132	$192	$202	$206
Ages 3-9	$56	$110	$160	$168	$169

Base Ticket admits the guest to one theme park each day of use: Magic Kingdom, Epcot, Disney's Hollywood Studios, Animal Kingdom.

Add: **Park Hopper**	$45	$45	$45	$45	$45

The Park Hopper option entitles guests to visit more than one theme park on each day of use: Magic Kingdom, Epcot, Disney's Hollywood Studios, Animal Kingdom.

Add: **Water Park** **Fun and More**	$50	$50	$50	$50	$50
(visits)	3	3	3	4	4

The Water Park Fun and More option entitles a guest to a specified number of visits (3-6) to a choice of entertainment and recreation venues: Blizzard Beach, Typhoon Lagoon, DisneyQuest, Pleasure Island, Wide World of Sports.

Add: **No Expiration**	n/a	$10	$15	$40	$55

No expiration means unused admissions on a ticket have no expiration date. All tickets expire 14 days after the first use unless you buy the No Expiration option.

Advance Purchase Savings					
Ages 10 and up	n/a	n/a	n/a	$2/$12	$5/$15
Ages 3-9	n/a	n/a	n/a	$2/$10	$2/$10

Advance Purchase Savings occur when you buy 4-10-day tickets with Park Hopper and/or Water Park Fun and More domestically outside of Florida before arrival at Walt Disney World Resort. (Savings to the left of the slash are with one feature; savings to the right of the slash are with both features.)

- Seasonal passes: $223 ages 10 and up, $197 ages 3–9 (peak seasons and holidays are blacked out)

Florida residents are also granted a savings of 9–10 percent on one-day base tickets; $60.30 ages 10 and up, $51 ages 3–9.

More Disney Attractions

A single-day, one-park ticket at **Typhoon Lagoon** or **Blizzard Beach** is $36 for ages 10 and up, $30 for ages 3–9. A **water park Park Hopper annual pass** is $99.95 for ages 10 and up, $80.50 for ages 3–9, which allows guests full access to both water parks for a year.

A one-day ticket at **DisneyQuest** is $36

TICKET Base Ticket	6-DAY	7-DAY	8-DAY	9-DAY	10-DAY
Ages 10 and up	$208	$210	$212	$214	$216
Ages 3-9	$171	$173	$175	$176	177
Add: **Park Hopper**	$45	$45	$45	$45	$45
Add: **Water Park** **Fun and More**	$50	$50	$50	$50	$50
(visits)	5	6	6	6	6
Add: **No Expiration**	$60	$90	$125	$150	$155
Advance Purchase Savings					
Ages 10 and up	$6/$16	$7/$17	$7/$17	$7/$17	$7/$17
Ages 3-9	$2/$10	$2/$10	$3/$11	$3/$11	$3/$11

for ages 10 and up, $30 for ages 3–9. A DisneyQuest annual pass is $89 for ages 10 and up, $71 for ages 3–9. There's also a combined **DisneyQuest/Water Park annual pass** ($129 ages 10 and up, $99 ages 3–9).

A pass to **Disney's Wide World of Sports complex** is $10.28 for ages 10 and up, $7.71 ages 3–9. **Pleasure Island** passes are $21.95 for one night and allow admission to multiple clubs, for ages 18 and up only ($55.95 for an annual pass).

Cirque du Soleil's **La Nouba** tickets range $63–112 for ages 10 and up, and $50–90 for ages 3–9.

FASTPASS

FASTPASS is a system created by Disney in 1999, the aim of which is to allow you to cut the line if you're a long-term and strategic thinker. It's a reservation system, essentially, that works like this: You walk up to a much-coveted attraction, Expedition Everest in Disney's Animal Kingdom, say, and you go to the FASTPASS ticket–dispensing machines near the ride entrance. Insert your park admission ticket briefly into the machine, and it spits out a chit that lists an hour-long window of time in which you are to return to Expedition Everest to ride. You return to the ride at the specified time and bypass the regular line, hopping instead into the shorter FASTPASS Return line after showing your FASTPASS ticket to a "cast member."

Not every ride takes FASTPASS. The FAST-PASS attractions are listed in each chapter, and those rides that are essential to FASTPASS are indicated. Planning your day around FAST-PASSing is smart—you can wait in line 15 minutes while other people languish in the other line for up to an hour.

FASTPASS tips: Send one person from your party to go directly to a busy FAST-PASS ride—give this person all of your park admission tickets so he or she can get FASTPASS chits for everyone in your party. It used to be a guest could hold only a single FASTPASS at a time; if you tried to insert a park ticket into another FASTPASS machine before the time shown on your previous FASTPASS, the machine would spit out a message saying that it was not yet time to obtain another FASTPASS. It's loosened up a little, and now additional FASTPASSes can be had sooner after one another. Just try it.

Re-Admission Policy

If you leave the park with the intention of returning, get your hand stamped at the exit. To reenter, present your ticket or Walt Disney World Resort ID and your hand stamp.

Resorts

Walt Disney World Resort has 32 different resorts, with more than 31,000 guest rooms and 784 campsites—this includes five Disney Vacation Club Resort properties and 10 resorts that are not Disney owned and operated. If the bulk of your time in Orlando will be spent at Walt Disney World Resort theme parks, it makes a lot of sense to stay in one of the Disney Resorts. They are offered at nearly every price point, many of them just adjacent to one of the parks, and there are a host of benefits afforded Disney Resort guests. There are also perks such as getting to use your Disney Resort ID like a credit card, or having a package delivered right to your room. Resort identification (your plastic Disney Resort ID) and theme park admission tickets are required to take advantage of these perks. To make a reservation at any Walt Disney World Resort, call 407/934-7639.

At all Disney Resorts, children under 18 stay at no additional charge. For more than two adults in a single room, value resorts charge an extra $10 per person, moderately priced resorts charge an extra $15 per person, and deluxe resorts charge an extra $25 per person.

Disney has five "seasons" at its Walt Disney World Resort hotels every year. Value Season is the least expensive and least crowded time, followed by Regular Season, Summer Season, Peak Season, and Holiday Season. These change year by year, and they change property to property, but generally they are roughly as follows:

- Value Season: January 1–February 14, August 5–October 3, November 25–December 19

- Regular Season: April 15–May 23, October 4–November 24

- Summer Season: May 24–August 4

- Peak Season: February 15–April 14

- Holiday Season: December 20–December 31

PRICE KEY

$ - Disney's value resorts
(from $82/night)
Amenities at value-priced resorts include food courts, pizza delivery, luggage service (hourly), swimming pools, and bus transportation.

$$ - Disney's moderate resorts
(from $145/night)
Amenities at moderate-priced resorts include full-service restaurants, food courts, room service (limited), luggage service, swimming pools with a slide and hot tub, on-site recreation, bus or boat transportation.

$$$ - Disney's deluxe resorts
(from $215/night)
Amenities include full-service restaurants, room service, luggage service, valet parking, swimming pools, beach access, on-site recreation, on-site childcare, monorail, boat, or bus transportation.

$$$$ - Disney Vacation Club resorts
(from $279/night)
Amenities at these resorts offer full-service restaurants, kitchen facilities, pizza delivery, luggage service, swimming pools, on-site recreation, front-door parking, flexible room arrangements, bus or boat transportation.

Value Season pricing can save you anywhere from $30 (at a value resort) to $120 (at select deluxe resorts) per night.

Disney Transportation
Disney transportation is a real benefit of staying at a Walt Disney World Resort. Staying on International Drive is fun, staying on U.S. Highway 192 in Kissimmee is cheap, but either way you're going to spend a great deal of time in traffic. At one of the Disney Resorts, you can park your car and hop a motor coach, water taxi, or monorail to the parks. Not only does this save gas and aggravation, but at parks such as Magic Kingdom it gives you a distinct advantage over nonresort guests because you are dropped off right at the main gate, not at the Ticket and Transportation Center with the rest of the hoi polloi.

Extra Magic Hour Benefit
The Extra Magic Hour benefit entitles resort guests to go to designated theme parks an hour early and to stay as much as an extra three hours after other park-goers have gone home. This perk also extends to Disney water parks. During high season, the reduced crowds during these hours is a real treat.

The Extra Magic Hour schedule is as follows: At Magic Kingdom it's Thursday mornings and Sunday evenings; at Epcot it's Tuesday mornings and Friday evenings; at Disney's Hollywood Studios it's Saturday mornings, and evening hours vary; and at Animal Kingdom it's Monday mornings and Wednesday evenings. The days do change, so check the website for up-to-date Extra Magic Hours and for those of the water parks.

Disney's Magical Express Service
Disney's Magical Express Service offers Disney Resort guests personalized luggage service (pet carriers are not included). Guests check their luggage at their hometown airport. The luggage then magically appears in your room at the resort—you don't have to retrieve it from baggage claim. Instead, hop on the Walt Disney World Resort motor coaches and go. The same thing works in reverse: Bags precede you to the airport and are checked through to your final destination. You can even have your resort print your boarding passes (domestic flights only). Disney's Magical Express Service may still be working out some of the kinks—word is, luggage doesn't always find its rightful home—but certainly Disney will fix any little bobbles in the system.

Resort Dining
Disney has always taken food fairly seriously—it used to have a culinary school open to the public for recreational cooking classes. In

recent years, an influx of celebrity chefs, luxury resort properties, and sophisticated convention business has upped the ante. In high season (summer, spring break, winter holidays), reservations are a must at top Disney restaurants. They aren't called reservations per se, but "priority-seating arrangements" can be made by calling 407/939-3463 up to 90 days in advance. All are nonsmoking. Dress code is universally casual at all Disney properties with the exception of Victoria and Albert's at Disney's Grand Floridian Resort (jackets for men, dresses or equivalent for women).

The **Magic Your Way Package Plus Dining Package** (a discount package that includes resort accommodations, tickets, and food) allows you to choose from 100 Disney restaurants for one table-service meal, one counter-service meal, and one snack per person per day of your package stay. Longtime Disney enthusiasts complain that service in many restaurants tends to get a little lax when they realize you're using a dining package (not as great an opportunity for a big tip as regular à la carte dining).

It's something to consider if dining is an important part of your travel experience.

MAGIC KINGDOM

Every night Magic Kingdom–area resort guests are treated to a special show when the **Electrical Water Pageant** glides around Seven Seas Lagoon and Bay Lake. The aquatic parade of 14 lighted barges carry a 25-foot-tall screen of lights with a music-and-light show. As of 2007, the schedule was: Polynesian Resort 9 P.M., Grand Floridian 9:15 P.M., Wilderness Lodge 9:35 P.M., Fort Wilderness 9:45 P.M., and Contemporary Resort 10:05 P.M. Note that the pageant is not held in bad weather.

Disney's Fort Wilderness $-$$$
Resort and Campground

Disney's Fort Wilderness Resort and Campground (campsites from $41 per night, cabins from $249–365 per night) has 784 campsites and 409 cabins in a lovely 700-acre wilderness setting. Campsites are level, paved pads with electric, water and sewer hookups, charcoal

a wilderness cabin at Disney's Fort Wilderness Resort and Campground

© DISNEY

grills, and picnic tables. All campsites have easy access to air-conditioned bathrooms with private showers, coin laundry, vending machines, and telephones.

Wilderness cabins are air-conditioned accommodations that sleep up to six guests and feature vaulted ceilings, fully equipped kitchens, full bathrooms, television, VCR, outdoor grills, picnic tables, and a private patio deck. Amenities include watercraft, beach, fishing, tennis courts, two heated swimming pools, arcade game room, laundry facilities, and kennel. There's a nightly campfire and marshmallow roast with Disney characters and a Disney movie, and a nightly dinner show is available at Pioneer Hall's Hoop-Dee-Doo Musical Revue.

RESTAURANTS

The **Hoop-Dee-Doo Musical Revue** ($50.99–58.99 adults, $25.99–29.99 children) is the big dining kahuna here, and reservations are a must far in advance (make them up to 180 days in advance by calling 407/939-3463). It's an all-American hoedown with family-style barbecue ribs, corn, baked beans, draft beer, wine, and soft drinks, all enjoyed with a musical comedy review that always gets highest marks from longtime Disney fans. It's one of the longest-running shows at Walt Disney World. There are three shows nightly at 5, 7:15, and 9:30 P.M. There's also **Mickey's Backyard BBQ** ($44.99 adults, $26.99 children; make reservations), with a country-western–themed all-you-can-eat character picnic.

For just regular dining, **Crockett's Tavern** features pizza, appetizers, smoothies, and a full-service bar, and **Trail's End Restaurant** in rustic Pioneer Hall has a down-home buffet.

Disney's Wilderness Lodge $$$

Disney's Wilderness Lodge ($215–675) has 728 rooms with 27 suites in a woodsy, national parklike setting (think Old Faithful Inn at Yellowstone Park). The six-story lobby has tepee-topped chandeliers, totem poles, and an 82-foot-tall stone fireplace. The swimming area features hot and cold spas and a geothermal "geyser" erupts hourly at the edge of Bay Lake. Recreation and amenities include bike and boat rentals, pools, and playground.

RESTAURANTS

Artist Point (entrées $30–50) at Disney's Wilderness Lodge specializes in foods of the Pacific Northwest—cedar plank salmon, great wines from Oregon and Washington—but it's a little ho-hum in my book and fairly pricy for what you get.

Disney's $$$
Contemporary Resort

Disney's Contemporary Resort ($259–755) was one of the original deluxe resort hotels in Disney's lineup. When it opened in 1971 its Death Star–like black glass-and-concrete pyramidlike design was the height of state of the art. It's ironic, really, that the hotel seems a little retro in its design now—not particularly contemporary at all. That's not to say it's not a lovely hotel. A recent remodel has updated and glamorized the 1,008 rooms and suites in the 14-story deluxe resort. Cinderella Castle and all the hubbub of Magic Kingdom is within eyesight of the hotel, which boasts an interior monorail station. An atrium lobby is filled with modern art, and recreational amenities include waterskiing, boat rentals, six lighted tennis courts, jogging, volleyball, parasailing, playground, and two swimming pools. The 90,000 square feet of meeting space includes a 44,300-square-foot grand ballroom.

RESTAURANTS

Making lists of Orlando's top restaurants nearly every year, **California Grill** (entrées $30–50) at Disney's Contemporary Resort draws locals as well as tourists. It was one of Disney's earliest efforts at luxurious destination dining, with panoramic windows of Magic Kingdom (and its fireworks) and a dynamic open kitchen. The food is a very apt facsimile of what made San Francisco such a culinary mecca in the late 1980s—flatbreads, Sonoma goat cheese ravioli, grilled pork tenderloin with polenta and balsamic-sparked cremini mushrooms—simple, bright flavors with a heavy reliance on seasonal produce. The wine list is a treasure trove for the California cab-ophile, even by the glass. My only complaint about California Grill is the somewhat cold and antiseptic, strangely art nouveau interior. Other dining options include **Concourse Steakhouse** (entrées $15–29) and **Chef Mickey's** (breakfast and dinner buffets $15–29), two lounges, two snack bars, and room service.

The Villas at Disney's Wilderness Lodge $$$$

A Disney Vacation Club time-share resort that opened in 2000, the Villas at Disney's Wilderness Lodge ($305–1,075) have 136 units/181 rooms, including studio, one-, and two-bedroom villas, next to Disney's Wilderness Lodge. Complete with totem poles and geysers in an American West railroad motif, the property has rooms that include wet bar, microwave, and small refrigerator, or a full kitchen. It offers a health club and pool. Guests have access to the restaurants at Disney's Wilderness Lodge.

Disney's Polynesian Resort $$$

Disney's Polynesian Resort ($329–815) is one of the historic original resort hotels at Walt Disney World, planned by Walt himself. Construction started in 1971, with 39 acres of waterfalls and lush gardens to give this lavish hotel a South Pacific Island magnificence. Monorail service is available to Magic Kingdom, which is just across the Seven Seas Lagoon. This deluxe, 847-room hotel features a pool area with waterfalls, white-sand beach, and a complete array of dining and recreational options that include swimming, boating, jogging, playground, and a game room. A recent remodel has maintained the hotel's luxury standards, but many guests blanch a little at the very high prices.

RESTAURANTS

On the second floor of the Great Ceremonial House, **'Ohana** (breakfast and dinner $15–29 per person) offers a character breakfast with Lilo and Stitch and a family-style feast with Hawaiian-style appetizers and Polynesian, three-foot grilled skewers cooked over an 18-foot wood-burning fire pit, all overlooking the Seven Seas Lagoon. The **Tambu Lounge** is a fun bar for froufrou tropical cocktails, connected to 'Ohana on the second floor of the Great Ceremonial House. Then there's **Disney's Spirit of Aloha** dinner show (at 5:15 and 8 P.M. Tues.–Sat., $50.99–58.99 adults, $25.99–29.99 children) with traditional Polynesian music, dancing, and costumes, and an all-you-can-eat buffet.

Fueled by Kona coffee, the 172-seat **Kona Cafe** (entrées $14–25) serves appealing breakfasts, lunches, and dinners with an eye to healthy preparations and an Asian-inflected palate. It's a very pretty restaurant, a delight whether you're popping in for a sweet (an exceptional array comes out of the gorgeous dessert kitchen) or for Auntie Kaui's Tonga Toast, a Polynesian breakfast original of banana-stuffed sourdough bread, rolled in cinnamon sugar, and fried crisp. **Captain Cook's Snack Company** purveys straightforward ice creams, pizzas, and sandwiches 24 hours; the **Barefoot Pool Bar** serves snacks and drinks to those sunning and swimming.

Disney's Grand Floridian Resort and Spa $$$

(Disney's Grand Floridian Resort and Spa ($375–910) is indeed grand, with nearly 900 rooms in this luxury resort on the shores of Seven Seas Lagoon. The closest hotel to Magic Kingdom, it boasts a soaring five-story lobby and a stately turn-of-the-20th-century Victorian theme. It's the splurge, pull-out-all-the-stops choice. Built in 1988 and considered the Disney flagship resort, it was modeled after the Hotel del Coronado in San Diego, with red gabled roofs and six lodge buildings. Concierge service has expanded to one of the resort's lodge buildings, adding 95 deluxe-service rooms and suites. Recreation possibilities include boat rentals featuring *Grand 1*, a 45-foot Sea Ray yacht, two swimming pools (one with slide and waterfall), playground, health club, game room, a full-service spa, fishing excursions, and preferred access to Disney's six golf courses. There's also 40,000 square feet of meeting and con-

Disney's Grand Floridian Resort and Spa

© DISNEY

vention space. Transportation is provided by monorail, water taxis, and buses.

RESTAURANTS

Disney's Grand Floridian Resort has a couple of notable restaurants, the fanciest of which is undoubtedly **Victoria and Albert's** (more than $100 per person). Frette linens, Riedel crystal—it's a pull-out-all-the-stops kind of place, the only AAA Five-Diamond restaurant in Central Florida. It's on a much more intimate scale than many of the Disney Resort restaurants, with only 18 tables in the main dining room and another five in the private fireplace room, plus a chef's table in the kitchen. Ladies get a red rose upon departure, a harpist glides through mellifluous ditties, service is formal—in all, it's a kind of old-timey fancy restaurant ambience, but chef Scott Hunnel's culinary vision is emphatically 21st century. He does those trendy flavored foams (it's a trend I hope will fade quietly), amazing things with Hudson Valley foie gras, and gutsy, vibrant dishes such

as Virginia black bass with asparagus risotto and English peas. There are two seatings daily September through June, one seating daily July through August. The chef's table seating is 6 P.M. daily. Dinner is $100 per person, $155 with wine pairing; chef's table is $150 per person, $215 with wine pairing. Reservations can be made up to 90 days in advance for the dining room and 120 days in advance for the chef's table.

The Grand Floridian has a couple of other notable eateries, **C Citricos** (entrées $30–50) being the next most impressive. The dining room is a lovely riff on warm Mediterranean colors, with an open kitchen that follows suit with the cuisine. Part Provence, part Tuscany, and a dash of Spanish Riviera, the seasonally changing menu may feature classic warm goat cheese salad with arugula, frisée, and crispy lardons of bacon; or warm onion tart with walnut vinaigrette; or hearty braised veal shank. The house martinis are excellent, especially the Citropolitan with lemon and lime liqueur. It's fairly quiet and rarefied, so kids might prefer elsewhere (except that the view from here of Magic Kingdom's evening fireworks is fab).

Where kids prefer, actually, is **1900 Park Fare** (entrées $15–29), which does a Cinderella and friends buffet character breakfast and dinner. It's a hoot and the array of carving stations, pastas, and salads are much better than the dreaded word "buffet" often warrants. There's also seafood at **Narcoossee's** (dinner nightly, $30–50) and **Grand Floridian Café** (lunch and dinner daily, $10–18) for more casual fare.

EPCOT AND DISNEY'S HOLLYWOOD STUDIOS
Disney's Caribbean Beach Resort $$

Disney's Caribbean Beach Resort ($145–225) features 2,112 rooms spread in five low, two-story "villages" on the banks of 42-acre Barefoot Bay, a man-made lake. Pastel colors and Caribbean names (Barbados, Jamaica, Martinique, Aruba, and Trinidad) make this one all about da islands, mon. There are sandy beach-rimmed swimming pools, equipped with hammocks for serious relaxation, outside each building, and the resort's main pool is kitted out with a cool pool bar and water slide. A lakeside recreation area offers sailboat and small watercraft for hourly rental, and there are a jogging track, nature trails, and bicycling. At the center of the lake is Parrot Cay Island with an aviary of tropical birds.

Of the moderately priced Disney hotels, this one has the largest rooms. The resort is fairly vast, necessitating an internal bus system to ferry guests around.

RESTAURANTS
Shutters (entrées $15–29) is the only upscale, sit-down, dinner-only restaurant on the property, with a familiar menu that runs to prime rib and simple fish preparations, some with accessible Caribbean embellishments. **Old Port Royale Food Court** is more geared to families, with six different counter-service restaurants catering to a range of tastes—but all of them fairly pedestrian tastes (pizza, burgers, sandwiches, and so on). There is also room-service pizza.

Disney's Beach Club Resort $$$
Disney's Beach Club Resort ($315–710) is one of Disney's splurge hotels, between Epcot and Disney's Hollywood Studios and close enough to walk to either one (although there's also boat transportation across the lagoon that runs to both parks). The resort's 576 rooms and suites are in a New England beach cottage style with a slight nostalgic 19th-century patina. The lobby features white wicker furniture and 24-foot-high ceilings. With its neighbor Disney's Yacht Club Resort, it shares Stormalong Bay, with three lagoon areas, a deep "lazy river," an enormous water slide, and whirlpools (the largest pool complex in all of Disney, it requires guests to wear wristbands to keep out eager interlopers). It also shares a health club with steam, sauna, massage, weights, and aerobics rooms, and a marina with motorized watercraft.

RESTAURANTS
Steamed shellfish takes center stage at the casual indoor evening clambake held at **Cape May Café** (buffet breakfast, $15–29, buffet dinner $15–29), which also hosts a meet-and-greet character breakfast with Goofy and friends. Kids will like the **Beaches and Cream Soda Shop** with its signature diner-style jukebox and massive sundaes, while adults may prefer a tipple at **Martha's Vineyard Lounge**.

Disney's Yacht Club Resort $$$
Disney's Yacht Club Resort ($315–710) is the sister property to Disney's Beach Club Resort, with which it shares a 73,000-square-foot convention center and the three-acre sandy-bottomed Stormalong Bay pool complex with its charming beached shipwreck. The theme here is still the beach, but it's more a buttoned-up New England nautical idiom with oyster-gray clapboard buildings set around 25-acre Crescent Lake, all rooms with French doors that open onto porches or balconies. Designed by architect Robert A. M. Stern, the resort's 621 rooms and suites are more understated than their counterparts at the Beach Club. Hardwood floors, a wide wraparound porch with wicker rockers, and quiet walkways

give it a more contemplative, adult air. Guests enjoy a big croquet lawn in view of a lovely oh-so-New England marina lighthouse.

Boats run to Epcot and Disney's Hollywood Studios; Epcot is a short, 10-minute walk. Buses take guests to the other parks (no extra charge). Epcot's nightly IllumiNations show is visible from the beach of the Yacht Club/Beach Club complex.

RESTAURANTS

The **Yachtsman Steakhouse** (entrées $30–50) serves well-executed dry-aged steaks with creamed spinach and all the usual suspects on the side—it's a classic steak house in a rarefied ambience. More casual is the **Yacht Club Galley** (entrées $11–21), serving sturdy, familiar American food for breakfast, lunch, and dinner.

Disney's BoardWalk Inn $$$

Also alongside Crescent Lake, Disney's Board-Walk Inn ($315–750) is a resort and entertainment complex reminiscent of a 1930s mid-Atlantic seaside beach town. The central draw is, as the name suggests, a long boardwalk dotted with restaurants, shops, and other festive entertainment. It's within walking distance of the International Gateway entrance to Epcot. Some of the 372 rooms feature views of Crescent Lake, over which guests can watch Epcot's evening fireworks and laser display (although these rooms also overlook the boardwalk, which can be loud fairly late into the evening). Four-story white buildings with pale green shingled roofs and private courtyards give this property real charm, with amenities such as a children's activity center, health club, tennis courts, themed pool, and a 20,000-square-foot conference center.

RESTAURANTS

Flying Fish Café (entrées $30–50) at Disney's BoardWalk is another one that foodies have been flocking to, or maybe "schooling" in. It's an underwater fantasy with lights that dangle from oversize fishhooks and shimmery fish-scale walls. Not goofy at all, the restaurant theming is gorgeous, with a huge exhibition kitchen for added drama. It's been through a couple of chefs, but the kitchen keeps seamlessly sending out exceptional, seafood-heavy fare. The signature is crispy, potato-wrapped Florida red snapper napped with creamy leek fondue and red wine-butter sauce, but the peeky-toe crabcake is lush, as is the crème brûlée–sandwiched banana napoleon. It has a great champagne list.

Spoodles (entrées $15–29) is the Board-Walk's family-oriented restaurant, also very worthwhile. Big stacks of Fiestaware, wide wooden tables, and another open kitchen make it lively and fun. The best way to dine here is by working your way through the Mediterranean small plates accompanied by a pitcher of sangria. **Big River Grille and Brewing Works** (lunch and dinner daily, $15–29) features handcrafted beers in a fun atmosphere with nice outdoor dining; there's also an **ESPN Club** sports bar for all your game-viewing needs.

Disney's Beach Club Villas $$$$

The fourth of the five Disney Vacation Club Resorts to be built, Disney's Beach Club Villas ($315–1,105) contains 208 units/280 rooms in studio, one-, and two-bedroom vacation villas in a Cape May style and pastel colors. As with all the vacation club properties, it shares its amenities with its corresponding traditional hotel, in this case with Disney's Beach Club Resort. At approximately the same prices as the Beach Club Resort, the timeshare villas, opened in 2002, have the added benefit of full kitchens (all the better to throw together breakfasts or quick dinners before or after a day at the theme parks) and larger living spaces. These five-story villas reflect the same design motifs as Disney's Beach Club Resort with pastel colors and a charming "stick-style" architecture, sharing also the three-acre Stormalong Bay (as well as two "quiet pools," spa, and kiddie pool), the Ship Shape Health Club, Lafferty Place Arcade, and watercraft rentals—all accessible via lovely breezeways. Guests can also enjoy fishing, beach volleyball, croquet, or tennis. The villas share **Cape May Café, Beaches and**

Cream Soda Shop, and **Martha's Vineyard Lounge** with Disney's Beach Club Resort.

Disney's BoardWalk Villas $$$$

Another entry in Disney Vacation Club time-shares, Disney's BoardWalk Villas ($315–2,090) has 383 units/532 rooms in one-, two-, and three-bedroom pale pastel-colored villas with full kitchens that all reflect the theme of the deluxe Disney's BoardWalk Inn. Outside enjoy the carnival sights and ragtime sounds of the boardwalk at the edge of Crescent Lake. Modeled after an Atlantic seaboard resort of the 1930s, the villas are near the Yacht and Beach Club Resorts as well as the Dolphin and Swan Hotels, within walking distance of Epcot. The pools, shared with Disney's BoardWalk Inn, are in an area called Luna Park, which boasts a 200-foot waterslide and a "quiet pool." A children's playground, Side Show Games video arcade, and bike rentals make this a great one for families with elementary or middle school-age kids. For adults, there's the Muscles and Bustles Health Club, tennis, and watercraft rentals (it has cool "WaterMouse" boats you can rent by the hour). The restaurants **Flying Fish Café, Spoodles, Big River Grille and Brewing Works,** and the **ESPN Club** are shared with Disney's BoardWalk Inn.

As with all Disney Vacation Club properties, anyone can rent time-share rooms—you don't have to be a member or owner in the club.

DISNEY'S ANIMAL KINGDOM

Disney's All-Star Movies Resort $

One of three sprawling "All-Star" budget resort complexes, Disney's All-Star Movies Resort ($82–141) is in the southern part of the Disney complex and features 1,920 rooms. Each individual building is tricked out with specific Disney film-obilia, with characters from *101 Dalmatians, Toy Story, Fantasia, The Love Bug,* or *The Mighty Ducks* adorning the hotel, mostly via giant Disney film icons affixed to the sides of the low-rise buildings. (Is a 35-foot-tall Buzz Lightyear really a good thing as a design embellishment?) Rooms are com-

fortable but somewhat bare-bones and small (260 square feet). If your aim is to spend most of your days at the parks, this is a perfectly acceptable concession in the name of parsimony. Kids don't seem to notice, maybe because the resort has in-room pizza delivery, a *Fantasia* pool, a *Mighty Ducks*–themed pool, a big playground, and a video arcade. It has no sit-down restaurant, so guests are limited to a quick-service movie-themed **World Premiere Food Court** that runs to hamburgers and salads.

Buses travel between all three All-Star properties and the theme parks, but Disney's All-Star Movies is the last stop, meaning the buses are sometimes filled nearly to capacity by the time they arrive here—you may be forced to stand during your bus ride.

Disney's All-Star Music Resort $

Get rid of all those Disney film characters and all that sporting equipment (below), substituting instead some giant musical icons—jukeboxes, top hats, speakers, and, somewhat strangely, a huge pair of cowboy boots. It's Disney's All-Star Music Resort ($82–141), suites to $285), also with 1,920 rooms but boasting 214 "family suites" in three-story, low-rise buildings decorated with oversize musical instruments and symbols. Of the family suites, 192 sleep up to six people and feature two bathrooms, a kitchenette, and private master bedroom—it's definitely a good deal for larger families. Each building cluster features its own name and theme, such as Calypso and Jazz.

The best part of Disney's All-Star Music Resort is the piano pool, shaped like a huge grand piano with drawn-on piano keys (there's a second one shaped like a guitar), but there's also a Note'able Games arcade in Melody Hall, right across from Intermission Food Court (pasta, rotisserie chicken, and sandwiches).

Disney's All-Star Sports Resort $

Now sub out sports equipment for Disney film characters and you've got the budget Disney's All-Star Sports Resort ($82–141), again with 1,920 clean but plain rooms, most with two double beds. The complex celebrates sports ex-

DISNEY WORLD PLANNING

uberantly with huge pennants, basketball, tennis, baseball, surfing, and football apparatus decorating the 10 buildings, which are divided into five sections, each with its own prevailing theme. You'll find a baseball-themed Grand Slam Pool, another called SurfBoard Bay, and a kiddie pool. A video arcade and extensive playground appeal to young children. Stadium Hall houses the **End Zone Food Court** (decorated with surfing and football scenes; food runs to burgers and rib-sticking "blue-plate specials"), registration desk, store, and arcade. Disney's All-Star Sports Resort is the first resort you come to on West Buena Vista Drive; it's on a 246-acre site at the northwest quadrant of the World Drive and U.S. Highway 192 interchange.

Disney's Coronado Springs Resort $$

C **Disney's Coronado Springs Resort** ($145–225) is inspired by the American Southwest and regions of Mexico and encircles a 15-acre lagoon. The name and theme are loosely linked to the explorations of Francisco de Cor-

onado, with a five-story Mayan pyramid at the center. The tiled lobby is lovely, showcasing the spring-fed Fountain of the Doves (La Fuente de Las Palomas); the 1,921 guest rooms are scattered in three village areas: the Casitas (three- and four-story buildings), the Ranchos (two- and three-story villas), and the Cabanas (two-story buildings). The Casitas or "little houses" would look right at home in Santa Fe, with lots of rustic stucco buildings and terracotta roofs. Buildings are separated by colorful plazas and inviting, palm-shaded courtyards.

It's first and foremost a convention property, because it houses a 220,000-square-foot convention center with the 60,214-square-foot Coronado Ballroom. But for families, the Mayan ruin–themed Dig Site pool is a huge draw—great water slide—as are the Jumping Beans Arcade and the 20,000-square-foot sandy playground/fake archaeological site.

RESTAURANTS
The full-service option here is the **Maya Grill** (entrées $30–50), with a Nuevo Latino culinary

© DISNEY

Disney's Coronado Springs Resort

DISNEY WORLD PLANNING

flair, a huge exhibition grill, and attractive Mayan-inspired decor. A second restaurant, **Pepper Market,** is an open-air quick-service spot for pizza, pasta, burgers, and familiar stalwarts.

Disney's Animal Kingdom Lodge $$$

The big draw at Disney's Animal Kingdom Lodge ($215–635) is the 33-acre wildlife reserve out the windows of the 1,293 rooms in the six-story luxury resort. Rooms are arrayed in a horseshoe shape after a kraal African village design, mostly to maximize guests' views of free-roaming mammals and tropical birds on the lush savanna. It pays to get the "savanna-view" rooms, in which guests step out through sliding glass doors onto private balconies to get a ringside view of giraffes, zebras, wildebeests, and ostriches.

Meanwhile, indoors has lot to look at, too. The resort features hand-carved furnishings and art, African tapestries, and a giant fireplace in a soaring lobby. It's a truly stunning resort in a vibrantly colored African motif that somehow never seems overly contrived. The Uzima zero-entry pool features a 67-foot water slide, separate wading pool, two spas, and a nearby playground. A fitness center, clubhouse for kids in the evening (essentially a babysitting service), and video arcade are added allures, but the resort offers a unique animal program that makes this something special: You use night vision to view the animals on the savanna at dusk, watch animal handlers feed the pelicans and flamingos, and more.

RESTAURANTS

At Disney's Animal Kingdom Lodge, **Jiko–The Cooking Place** (entrées $30–50) is the top offering, with a broad palette of cuisines that range across the Mediterranean, Europe, and the 52 countries on the African continent. It's a lovely dining space, vaguely evocative of *The Lion King,* enlivened by two huge wood-burning ovens. Appetizers tend to be more imaginative than entrées (Jiko can't get too adventurous with the fairly meat-and-potatoes clientele), and the array of wines from South Africa is laudable. **(Boma** (entrées $15–29) is the lodge's more casual, family-friendly dining option, with a breakfast and dinner buffet that feature more dishes from Africa (and some American faves for the gastronomically timid), served in a thatched-roof space with hosts actually hailing from Africa. You'll also find quick counter-service burgers and pizzas at **The Mara** food court.

DOWNTOWN DISNEY
Disney's Port Orleans Resort French Quarter $$

New Orleans's French Quarter is the jumping-off point for this 1,008-room midpriced resort. Disney's Port Orleans Resort French Quarter ($145–225) is on a 325-acre woodland site between Epcot and Downtown Disney Marketplace, with seven three-story buildings connected by cobblestone "streets" illuminated by gas lamps. Magnolia trees and elaborate wrought-iron railings capture the Big Easy at around the turn of the last century. Guests check in at the "Port Orleans Mint," designed

© DISNEY

Disney's Animal Kingdom Lodge

to look like an old-timey bank with tellerlike windows. Very nice, but outside in the Jackson Square–like courtyard the huge jesters and Mardi Gras icons are a little heavy-handed.

The landscaping is lovely at this property, all bougainvillea and tinkling fountains; the rooms are pleasant and of ample size, but they're not anything to write home about. Still, it's got some real charm, with the Sassagoula River adding romance—you can take horse-drawn carriage rides alongside it or rent a boat (canopy boat, pontoon, or Sea Raycer) and get out on it. Kids enjoy the Doubloon Lagoon pool area, the video games at South Quarter Games, or the playground across from the spa. Joggers opt for the one-mile jogging trail along the Sassagoula River, which bikers or surrey renters can explore as well. Transportation to the Downtown Disney Marketplace in flat-bottomed boats departs every 30 minutes from 10 A.M. to 4 P.M. and then every 15 minutes until 11:30 P.M., making it easy to hop over there for dinner.

RESTAURANTS
Sharing with its sister property Disney's Port Orleans Riverside Resort next door, the French Quarter Resort offers home-style Southern fare at **Boatwright's Dining Hall** (entrées $15–20). The motif here is that you're dining in a restored boat-construction warehouse (somehow relating to the Sassagoula River), but the culinary focus is very pleasant prime rib, pot roast, cornbread, and rib-sticking potatoes. Breakfast features "tin pans," a kitchen-sink approach to egg dishes. A converted Mardi Gras warehouse setting contains **Sassagoula Floatworks and Food Factory Food Court,** for quick-service pizza, pasta, hamburgers, rotisserie chicken, barbecue ribs, Cajun meat loaf, and sandwiches. Easy access to Downtown Disney exponentially increases guests' dining options.

Disney's Port Orleans $$
Riverside Resort
It used to be called Dixie Landing before it aligned itself more closely with its neighbor, Port Orleans Resort French Quarter in 2001.

Disney's Port Orleans Riverside Resort ($145–225) spreads 2,048 rooms throughout three-story Southern-style mansions in Magnolia Bend and more rustic two-story tin-roof Alligator Bayou dwellings. The former fits a Mississippi plantation theme; the latter is more Cajun backwoods. Alligator Bayou rooms offer a trundle-bed option to fit in a fifth guest, good for bigger families. Still, some folks claim this resort is quieter than most, making it ideal for adults traveling without kids.

Many of the recreational possibilities are the same as at the neighboring French Quarter, but there's a wonderful 3.5-acre old-fashioned swimming hole with slides, rope swings, and playgrounds, all called Ol' Man Island. Boat rentals, a river path for jogging or biking, and cane pole catch-and-release fishing in the stocked fishing pond render this a relaxing change of pace from theme park–going. Again, riverboats (no extra charge) take guests to Downtown Disney and Pleasure Island all day long.

RESTAURANTS
Disney aficionados claim that the **Riverside Mill** food court is among the best in all of Disney. It's got a large paddle wheel and accoutrements such as an operating cotton mill. Foodwise, it serves most of the standards you'll find at all of Disney's food courts (burgers and so forth) but with the addition of red beans and rice and very competent Louisiana-style pralines. Guests also have access to **Boatwright's Dining Hall** (see *Disney's Port Orleans Resort French Quarter*). There's a poolside quick spot called **Muddy Rivers** for hot dogs or drinks, and the **River Roost** lounge offers cocktail service and a menu of hors d'oeuvres.

Disney's Old Key $$$$
West Resort
The Conch Republic isn't flogged too vigorously at Disney's Old Key West Resort ($279–1,595), another Disney Vacation Club time-share resort, with 761 rooms in studios, one- and two-bedroom homes, and two-story, three-bedroom grand villas that sleep up to

12. Pastel pinks, blues, and greens with gingerbread woodwork detailing are reminiscent of Key West during Hemingway's tenure in America's southernmost city, but it's understated when compared to someplace like the All-Star Resorts. Generally, this huge, sprawling resort built in 1991 (the first Vacation Club) is quiet and low key, with nautical decorations, wicker furniture, and wide paddle fans in the generously sized rooms.

An on-property marina rents watercraft, and there's a canal leading to the Sassagoula River, by which guests can travel to other resorts and the Downtown Disney complex. A lighthouse anchors the sprawling pool area, and recreation includes volleyball, basketball, and access to nearby golf. A saltwater harbor plays home to some friendly dolphins.

RESTAURANTS

Dining includes **Olivia's Café** (entrées $10–20), a family-style restaurant with a Key West inflection (think Key limes), poolside fare at the **Gurgling Suitcase,** or waterside counter service that can be enjoyed at a nearby picnic table at **Good's Food to Go.**

Disney's Saratoga Springs Resort and Spa $$$$

It's Disney's biggest, newest Vacation Club Resort, all villas. Again, it's technically a timeshare, but anyone can stay, not just owners. Disney's Saratoga Springs Resort and Spa ($279–1,595) increased dramatically in size in 2007, with the completion of its third phase of construction. There are now 828 studio, one-, two-, and three-bedroom vacation homes in Victorian cottages in a slightly equestrian upstate New York lakeside resort motif. It's named for the natural mineral hot springs found in Saratoga Springs, New York, so it's not surprising that there's an extensive on-site spa, with Swedish massage, Adirondack stone therapy, and lots of other indulgences.

What used to be called the Villas at the Disney Institute, Saratoga Springs still seems to be a little bit of a work in progress. It lacks some of the amenities of most other Disney prop-

erties (a sit-down restaurant or varied dining options), and the "Health, History, Horses" theming is a bit vague. Still, for people aiming to save some money by preparing meals at "home," there are deals to be had here, especially on the smaller villas.

RESTAURANTS

The only on-site dining option is **The Artist's Palette** counter-service food court and market, featuring the same array of salads, burgers, sandwiches, and pastas you find at many Disney food courts. Easy access to Downtown Disney, via a short walk or free ferry service, increases the dining options tremendously.

DISNEY'S WIDE WORLD OF SPORTS
Disney's Pop Century Resort $

The most recent addition to Disney's value resorts, 【 **Disney's Pop Century Resort** ($82–141) features 2,880 rooms that pay tribute to 20th-century pop culture. The lodge buildings and furnishings are inspired by decades from the 1950s to the 1990s, festooned with icons from each decade (four-story Rubik's cubes to 65-foot-tall bowling pins). Rooms are compact but adequate, with pleasant decor (a little less garish and goofy than the All-Star properties). Kids enjoy the two 5,000-square-foot arcades, the Pop Jet Playground, three heated, kooky-shaped pools, and a recreational path for biking or surrey riding around Hourglass Lake.

RESTAURANTS

Disney's Pop Century Resort is the first to have an integrated food/drinks/shopping court, which is called the **Everything Pop Shopping and Dining Food Court.** Offerings are similar to those at all the food courts (sandwiches, quick breakfasts, salads, pizza). For cocktails, there are the **Classic Concoctions Lounge** and **Petals Pool Bar.**

SHADES OF GREEN

Shades of Green on Walt Disney World Resort (formerly The Disney Inn, 586 rooms) is a U.S. Armed Forces Recreation Center for the exclusive use of vacationing servicemen and women from all branches of the armed forces. It overlooks pools, gardens, and two PGA championship 18-hole golf courses and nine-hole walking course adjacent to this property. For reservations, call 407/824-3600.

OFFICIAL NON-DISNEY HOTELS

All of the previously mentioned hotels are owned and operated by Disney, with all the good and bad that that entails. Extra Magic Hours, Magic Express service to and from the airport, character meals, special modes of transportation to and from the theme parks, and so forth are available only to guests staying at official Disney-owned hotels. They are lavishly decorated with Disney-obilia, almost always in a very narrow theme or idiom. The downside? Televisions seem to broadcast a nonstop array of Disney promotions and infomercials, food courts contain Disney-brand foods (you can't buy a Hershey bar, only a Mickey version not nearly as tasty), and the in-room soaps are often low-quality Mickey-shaped bars—in short, Disney infiltrates every element of your stay. The biggest downside, though, is that they are often more expensive than their equivalent non-Disney counterparts.

If you want a respite from Disney culture, or you just want to save a few bucks, you can still stay within Walt Disney World Resort at one of a number of non-Disney–owned hotels. The Grosvenor, for example, is within walking distance of Downtown Disney, while the Disney-owned All-Star Resorts are fairly remote from most things (and they have no restaurants on-site other than perfunctory food courts).

These hotels have been Disney sanctioned—often offering package deals that include park admission. If you belong to a hotel chain's frequent visitor club (Hilton HHonors points or others), these independent on-site properties also allow you to take advantage of any special discounts you might be entitled to. Most of these are considered Downtown Disney Resort Area Hotels. This list may grow shortly, as Four Seasons and Walt Disney World Resort

announced plans for an on-property 900-acre luxury Four Seasons Resort. The new hotel is expected to open in 2010, and the current Osprey Ridge golf course will be renovated and rebranded as a Four Seasons property.

All official non-Disney hotels offer continuous or scheduled transportation to the theme parks at no extra charge.

Under $100

Grosvenor Resort (1850 Hotel Plaza Blvd., Lake Buena Vista, 800/624-4109, from $95) boasts 626 rooms in a lakeside resort. A $24 million makeover and name change will be completed in Novemeber 2007, and will include tennis, shuffleboard, two swimming pools, playground, game room, and fitness center.

With great views of the IllumiNations nightly show at Epcot, **Best Western Lake Buena Vista Resort Hotel** (2000 Hotel Plaza Blvd., Lake Buena Vista, 407/828-2424, from $98) is a 331-room Caribbean-style resort featuring a game room, fitness center, swimming pool, and playground. The 18-story hotel is configured in an arced semicircle to maximize the view from most rooms.

$100–150

Hotel Royal Plaza (1905 Hotel Plaza Blvd., Lake Buena Vista, 407/828-2828, from $109) reopened in summer 2006 after a massive renovation, with 394 rooms in a boutique-style high-rise very close to Downtown Disney. Roomy standard rooms sleep five, and kids eat free at breakfast. The property has versatile conference facilities, swimming pool, tennis courts, and a fitness center.

Doubletree Guest Suites Resort (2305 Hotel Plaza Blvd., Lake Buena Vista, 407/934-1000, from $129) is the only all-suites hotel in the Downtown Disney area, with 241 units that sleep up to six people. Each has a living room and separate bedroom, and the property has a swimming pool, whirlpool, game room, and children's theater.

Even though the **The Hilton** (1751 Hotel Plaza Blvd., Lake Buena Vista, 407/827-4000, from $139) is a non-Disney–owned hotel, the

23-acre AAA Four-Diamond hotel offers access to Extra Magic Hours. It's in the Downtown Disney area, with 863 rooms, seven restaurants and lounges, three swimming pools, and a tropical outdoor spa. Standard rooms sleep up to four people. The Hilton tends to be primarily a business and convention hotel; in May 2006 it expanded to 75,000 square feet of meeting and banquet space.

Some might say that the **Walt Disney World Swan** (758 rooms, operated by Westin) and **Walt Disney World Dolphin** (1,509 rooms, operated by Sheraton) are the archetypal fancy Disney hotels with all the attendant bells and whistles. Not owned by Disney, both properties (both at 1500 Epcot Resorts Blvd., Lake Buena Vista, 888/828-8850, from $150) do offer Extra Magic Hours service to their guests. Between the two hotels, there are 2,267 luxury rooms and 254,000 square feet of meeting and exhibition space. They share 17 restaurants and lounges, four swimming pools, two health clubs, and a wide range of recreational activities.

The Walt Disney World Dolphin houses an outpost of **Shula's Steakhouse** (entrées $30–50), a classic purveyor of slabs of rosy beef and creamed spinach, but also with very nice potato pancakes and a drool-worthy wine list. The real star at the Dolphin, though, is **⟨ Todd English's bluezoo** (entrées $40–60), another underwater-themed, but gorgeous, restaurant. Todd English has justifiably come to fame for his seafood-laden cuisine drawn from coastal areas around the world. It's the best kind of example of fusion cuisine, heavy on the fish, with price tags that seem to draw conventioneers whooping it up on an expense account.

Over $150

The luxury-oriented **Buena Vista Palace** (1900 Buena Vista Dr., Lake Buena Vista, 866/397-6516, from $239) pairs 1,013 rooms and suites with 90,000 square feet of meeting space in a 27-story, lakeside setting. The property also contains a European-style spa, beauty salon, fitness center, five restaurants and lounges, three pools, tennis courts, volleyball courts, and a marina with boat rental.

MAGIC KINGDOM

A giddiness overtakes people at Magic Kingdom. Irrespective of age, country of origin, or any genetically encoded sense of gravitas, there will be people skipping, whooping, and wearing hats with ears (now available equipped with bridal veils and other accessories). This is because Magic Kingdom is unmistakably Disney's epicenter. Cinderella Castle looms over it all, stunning in its grandeur from far away, but also giving up countless tiny treasures upon close investigation of its lush mosaic tile murals or sweeping Gothic columns.

More than any of Orlando's other theme parks, Disney or otherwise, Magic Kingdom allows kids to be their most innocent selves, and for adults to tap into a time when they themselves were such creatures. Because some of the park's attractions are so beloved, change comes more slowly to this park—rides that were original to the park in 1971 are usually renovated and updated as opposed to being bulldozed for something cutting-edge. Technology here is more focused on lifelike movement of animatronic figures, not increasing the g-forces on a loop-di-loop thrill ride. Thus, little kids and older adults may find Magic Kingdom the most charming of Disney's four parks, while teenagers may be left unimpressed.

More than 16 million visitors go to Magic Kingdom annually (10 million to Epcot, nearly nine million to Disney's Hollywood Studios, and a little more than eight million to Disney's Animal Kingdom). Why is Magic Kingdom the single most popular park in the world? Its greatest accomplishment is how easily it enables people of all ages to suspend disbelief.

© DISNEY

HIGHLIGHTS

LOOK FOR (TO FIND RECOMMENDED SIGHTS, ACTIVITIES, DINING, AND LODGING.

(**Pirates of the Caribbean:** Johnny Depp's Jack Sparrow now makes several appearances in the many animatronic scenes of this classic pirate-themed dark ride (page 67).

(**Big Thunder Mountain Railroad:** More than any other Disney park, Magic Kingdom manages to entertain several generations with the same attraction. This tame, well-themed coaster is a perfect example, offering something for everyone in an imaginative three-minute ride (page 69).

(**Peter Pan's Flight:** Dating to 1971, this animatronic-heavy ride maintains its charm – one flies over London, then to Never Land and Skull Rock, Hook's 48-foot pirate ship, the Lost Boys camp, and Mermaid Lagoon, all populated by Captain Hook, Mr. Smee, Princess Tiger Lily, and the gang (page 73).

(**Mickey's PhilharMagic:** Immerse yourself in what is perhaps Disney's best 3-D movie effort, with lots of added "4-D" touches such as smells, smoke, wind, and water (page 74).

(**Space Mountain:** Rocket into another galaxy aboard a not too fast but plenty bumpy dark-ride roller coaster before it's too late. Rumor has it this classic ride will undergo a major update soon (page 79).

(**Wishes Nighttime Spectacular:** Longtimers say the current nighttime fireworks extravaganza is the most lavish yet, replacing Fantasy in the Sky, which made its debut in 1976. It's a nightly parkwide party presided over by Jiminy Cricket, Pinocchio, Cinderella, Ariel, Peter Pan, and others (page 83).

Each of the park's seven themed areas creates a world-within-a-world, with its own flora, architecture, and themes. Inhabit a tropical jungle, leap back to the American Revolution, or dodge tumbleweeds and feisty cowboys in the Old West. Disney has long capitalized on the transformative power of "believing." The magic of Magic Kingdom is the ease with which guests do just that.

HISTORY

The park that is synonymous with Walt Disney World, Magic Kingdom really started it all for Central Florida's theme parks. Ground was broken in 1967 on what had been swampland with scrubby patches of palmetto, cattle pasture, and the odd citrus farm because, as Walt Disney famously said, "Here in Florida, we have something special we never enjoyed at Disneyland... the blessing of size. There's enough land here to hold all the ideas and plans we can possibly imagine." The Magic Kingdom opened on this former backwater on October 1, 1971.

Disneyland had opened in Anaheim, California, in 1955, and much to Disney's chagrin, the slow creep of ticky-tacky motels, greasy spoons, neon signs, and everyday commerce threatened to encroach on the dream world he had created.

Using dummy corporations, he quietly bought up 47 square miles of land in this sleepy backwater. Magic Kingdom would be like California's Disneyland in its design, but with sprawling land on all sides to provide a buffer zone for guests, to help preserve the delicate fantasy he and his Imagineers envisioned. For a long time, Magic Kingdom was all there was—Epcot came later, in 1982, Disney's Hollywood Studios in 1989, and Disney's Animal Kingdom in 1998.

These days, Magic Kingdom takes up 107 acres and is visited annually by more than 16 million people, making it the most visited park in the world. At its opening, Walt Disney World Resort employed around 5,500 cast members, while today that number hovers around 58,000, with more than $1.1 billion in payroll. The company is the largest single-site employer in the country.

It took 9,000 workers to build Magic Kingdom, which has an elaborate system of underground "utilidor" tunnels to allow cast members to move between themed areas without guests' seeing them. The park opened with six lands: Main Street, U.S.A., Adventureland, Frontierland, Liberty Square, Fantasyland, and Tomorrowland (Mickey's Toontown Fair came later), each with its own theme, background music, and architecture.

Planning Your Time

The Magic Kingdom is not huge (Epcot is twice the size), but its seven themed lands are dense with attractions. It's very difficult to see and do everything in a single day. The park is decidedly all-ages, without a ton of height-restricted thrill rides. Preschool and elementary-age kids will find attractions geared to their interests in every part of the park, while adults are charmed by the nostalgic "classic" rides and educational attractions.

Magic Kingdom, more so than the other three Disney theme parks, relies heavily on slow ride-throughs of animatronic-heavy landscapes ("it's a small world", Pirates of the Caribbean, The Haunted Mansion, Peter Pan's Flight). This means a couple of things: These indoor rides are out of the hot Florida sun and invariably air-conditioned, and each provides an opportunity to rest your legs. Thus, Magic Kingdom may be the best park for the elderly, those with disabilities, or just anybody who has a hard time pounding the hot pavement all day long. Most of the rides at this park require that guests in wheelchairs or ECVs transfer to ride seats, so there's quite a bit of standing up and sitting down to contend with.

Aside from the afternoon parade and the fireworks at night, Magic Kingdom is not heavy on live shows.

Magic Kingdom is particularly navigable, because it is laid out like a wheel with "spokes" leading to the various themed areas from the central hub that is Main Street and the Cinderella Castle, the monumental symbol of the park. From the park entrance, guests enter onto **Main Street, U.S.A.,** a recreation of an early 20th-century Mayberry-ish American town. The first walkway on your left takes you to **Adventureland,** a loosely jungle-theme area (making the Middle Eastern bazaar part of it, um, bizarre). Due north of this is **Frontierland** with its Wild West theme. North and east of that is **Liberty Square,** a tribute to the country's colonial history. East of that, directly behind the Cinderella Castle, **Fantasyland** is all about princesses, fairies, and little-kid dreams. Still east of that, **Mickey's Toontown Fair** is another little-kid area, this one a little less fantasy oriented and more like a classic carnival midway. And, finally, in the easternmost part of the park, **Tomorrowland** is devoted to space and technology.

Veteran park-goers are of different minds about how to navigate this park. Because it can be absolutely packed, some say arrive early and race immediately to the park's biggest attractions (Space Mountain, Splash Mountain, Big Thunder Mountain Railroad). Others say start in Tomorrowland and work your way counterclockwise around the park—because this park doesn't feature lots of scheduled shows, you won't be crisscrossing back and forth across the park to meet particular showtimes. And if you're staying at a Disney resort, take advantage of Extra Magic Hours.

CHARACTER GREETINGS

Magic Kingdom is fairly crawling with characters, their whereabouts listed daily on the *Character Greeting Times Guide,* which you can pick up at City Hall in Town Square, at the main tip board on Main Street, U.S.A., and at all the character greeting locations. The guide tells you which "kind" of characters to expect, not the exact ones (it will say "characters from *Peter Pan,*" not "Captain Hook").

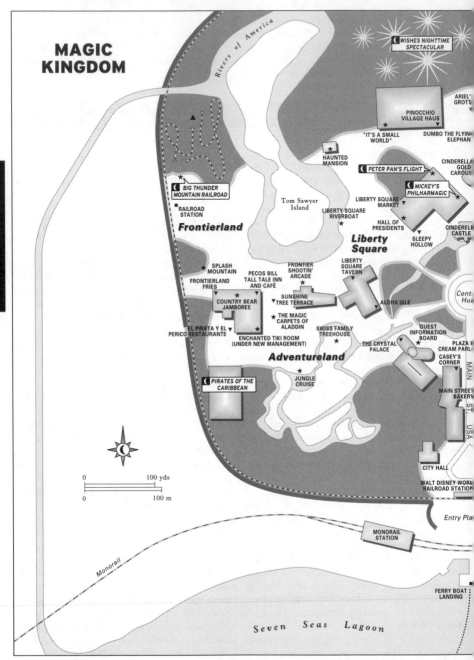

MAGIC KINGDOM

MAGIC KINGDOM

Rivers of America

WISHES NIGHTTIME SPECTACULAR

ARIEL'S GROTTO

PINOCCHIO VILLAGE HAUS

"IT'S A SMALL WORLD"

DUMBO THE FLYING ELEPHANT

HAUNTED MANSION

PETER PAN'S FLIGHT

CINDERELLA'S GOLDEN CAROUSEL

BIG THUNDER MOUNTAIN RAILROAD

MICKEY'S PHILHARMAGIC

RAILROAD STATION

Tom Sawyer Island

Frontierland

LIBERTY SQUARE MARKET

LIBERTY SQUARE RIVERBOAT

HALL OF PRESIDENTS

CINDERELLA CASTLE

Liberty Square

SLEEPY HOLLOW

SPLASH MOUNTAIN

FRONTIER SHOOTIN' ARCADE

LIBERTY SQUARE TAVERN

FRONTIERLAND FRIES

PECOS BILL TALL TALE INN AND CAFÉ

SUNSHINE TREE TERRACE

ALOHA ISLE

Central Hub

COUNTRY BEAR JAMBOREE

THE MAGIC CARPETS OF ALADDIN

SWISS FAMILY TREEHOUSE

GUEST INFORMATION BOARD

PLAZA ICE CREAM PARLOR

EL PIRATA Y EL PERICO RESTAURANTE

ENCHANTED TIKI ROOM (UNDER NEW MANAGEMENT)

THE CRYSTAL PALACE

CASEY'S CORNER

Adventureland

MAIN

MAIN STREET BAKERY

PIRATES OF THE CARIBBEAN

JUNGLE CRUISE

ST.

USA

CITY HALL

WALT DISNEY WORLD RAILROAD STATION

Entry Plaza

0   100 yds

0   100 m

MONORAIL STATION

Monorail

FERRY BOAT LANDING

Seven Seas Lagoon

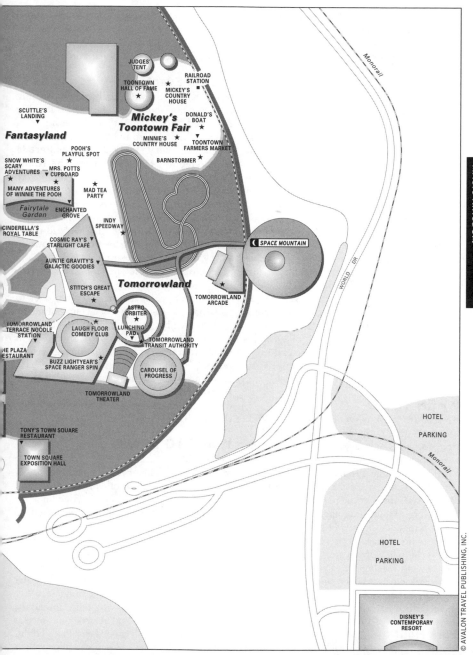

MAGIC KINGDOM

JUDGES' TENT

TOONTOWN HALL OF FAME

RAILROAD STATION

MICKEY'S COUNTRY HOUSE ★

SCUTTLE'S LANDING ▼

Fantasyland

DONALD'S BOAT ★

Mickey's Toontown Fair

POOH'S PLAYFUL SPOT ★

MINNIE'S COUNTRY HOUSE

TOONTOWN FARMERS MARKET ★

SNOW WHITE'S SCARY ADVENTURES ★

MRS. POTTS CUPBOARD ▼

BARNSTORMER ★

MANY ADVENTURES OF WINNIE THE POOH ★

MAD TEA PARTY ★

Fairytale Garden

ENCHANTED GROVE

INDY SPEEDWAY ★

CINDERELLA'S ROYAL TABLE

COSMIC RAY'S STARLIGHT CAFÉ ▼

☾ SPACE MOUNTAIN

AUNTIE GRAVITY'S GALACTIC GOODIES ▼

Tomorrowland

STITCH'S GREAT ESCAPE ★

TOMORROWLAND ARCADE

TOMORROWLAND TERRACE NOODLE STATION

ASTRO ORBITER ★

LAUGH FLOOR COMEDY CLUB ★

LUNCHING PAD ▼

THE PLAZA RESTAURANT

TOMORROWLAND TRANSIT AUTHORITY ★

BUZZ LIGHTYEAR'S SPACE RANGER SPIN ★

CAROUSEL OF PROGRESS ★

TOMORROWLAND THEATER

TONY'S TOWN SQUARE RESTAURANT

TOWN SQUARE EXPOSITION HALL

Monorail

WORLD DR.

HOTEL PARKING

Monorail

HOTEL PARKING

DISNEY'S CONTEMPORARY RESORT

© AVALON TRAVEL PUBLISHING, INC.

You'll tend to find classic Disney characters such as **Mickey** along Main Street, U.S.A.; characters from **Peter Pan** outside Pirates of the Caribbean; **Ariel and friends** at Ariel's Grotto in Fantasyland; and **Rafiki, Timon,** and other *Lion King* characters outside the Sunshine Tree Terrace in Adventureland. Mickey's Toontown Fair has an established character queue with loads of characters cycling through during the course of the day, both at the Toontown Hall of Fame Tent and the Judge's Tent (Mickey is often hanging out in there).

As with all character greetings at the Disney parks, be ready when you reach the front of the line: Have your autograph book and pen ready (a fat pen, so the gloved characters can grip it easily), make sure the lens cap is off, and that your camera is on. If you reach the front of the line and your child is frankly terrified of the whole thing, don't force the issue. Try again with a less intimidating character. If you or your child is desperate to meet a particular character, people in Guest Relations can help track down characters' exact locations throughout the day.

This park also features some of Disney's most entertaining and lavish character dining, mostly with food that is better than it has to be. For reservations, call 407/939-3463.

WHEN TO GO

Because this park is synonymous with Walt Disney World, most visitors make this their first stop—it's busy at the beginning of the week, with Friday and Saturday tending to be a little slower. The difference between a busy day and a slow day can be vast, doubling or tripling wait times at the popular attractions. Extra Magic Hours draw enormous crowds to Magic Kingdom, so the advantage of an extra couple of hours may be offset by the additional time spent in line. If you are a resort guest, one way to work the angle is to visit Epcot or another park during the day and park-hop over to Magic Kingdom for the evening's fireworks and extended Extra Magic Hours.

Park Hours

Magic Kingdom opens each day at 9 A.M. It stays open later than most of the other parks, closing as early as 7 P.M. but as late as midnight, depending on the season. Check the website for the calendar of park hours.

Special Events

Magic Kingdom is especially magical during the December holidays. The park is lavishly decorated, there's a nightly tree-lighting ceremony on Main Street, and the afternoon parade is called the **Very Merry Christmas Parade** for the month. **Mickey's 'Twas the Night Before Christmas** is performed at the Galaxy Palace Theater and there's a hard-ticket event (that means it's a dated ticket, separate from admission to the park) called **Mickey's Very Merry Christmas Party.** Another hard-ticket event is the annual **Not-So-Scary Halloween Party,** with trick-or-treating, a Halloween parade, costumed dance parties, and so forth, held many nights during October.

In recent years, the park is given over to Christian music concerts for a couple of nights each September (another hard-ticket event), and at the end of April the park hosts all-night **Grad Nights** parties for graduating high-school seniors. At the beginning of 2007, the park launched a new special event called **Disney's Pirate and Princess Party,** a nightly treasure hunt through the park—it's unclear whether this will be an annual hard-ticket event.

WHAT TO BRING

Because Magic Kingdom is fairly compact with lots of shaded, indoor rides, it's less physically taxing than some of the other parks. That said, comfortable shoes are always advised for a day at the park. Few rides will get you soaked, so ponchos or self-sealing bags are unnecessary; however, regular afternoon thunderstorms make an umbrella a wise item to bring. Because a number of attractions are "dark rides," guests with glasses should consider bringing regular glasses as well as prescription sunglasses. I've made the mistake of having only sunglasses, rendering me nearly blind in attractions such as Pirates of the Caribbean or Peter Pan's Flight. Multiple cell phones or a pair of walkie-talkies ensure that you'll find each other again if your party splits up.

PRACTICALITIES
Alcohol and Smoking
Be advised that Magic Kingdom is dry. No beer, no wine, no booze—not at fancy character dinners, not at grab-'n-go stands. It is the only one of the four Disney parks to favor this stringent level of temperance. Smoking is allowed, but only in designated smoking areas, indicated on the park map.

Camera Services
There is a camera center at Exposition Hall at Main Street, U.S.A.

First Aid
First Aid is next to The Crystal Palace restaurant on Main Street, U.S.A. This is also where the Baby Care Center is for nursing mothers or diaper-changing facilities.

Guest Relations
The Guest Relations headquarters is at City Hall. It provides the following services: messages for separated parties and the lost and found; information for guests with disabilities and sign-language services; character greeting information and dining priority seating; tour information; park maps; and foreign currency or Disney Dollar exchange. There's a Bank One ATM on the right side of the ticket booths at the Transportation and Ticket Center, as well as ATMs at the park entrance near the locker rentals, near City Hall, at the Frontierland/Adventureland Breezeway near the shooting gallery, at Fantasyland near the Pinocchio Village Haus restrooms, and inside the Tomorrowland Arcade.

Kennels
Pet-care facilities are just outside the park entrance, adjacent to the Transportation and Ticket Center. The staff will feed your pet, but you are advised to walk your dog twice during the day. Dogs must have proof of rabies, DHP, parvovirus, and bordetella shots, while cats must have proof of rabies, panleukopenia, rhi-

notracheitis, and calcivirus shots. There is no on-site veterinarian. All dogs and cats must be at least eight weeks old to be kenneled and no exotic animals are allowed. The kennels open one hour before and after the park hours. Call 407/824-6568 to reserve; the cost is $10 per pet per day ($13 for overnight if you are a Disney Resort guest, $15 for nonguests).

Rentals
Strollers are available for rent at the Stroller Shop inside the park entrance. Single strollers cost $8 with a Disney Dollar deposit back when you turn it in; doubles are $15 with a Disney Dollar back.

Wheelchairs are also available at the Stroller Shop. Rentals are $10 per day with no deposit, and motorized ECVs are $35 per day with a $5 refundable deposit. Because there are a limited number of wheelchair and ECV rentals, get to the park early to ensure getting one. Be advised that nearly all of the seated rides and attractions at Magic Kingdom require that those in wheelchairs and ECVs be reseated in the ride seating.

Lockers are near the Transportation and Ticket Center or on the ground level of the Main Street Railroad Station. The cost is $7, $2 of which is a refundable deposit on the key (and if you go to a second park, you can bring your locker receipt and just put down an additional $5 deposit for a locker there).

GETTING THERE AND AROUND
Walt Disney World Resort is southwest of Orlando, off I-4, west of the Florida's Turnpike. Magic Kingdom is in the northern part of Walt Disney World Resort. Take Exit 64 off I-4. Once you arrive in the Magic Kingdom parking lot and have taken the tram to the Ticket and Transportation Center (TTC), you're still 1.5 miles from the real entrance to Magic Kingdom. Get there via ferry or monorail: Monorail is a little faster (4–5 minutes); the ferry is more picturesque (6–7 minutes). For the full experience, take the ferry one direction and the monorail the other.

More than any other theme park in Orlando,

MAGIC KINGDOM

Magic Kingdom is serviced by a vast number of modes of transportation: Buses go to all Walt Disney World Resorts; ferry boats go to the Transportation and Ticket Center; monorails go to Disney's Contemporary Resort (although it's close enough to walk), Disney's Polynesian Resort, Disney's Grand Floridian Resort and Spa, and to the Transportation and Ticket Center; water launches go to Disney's Polynesian Resort, Disney's Grand Floridian Resort and Spa, Disney's Wilderness Lodge, and Disney's Fort Wilderness Resort and Campground.

Guests staying on Disney property have a major advantage because they can take Disney transport directly to the Magic Kingdom turnstiles and bypass the Ticket and Transportation Center, saving 10–15 minutes.

Parking

Parking costs $10 but is free to all Walt Disney World resort hotel guests. If you are park-hopping, your parking receipt will be honored at the other parks. Trams take visitors from the parking lot to the park entrance. There is also wheelchair-accessible parking available for vehicles with a valid Disabled Parking Permit—ask at the auto plaza where you pay for parking. Should your vehicle become disabled during your visit, free towing is available from AAA during park hours.

Parking areas are marked with a character (for example, Pluto) and a row (for example, 17), a combination that is drilled into your head by the tram drivers. Write it down somewhere.

If you elect to park-hop, air-conditioned Disney transportation (trams, monorail, or buses) will take you between parks swiftly and with a minimum of fuss. Disney's monorail runs between the Magic Kingdom, Disney's Contemporary Resort, Disney's Grand Floridian Resort and Spa, Disney's Polynesian Resort, and the Transportation and Ticket Center (adjacent to the Magic Kingdom parking lot). A connecting monorail takes people from the Transportation and Ticket Center to Epcot. Between the other parks a bus system runs approximately every 20 minutes. Express buses go strictly between the parks, while nonexpress buses loop around through the various resort hotels. During peak season, there can be long waits to board buses, so it may save time to drive between parks.

Park Maps

Pick up free guide maps just inside the park. They are offered in English, Spanish, French, Portuguese, German and Japanese, as well as in Braille (at Guest Relations).

Tours

Railroad enthusiasts will jump at the chance to experience **Disney's the Magic Behind Our Steam Trains Tour** (three hours, $40 per person, must be 10 or older). Guests arrive before the park opens and accompany the railroad engineers backstage at the roundhouse as they prepare the steam trains for the day.

The **Disney's Family Magic Tour** (2.5 hours, $27 for ages three and up) is essentially a scavenger hunt around the park with Disney trivia.

Diehard Disney fans will opt for the **Disney's Keys to the Kingdom Tour** (4.5–5 hours, $60 per person, must be 16 years or older, lunch included). It's an outdoor walking program that takes you backstage at a range of favorite attractions. Guests get insider secrets about the park and lots of history about Walt Disney the man.

Mickey's Magical Milestones Tour (9 A.M. Mon., Wed., and Fri., two hours, $25 per person) is for Mickey fans. Guests tour the park with a guide who recounts the mouse's history from the first doodle, through Steamboat Willie cartoons, and up through Mickey's PhilharMagic and the mouse of the moment.

The top-of-the-line tour is **VIP Tour Services** (six-hour minimum, $125 per person per hour, special discounts for resort guests), really only worthwhile during busy periods at the park. A guide plans your day's itinerary, gets you the best seats in the house for live shows, and generally makes sure you don't have to fraternize with the hoi polloi.

All tours may be booked in advance by calling 407/WDW-TOUR (407/939-8687). Tour costs do not include admission to Magic Kingdom.

Main Street, U.S.A.

Main Street, U.S.A. is two long blocks of nostalgia that stretch from the train station at the park's front entrance to Cinderella Castle in the north. You can traverse this area by foot or via a little sexier mode of transportation: horse-drawn trolleys, antique cars (you can call them horseless carriages), street cars, a replica of an early fire engine, and jitneys scoot up and down the street as part of the **Main Street Vehicles** attraction. Supposedly inspired by Walt's memories of his hometown at the turn of the 20th century, Main Street, U.S.A. has a stately **City Hall,** which is home to Guest Relations, Information, and the lost and found, and the **Town Square Exposition Hall,** where you can buy film and camera accoutrements or peruse a teensy motion-picture museum. There's a flag-lowering ceremony at 5 P.M. daily in the **Town Square's Municipal Park** (American

veterans can volunteer to be the Veteran of the Day), occasional **Main Street Trolley Parades,** and itinerant performers who roam the street dancing and/or singing.

At the end of Main Street, closest to Cinderella Castle, a **Guest Information Board** lists wait times for rides and which attractions are not operational.

WALT DISNEY WORLD RAILROAD

Guests board the Walt Disney World Railroad at the very foot of Main Street. The old-timey narrow-gauge steam locomotives, built in the 1910s and 1920s, make a 20-minute, 1.5-mile loop around the perimeter of the park, with stops in Mickey's Toontown Fair and Frontierland. (First thing in the morning, get off at Frontierland to make a beeline to Splash Mountain or Big Thunder; hop off at Toontown to put yourself close to Space Mountain.)

Walt Disney was an enormous train enthusiast (as a young man he built a half-mile scale model railroad in his backyard), and thus this was one of the first attractions he planned. The sound of the train whistle and chugging engines can be heard all over the park, and the cheery, brightly painted (one red, one blue, one yellow, and one green) locomotives are kept in pristine condition. No wonder it's one of the busiest steam-powered railroads in the nation, with more than 1.5 million passengers annually. Each locomotive pulls five passenger cars with a capacity of about 350 people, so lines are never long and trains run continuously.

FOOD

There are lots of dining options here, because it's the first place you go upon arrival at the park and the last place you see in the evening. **The Plaza Restaurant** (à la carte $15–29) is probably the top offering. The sit-down, table-service restaurant has a nostalgic turn-of-the-20th-century vibe and serves pleasant deli

Main Street, U.S.A., with Cinderella Castle in the background

© DISNEY

MAGIC KINGDOM RIDE GUIDE

FASTPASS RIDES

Listed in order of importance, these are the rides and shows to FASTPASS:

1. Space Mountain
2. Splash Mountain
3. Jungle Cruise
4. The Many Adventures of Winnie the Pooh
5. Peter Pan's Flight
6. Big Thunder Mountain Railroad
7. Mickey's PhilharMagic
8. Buzz Lightyear's Space Ranger Spin
9. Stitch's Great Escape!

RIDE RESTRICTIONS

- **Splash Mountain:** Riders must be at least 40 inches tall, and they will get wet.
- **Big Thunder Mountain Railroad:** Riders must be at least 40 inches tall.
- **Tomorrowland Indy Speedway:** Riders must be at least 52 inches tall to ride solo.
- **Space Mountain:** Riders must be at least 44 inches tall; some children find it dark and scary.
- **Stitch's Great Escape!** Riders must be at least 40 inches tall; children find the ride scary and the restraints hurt.

ACCESS RESTRICTIONS

On the following attractions, guests in wheelchairs or electronic convenience vehicles (ECVs) will have to transfer to a ride chair:

- Astro Orbiter
- Big Thunder Mountain Railroad
- Buzz Lightyear's Space Ranger Spin
- Cinderella's Golden Carousel
- Dumbo the Flying Elephant
- The Haunted Mansion
- "it's a small world"
- Mad Tea Party
- Magic Carpets of Aladdin
- Main Street Vehicles
- The Many Adventures of Winnie the Pooh
- Peter Pan's Flight
- Pirates of the Caribbean
- Snow White's Scary Adventures
- Space Mountain
- Splash Mountain
- Stitch's Great Escape!
- Tomorrowland Indy Speedway
- Walt Disney World Railroad

sandwiches, burgers, salads, and scoop-shop ice cream. Elsewhere in this area, head to **Tony's Town Square Restaurant** (entrées $11.19–25.49, kids' menu $4.99–5.49), with a very *Lady and the Tramp* interior, for sit-down, table-service Italian *panini* or salads. **Casey's Corner** is perfect for a quick hot dog or fries, or check out **Main Street Bakery** for ice cream and sweets. **Plaza Ice Cream Parlor** always seems to have a very long line for hand-scooped treats.

Character Dining

The buffet at the **Crystal Palace** ($15–29 per person, 407/939-3463) for breakfast, lunch, and dinner shows a real focus on fresh, healthy ingredients prepared with an eye to presentation. This is not a tired steam-table buffet—too bad you can't have a glass of wine with your lively Mediterranean salads, pasta bar, or mixed grill.

The Winnie the Pooh gang, with a bouncy Tigger and a doleful Eeyore, drift from table to table, mugging, hugging, signing autographs, and posing for photos. (Remember, they have taken a vow of silence that is nearly as sacrosanct as a spiritually motivated one.) I've heard sliding them a little extra cash encourages them to linger tableside, but I've never had the nerve to try it out. If characters miss your table, feel free to send your kids over to wherever they are in the dining room. Sometimes you'll find characters assembling an impromptu conga line or clustering around a birthday boy or girl for a little extra attention, but for the most part their mission is to quickly hit one table after the next, kind of like the bride at a wedding reception.

SHOPPING

Main Street, U.S.A. is commerce intensive, with the **Engine Co. 71-Firehouse Gift Shop, Arribas Brothers Crystal Arts, Disney** **Clothiers, Main Street Toy Store, Uptown Jewelers** (good snow globes), and a major **Pin Station.** All of these sell fairly self-explanatory merchandise, most festooned with Disney characters. The neatest shop in this area is the **Harmony Barber Shop,** a real old-time barber shop that specializes in "first haircuts" for kids. Bill it as a "shear adventure" if it seems to be a hard sell, but who can blame young kids for being a little squeamish about going to the barber? At this shop, though, the shorn receive a free set of Mickey ears with "first haircut" embroidered on the back to soften the blow. A barbershop quartet performs daily.

Adventureland

It's a jungle out there. Which jungle is a matter of debate, because Adventureland combines elements of Southeast Asia, Africa, Polynesia, South America, and the South Pacific in its luxuriant foliage and exotic architecture. The overall theme seems to be the exploration and mystery of an unspecified tropical paradise. A Caribbean town square anchors the land, and the core attractions (Pirates of the Caribbean, Jungle Cruise, Swiss Family Treehouse) revolve around man's attempts, often futile, to tame the lush wilderness.

PIRATES OF THE CARIBBEAN

Pirates of the Caribbean is the top offering in this area, by a mile. Its history is a weird stew of life imitating art—or maybe art imitating art. Originally a classic Disney theme park ride, it was then co-opted and liberally interpreted in the film *Pirates of the Caribbean: The Curse of the Black Pearl* and the cliffhanger *Pirates of the Caribbean: Dead Man's Chest* (has there ever been a less satisfying ending to a movie?). The ride, in turn, was shut down and revamped in time for the release of the second film, incorporating Johnny Depp's inspired rendering of Captain Jack Sparrow, heavy on the eyeliner, and Geoffrey Rush's deliciously menacing Captain Barbossa. After boarding a 15-person boat, you're transported to a pirate jamboree set in 1700s West Indies. More than 125 animatronic pirates, villagers, and animals seem to do a lot of boozing, singing, and fighting. The ride, which originally opened in 1973, is 8.5 minutes of good fun, winding through a port city under pirate attack, through a town overrun by pirates, and then finally through a treasure room presided over by a gleeful Jack Sparrow.

Nothing is particularly frightening for young children, but there is a slight drop at the beginning of the ride that tends to take people by surprise.

JUNGLE CRUISE

Adventureland's jungly, Caribbean motif may have been prompted by Pirates of the Caribbean, but it's carried through with other attractions. Jungle Cruise is another animatronic-heavy ride, this time viewed from a canopied boat (à la *African Queen*) piloted by a live skipper. The skippers are the best part, quick with the puns and hammy jokes. The tour is a geographically incoherent cruise along the Amazon, the Nile, and the Mekong Rivers. What these rivers seem to share is a propensity for picturesque ruins,

MAGIC KINGDOM

© DISNEY

Adventureland's Jungle Cruise

herds of animals (some disgruntled), and restless natives.

Tips: The nine-minute ride dates back many years and is starting to look a little wilted around the edges—still, it's a FASTPASS attraction, which you should take advantage of because lines can be excruciatingly long. Little kids may be frightened during one small stretch of darkness in the cave temple.

SWISS FAMILY TREEHOUSE

The Swiss Family Treehouse is something else entirely. Only for the robustly ambulatory, the attraction is a 60-foot re-creation of the Robinson family's massive tree house. Most kids have never seen the 1960 Disney classic, but this doesn't numb their appreciation for the ingenious, multilevel tree house made of shipwreck-salvaged flotsam and jetsam (I guess, technically, it's just flotsam, all from the wreck of the *Swallow*). While the attraction opened here in 1971, it's been recently and expertly refurbished. Bedrooms with hammocks, a library, a kitchen, and so forth are arrayed up countless flights of wooden stairs. There's not much to do here beyond ascending and descending, but it's a nice contrast with all the other, more passive attractions in Adventureland.

THE MAGIC CARPETS OF ALADDIN

From the top of the Swiss Family Treehouse, all of Adventureland is laid out in its lush jungle foliage. The motif is fairly convincing, which is why it's jarring to come upon The Magic Carpets of Aladdin, set resoundingly in the arid Middle East. It's a hub-and-spokes ride in which the hub is a massive genie bottle and the spokes are four-person "flying carpet" vehicles. You can raise or lower your carpet, preferably out of spitting range of the large golden camel that jets water onto less vigilant riders (that's me).

Tips: The queue isn't too long, but the ride lasts a mere 80 seconds, so don't bother if it looks crowded. It's really the exact same ride as the Dumbo ride in Fantasyland, subbing a carpet for an elephant.

THE ENCHANTED TIKI ROOM—UNDER NEW MANAGEMENT

Magic Kingdom has numerous singing-oriented animatronic shows—"it's a small world", Country Bear Jamboree, and The Enchanted Tiki Room-Under New Management in Adventureland. The songs in this last show appeal to a broad range—Miami Sound Machine to Cole Porter—but the plotline is nearly incoherent to younger audiences. A cast of animatronic birds has evidently put on a regular show, but the new owner, Iago from Aladdin, thinks their act is tired. He wants to pep it up, but the tiki gods ominously insist "if it ain't broke, don't fix it." What ensues is a couple of bird-brained singing numbers augmented with lip-flapping totem poles and disco balls. It's an all-ages 10-minute show, but the fierce tiki goddess may be scary for little kids. The version of this show at Disneyland in the 1960s was the first show to use animatronics.

FOOD

El Pirata y el Perico Restaurante (entrées $8–10) is the top restaurant here, with very respectable tacos and taco salads, but it tends to be closed during low times at the park (September, October, January, and February). Otherwise it's slim pickings, with pineapple-oriented delights at **Aloha Isle** and coffee drinks and ice cream at **Sunshine Tree Terrace.**

SHOPPING

Adventureland's shops stock the major "essentials": Grass skirts and island apparel can be found at **Island Supply;** Middle Eastern costumes and swords fill **Agrabah Bazaar;** and pirate supplies are the booty at **Pirate's Bazaar.** Buy the dreadlock wig/hat combo to look just like Jack Sparrow.

MAGIC KINGDOM

Frontierland

Appropriately situated at the westernmost edge of the park, this area is steeped in the American Old West, with rough-hewn dance hall, log cabins, and a shooting range (even the gift shops are heavy on the rifles and ammo—now there's family values). Fittingly, all the attractions in this area have a homey, aw-shucks Western appeal.

◖ BIG THUNDER MOUNTAIN RAILROAD

To my mind, the very best offering is Big Thunder Mountain Railroad. It's a long, 3.5-minute coaster ride with exceptional theming, but it dates all the way back to 1980, so it doesn't have the g-forces, inversions, corkscrews, or bells and whistles of Disney's other, newer monster coasters. The Southwestern landscape is the big draw, with buttes, waterfalls, old mines, caves, and animatronic mules, goats, and possums to ogle as you wend your way at speeds up to 30 mph. The accompanying soundtrack

Big Thunder Mountain Railroad

© DISNEY

completes the illusion, with chestnuts such as "Big Rock Candy Mountain" and "My Darling, Clementine."

Tips: There's a 40-inch height requirement; nonriders can enjoy the theming (and possibly glimpse the riders in their party) by walking up to the observation point on Nugget Way. FAST-PASS this ride or Splash Mountain, and do the other while waiting for your assigned time.

SPLASH MOUNTAIN

Splash Mountain is the next-best attraction, really a monster log flume ride with a five-story drop at the end. Right next to Big Thunder Mountain, the ride bears the distinction of eliciting the most audible screams of any attraction in the park. Still, it's not that scary—themed around Brer Rabbit, Brer Fox, and all the other characters from *Song of the South,* it's an 11-minute ride on an eight-person log. The long queuing area winds through Chickapin Hill, where you find out that Brer Rabbit has decided to leave the briar patch in search of adventure, with the fox and lunkheaded bear in hot pursuit. The ride is themed with 65 animatronic characters and liberal use of the song "Zip-a-Dee-Doo-Dah."

Tips: FASTPASS this ride. The height restriction is 40 inches (pregnant women and those with back problems are discouraged). You will get wet, especially at the front of the log. Nonriders can watch the plunge of their friends and family from the bridge below (where you will also get wet).

TOM SAWYER ISLAND

Tom Sawyer Island is the antidote to the sit-down-and-strap-in kinds of rides in Frontierland. A short raft ride across the Rivers of America takes you over to the island, where kids can explore on their own and adults can sit in a rocker on the dock and regroup for a bit. Paths branch out in all directions (maps are posted), leading through caves and a mine shaft, woods and an old fort (with cannons, air rifles, and an escape tunnel), a rope bridge and a floating-barrel bridge. A Disney veteran told me that whitewash brushes are secreted around

the island—if you find one and turn it in you get a prize (I didn't find any). **Aunt Polly's** on the island is a great spot to grab a drink or ice cream. Note that Tom Sawyer is impossible to navigate if you're not ambulatory.

COUNTRY BEAR JAMBOREE

I don't get the appeal of this tired animatronic show of another era. But I am not the only one. During my visit, countless children were heard asking plaintively, "Is this almost over? When is it going to be over?" Fifteen minutes seldom seem as long as they do listening to the country musical stylings of animatronic Big Al, Liver Lips McGraw, and guys named, if I remember correctly, "Zeke and Zed and Ted and Fred, and a bear named Tennessee." They do hokey, nasal versions of songs such as Homer and Jethro's "Mama Don't Whup Little Buford" or Tony Kraber's dour "Blood on the Saddle," some playing a one-string bass or blowing a corn whiskey jug. There's no plot per se; it's just a country music show that was replaced for some years and then strangely resurrected. A slightly better Christmas Special is shown in December. Time this for the hottest part of the day, because Grizzly Hall is always cool.

FRONTIER SHOOTIN' ARCADE

The arcade itself looks like a Lincoln Log log cabin—belly up to the bar, pay your $0.50, and get a few shots at a fun, Old West tableau of cacti, tumbleweeds, buzzards, ghost riders, and tombstones. It's the classic state fair shooting arcade. Peer down the sights on the realistic-looking hunting rifle (it shoots infrared light beams) and hit the 100 or so targets on the pop-up, moving, and stationary figures.

LIVE ENTERTAINMENT

New to Frontierland in 2006, **Woody's Cowboy Camp** is staged right on the street with Jessie, Bullseye, Woody, and Sam the Singin' Cowboy dancing and singing through some Western numbers. The cast rides in on a wagon, runs through some songs, gets everyone square-dancing, and then hands out wooden stick horses for kids to navigate a cowboy obstacle course. Some audience members are drafted into wearing cactus or rattlesnake hats. It's all good fun, especially for little kids (but fairly withering on a hot day with no shade). The show lasts 20 minutes and occurs daily at 10:20 A.M., 11:10 A.M., noon, 12:50 P.M., 1:40 P.M., and 3:50 P.M. Because showtimes change, check the daily calendar.

FOOD

Tamp down those hunger urges with McDonald's fries from the **Frontierland Fries** stand, or for a more substantial meal, grab a most excellent burger from the counter-service **Pecos Bill Tall Tale Inn and Café** (entrées

$7–9). What makes this especially good is that it offers a fixings bar that includes freshly caramelized onions and sautéed mushrooms as burger toppings. The vaguely Southwest-inflected chicken salad with lime vinaigrette is also commendable.

SHOPPING

In Frontierland, beyond the strange Frontierland Shooting Arcade and its **Frontier Mercantile** that stocks lots of cap guns, you'll find jelly and preserves at **Prairie Outpost and Supply,** Winnie-the-Pooh souvenirs at **Briar Patch,** Splash Mountain souvenirs and ride photos at **Splash Court,** and a nice little hat shop.

Liberty Square

Frontierland offers access to Adventureland to its south and Liberty Square to its northeast, where you can make a brief pit stop to pay tribute to our colonial heritage. It's the smallest land in the kingdom, thankfully, as it's generally thought of as the least interesting. Its architecture is a riff on an American Revolutionary town, with a cluster of little shops and restaurants. It seems to be where lots of people take a bathroom break, regroup, and grab a drink before heading on to Fantasyland. As for attractions, kids often balk at watching the old-timey and educational show at the Hall of Presidents, and they are underwhelmed by the slow cruise aboard Liberty Square Riverboat. Thankfully, Liberty Square's Haunted Mansion has broad appeal for kids and adults alike.

THE HAUNTED MANSION

The most entertaining attraction in this area is The Haunted Mansion, a dark ride in two-person "doom buggy" through a moderately scary haunted house. The queue winds up a path, through creepy wrought-iron gates and past tombstones (read them, they're funny, and one of them opens its eyes), and finally into a spooky Tudor manse. The ride is a classic,

here since 1971, but the eight-minute adventure remains a hoot as you enter the house on foot and descend in a spine-chilling elevator to the boarding area. Each two-person vehicle is equipped with a speaker from which your "Ghost Host" narrates the journey. Animatronic ghosts and skeletons, holographic ghost dancers, and other ghouls populate the hallway, library, conservatory, ballroom, and graveyard through which you pass. At the end, you slide by a mirror only to see your reflection seated next to a "hitchhiking" ghost.

Tips: Watch your step getting off your doom buggy onto the moving walkway—it's dark and a little tricky. Children older than six or seven should be fine on this ride, but discuss the ride first, explaining that there will be bats, spiders, skeletons, and ghosts that jump out but don't ever touch you or do anything particularly scary.

HALL OF PRESIDENTS

The Hall of Presidents is another absolute classic at Magic Kingdom, but it's not for everyone (read Sarah Vowell's hilarious essay on the subject in *Take the Cannoli: Stories from the New World*). All the U.S. presidents are represented as animatronic figures who

Liberty Square Riverboat cruises down Rivers of America

© DISNEY

nod and wave at roll call, some of them giving little speeches (Lincoln and, alas, George W. Bush). The 700-seat, air-conditioned theater never seems to be at capacity, which signals how many families eschew this attraction in favor of more thrilling fare. Still, the short patriotic film, about the Constitution and the presidency, shown at the beginning of each 25-minute show is quite moving, and the lobby contains nice portraits of each president.

LIBERTY SQUARE RIVERBOAT

The Hall of Presidents and Liberty Square Riverboat are about halfway through the park coming from either direction and are often touted as good places for a rest or even a nap. The Liberty Square Riverboat is certainly conducive. A slow cruise down Rivers of America on an ornate, wooden, three-level steam-powered stern-wheeler, it circles Tom Sawyer Island for a leisurely 17-minute ride out of the hot sun (unless you opt for the top deck).

Tips: The boat has insufficient seating for all passengers, so many must stand for the duration. Don't bother if the lines look long. During special events and in peak season there are sometimes characters and entertainment onboard.

FOOD

In Liberty Square, fairly dense with commerce of all kinds (Smucker's jam shop, anyone?), the best restaurant is Liberty Tree Tavern (below). Beyond that, it's funnel cakes at **Sleepy Hollow** or fish and chicken baskets and clam chowder at **Columbia Harbour House** (counter service, $6–10).

Character Dining

Patterned after an 18th-century colonial inn, **Liberty Tree Tavern** (lunch $15–20, buffet character dinner $27.99 adults, $12.99 kids 3–9) hosts character dinners with Minnie, Goofy, Pluto, and other classic characters. The food is fairly traditional roast-oriented fare, with mashed potatoes and stuffing; vegetarians are a little stymied for good options. For lunch, the Liberty Tree offers more 21st-century menu options, such as crab cakes, appealing salads, and sandwiches with an eye to contemporary tastes.

SHOPPING

Liberty Square has **Ye Olde Christmas Shoppe,** cooking and kitchen accessories at **Yankee Trader,** and early-American-inspired flags, T-shirts, and gifts at **Heritage House.**

Fantasyland

Fantasyland is the core of Magic Kingdom and directly behind Cinderella Castle. The castle itself informs and anchors the area, lending it a medieval carnival vibe in which princes and princesses look right at home (you'll see Disney's versions of both strolling here with regularity). Of the land, Walt once said, "Fantasyland is dedicated to the young at heart and to those who believe that when you wish upon a star, your dreams come true."

There must be many of us who fit that description because Fantasyland is often among the busiest parts of the park, with a good amount of shade and ride entrances with excellent viewing areas to allow little kids to check rides out before committing. It has an intimidating number of attractions, mostly linked by their reliance on classic fairytales and their appropriateness for the very young (no attraction in this area is overly scary or has height limitations). When you tick off the top offerings—"it's a small world", the teacups, Dumbo the Flying Elephant, the carousel—it quickly becomes apparent that Fantasyland has the greatest share of the park's most beloved rides, those that little kids are most eager to visit, but that also harbor the most nostalgia for adults.

Longtime Disney fans will often advise first-timers to enter the park, hightail it up Main Street, go straight through the castle, bear left slightly, and start the day at "it's a small world". This is practical as a strategy for beating the crowds, but it also sets a tone of childlike wonderment and innocence that is really the core virtue of Fantasyland. Attractions are listed here from most notable to least.

◖ PETER PAN'S FLIGHT

Were it not for the interminable lines (always FASTPASS this), Peter Pan's Flight might be my favorite attraction in the park. Clearly most people feel this way: After "it's a small world", it's the second-most ridden attraction in the park. A faithful retelling of the 1953 classic (purportedly Walt Disney's favorite of his animated features), the ride begins aboard a three-passenger pirate galleon with a red seat, billowed red-and-blue "sail," and lots of gilded woodwork. Tinker Bell sprinkles a little fairy dust over the assembled crew and soon you're flying over nighttime London where Big Ben and other famous sights are beautifully illuminated. The ride swoops through the Darling family's nursery—there are the beds and Nana, and through the window you can see the kids flapping along behind Peter. From there you reach Never Land, swooping around Mermaid Lagoon and Skull Rock where Smee, Captain Hook, the Lost Boys, and the hungry croc are all rendered in very lifelike models.

Tips: Unfortunately this is a short ride, only a little more than two minutes long—not a good payoff if you've waited in a 90-minute line. I repeat, FASTPASS this one.

"IT'S A SMALL WORLD"

The Magic Kingdom's iconic attraction, "it's a small world", gives me a full-body rash. It makes me queasy and sweaty, with dry-mouth and random stabbing pains. Worst of all, it reliably causes my brain to fill with an endless loop of the high-pitched voices of children singing the dreaded song, each in his or her own native tongue.

Other people love this ride and are passionately devoted, making annual pilgrimages.

Some people actually like the song, unperturbed by the fact that you hear it 7,000 times during the course of the queue and the duration of the 10.5-minute ride. This is a striking testament to how different we humans can be—which, in essence, is what the ride is all about. That is why it is listed near the top of my Fantasyland lineup, despite my own revulsion.

Little kids and their parents wind through the queuing area before boarding 20-person boats that dip and bump along through many countries of the world, and some countries that may be on other worlds. Nearly 300 animatronic dolls, each and every one of them smiling, sing along to the song in English, Japanese, Spanish, Italian, or Swedish in tableaux that are supposed to represent the indigenous culture, dress, flora, and fauna of various countries.

Tips: Original to the park in 1971, "it's a small world" is regularly maintained and gussied up (it was closed in 2004 for refurbishment and reopened in 2005), but it still seems fairly low-tech by today's standards. Older kids will be eye-rolling and snarky. The ride does not offer FASTPASS, but it manages to move the hordes through fairly quickly.

◖ MICKEY'S PHILHARMAGIC

Just down the street a bit, Mickey's PhilharMagic opened in October 2003 and has quickly become one of the most popular attractions in the park. At 150 feet, the screen is supposedly the largest seamless projection screen in the world and the 12-minute 3-D movie it projects is a real treat for all ages. The film uses all of the typical Disney 3-D effects elegantly, bombarding audiences with smells (think pies, not chili-dog burps), vibrations, smoke, wind, and water to deepen the experience.

The plotline follows the bumbling efforts of stagehand Donald Duck as he puts on Sorcerer Mickey's hat and tries to conduct. First, you hear Goofy running around backstage, next Donald gets in a scuffle with anthropomorphic orchestra instruments, but then it's smooth sailing. It's a completely computer-animated movie with cameos by all kinds of Disney characters, from Aladdin to Peter Pan

and Ariel. The music skims through a number of major Disney crowd pleasers. Kids may be a little disturbed by the ending, in which Donald appears to be blown from a tuba only to smash into the back wall of the theater. The theater itself is quite lovely and the long mural in the lobby is worthy of some scrutiny.

Tips: The "concert hall" seats 500 people, but FASTPASS it because the lines are long.

CINDERELLA'S GOLDEN CAROUSEL

Cinderella's Golden Carousel is a very pretty, very traditional carousel built in 1917, with 90 lavishly decorated horses going up and down. It is utterly festooned with twinkling lights and 18 hand-painted scenes from *Cinderella*. Each ride is two minutes long, accompanied by classic Disney songs such as "Feed the Birds" from *Mary Poppins*. Lines aren't long; parents can sit on a bench and wave.

MAD TEA PARTY

The Mad Tea Party hosts the classic teacups, one of the park's original attractions. The four-person cups can be whipped into a spinning frenzy by hand-cranking the metal wheel at each car's center. The cups are pretty pastel colors decorated with geometric designs; at the center of the ride is a teapot from which the Dormouse appears.

Tips: Lines move quickly for this two-minute ride, which is suitable for all ages, assuming you don't get queasy easily.

DUMBO THE FLYING ELEPHANT

Dumbo the Flying Elephant is a hub-and-spokes ride in which guests board one of 16 identical big-eared gray elephants and circle around and around, occasionally also going up and down. This is a very short ride with nothing much to see, often with very long lines. For some reason most little kids insist upon riding this baby, so their attendant adults must sweat it out dutifully in line. As you get closer to paydirt, the line snakes around underneath the protection of an overhang, but farther out you're standing in the sun. If one adult bites the bullet and waits it out with young ones (in fact, a single elephant is a very tight squeeze with two adults and a child, so one adult and one or two little ones works best), everyone else can head over to the Pinocchio Village Haus nearby for a snack.

THE MANY ADVENTURES OF WINNIE THE POOH

This dark ride is a lot like Peter Pan's Flight or "it's a small world"; visitors board four-person "hunny pots" and then bounce along through the Hundred Acre Wood. As Pooh and Piglet take you on the ride, a storm moves in, and animatronic Owl, Roo, Kanga, Tigger, Eeyore, and Rabbit come to the rescue to save Piglet from falling over Floody Place Falls. The ride touches on lots of the core Pooh stories, with a fun opportunity to bounce with Tigger.

Tips: The Many Adventures of Winnie the Pooh replaced Mr. Toad's Wild Ride back in 1999, right there a strike against it in diehard Disney fans' books. Still, it's hugely popular, so FASTPASS it. The ride lasts about four minutes and is appropriate for all ages.

SNOW WHITE'S SCARY ADVENTURES

Similar but less successful, Snow White's Scary Adventures is thought of by many families as too scary for little kids but too childish and slow for big kids. So, who's it for? A show called Snow White's Adventures was original to the park, and then the park closed it, made it less scary, and reopened it as the Scary Adventures version in 1994. You see all the dwarves, Snow White hooks up with the prince, and it all works out in the end. Still, little kids seem freaked by this ride.

Tips: The witch still makes lots of little kids cry, and the diamond mine carts in which you ride are very bumpy. It doesn't offer FAST-PASS, so if lines are long, skip it. Rumor has it the ride will be replaced soon.

CINDERELLA CASTLE

At the center of it all is Cinderella Castle, a Gothic palace of gray and royal blue that stands 189 feet tall. Inspired by Versailles, Neuschwanstein Castle, Fontainebleau, and other famous chateaux, the castle is a study in forced perspective (windows up high are smaller to make them look farther away) and trompe l'oeil (it looks like brick, but it's all concrete and steel). As part of 2007's "Year of a Million Dreams," a suite in the castle has been opened to play overnight host to lucky families who have won part of the Disney Dreams Giveaway.

POOH'S PLAYFUL SPOT/ ARIEL'S GROTTO

The least interesting parts of Fantasyland are Pooh's Playful Spot and Ariel's Grotto, which are adjacent to each other. The former is a new addition to the park, a "fly and be free" playground for preschoolers. At the center of the Hundred Acre Wood–themed play area is a tree, which looks like a house from the back. There's nothing really to do in the tree, nor is there much to do outside on the soft-floored play area. A couple of little fountains shoot up to douse the toddlers milling about, and there

Cinderella Castle

© DISNEY

MAGIC KINGDOM

MAGIC KINGDOM

are tipped-over "hunny pots," their function utterly puzzling. There are also a lot of misspelled, poorly lettered signs, ostensibly written by Pooh—but not too amusing for a prereading crowd.

Ariel's Grotto is really just a covered seating area where people wait for a meet-and-greet with Ariel. It's also a good place to hang out for a bit of respite during the hottest part of the day. Look for the gold scallop shell for the number of minutes until the next Ariel appearance. Because she appears regularly throughout the day, lines tend to be fairly short and move briskly.

LIVE ENTERTAINMENT

Reserved for 20-minute storytime sessions with Belle is the **Fairytale Garden,** where she retells the *Beauty and the Beast* story incorporating audience members as the cast. **Dream Along with Mickey** made its debut in September 2006 on the Castle Forecourt Stage, just in front of Cinderella Castle. The 20-minute show is performed four or five times each day,

with a song spectacular in which—something totally new—the characters' mouths actually move in time to the music, and their eyes swivel around. It's Mickey, Minnie, Goofy, and Donald Duck, all dressed in shades of blue, dancing and whooping it up with three princesses and their beaux. Captain Hook, Smee, and Maleficent make appearances. It's not a great show, but the princesses mingled with the audience for quite a while afterward. This show seems to be replacing the Cinderellabration, which was staged at the same place and featured an original song titled "A Little Bit of Me."

Just behind Cinderella Castle, **The Sword in the Stone** is performed, in which some lucky audience member gets to pull Excalibur from the stone (it comes with perks— the sword-puller is dubbed temporary ruler of the realm).

FOOD

Pinocchio Village Haus (entrées $6–8)— why the German spelling of "Haus" when Gepetto and Pinocchio were Italian?—sends

© DISNEY

releasing Excalibur at The Sword in the Stone

CHARACTER MEALS

I've eaten meals with quite a number of goofballs in my day. At Disney you pay extra to do so. Well, maybe not goofballs, but certainly Goofy, and maybe even Dopey, Grumpy, and Bashful. The phenomenon of character dining is unique to Disney, with its own attendant rules and etiquette.

The idea is basic: Make reservations at one of the Disney restaurants featuring character meals, and then sit and dine while dressed-up characters roam the room, with a vow to stop at each table. Beyond eating, you spend your time gathering autographs, posing with the characters for keepsake photos, and maybe giving or receiving a hug. Each character meal features its own cast of characters or themes, and prices range wildly. Meals generally are buffet-style. For reservations at any of the restaurants, call 407/WDW-DINE (407/939-3463).

MAGIC KINGDOM

There are two character dining options at Cinderella's Royal Table in Cinderella Castle. The first is **Once Upon a Time Breakfast** with Cinderella and friends, which includes a photo imaging package and an entertainment magical moment (8-10:20 A.M.). The cost is $31.99 ages 10 and over, $21.99 ages 3-9, plus theme park admission. A little later in the day is **A Fairytale Lunch** with Cinderella and friends, which also includes a photo imaging package and an entertainment magical moment (12-3 P.M.). The cost is $33.99 ages 10 and over, $22.99 ages 3-9, plus theme park admission.

Dine with Winnie the Pooh and friends at the buffet at **The Crystal Palace** (breakfast 8-10:30 A.M., $18.99 ages 10 and over, $10.99 ages 3-9; lunch 11:30 A.M.-3 P.M., $20.99 ages 10 and over, $11.99 ages 3-9; dinner from 4 P.M.-closing, $27.99 ages 10 and over, $12.99 ages 3-9). Theme park admission is required.

Another dinner option is **Goofy's Liberate Your Appetite Character Dinner** at Liberty Tree Tavern in Liberty Square, with Goofy, Minnie, Pluto, and friends (4 P.M.). The cost is $27.99 ages 10 and over, $12.99 ages 3-9, plus theme park admission.

EPCOT

Epcot is home to **Chip 'n' Dale's Harvest Feast** at Garden Grill in The Land, with Mickey and friends (lunch 11 A.M.-3 P.M., $20.99 ages 10 and over, $11.99 ages 3-9; dinner 4:30 P.M.-closing, $27.99 ages 10 and over, $12.99 ages 3-9). Theme park admission is required.

Got a princess in your party? She'll love the **Princess Storybook Dining** at Akershus Royal Banquet Hall in the Norway pavilion, with Belle, Jasmine, Snow White, Sleeping Beauty, Mary Poppins, Pocahontas, Cinderella, Ariel, Alice, and Mulan (breakfast 8:30-10:10 A.M., $22.99 ages 10 and over, $12.99 ages 3-9; lunch 11:40 A.M.-2:50 P.M., $24.99 ages 10 and over, $13.99 ages 3-9; dinner 4:20-8:40 P.M., $28.99 ages 10 and over, $13.99 ages 3-9). Theme park admission is required.

DISNEY'S HOLLYWOOD STUDIOS

Playhouse Disney's **Play 'n Dine at Hollywood and Vine** features JoJo and Goliath from *JoJo's Circus* and June and Leo from *Little Einsteins* (breakfast 8-11:20 A.M., $22.99 ages 10 and over, $12.99 ages 3-9; lunch 11:40 A.M.-2:25 P.M., $24.99 ages 10 and over, $13.99 ages 3-9). Theme park admission is required.

DISNEY'S ANIMAL KINGDOM

Donald's Breakfastosaurus at Restaurantosaurus in DinoLand U.S.A. features a buffet with Donald Duck and friends (from park opening to 10:30 A.M.). The cost is $18.99 ages 10 and over, $10.99 ages 3-9 and theme park admission is required.

Beyond the four theme parks, many of the resort properties also host character meals:

- Disney's Beach Club Resort hosts the Beach Club Buffet.
- Disney's Contemporary Resort is home to the Chef Mickey's Fun Time Buffet.
- Disney's Grand Floridian Resort and Spa's 1900 Park Fare has the Supercalifragilistic Breakfast, Wonderland Tea Party, and Cinderella's Gala Feast.
- Disney's Polynesian Resort's 'Ohana Best Friends Breakfast features Lilo and Stitch.

out competent pizza, sandwiches, and salads. Kids can opt for mac-and-cheese or pbj's. For an icy cold drink or snack, you'll find frozen Coca-Cola at **Scuttle's Landing,** ice cream at **Mrs. Potts' Cupboard** (long lines on a hot day), and cold drinks at **Enchanted Grove.**

Character Dining
Cinderella's Royal Table ($30–50 per person for buffet breakfast, lunch, or dinner, reserve up to 180 days in advance, 407/939-3463) is the place to go for a pull-out-all-the-stops character meal. Dining here means a personal photo with Cinderella, and then kids are given a light-up wishing star for a wishing ceremony. Along with the sophisticated New American cuisine, you get tableside meet-and-greets with Cinderella, the Fairy Godmother, Sleeping Beauty, Belle, and other major players in the Disney pantheon. This is the priciest dining in the kingdom, but it's worth it if you have a princess fan in your entourage.

SHOPPING
In Fantasyland, **Fantasy Faire** is devoted to Mickey's PhilharMagic merchandise. You'll find another Pooh merchandise shop called **Pooh's Thotful Shop,** a Tinker Bell shop called **Tinker Bell's Treasures,** and **Sir Mickey's,** a Mickey snow globe and costume shop. There's also a kiosk to buy or process film.

Mickey's Toontown Fair

This area was originally called Mickey's Birthdayland, so it should come as no surprise that this is where to go if you're dead set on meeting the Mouse. Behind Fantasyland, this area of the park is a hike from everything else—you may want to take the Walt Disney World Railroad here from Main Street, U.S.A. or Frontierland. Mickey's Toontown Fair contains Minnie's Country House and Mickey's Country House, both an easy walk-through.

In general, Toontown Fair is geared to younger children, and since just about everything in this area is a walk-through, stamina is important (although the walk-throughs are wheelchair-accessible).

MICKEY'S COUNTRY HOUSE AND THE JUDGE'S TENT
Mickey's House tends to perpetuate all kinds of stereotypes about the slovenliness of the average male living alone: The state of his kitchen leads houseguests to believe he must be strictly a take-out man; a game room has the requisite bachelor diversions such as a Ping-Pong table and darts; and the living room radio broadcasts news of his beloved Duckburg University football team. All in all, the four-room house contains lots of subtle, funny touches. Still, it doesn't boast as many interactive bells and whistles as Minnie's Country House and requires only a brisk five minutes or so to tour.

Once through Mickey's house, at the Judge's Tent you have the opportunity to queue up to meet the Mouse who started it all. Lines can occasionally be long, in which case head over to the Toontown Hall of Fame and meet whichever characters are hanging out there first (the schedule is listed in the daily *Times Guide*). Disney employees keep the line moving—lingering for a protracted schmooze is not an option—and assist in orchestrating the meetings between Mickey and shy kids as well as directing the requisite photo shoots and autograph signings. The Judge's Tent is decorated with "prize-winning" fruits and vegetables, state fair–style, and a video of Mickey's adventures at the fair entertain the troops as they wait in line.

Tips: The lines can be long but move briskly; because it's enclosed, head for this in the hottest part of the day.

MINNIE'S COUNTRY HOUSE
Minnie's Country House is, of course, lavender and bubble-gum pink and inside you can riffle through the contents of her refrigerator, jump on

her furniture, pop a little noisy popcorn, check her answering-machine messages, or bake a cake at the touch of a button. Minnie is nothing if not the 21st-century working girl; she's also the editor of *Minnie's Cartoon Country Living Magazine,* which you can check out in her office.

THE BARNSTORMER AT GOOFY'S WISEACRE FARM

In keeping with Toontown's littler-kid orientation, The Barnstormer at Goofy's Wiseacre Farm makes for a gentle first coaster experience, and the theming is sweet. Climb aboard a 1920s-style crop duster (two or three to a car, eight cars on the train) which takes you through cornfields and smack through the middle of a barn.

Tips: The ride lasts just about a minute, with top speeds of 25 mph—don't wait more than 20 minutes in line for this one. The height requirement is 35 inches.

SS *MISS DAISY*

Donald's Boat is the cool-looking wreck of the SS *Miss Daisy.* Mostly a meet-and-greet spot for Donald, this area is billed as a playground for little ones, but there isn't much to do except stand there and get squirted with random sprays of water. Inside the boat, activities are limited to spinning the captain's wheel or clanging a bell.

TOONTOWN HALL OF FAME

The area has a county-fair motif, with a cluster of candy-striped tents in which you'll find an array of Disney characters assembled for meet-and-greets. There are three separate rooms, each with its own line. You'll encounter a rotating cast of characters at the end of each: maybe Pooh, Tigger, or Piglet at one; Goofy and Pluto at a second; and a changing lineup of princesses at the third, which is called, aptly, The Princess Room. Lines are long but move quickly; while waiting, explore the County Bounty, a Disney character memorabilia and stuffed animal shop that shares the building with Toontown Hall of Fame. This is appropriate for all ages intent upon collecting autographs and photos of Disney characters.

FOOD

Though there's not much here foodwise, hungry visitors can pick up fruit, yogurt, or a drink at **Toontown Farmers Market.**

SHOPPING

In Mickey's Toontown Fair, children's clothing and stuffed toys make up the bulk of the wares at **County Bounty,** inside Toontown Hall of Fame, and Mickey-specific souvenirs can be picked up at nearby **Mickey's Toontown Fair Souvenirs.**

Tomorrowland

The most physically unattractive part of Magic Kingdom, Tomorrowland is strictly devoted to space, aliens, and the future. Partly because of the theme, it lacks any landscaping or greenery and is awash in great slabs of unshaded concrete. The plaza around the Astro Orbiter is the core of the area, with people milling about, regrouping, having an ice cream, or waiting for members of their group who have gone to Space Mountain.

◖ SPACE MOUNTAIN

Space Mountain takes up the interior of a huge, white accordioned structure that can be seen from pretty much anywhere in Magic Kingdom. Inside the space-age dome, you board six-seat rockets and blast off into space. The ride made its debut in 1975 as one of the world's first dark-ride coasters, and thus it reflects slower speeds (28 mph) and less slick ride technology (no inversions but a very bumpy ride). That said, the strobe light tunnel, the galaxies and shooting stars, luminous planets, and plain exhilaration of not knowing what's around the next bend make this an exciting and memorable ride. Unlike many Disney rides, there are no characters

© DISNEY

MAGIC KINGDOM

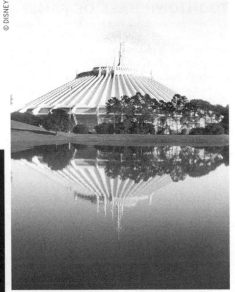

Space Mountain®

involved and no discernible storyline. Just you, launched into the vastness and darkness of space for 2.5 minutes.

The postride theming is great: Riders exit onto a moving sidewalk that glides past exhibit rooms of astronauts and space gewgaws—occasionally you glimpse the coaster "rockets" swooping around above you, their long phosphorescent-striped exteriors making streaks in the dark space.

Tips: Space Mountain is decidedly the top offering in Tomorrowland, but lines are intolerable if you don't use FASTPASS. Also, it occasionally malfunctions, leaving hundreds of people packed in a fairly tight queue and some people dangling in coaster seats high in the dark. The height requirement is 44 inches. Don't ride if you have back issues or are pregnant.

BUZZ LIGHTYEAR'S SPACE RANGER SPIN

A three-minute interactive ride/attraction, Buzz Lightyear's Space Ranger Spin is fun for all

ages. The pre-ride queue prepares you for your mission to stop evil Emperor Zurg from stealing the universe's systolic-fusion-something-or-other supply (batteries, essentially). Board a two-person space cruiser and head out at a tame speed for a 4.5-minute shooting spree in a colorful, black-light environment. You train your laser sights on huge robots and on a series of Emperor Zurg's circles marked with the letter Z, moving your laser cannon and spinning your cruiser to get as many as possible. Your score is kept on the dashboard, which you can evaluate on the Space Ranger chart to find your rank. (Tip: Far-away targets and moving targets tend to be worth more points.)

Tips: FASTPASS this ride and ride on the Tomorrowland Transit Authority while you wait for your assigned time window.

TOMORROWLAND TRANSIT AUTHORITY

Tomorrowland Transit Authority (TTA) is basically an elevated transportation system of four-person cars that glide for 10 minutes above Tomorrowland. You get to see inside Space Mountain and Buzz Lightyear's Space Ranger Spin, and you generally get out of the sun and rest your feet. It's also a good way to see which attractions seem to have the longest lines. The TTA seldom has lines and it's especially pretty at night.

WALT DISNEY'S CAROUSEL OF PROGRESS

Walt Disney's Carousel of Progress is one of the most charming parts of Tomorrowland. It's a 20-minute animatronics show on a rotating carousel theater, with four acts that follow the life of a single family, from the turn of the last century, to the 1920s, to the 1940s, and finally some time that is roughly contemporary. The basic idea is a chronicling of how mankind's world has been improved through technologies such as electricity and indoor plumbing.

Tips: I hesitate to hype this ride too much because the last few years have seen it open and close a number of times; it is now open seasonally. Rumor has it the attraction based on the

© DISNEY

Astro Orbiter spins high atop Tomorrowland.

famous "Progressland" at the 1964 New York World's Fair will be permanently closed one of these days.

ASTRO ORBITER

The Astro Orbiter is really the centerpiece of Tomorrowland; it's a great-looking rocket ride high above the land with planets and stars. Once you're on board, though, it's a lot like The Magic Carpets of Aladdin or Dumbo the Flying Elephant—it's a hub-and-spokes two-person rocket ride that circles for 1.5 minutes.

Tips: Don't bother if the line looks long (although it gives little kids something to do while they're waiting for their bigger siblings to get off Space Mountain).

TOMORROWLAND INDY SPEEDWAY

An original attraction of the park, Tomorrowland's track size was shrunk a while back to 0.4 mile to accommodate Toontown. The park has gussied up the winding racetrack with items from the Indianapolis Motor Speedway (the scoring pylon, Gasoline Alley) for greater verisimilitude. Despite its cool theming, I've ridden lots of go-cart tracks that are more thrilling and with cars that are easier to steer (you see riders wobbling all over the place as they acclimate to the steering quirks). And the cars, powered by lawn mower–type gas engines, bang into each other with regularity and can cause some mild whiplash during the five-minute ride. Still, it's fun to watch kids, and adults, grin when they get the checkered flag as they putt past the finish line.

I tend to think the Speedway has some conceptual problems. First, what's space-age about Indianapolis 500–style race cars? Second, there's a 52-inch height limitation for drivers, so little kids, who might actually appreciate this slow, seven mph opportunity to drive around a wide track, are precluded from taking the wheel. They can be passengers, but certainly every kid's minivan back home can get a little more exciting than this.

Tips: Lines are tremendously long (no FAST-PASS, and it takes forever to load and unload riders), but the queue winds past replicas of racecars and photos of the history of the big three Indy events: the 500, the Brickyard 400, and the Grand Prix. Real auto-racing enthusiasts will want to head outside the main gate of Magic Kingdom to the **Walt Disney World Speedway,** where they can enjoy one of the racing programs at the **Richard Petty Driving Experience** (for a description, see *Daytona Beach* in the *Excursions* chapter).

STITCH'S GREAT ESCAPE!

The biggest dud in Tomorrowland is the 2004 addition of Stitch's Great Escape! at the site of the former Alien Encounter. Guests are herded into the holding chamber, where they are briefed: You are recruits to the guards of the Galactic Federation, assigned to guard a Level 3 prisoner. Everyone heads into the theater in the round, at the center of which is a teleportation device. You are restrained in your chair (the shoulder restraints actually hurt) and the prisoner is revealed. An animatronic Stitch is appropriately mischievous and menacing, everything goes dark, plasma cannons misfire all over the place, and the prisoner escapes. Various effects conspire to make you think Stitch is right over you, bouncing on your shoulder restraints and burping foul chili-dog smells in your face. He spits some kind of noxious acid on you, makes those horrible Stitch noises, and generally behaves like the selfish, unsympathetic character that Disney has created for him (why is it that classic all-id-no-superego characters such as Woody Woodpecker are not quite as unappealing?).

Tips: Stitch's actions are not nice and kids are terrified. The minimum height requirement is now 40 inches. While it offers FASTPASS, lines recently haven't been too long.

MONSTERS, INC. LAUGH FLOOR COMEDY CLUB

In spring 2007, Magic Kingdom opened the Monsters, Inc. Laugh Floor Comedy Club, a 15-minute hybrid live show/attraction across from Stitch's Great Escape! After watching a short preshow movie starring Roz in the holding pen, folks are let into the auditorium. Audience members are encouraged to text-message their favorite joke to the monsters, who actually incorporate them into the show. An animated Mike Wazowski introduces three acts, one by his nephew, the other two by unfamiliar monsters, who then run through comedy routines that rely heavily on mocking the audience—the monsters ask audience members questions, and then the audience is asked to judge the monsters' performances.

FOOD

Tomorrowland Terrace Noodle Station (counter service, $6–12) offers the healthiest, most interesting food in the park, with chicken noodle bowls with broth, vegetarian noodle bowls with tofu and broth, chicken teriyaki, beef and broccoli, and Caesar salad with chicken. **Cosmic Ray's Starlight Café** (entrées $7–14) has counter-service burgers, ribs, and chicken. The **Lunching Pad** serves takeaway smoked turkey legs, while **Auntie Gravity's Galactic Goodies** purveys ice cream and smoothies.

SHOPPING

In Tomorrowland there are space-oriented stores such as **Merchant of Venus** (toys, Stitch merchandise) and **Mickey's Star Traders** (souvenirs and clothing).

Entertainment

DISNEY'S DREAMS COME TRUE PARADE

A parade winds its way from Frontierland to Main Street, U.S.A. at 3 P.M. daily. The parade begins with a float topped by an animator (a young Walt?) sketching Mickey, who follows in the next float. More than 100 cast members wave from floats and on foot—but some of the float pairings are odd. Why is Pooh piling on with Aladdin? The whole parade lasts 10 minutes, with viewing spots all along the route (guests with disabilities get a special viewing area in the circle in front of Cinderella Castle).

The current version, new as of August 2006, has a few problems. First, the parade announcement and official grand marshals strut their stuff a full 10 minutes before the parade really gets under way. So people on Main Street, U.S.A. are left milling around and a little confused (many non-English-speaking guests timidly try to ascertain whether this little flurry constituted the whole parade). Then, music begins to emanate from speakers on either side of Cinderella Castle. Because this music overpowers that coming from the parade itself, you don't know exactly where the parade will appear.

◖ WISHES NIGHTTIME SPECTACULAR

Each evening at the park ends with a firework spectacular—a rare instance when that noun is not hyperbole. Every night it's like the best Fourth of July pyrotechnics display ever—on steroids. It may seem grueling to stay to the bitter end after a long day at the park, but it's worth it. The current show, Wishes, made its debut near the end of 2003 and replaced the long-running Fantasy in the Sky. It runs 12 minutes with more than 600 fireworks bursting above the castle and a storyline narrated by Jiminy Cricket. The voices of Snow White and the Evil Queen, Peter Pan, Cinderella, Aladdin, and Ariel assist in conveying the fairly simple message about making dreams come true, while snippets of a dozen classic Disney songs fit seamlessly with the firework

display. The finale is unbelievable, and then a real, live Tinker Bell "flies" down from the top of Cinderella Castle. The IllumiNations show at Epcot pulls out all the stops, but Magic Kingdom is still the reigning leader for sheer spectacle.

There are no "bad seats" from which to watch the show, but many people favor standing right on Main Street, U.S.A. with the castle dead ahead. On the other hand, the fireworks can be viewed from rides such as Big Thunder Mountain Railroad or Splash Mountain for a more dynamic experience.

SPECTROMAGIC

During the busiest times of the year, the fireworks display is preceded by a shimmering, lighted parade called SpectroMagic. Floats illuminated by thousands of tiny lights include Cinderella's coach, a carousel, Ursula from *The Little Mermaid*, and others, all set to music. The 15-minute parade trails down Main Street, U.S.A., circles around in front of the castle, travels onward through Frontierland, and finishes on the left side of Splash Mountain. The best vantage spots are on either side of Main Street, U.S.A. or on the periphery of the castle front.

ELECTRICAL WATER PAGEANT

Every night Magic Kingdom–area resort guests are treated to a special show when the Electrical Water Pageant glides around Seven Seas Lagoon and Bay Lake. The aquatic parade of 14 lighted barges carry a 25-foot-tall screen of lights with a music-and-light show. The schedule is usually as follows, but it can be canceled on account of rain: It begins at 9 P.M. at the Polynesian Resort; 9:15 at the Grand Floridian; 9:35 at Wilderness Lodge; 9:45 at Fort Wilderness; 10:05 at Contemporary Resort. During Magic Kingdom extended hours, the parade finishes around 10:20 at Magic Kingdom. If you're not staying at one of these resorts, consider having dinner at one of their restaurants, timed to catch the parade. Resort employees will direct you to the best viewing areas.

EPCOT

Formerly called EPCOT (an acronym for Experimental Prototype Community of Tomorrow), the 300 acres of attractions, shows, food vendors, and exhibits loosely celebrate human achievement. Walking around the park, visitors get a decidedly nostalgic view of the future—many of the structures and attractions resemble a more naive, wide-eyed view of technology's role in our world and all of the wrongs it could right (much in the way *The Jetsons* is at once retro and futuristic).

This isn't by accident. Housed in a series of "pavilions," attractions resemble the kinds of exhibits that were popular at World's Fairs toward the beginning of the 20th century, specifically the famous 1939 New York World's Fair. The park is huge (twice the size of Magic Kingdom), but the scope of the attractions and the fact that they are largely indoors and air-conditioned make Epcot a great all-ages park. There are not as many thrill rides as at Disney's Hollywood Studios, but there are not as many animatronics shows as at Magic Kingdom. Adults tend to gravitate toward Epcot because much of it is overtly educational, and because several annual events cater specifically to adult interests. That said, kids will still find plenty to entertain them, and they might even walk away a little bit smarter.

There are two distinct lands in the park: Future World and World Showcase. Future World showcases new ideas and technology, with the huge golf ball–like Spaceship Earth anchoring the rough circle of imposing metal, glass, and concrete pavilions. World Showcase is arranged in villages celebrating 11 nations (and

© DISNEY

HIGHLIGHTS

LOOK FOR (TO FIND RECOMMENDED SIGHTS, ACTIVITIES, DINING, AND LODGING.

(**Mission: SPACE:** About as close as most of us come to being astronauts, this is a simulated rocket trip to Mars, with four people in each capsule performing their assigned jobs (to take the astronaut personality test and find out which role you'd be suited for, visit disney. go.com). Not for those with weak stomachs (page 94).

(**Soarin':** A gentle motion simulator with a breathtaking film of California's most beautiful scenery, this 10-seat hang-glider ride has become an instant classic (page 96).

(**Turtle Talk with Crush:** It's really a digital puppet controlled by a puppeteer, but what kids believe is that the animated surfer turtle from *Finding Nemo* has swum up and started talking specifically to them. He even knows their names as he answers questions (page 97).

(**Maelstrom:** The Lofoten Maelstrom on the northern coast of Norway has long been noted for its strength and dangerous whirlpools. Disney's version is a gentle thrillish ride in the World Showcase area (page 99).

(**IllumiNations:** Every evening, the 40-acre artificial lake in Epcot explodes with pyrotechnics in a pull-out-all-the-stops fireworks, lasers, fire, water, and music show. Environmentalists take note: Disney engineers have pioneered a new method of launching fireworks with air compression, which cuts down on ash, smoke, and pollutants (page 105).

their beers), all situated along a 1.3-mile promenade that encircles the 40-acre World Showcase Lagoon. Generally speaking, the big rides and attractions are in Future World, while the densest concentrations of food and shopping are to be found in World Showcase.

HISTORY

Walt Disney envisioned a utopian land, where people lived in harmonious equanimity in a futuristic domed and air-conditioned city with cutting-edge technology at every turn. He envisioned it as a planned community in which everyone rented and worked, and where no one was impoverished. Most people would walk to the city center along people-movers, and monorails would supplant cars. Laid out on a hub-and-spokes design, the city would have abundant public green space, a 30-story hotel and convention center, and nubile dancing girls on every corner. (All right, I made up the dancing girls.)

Ground broke on the park in 1979. At the time it was built, it was the largest construction project on the planet. Epcot opened in 1982, years after the death of Walt and his brother Roy. As with all Disney theme parks, it's still a work in progress, with attractions retired and new ones added regularly. It may not be exactly the futuristic city of Walt's specifications, and one wonders what he might think of it today, but his original notions about honoring technology and human achievement continue to be at the forefront of all that happens at Epcot.

EPCOT

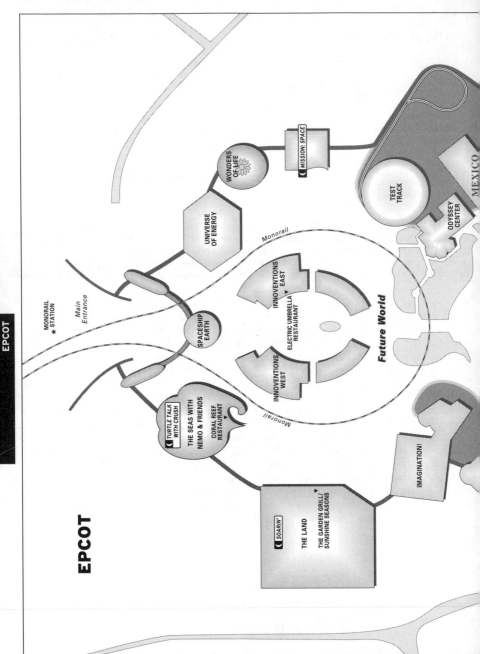

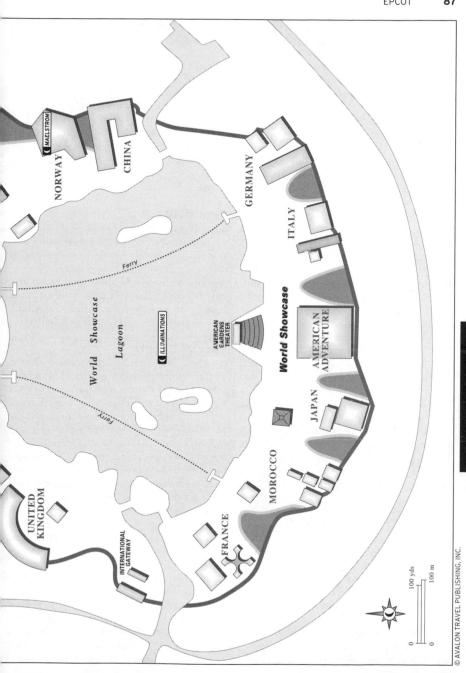

EPCOT

© AVALON TRAVEL PUBLISHING, INC.

Planning Your Time

Because of Epcot's size, many park-goers think it can't adequately be seen in a single day. I disagree: First of all, it is not prudent, or even fun, to visit every single food and beverage purveyor in World Showcase. Second, small children will balk if you attempt an exhaustive viewing of all the exhibits at Innoventions or a slow perusal of all the art and tchotchkes in World Showcase. If you pick and choose instead, then voilà, you're done in a single day.

Epcot is unique among Disney parks because it has two entrances. The original entrance feeds Epcot's 162-acre parking area and the Epcot monorail station (the monorail runs between Epcot and the Magic Kingdom Transportation and Ticket Center, which is three miles to the north). A second entrance opened in 1990 near the France pavilion in World Showcase. This International Gateway entrance provides park access to guests staying in Disney resort hotels close by (Disney's BoardWalk, Disney's Beach Club Resort, Disney's Yacht Club Resort, Walt Disney World Swan, and Walt Disney World Dolphin). If you use the main entrance, you will find yourself in **Future World,** a good place to start. Because Epcot is huge and spread out, it never seems mobbed and lines are seldom excruciating (maybe a little painful at Test Track, Mission: SPACE, and Turtle Talk with Crush). Head to **World Showcase** when you're hungry, or when you just need some time to sit and rest your feet.

CHARACTER GREETINGS

Epcot is not as crawling with characters as some of the other Disney parks. Mickey and friends sometimes hang out at The American Adventure, **Belle** and **the Beast** appear in France, **Snow White** can be seen in Germany, and **Jasmine** and **Aladdin** wander through Morocco. For a heavy dose of girl power (Snow White, Sleeping Beauty, Cinderella, and their nonprincess friends Belle, Jasmine, Ariel, Alice, Mulan, Mary Poppins, and Poca-

hontas), there's Princess Storybook Dining for breakfast, lunch, and dinner at Akershus Royal Banquet Hall in Norway. Make reservations through 407/WDW-DINE (407/939-3463).

WHEN TO GO
Mondays and Tuesdays are often the best days to visit Epcot because the masses train their sights on Magic Kingdom at the beginning of the week.

Park Hours
Epcot is generally open 9 A.M. to 9 P.M. daily, with Future World remaining open until 7 P.M. and World Showcase staying open to 9 P.M. or later. IllumiNations is shown nightly, at closing, around the World Showcase Lagoon. On busy holidays (Easter, Fourth of July, Christmas), Epcot may stay open until 10 P.M. Check the website for the calendar of park hours.

Special Events
A couple of annual events cement Epcot as the theme park for adults. The **Epcot International Flower and Garden Festival** now runs 60 days between the beginning of April and the beginning of June. Each year the park fills with more than 70 topiaries (many of them Disney characters), and gorgeously designed flower beds, rose gardens, bonsai, and blossoms are everywhere. The festival also hosts celebrity guest speakers, seminars, and other gardening exhibits. For the most part, kids ignore the whole thing, but they manage to get just slightly excited by the butterfly garden, the "I Dig Bugs" weekend, and the daily ladybug release. For more information, call 407/934-7639 or visit disneyworld.com/flower. The festival is included in regular Epcot admission.

Each year from the end of September through the middle of November there's the **Epcot International Food and Wine Festival.** Taking place in both Future World and World Showcase, the festival hosts wine and beer tastings and seminars, international marketplaces serve small tastes of regional specialties ($1.50–4.50), and winemakers and chefs are brought in for dinners, wine school, and cooking classes (more than 250 chefs stop in for demos). More than 100 wineries offer free samples, and there are beer and tea tastings. Live bands get things jumping at night. Included in the regular price of Epcot admission are the wine and beer seminars, the concerts, and the cooking demos. The weekly grand "Party for the Senses" tasting, the food and wine pairing classes, special dinners, The Odyssey Cooking School, Wine Schools, Lunch and Learn series, and several other events require a separate ticket and reservations. For more information, call 407/939-3378.

The Christmas holidays are celebrated in style at Epcot, with lovely decorations and a series of regular events. There are international holiday storytellers in each pavilion around World Showcase during the day, and then at 6 P.M. each evening there's a tree-lighting ceremony with Mickey at the World Showcase Plaza Tree Stage. Going strong since 1970, the **Candlelight Processional** is a nightly reading of the Christmas story by a celebrity narrator (real celebrities, such as Gary Sinise or Edward James Olmos) accompanied by a choir and 50-piece orchestra. It runs from near the end of November through the month of December, with three shows, at 5 P.M., 6:45 P.M., and 8:15 P.M. daily. A Candlelight Dinner Package is offered at most of the sit-down restaurants in World Showcase ($28–45 for adults); these sell out months in advance, so begin calling in August for December dates.

WHAT TO BRING

Guests do tons of walking at Epcot, so comfortable shoes are a must. The park's many indoor shows are air-conditioned, some might even say overly so. If you chill easily, you may want to bring a sweatshirt to toss on indoors. While you're not supposed to bring food in from outside the park, tuck some extra snacks in your backpack to cut down on in-park expenditures. Cell phones or walkie-talkies ensure that you'll find each other again if your party splits up.

PRACTICALITIES
Camera Services
CD burning and other camera services are available at the Camera Center in the main entrance plaza.

First Aid
The First Aid Center, staffed by registered nurses, is near the Odyssey Center in Future World.

Guest Relations
The Guest Relations offices are outside the park at the turnstiles, inside the park to the right after you go through the gates, and also behind Spaceship Earth to the left. They provide the following services: messages for separated parties and the lost and found; information for guests with disabilities and sign-language services; character greeting information and dining priority seating; tour information; park maps; and foreign currency or Disney Dollar exchange. There are ATMs presented by Bank One near the park entrance on the left near the kennels, at the bridge between World Showcase and Future World near the Disney Vacation Club kiosk, and at the American Adventure near the restrooms.

Kennels
Pet care facilities are just outside the entrance plaza. It is open one hour before and after the park hours. Call 407/824-6568 to reserve; it's $10 per pet per day ($13 for overnight if you are a Disney Resort guest, $15 for nonguests). The staff will feed your pet, but you are advised to walk your dog twice during the day. There is no on-site veterinarian. Dogs must have proof of rabies, DHP, parvovirus, and bordetella shots, while cats must have proof of rabies, panleukopenia, rhinotracheitis, and calcivirus shots. All dogs and cats must be at least eight weeks old to be kenneled. No exotic animals are allowed.

Rentals
Strollers can be rented from special stands on the east side of the entrance plaza and at

EPCOT

World Showcase's International Gateway. Single strollers cost $8 with a Disney Dollar deposit back when you turn it in; doubles are $15 with a Disney Dollar back.

Wheelchairs are available at the same places, with $10 per day rental with no deposit, and motorized ECVs are $35 per day rental with a $5 refundable deposit. Because there are a limited number of wheelchair and ECV rentals, get to the park early to ensure getting one.

Lockers are near the west side of Spaceship Earth. Or try the unattended lockers at the International Gateway or the oversize lockers at Bus Information. Cost is $7, $2 of which is a refundable deposit on the key (and if you go to a second park, you can bring your locker receipt and just put down an additional $5 deposit for a locker there).

GETTING THERE AND AROUND

Walt Disney World Resort is southwest of Orlando, off I-4, west of the Florida's Turnpike. Take Exit 67 off I-4 for Epcot and Downtown Disney. Epcot is accessible by bus from Walt Disney World Resort hotels and accessible by boat from Disney's BoardWalk Inn and Villas Resort, Disney's Yacht Club, Disney's Beach Club Resorts, Walt Disney World Swan, and Walt Disney World Dolphin Hotels. It is also accessible by monorail via the central Transportation and Ticket Center.

Parking

The cost is $10 but free to all Walt Disney World Resort hotel guests. If you are park-hopping, your parking receipt will be honored at the other parks. Trams take visitors from the vast parking lot to the park entrance, but much of the parking is close enough to the entrance to walk it. Parking sections are named for themes (Energy, Harvest, and so on), and the aisles are numbered.

Park Maps

Pick up free guide maps just inside the park. They are offered in English, Spanish, French, Portuguese, German and Japanese, as well as in Braille (at Guest Relations).

Tours

Epcot offers more tours than any other park, many of them educational, many of them behind the scenes, and many of them geared to adults.

AROUND THE WORLD AT EPCOT

The coolest tour is a fairly recent addition to the lineup: the "Segway" Around the World at Epcot (at 7:45 A.M., 8:30 A.M., 9 A.M., and 9:30 A.M. daily, two hours long, $85 per person, must be at least 16 years old and weigh 250 pounds or less). Guests ride upright, two-wheel Segway Human Transporters on an outdoor tour around the World Showcase. It includes a lesson on how to ride the things—trickier than it looks.

AQUATIC TOURS

There are several aquatic tours, the least expensive of which is the **Seas Aqua Tour** (2.5 hours, with the in-water experience lasting 30 minutes, $100, theme park admission is neither required nor included, guests 8–16 must be accompanied by a parent or legal guardian). Guests don swimsuits and then wet suits before plunging into the six-million-gallon The Seas with Nemo and Friends aquarium, which contains more than 65 species of marine life in a coral reef environment. Admission includes gear, refreshments, a T-shirt, and a group photo.

For those with scuba certification, **Epcot DiveQuest** (three hours with the in-water experience lasting 40 minutes, $140, includes all gear and a limited-edition T-shirt, ages 10 and up) is a scuba-aided exploration of the same aquarium. **Dolphins in Depth** (three hours, $150, must be 13 or older) gets folks wet up to the waist in The Seas with Nemo and Friends area, but this time it's for a one-on-one with the dolphins. You do not need to swim or be scuba certified, and again, theme park admission is neither required nor included for this event. At the end you get a photograph with the dolphin, refreshments, and a T-shirt.

BEHIND THE SEEDS

Avid gardeners enjoy the **Behind the Seeds at Epcot** tour (one hour, $12 ages 10 and up, $10 ages 3–9), which takes guests through the greenhouses in The Land pavilion. Kids enjoy the part where they spy on alligators and release ladybugs. The **Gardens of the World** tour (three hours, $59, must be 16 or older) is a more in-depth look at the gardens of World Showcase and an examination of Disney's landscaping design elements.

BACKSTAGE TOURS

A trio of tours take guests essentially "backstage" at the park. The **UnDISCOVERed Future World** tour (4.5 hours, $49, must be 16 or older) explores Walt Disney's original vision for the park—the EPCOT city of the future; **Hidden Treasures of World Showcase** (3.5 hours, $59, must be 16 or older) explores the art, architecture, and costumes of the 11 countries represented. And if you want to understand some of the technology at work in the parks, **Backstage Magic** (seven hours, $199 includes lunch at Mama Melrose's Ristorante, must be 16 or older) takes you behind the scenes at Epcot, Disney's Hollywood Studios, and Magic Kingdom.

The **VIP Tour Services** is offered at all the parks; it's really just a way to have a guide take care of planning your itinerary, enabling you to hop to the fronts of lines and get the best seats in the house for shows. In addition to your regular park admission, this service is $125 per hour, with a minimum of six hours. It's very steep, but there are discounts for resort guests.

Future World Pavilions

If Walt Disney envisioned this park as the Experimental Prototype Community of Tomorrow, the Future World Pavilions represent the "Tomorrow" part. In each of the discrete nine pavilions, attractions explore some element of technological advancement. If that all sounds too educational, never fear. This part of the park has plenty to make you yell "whoo" with your hands in the air: Become a crash-test dummy at high speeds in Test Track, sign on as one of four crew members on a simulated voyage to Mars in Mission: SPACE, or get really, really small at Honey I Shrunk the Audience.

There's a lot of whimsical, all-ages fun to be had in Future World, each huge pavilion containing usually containing two or three attractions in a particular theme (human health, scientific advancement, the environment). Attractions are primarily indoors and air-conditioned, making it a good destination on a hot or rainy day.

Pavilions are listed here clockwise around the park from the left of the entrance. Because specific showtimes don't play a huge role in scheduling your day, a simple clockwise approach works fine (attractions such as Mission: SPACE and Soarin' run out of FASTPASSes on very busy days, so you may want to head to them upon arrival).

SPACESHIP EARTH

An old-timer at the park, dating to 1982, Spaceship Earth is the landmark pavilion right at the entrance of the park, its 180-foot space-age golf ball/geosphere visible from all over the park. Inside is a sphere within a sphere that contains the attraction of the same name.

Guests board continuously loading small "time vehicles" that rotate as they glide through the gentle 16-minute dark ride. Narrated by the ever-patrician Jeremy Irons, the animatronic-heavy attraction focuses on the history of communications—going back as far as the Stone Age, then on to papyrus in Egypt in the 9th century, up through the development of the printing press and the Age of Enlightenment. The narration may not be of particular interest to young kids, but this all-ages ride has enough drama and excitement to hold anyone's

EPCOT

© DISNEY

Spaceship Earth

interest (there's a stunning star-filled night sky scene, and another with Michelangelo painting the Sistine Chapel).

Introduced for the Millennium Celebration, **Leave a Legacy** gives guests a chance to have their photographic images etched onto a steel tile and then incorporated into a huge stone sculpture in the Leave a Legacy Plaza. The cost is $35 for one tile.

Tips: Parts of the ride are very dark, and sometimes the vehicles are turned backward. Lines are seldom long except for right at the start of the day, and its air-conditioning is quite a respite on a hot day. There are no height restrictions.

UNIVERSE OF ENERGY

To the left of Spaceship Earth is the Universe of Energy, a stunning, mirrored pyramid. While the pyramid has been here since 1982, the show it contains is of much more recent vintage. It's appropriate that **Ellen's Energy Adventure** addresses issues of diminishing fossil fuels: The entire roof of the Universe of

Energy pavilion is covered in solar panels, partially powering the ride.

Ellen's Energy Adventure

This 45-minute film/ride begins with a movie called *Ellen's Energy Adventure,* starring Ellen DeGeneres, with Jamie Lee Curtis and Bill Nye the Science Guy. The comic plotline is that DeGeneres dreams she's on *Jeopardy* pitted against her college rival, Dr. Judy Peterson (Curtis). Bill Nye brings DeGeneres up to speed quickly on the Big Bang, fusion, and other scientific issues related to energy (the *Jeopardy* category she faces). All this time guests have been seated in a 600-seat theater, concluding this segment with a very brief history of the universe playing across the three enormous screens.

The theater then rotates and divides into six huge "cars" in which guests accompany Ellen and Bill on a journey through prehistoric times—roaring audio-animatronic dinosaurs, visual effects, dramatic lighting, cold air in a primeval forest, volcanoes erupting, and all while Ellen and Bill keep up a little comic patter. At one point Ellen even appears as an animatronic figure.

Tips: It's the most technologically advanced attraction at Epcot and about the longest ride in all of Disney. There are no ride restrictions; young children will be frightened of the dinosaurs. Because it's long and all indoors, time it for the hottest part of the day.

WONDERS OF LIFE

A giant double helix sculpture outside provides a major clue: The Wonders of Life pavilion contains attractions that relate to human life, fitness, and health. It's a huge golden geodesic dome, opened originally in 1989 between the Universe of Energy and Mission: SPACE.

Tips: The attractions contained therein open only during peak season at this point (spring break and the December holidays); the rest of the year this dome is used for special events.

Body Wars

If visiting during a busy season, take a ride on the motion simulator Body Wars. Scientists—

EPCOT RIDE GUIDE

FASTPASS RIDES

Listed in order of importance, these are the rides to FASTPASS:

1. Soarin'

2. Test Track

3. Mission: SPACE

It's not necessary to FASTPASS the following rides unless it's high season:

4. Honey, I Shrunk the Audience

5. The Maelstrom

6. Living with the Land

RIDE AND ACCESS RESTRICTIONS

* **Body Wars:** Riders must be at least 40 inches tall; pregnant women or those with back or neck problems should not ride; children younger than six might find it scary.

* **Maelstrom:** Riders must be three years old or older.

* **Mission: SPACE:** Riders must be at least 44 inches tall; pregnant women and those who experience motion sickness or have back problems should not ride.

* **Soarin':** Riders must be at least 40 inches tall.

* **Test Track:** Riders must be at least 40 inches tall.

    On Body Wars, Mission: SPACE, Soarin', Maelstrom, Living with the Land, and Test Track, guests in wheelchairs or electronic convenience vehicles (ECVs) will have to transfer to a ride chair.

that's you—are miniaturized to the size of a single cell and propelled through the bloodstream. Think Star Tours flight simulation, but more like the 1966 sci-fi film *Fantastic Voyage*. Guests walk through a preshow tunnel before being seated and buckled into the 44-seat flight-simulation theaters. What starts as a routine medical probe to assist a scientist already miniaturized becomes a hair-raising mission through the bloodstream.

Tips: Visual effects and seats that bump and rock appropriately (which in turn are set in four theaters that themselves move) make this a somewhat nausea-inducing five-minute ride. There is a 40-inch height requirement, and pregnant women or those with back or neck problems should not ride. Young children may find this scary. The film, directed by Leonard Nimoy, is looking a little tired and in need of replacement.

Cranium Command

A similarly educational attraction, but more comic and with animatronics, is Cranium Command, a show about adolescent insanity and how a 12-year-old boy's brain works as he attempts to ask a girl out.

Guests enter the lobby and stand in the pre-show area for a short film with educational information about the brain (fairly simplistic, but comprehensible even to young children), complete with lots of brain puns and jokes. From there, guests enter the theater and settle in for a 17-minute show in an air-conditioned theater with long benches for seating. An animatronic Captain Buzzy starts the show, alerting guests to the fact that we are now in the "unstable craft" that is Bobby's brain. Different parts of Bobby's "command crew" are voiced by famous actors—Charles Grodin is Left Brain, Jon Lovitz is Right Brain, Dana Carvey and Kevin Nealon play parts of the heart, and Bobcat Goldthwait plays Adrenal Gland (why does that seem so appropriate?) for the film.

Tips: Little kids won't get the jokes about the hypothalamus, but it's still an all-ages show from which different age groups just get different things.

EPCOT

The Making of Me

A third attraction, The Making of Me is a 15-minute film about romance, marriage, and how that sometimes results in children. Disney's coy attempt to discuss human reproduction, the film stars Martin Short trying to ask questions such as "Where did I come from?" and "What's it like being born?" without saying anything indiscreet.

Tips: This film, released in 1989, is rumored to retire permanently in the near future. Young children won't exactly understand what this is about, and it's appropriate only for older children who have a passing familiarity with the birds and the bees.

MISSION: SPACE

Launched, so to speak, in 2003, Mission: SPACE had a nice addition in 2006 that allows guests to choose between the full-bore experience or a milder alternative. This is a major, gut-lurching space-travel simulator, using the same centrifuge-type technology used to train astronauts to handle high G-forces. The four-person mock space capsule ride to Mars is the first part of the attraction (each of the four "crew members" gets an assigned "job" during the flight, which mostly means pressing buttons that don't do anything in particular). After disembarking from the simulator, guests can get involved in the collaborative, team Mission: SPACE Race game in the Advanced Training Lab. That part is super fun, with Team Triton and Team Orion battling to fix their rocket's problems before the other team. Outside, the Planetary Plaza is a great place for little kids to play while waiting for family members who are riding Mission: SPACE.

Tips: The simulator has a height requirement of 44 inches and is not appropriate for those with high blood pressure or anyone significantly overweight. The simulator's blastoff and weightlessness are very cool but are prone to inducing motion sickness, and the five-minute ride has been linked to at least two deaths at the park. Be sure to FASTPASS this ride early in the day because FASTPASSes can run out by early afternoon.

TEST TRACK

Thrill seekers were gaga over this attraction when it opened in 1999. A collaboration with General Motors, the racing-theme dark ride/coaster has been surpassed in recent years by lots of other Disney and Universal attractions. The indoor queuing area leads guests through a GM testing laboratory, with lots of loud equipment and cool machines testing the safety of brakes, airbags, suspensions, and other car parts. Guests then assume the role of crash test dummy, boarding six-passenger cars that squeal up a three-story "hill climb test" before doing a slow loop and then a high-speed, 65-mph loop around the track for a "ride handling test." Additional tests of the brakes and suspension add some bumps and drama, as do the temperature tests—the noteworthy "barrier test" will grab your attention.

Tips: Test Track is a long ride (5.5 minutes), but lines can be daunting, so FASTPASS this attraction. There is a height requirement of 40 inches and a single-rider line that solo travelers should take advantage of. Be warned that

Test Track

© DISNEY

the attraction breaks down with unfortunate regularity and the postride exhibit of GM cars and a short cartoon are ho-hum. Young children or those with bad backs will find this ride unpleasant.

INNOVENTIONS

This is where to wait for your FASTPASS window at Test Track; it's an indoor hall reminiscent of your hometown science center. Disney has partnered with a number of companies through the years in this ever-changing walk-through exposition of scientific gizmos that opened in 1994. It's divided into Innoventions West and Innoventions East, and the overarching aim is to celebrate human achievement.

Innoventions West, designated with blue signs, contains the **ThinkPlace Presented by IBM,** with interactive computers, voice recognition, and Internet postcards you can send to your friends. There's also a large, multiplayer video game in which people work together to build a machine. Another video game area is called **Video Games of Tomorrow;** it has a range of games based on Disney film characters. Also in Innoventions West cast members demonstrate **Segways,** those upright, two-wheeled human transporters. **The Great American Farm** hosts a ladybug release each day every hour beginning at 11:30 A.M.; and families can while away a bit of time playing the interactive **Where's the Fire?,** a fire safety game that educates everyone about fire hazards in the home.

Innoventions East, designated by green signs, clusters the **Fantastic Plastic Works** (design your own plastic robot that then competes in a race; watch molded plastic parts being made); **Test the Limits Lab** (in six kiosks, kids experiment hands-on with the safety of products—in a "shatter lab," an "impact lab," a "drop lab," and so forth); and the **Innoventions Internet Zone Presented by Disney.com** (visitors can send video email to friends back home or play a game of Toon Tag).

Exhibits change with regularity (for a while there was a cool nanotechnology exhibit sponsored by Cornell), but there's usually something that will capture the interests of visitors from toddler-age up through adults.

Tips: The Innovention Fountain in the plaza outside may be more entertaining for the very young; it puts on a "show" set to music every 15 minutes.

IMAGINATION!

Two conjoined gleaming glass pyramids, opened in 1982 and sponsored by Eastman Kodak, contain three attractions linked by their reliance upon the human imagination. This part of the park has changed quite a bit through the years, but the current lineup—a film called **Honey I Shrunk the Audience,** a ride called **Journey into Imagination with Figment,** and a small interactive **ImageWorks** lab—appeal to an all-ages audience.

Honey I Shrunk the Audience

One of Disney's earlier efforts with 4-D (that fourth dimension being one that allows audiences to feel and smell what's going on on-screen), Honey I Shrunk the Audience doesn't seem exactly cutting-edge these days. Still, it's a 20-minute romp of a movie, with Professor Wayne Szalinski (Rick Moranis) accepting the Inventor of the Year Award for his Dimensional Duplicator and Incredible Shrinking Machine. Needless to say, the shrinking machine malfunctions and the audience gets very tiny.

Tips: The film itself is looking a little fuzzy these days, but a dog sneeze and rats scuttling on the floor spice things up. This attraction offers FASTPASS and is appropriate for all ages.

Journey into Imagination with Figment

This attraction had a recent refurbishment that makes it more like the original attraction to the park. The ride travels through labs for studying the senses—sight, smell, and sound all get a workout while Figment, a purple dragon character, gums up the works. At the end, Figment invites guests into his perspective-skewing upside-down house. Overall, the dialogue is a little hackneyed, but little kids seem to love this ride and there are seldom long lines.

EPCOT

ImageWorks—The Kodak "What If?" Labs is at the end of the Figment ride and features an interactive area where you can conduct an orchestra, create sounds, and goof around in front of funhouse mirrors.

THE LAND

The Land spreads across six acres, making it the largest of Epcot's pavilions; the central idea here is the majesty and grandeur of our planet and a reminder of our obligation to take care of it. The huge, greenhouselike structure contains several notable attractions, the most popular of which is the **Soarin'** flight simulator added in 2005. Mostly beloved for its feeling of flying, it shows gorgeous scenes of California coastline, a good preamble to the environmental message of the little-kid-friendly *Circle of Life* film, or the all-ages tour of Epcot's greenhouses (yes, the workers produce cucumbers in the shape of Mickey heads, but they do other, more serious agricultural work with hydroponics and pest-resistant plants).

◖ Soarin'

The top offering in this six-acre pavilion,

Soarin' is a flight simulation film with an 80-foot domed projection screen. Guests are lifted 40 feet into the air, with swooping and tilting to re-create the sensation of flying. Gorgeous scenes of California—the redwoods, Golden Gate Bridge, Yosemite National Park—are accompanied by breezes and even smells that create an authentic flying experience. The front row provides the best view.

Tips: Despite the fact that Soarin' opened in 2005, the screen itself is starting to look a little worn, but guests are still enthusiastic so FASTPASS this ride. This is an all-ages kind of attraction, but there is a 40-inch height requirement. The ride itself is almost five minutes long, but with the preflight briefing the experience is 10 minutes.

Living with the Land

After winding through vignettes with animatronics illustrating the history of agriculture, a narrator explains all about Epcot's four greenhouses and the aquaculture facility as you glide through them on a 14-minute boat ride. There are the Tropics Greenhouse with crops such

Soarin' lets guests do just that.

© DISNEY

EPCOT

as rice and bananas grown under the 60-foot dome; the Temperate Greenhouse with its focus on sustainable agriculture and integrated pest management; the Production Greenhouse that produces lettuce, tomatoes, and other produce for the Garden Grill Restaurant and elsewhere in Epcot; the Creative House that experiments with wacky, space-age ways of growing crops; and the Aquacell, a fishery specializing in species such as tilapia and bass. Sound a little dry? It's not. Despite heavy messages about sustainable agriculture, intercropping, pest management, and our stewardship of the land, it's a breezy, fun ride with lots to look at from one of five benches on each canopied boat.

Tips: All-ages appropriate, it's a nice opportunity to get off your feet for a bit. This attraction also offers FASTPASS.

Circle of Life

The environmental message gets driven home with gusto in the 20-minute film *Circle of Life,* starring three characters from *The Lion King.* The Harvest Theatre holds nearly 500 people in delicious air-conditioning; still, it never seems to have too long a line. The story, most appropriate for elementary-age kids, tells how, in the name of progress, Pumbaa and Timon are cutting down trees and damming a river, until Simba sets them right. The film marries live action with animation.

THE SEAS WITH NEMO AND FRIENDS

Formerly The Living Seas, this pavilion had an overhaul in 2004, with a six-million-gallon aquarium stocked with thousands of tropical fish, dolphins, sharks, and manatees. Against this coral reef background, the characters from *Finding Nemo* appear to be swimming with the live fishes. Guests board "clam mobiles" and go on a journey for Nemo through a series of animated vignettes.

(Turtle Talk with Crush

The biggest draw in this pavilion is Turtle Talk with Crush, an interactive show in which visitors have a 3-D, 10-minute "conversation" with Crush.

Adults are seated on benches in a small theater that holds about 50 people; kids sit up front on the floor. A huge screen at the front shows an underwater scene. A cast member comes out and introduces the animated Crush, who then swims to the front of the screen and starts chatting. He picks people out of the audience to talk with—asking people their names, identifying them by what they're wearing (there must be a "man behind the curtain," in *Wizard of Oz* parlance). He jokes around, seems to "listen" to the audience, his facial expressions changing appropriately. He even moves to the closest part of the screen when talking to a particular audience member. Kids are absolutely wild about chitchatting with the cool surfer-dude turtle, so lines are long.

Tips: The 10-minute show is all-ages appropriate, but young children will like it best. The same goes for the small hands-on shark-themed play area called **Bruce's Sub House** adjacent to Turtle Talk with Crush.

FOOD

Dining is such a central part of experiencing World Showcase that sometimes the dining options in Future World get short shrift. It's a shame, as there are several offerings that rival restaurants at any of the other Disney theme parks.

The **Garden Grill Restaurant** (lunch and dinner, $15–29) is a rotating restaurant in The Land pavilion that overlooks scenes from the Living with the Land attraction; all produce is grown in The Land's greenhouses. The restaurant offers a character meet-and-greet meal with Mickey, with appealing fried catfish and rotisserie meats. The (**Coral Reef Restaurant** (lunch and dinner, $30–50), in The Seas with Nemo and Friends area, is fairly pricey but rivals Sharks Underwater Grill at SeaWorld Orlando for underwater drama and excitement. Something seems a little coldhearted about eating flounder or mahimahi while watching the fish swim in the saltwater aquarium, but the restaurant is usually mobbed.

For more casual dining, there are deli sandwiches, salads, and very competent burgers at the **Electric Umbrella Restaurant** at the

© DISNEY

Coral Reef Restaurant offers guests an underwater peek at the park.

center of Innoventions. Healthy soups, salads, pastas, and baked potatoes can be found at the **Sunshine Season Food Fair** food court in The Land pavilion.

SHOPPING

Shopping options are so varied and numerous in World Showcase that Future World seems like slim pickings. Future World has **The Art of Disney** collectibles and cels, as well as the huge, multifloor **MouseGear** for Epcot logo clothing and souvenirs. There's a camera center under Spaceship Earth; gardening books and gifts in the food court at The Land; and aquatic-themed gifts in the gift shop at The Seas with Nemo and Friends.

World Showcase Pavilions

Four continents and 11 countries—no passports, no security checks, no complicated foreign currencies. All right, so strict verisimilitude is not always the goal in these 11 pavilions arrayed on a 1.3-mile promenade around World Showcase Lagoon, but each gives some plausible national flavor through its architecture, wares for sale, ethnic cuisines, shows, and "ambassadors." Disney has taken pains even to reflect indigenous flora in its landscaping. And did I mention the beer? Pavilions are listed here clockwise around

the promenade. Each one has a special "Kidcot" area where kids can do a craft or interact with a native of the country in question.

If you plan to eat a sit-down lunch or dinner, make "Priority Seating" reservations (407/939-3463) or visit the restaurant early in the day to arrange it.

MEXICO PAVILION

Mexico is anchored by a pyramid modeled after an Aztec Temple of Quetzalcoatl, inside which is an assemblage of artifacts from different periods of Mexican history.

Mexico holds World Showcase's most appealing attraction for little kids, **Gran Fiesta Tour Starring the Three Caballeros.** This newly revamped seven-minute boat ride coasts through a shady lagoon filled with animatronic figures and a catchy song—all without all the long lines and attendant hoo-haw of "it's a small world."

Animales Fantasticos, a collection of Oaxacan folk art wood carvings of fantasy animals, is a fairly new addition to the pavilion. **Casa Mexicana** re-creates a traditional Mexican house that you can walk through. Outside the **Plaza de los Amigos** you'll occasionally see the 12-piece **Mariachi Cobre** strolling and playing—listen while perusing the baskets, pottery, leather goods, and clothing at the market.

Food

The pavilion's restaurant, **La Cantina De San Angel** (entrées $5–27) serves credible chicken mole (low on the spice) and also has a slushy margarita machine.

Shopping

The **Plaza de Los Amigos** offers small vendors' carts of Mexican souvenirs, from jewelry to pottery, piñatas, and big goofy sombreros. In the **Artesanias La Familia Fashions** you can browse casual Mexican clothing, and there are charming souvenirs and gifts from Northern Mexico at **El Ranchito del Norte.**

NORWAY PAVILION

A latecomer to the World Showcase, added in 1988, this 58,000-square-foot country contains the best dining around. Before you appease your stomach, wander through the 10th-century Viking village, with a town square that simulates Oslo, Bergen, Setesdahl, and Alesund.

(C Maelstrom

The Maelstrom adventure cruise is a little zestier than the boat ride in Mexico. The 12-minute journey on a 16-person, dragon-headed Viking ship through a mythical Norwegian forest isn't all a pleasure cruise. Bobbing along, you catch glimpses of audio-animatronic trolls and water spirits in a creepy Norwegian forest, who then cast a spell on your boat. You'll find yourself zooming backward through rapids, in the midst of an ocean storm, and finally in a calm Norwegian fishing village. The idea is that you are departing from a modern-day village on a Norwegian fjord, journeying through time over white-water rapids, narrowly avoid a waterfall, to a 10th-century Viking village. Finally, you disembark and are ushered into a theater for a short movie called *Norway, the Film* about this Scandinavian country's history. (The film is optional, but it's brief and pleasant.)

Tips: Maelstrom is the only thing that passes for a thrill ride in World Showcase, but it's appropriate for the whole family (children must be three years old or older to ride). You can also FASTPASS this ride. After the cruise, stroll through the re-creation of a **Stave Church** which contains cool Norse artifacts and weapons (it's heavily air-conditioned, nice on a hot day).

Food

The nearby **Kringla Bakeri Og Kafe** (under $14) bakery is a good spot to grab a pastry and a coffee, but then you'd miss out on the excellent **(C Restaurant Akershus** (reservations 407/939-3463, $15–27), which offers notably authentic Scandinavian food to accompany **Princess Storybook Dining** at breakfast, lunch, and dinner. Snow White, Sleeping Beauty, Belle, Jasmine, and others roam the room while guests try exotic *kjottkaker* (meat cakes), rutabaga mash, braised lamb, and lots of pickled fish. **Spelmanns Gledje** performs 15–20-minute shows of Norwegian folk music at intervals out on the street in the Norway Pavilion.

Shopping

Shopping in this area occurs at **The Puffin's Roost,** which carries a strangely broad array of hand-knit woolens, Norwegian books, fragrances, candy, and lots of troll merchandise.

EPCOT

Need a Viking helmet? You're in luck. It's the same with a "Troll Crossing" sign.

CHINA PAVILION

The most colorful and elaborate of the World Pavilions, China seduces with golden detailed roofing, bright red pillars, animal carvings, and the inviting triple-arched ceremonial Gate of the Golden Sun (styled after the main gate at the summer palace of Beijing, its bold primary colors comprise stunning mosaic stonework). Through the gateway, the dazzling Temple of Heaven appears on the right, flanked by tranquil ponds dotted with delicate lilies. The horticulturalist will have a field day in this pavilion, with rare weeping mulberries, corkscrew bonsai trunks, clumps of bamboo, and tallow trees.

Like many of the countries here, China offers a 20-minute film, inside the Temple of Heaven. This is a Circle-Vision 360 movie titled *Reflections of China,* shown on the half hour. It's a wide-eyed travelogue about the beauty and mystery of China without a lot of the messier political history. The film is projected onto nine moving screens in the circular theater, in which audiences stand for the duration. Outside the theater, the land is given over to serene templelike buildings, a small garden, and some good shopping and dining.

One of the buildings houses a new walk-through exhibit, **Tomb Warriors: Guardian Spirits of Ancient China,** which features a miniature re-creation of the tomb warriors arrayed in the 22-square-mile tomb of China's first emperor, Qin Shi Huang. The exhibit focuses on the Chinese approach to the afterlife, with selections from 2,000 years of Chinese funerary art. Kids won't be impressed, but they'll like the **Dragon Legend Acrobats** that perform at intervals or the occasional Chinese harpist.

Food

Nine Dragons Restaurant (entrées $15–29) is the sit-down restaurant with very predictable Chinese/American cuisine. The **Lotus Blossom Café** offers quick bites to grab and go.

Shopping

Shoppers will enjoy spending time sifting through the rugs, jewelry, and kitchenware at the **Yong Feng Shangdian Department Store.**

GERMANY PAVILION

In the central square you'll see the statue of **St. George and the Dragon,** and a clock tower contains a clock that strikes on the hour attended by Hummel figurines. Every October things get rocking in Germany, and St. Nicholas makes a lengthy appearance in December. The rest of the year, this pavilion is largely about shopping and eating, deftly catering to visitors' more sybaritic side.

Food

Food and shopping are the central draws in cheery, geranium-heavy Germany. At the heart of things is the (**Biergarten** (entrées $15–27), an indoor garden supposedly reminiscent of the 16th-century town of Rothenberg, with a hearty Bavarian Oktoberfest buffet (sau-

© DISNEY

China Pavilion

© DISNEY

St. George and the Dragon, Germany Pavilion

sages, potatoes, red cabbage, and sauerbraten), lent real panache by yodelers and the lederhosen-clad **Oktoberfest Musikanten** band. People seem to hang out here and whoop it up over several excellent beers. **Sommerfest** offers counter-service bratwurst and pretzels.

Shopping
Germany is major retail therapy: You'll find **Die Weihnachts Ecke** (that means the Christmas corner, with all the German Christmas ornaments that one might expect), **Glas und Porzellan** (glass and porcelain Hummel figures and the like), **Sussigkeiten** (meaning sweets, with classic German cookies and chocolates), **Volkskunst** (which means folk art—mostly hand-painted eggs and cuckoo clocks), and the **Weinkeller** for a sampling of German wine or wine accessories.

ITALY PAVILION
Built around a gorgeous piazza, the 83-foot campanile bell tower of St. Mark's Square, Venetian gondolas, and a replica of the 14th-

century pink-and-white Doges Palace in Venice make it clear: This land is a smorgasbord for the Italophile. The eye candy includes the bell tower, lustrous with real gold leaf, the piazza crowded with elegant statues, and little Venetian bridges and gondolas permanently moored to striped barber poles in World Showcase Lagoon. The architecture and the shops are the central draw here, making it a bit of a wipeout for kids. Kids are thrown a bone with **Sergio,** a juggler who performs regularly in the plaza.

Food
L'Originale Alfredo di Roma Ristorante ($30–50 at dinner) serves decadent fettuccine Alfredo. However, in September 2007 the restaurant will be replaced with a new venture from Patina Restaurant Group—one of the principals of which is celebrity chef Joachim Splichal, so this could turn culinary Big Time.

Shopping
Porcelain and fine crystal are arrayed at **Il Bel Cristallo,** and you'll find gourmet treats at **La Cucina Italiana** and chocolates and other Italian sweets at **Delizie Italiane.**

AMERICAN ADVENTURE
Centermost of the countries in World Showcase, American Adventure is elevated a little bit above the others, with robustly American landscaping and very lousy cheeseburgers. Still, it's a fun land with lots going on.

At the 30-minute historical stage show **American Adventure,** animatronic hosts Benjamin Franklin and Mark Twain speed through three centuries of the country's history in a lovely air-conditioned rotunda. Guests sit for the whole thing, which consists of a 72-foot-wide screen on which filmed images mix with moving sets, sound and lighting effects, and 35 audio-animatronic figures rising from the stage floor to tell the story of great events and people in America's past: Pilgrims and the Mayflower give way to the Boston Tea Party and the Declaration of Independence, then on to the Revolutionary War, slavery and the Civil War, the World Wars, and, briefly, the recent

EPCOT

past. Greats from Albert Einstein to Judy Garland and Bob Dylan get their moment—it's a swiftly moving, fun show, even for the history-nonplussed and the very young.

Just across from the American Adventure building, the outdoor **America Gardens Theatre** hosts a range of live stage shows, some patriotic and some not (such as the Candlelight Processional in December). A number of real, but nostalgic, bands play here each month in the evenings, from the Box Tops featuring Alex Chilton, to José Feliciano, Petula Clark, and the Guess Who. The **Spirit of America Fife and Drums Corp** makes regular appearances here in the outdoor space each day (check your Times Guide for times), whereas an a cappella group called **The Voices of Liberty** usually performs in American Adventure rotunda 15 minutes before the beginning of each American Adventure show, entertaining the crowds as they wait to enter the theater.

The new **American Heritage Gallery** houses a small, temporary exhibit called **Echoes of Africa** that attempts to explore the connection between historical African art objects and the work of contemporary African American artists. It's worth a brief swing through after seeing the American Adventure show; children may be bored. Celebrating its 25th anniversary in the fall of 2007, Epcot was to unveil an exhibit here called **National Treasures,** with significant artifacts in American history.

Food

If the food at **Liberty Inn** (under $14 per person) is our best foot forward with American cuisine, no wonder the rest of the world feels a little gastronomically smug. It's emphatically skippable hot dogs, cheeseburgers, and grilled chicken in a quick, counter-service setting. Hold off if you can until Japan—or feed the kids here with familiar fare and have the adults grab something more exotic in Morocco.

Shopping

A small gift shop will satisfy all your needs for bald eagle sculptures or replicas of the Declaration of Independence.

JAPAN PAVILION

Go directly from American Adventure through the red torii gates and you'll find yourself in a land of koi-filled pools, pagodas, samurai warriors, and much better food. The **Bijutsu-kan Gallery** always showcases some element of Japanese culture, such as an exhibit featuring tin toys, but exhibits change regularly. For kids' entertainment, there are regular performances by **Taiko drummers** and a longtime favorite, **Miyuki,** who specializes in candy artistry. During the annual **Epcot International Flower and Garden Festival,** Japan pulls out all the stops with a huge floral wall.

Food

The **Teppanyaki Dining Room** (entrées $15–29) gives you a Benihana-like experience with the shrimp-flipping shenanigans and very competent griddle cooking, the **Yakitori House** (entrées $6–10) proffers very respectable udon noodles (but, um, no yakitori), and the **Matsu-no-ma Lounge** serves competent sushi and cocktails.

Shopping

Mitsukoshi Department Store stocks freshwater pearls, Japanese dolls, toys, and bonsai trees.

MOROCCO PAVILION

This North African country is divided into two sections: the Ville Nouvelle (new city) and the Medina (old city), with structures that represent Casablanca, Fez, and Marrakesh. The 45-minute **Treasures of Morocco** tour is very educational, but it's a hard sell to kids (lots of history, some about the agricultural products of the country). Better for kids is the self-guided walk-through of **Fez House,** a re-creation of a Moroccan home with gorgeous mosaic tile work, or a quick run-through of the nearly hidden **Gallery of Arts and History,** which contains musical and technological artifacts from Morocco.

Food

Vegetarians are best accommodated in Morocco, with a kicky vegetarian platter of hummus, pita, and tabbouleh from **Tangierine**

Cafe (entrées $8–14), and serviceable but unexciting counter-service food from **Restaurant Marrakesh.** A belly dancer regularly adds quite a bit of spice to the dining experience. You'll also see a Moroccan rock band and characters from *Aladdin* who wander through occasionally.

Shopping

A bustling shopping plaza sells woven handicrafts, fezzes, planters, and sandals as the Koutoubia Minaret (prayer tower) looms overhead.

FRANCE PAVILION

In France, it doesn't seem as if you've journeyed just geographically—there's also been time travel. The centerpiece of France is an 18-minute film that whisks you through Paris, the Loire, Normandy, and the wine country, but everyone has resoundingly '70s hairdos and clothing. Though the movie, *Impressions de France,* is old, the soundtrack is a lovely stew of classical pieces. It might be somewhat tedious for little kids—especially if they've already sat through other World Showcase travelogue films. Still, there's seating and air-conditioning inside the **Palais du Cinema,** both necessary periodically during a hot Florida day. The Belle Epoque architecture of France is lovely, with a sidewalk café, a fragrance shop, and a Parisian marketplace. The park in this land is inspired by Georges Seurat's painting *A Sunday Afternoon on the Island of La Grande Jatte,* and the resident Eiffel Tower is one-tenth the size of the original.

Food

Lines are often too long to be tenable at **Boulangerie Patisserie** (under $14) pastry stand, so head for the cream puffs at **Les Chefs de France** (the rest of the food is ho-hum). Upstairs from there, the pricier **Bistro de Paris** (entrées $28–34) serves laudable renditions of classic French dishes, from a roquefort-topped mixed green salad with a walnut vinaigrette to duck confit and crêpe suzette. A street performer regularly puts on an amazing balancing act with chairs.

EPCOT

© DISNEY

France Pavilion, home to Orlando's Eiffel Tower

Shopping

Clustered to look like a real Parisian street scene, the shops in France are fairly sophisticated. At **Plume et Palette** you'll find designer fragrances, as you'll also find at **La Signature,** which stocks Guerlain perfumes along with cosmetics and accessories. The passage between these two shops is designed to look like a Parisian metro station. And while you may not be shopping for housewares, **Le Casserole** purveys tempting dinnerware and decorative tabletop doodads from the south of France. At **Vins de France,** you can peruse wines and accessories from B&G (Barton and Guestier), and in the **Galerie des Halles** you'll find souvenirs of the French impressionists.

UNITED KINGDOM PAVILION

There's a lot going on here. In the garden behind the western part of the United Kingdom pavilion you'll be entertained by **The British Invasion** Beatles imitators (the early, funny-haircuts-and-suits Beatles), while the **World Showcase Players** improv troupe regularly draws a crowd. Add to this cobbled streets, lovely flower gardens, and architecture that varies from Tudor to Georgian and Regency, and it's easy to see why this is a favorite land for many. But maybe it's just the Guinness, Bass, and Harp by the yard. Kids can play in the boxwood hedge maze, wander through the butterfly garden, or visit with the many Disney characters that seem to congregate in this area (Pooh characters, Mary Poppins, Peter Pan, and Alice in Wonderland folks are regulars).

Food

The excellent Pam Brody plays piano in the ◖ **Rose and Crown Pub and Dining Room** (entrées $12–24), which serves pleasant Harry Ramsden's fish-and-chips and a bang-up bangers and mash. Better than the food,

though, is the much-coveted patio seating, from which the evening fireworks can be viewed in all their splendor. Regular sing-alongs and a range of British ales, lagers, and stouts make this a favorite among Disney regulars.

Shopping

Shoppers will enjoy an inspection of **The Toy Soldier** for British toys, clothing at **Sportsman Shoppe,** or soaps and perfumes at **Queen's Table.**

CANADA PAVILION

Canada gets a raw deal here. But isn't that so often the case with Canada? If you've wended your way around World Showcase and arrive here last, you'll say, "What, another movie?!" It's true: The centerpiece of Canada is a 17-minute, 360-degree travelogue film called *O Canada!,* which goes coast to coast through the country's various regions. It's pretty good, if just slightly dated. There is no seating in the theater, so you must lean again the rails or be prepared to sit on the ground.

A lovely Victorian garden, a 30-foot Rocky Mountain waterfall, a Native American village with totem poles, and the Gothic **Hotel du Canada** all provide nice visuals and the band **Off Kilter** amps things up with Celtic rock.

Food

The best part of this area is **Le Cellier Steakhouse,** which doesn't seem particularly Canadian, but the steaks are good and the cheddar soup is better. Make priority seating arrangements for this one, as it tends to be very busy.

Shopping

Shoppers congregate at the **Northwest Mercantile** and **La Boutique des Provinces** for folk art, jewelry, and maple-flavored gewgaws.

Entertainment

𝕮 ILLUMINATIONS

The World Showcase Lagoon is the site of every evening's 13-minute finale that weaves fireworks, light, walls of flames, lasers, video display, fountains, and music. The current show, IllumiNations: Reflections of Earth, takes place at 9 or 9:30 P.M., depending on the park's closure time. There's a spherical illuminated Earth Globe at the center, with barges zooming around the lagoon shooting fountains of water and gigantic 40-foot propane flames in time to a swelling symphonic score. Is there a plot? Kind of: The first act has the fire shooting and is supposed to symbolize the Big Bang; then in the second act the Earth cools and the countries appear; the third act is a big hootenanny of a global celebration with fireworks. It's a very impressive show in its size and scope, but it lacks a bit of the Disney enchantment of Magic Kingdom's nightly show.

As to where to view it, opinions are mixed—some say over a pint at the Rose and Crown Pub, others say from the American Adventure Pavilion, the bridge at Italy, or a park bench in France. If you want to make a quick getaway at show's end, opt for a spot near the entrance to the World Showcase. For a really special experience you can rent a pontoon boat from the Yacht and Beach Club Marina and sit under the International Gateway Bridge to view the show.

EPCOT

DISNEY'S HOLLYWOOD STUDIOS

Walt Disney is said to have had the idea of a movie-oriented theme park years before Universal's parent company, MCA, got the notion. Regardless, it was a neck-and-neck race with this rival company that spurred Disney to open this 135-acre park in May 1989. While some of the park is devoted to television and movie production facilities, the rest is a tribute to, as Michael Eisner said at the dedication: "Not a place on a map, but a state of mind that exists wherever people dream and wonder and imagine, a place where illusion and reality are fused by technological magic. We welcome you to a Hollywood that never was—and always will be."

That's all fairly prescient, because the MGM association has clearly fizzled. The rumor was that the whole park is poised to change its name by 2008 to Disney's Hollywood Studios. The name change is engineered to reflect Hollywood's new entertainment—music, television, movies, and theater.

The park, by any name, is pretty sweet. It maintains a slightly nostalgic balance between attractions based on old classics (The Great Movie Ride, the Backlot Tour) and those reflecting a more 21st-century aesthetic (Rock 'n Roller Coaster Starring Aerosmith). Thus, it is more appealing to an all-ages crowd, with a suave art deco design that revisits the Hollywood of the 1930s. While Universal Studios throws mature crowds a bone with a single *I Love Lucy*–themed attraction, Disney's Hollywood Studios has a passel of attractions that feature a more historic (and educational) perspective on the cinema. That said, young children will really enjoy the park for its many live

© DISNEY

HIGHLIGHTS

LOOK FOR ((TO FIND RECOMMENDED SIGHTS, ACTIVITIES, DINING, AND LODGING.

((**Lights, Motors, Action! Extreme Stunt Show:** Disney's Hollywood Studios has doubled in size in the past 10 years, partly because of enormous attractions such as this, a thrilling car and motorcycle stunt show that made its debut in May 2005 and was imported from Disneyland Resort Paris (page 116).

((**The Twilight Zone Tower of Terror:** Recent changes to the program have meant that repeat Tower of Terror guests get a different thrill ride every time, winding through the creepy old Hollywood hotel only to be dropped, repeatedly, 13 stories from a "malfunctioning" service elevator (page 120).

((**Rock 'n Roller Coaster Starring Aerosmith:** You're "Crazy" to think that when Steven Tyler asks you to "Walk This Way" that what follows will be all "Sweet Emotion." "Dream On:" Thrill riders are "Livin' on the Edge" and "Don't Want to Miss a Thing" with this looping, corkscrewing, music-thumping coaster in the dark (page 121).

((**Beauty and the Beast – Live on Stage:** A short version of Disney's 30th animated classic comes to life on stage with fancy costumes, big dance numbers, and great voices telling "a tale as old as time" about a pretty girl who falls for a guy a little rough around the edges (page 121).

kiddie shows (Voyage of the Little Mermaid, Playhouse Disney-Live on Stage!) and enormous wealth of character-greeting possibilities (characters from *Toy Story, The Muppet Show, Star Wars,* and classic Disney films roam the park). This is definitely a park in which those expensive Disney autograph books can fill up fast—Disney characters helpfully congregate in a few hot spots in the park, like impalas on an African photo safari awaiting the cameras.

One increasingly annoying feature of the park is its uninhibited self-promotion—new and upcoming Disney movies and TV shows are flogged all around the park, by signs, rides, guides, and shows.

History

While the original idea was to operate a working TV and film production facility, recent years have been tough on the former Disney-MGM Studios. Near its beginning, the park was home to Walt Disney Feature Animation Florida, which produced several animated projects such as *Mulan, Lilo & Stitch, Brother Bear,* and parts of other Disney animated features. In 2003, all of Disney's animation efforts were consolidated in Burbank, California. The three soundstages of Walt Disney Studios Florida, the other production part of the studios, were the site of filming for episodes of *Superboy, Wheel of Fortune, Let's Make a Deal, Mickey Mouse Club,* and *Adventures in Wonderland,* and movies such as *House on Haunted Hill, Passenger 57,* and *Ernest Saves Christmas.* These days, the production facilities are mostly quiet, as is the radio studio on the property (it used to house Radio Disney, which is now headquartered in Dallas, Texas). It's a shame, because going "backstage" to see working film and animation facilities used to be one of the main attractions here.

DISNEY'S HOLLYWOOD STUDIOS

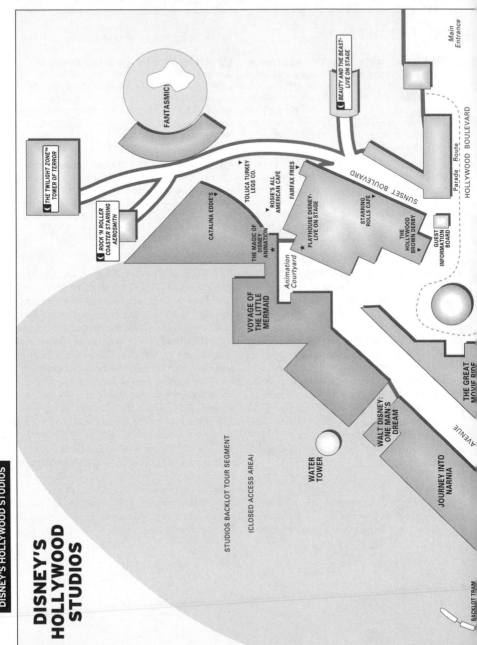

DISNEY'S HOLLYWOOD STUDIOS

THE TWILIGHT ZONE™ TOWER OF TERROR

ROCK 'N ROLLER COASTER STARRING AEROSMITH

FANTASMIC!

BEAUTY AND THE BEAST-LIVE ON STAGE

Main Entrance

CATALINA EDDIE'S

TOLUCA TURKEY LEGS CO.

ROSIE'S ALL AMERICAN CAFÉ

FAIRFAX FRIES

THE MAGIC OF DISNEY ANIMATION

Animation Courtyard

PLAYHOUSE DISNEY-LIVE ON STAGE

STARRING ROLLS CAFÉ

SUNSET BOULEVARD

THE HOLLYWOOD BROWN DERBY

GUEST INFORMATION BOARD

Parade - Route   HOLLYWOOD BOULEVARD

VOYAGE OF THE LITTLE MERMAID

STUDIOS BACKLOT TOUR SEGMENT

(CLOSED ACCESS AREA)

WATER TOWER

WALT DISNEY: ONE MAN'S DREAM

JOURNEY INTO NARNIA

THE GREAT MOVIE RIDE

AVENUE

BACKLOT TRAM

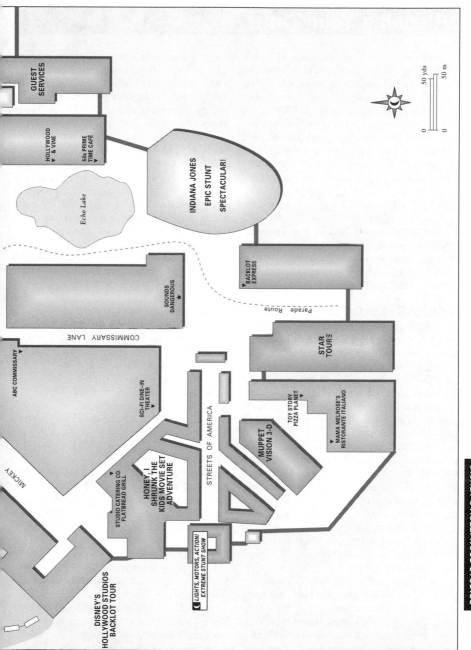

GUEST SERVICES

HOLLYWOOD & VINE

50s PRIME TIME CAFÉ

Echo Lake

INDIANA JONES EPIC STUNT SPECTACULAR!

BACKLOT EXPRESS

Parade Route

COMMISSARY LANE

SOUNDS DANGEROUS ★

STAR TOURS

ABC COMMISSARY ▸

SCI-FI DINE-IN THEATER ▸

STUDIO CATERING CO. FLATBREAD GRILL ▸

HONEY, I SHRUNK THE KIDS MOVIE SET ADVENTURE

MICKEY

STREETS OF AMERICA

MUPPET VISION 3-D

TOY STORY PIZZA PLANET ▸

▸ MAMA MELROSE'S RISTORANTE ITALIANO

LIGHTS, MOTORS, ACTION! EXTREME STUNT SHOW

DISNEY'S HOLLYWOOD STUDIOS BACKLOT TOUR

50 yds
50 m

DISNEY'S HOLLYWOOD STUDIOS

© AVALON TRAVEL PUBLISHING, INC.

Planning Your Time

Disney's Hollywood Studios is about the size of Magic Kingdom, but because scheduled shows comprise a lot of the entertainment, you'll find yourself doing a lot of walking, crisscrossing the park to make showtimes. As with Universal Studios, many of the park's attractions feature regular or 3-D movies, some with animatronic additions or live actors, some with a "ride" component for the audience. For this reason, it's sometimes hard to differentiate between a ride, a live show, or a walk-through attraction at this park. They are all listed together here, grouped by geographical area within the park, starting at Hollywood Boulevard and moving clockwise around the park from the left of the entrance. Grouped by area in the park, attractions are also listed in order of excellence, from greatest to most skippable.

CHARACTER GREETINGS

Character greetings at the park may have seen a temporary drop-off of enthusiasm in response to the much-publicized incident in 2006 involving a cast member dressed as Tigger punching a kid, the whole incident caught on videotape. Well, one bad cat doesn't spoil the menagerie. Disney's Hollywood Studios is positively crawling with characters, their exact whereabouts listed on the daily times guide.

In Mickey Avenue, you'll regularly see characters from *Little Einsteins*, **JoJo and Goliath, Kim Possible,** and **Mickey Mouse** himself. Most characters are of the costume-with-big-head variety, while others are just people in makeup and clothing meant to look like a particular character. They don't always nail it though: Kim Possible didn't look a whit like the character, and her totally exposed midriff was trampy to boot.

On Commissary Lane you'll likely see **Sulley** and **Mike Wazowski** from *Monsters Inc.;* they're fairly imposing and little kids seemed afraid. At Al's Toy Barn on New York Street you'll run into **Buzz Lightyear, Woody,** and the other guys from *Toy Story;* outside The

Magic of Disney Animation, **Elastigirl** and the other **Incredibles** regularly mill around. *Star Wars* **characters** show up on special *Star Wars* weekends, the **cars** from *Cars* rev regularly near Sounds Dangerous, and the **Power Rangers** roam the Streets of America.

WHEN TO GO

Park hours are usually longer during peak seasons (an advantage) but the lines are longer (a disadvantage). The busiest days of the week for this park tend to be Tuesdays, Wednesdays, and Saturdays. Because people often start their Disney exploration in Magic Kingdom, Mondays tend to be a little quieter for Disney's Hollywood Studios. Days on which there are Extra Magic Hours draw bigger crowds, but they are spaced over a longer day, so it often evens out.

Park Hours

While Disney's Hollywood Studios generally opens at 9 A.M., closing hours change during the course of the year. The park closes at 7 or 8 P.M. during off-season, but in March, April, and the summer it is generally open until 10 P.M. Check the website for the calendar of park hours, dates of Extra Magic Hours, and also the "operational list" for any ride closures.

Special Events

Usually held in early March, **ESPN The Weekend** features ESPN telecasts from the park, star motorcades, and panel discussions and question-and-answer sessions with professional athletes, Olympic athletes, and ESPN personalities. Admission is included with regular park admission.

For four consecutive weekends in May and June, the park hosts **Star Wars Weekends** that draw *Star Wars* fans and celebrities together. There are light saber training classes for kids, Stormtroopers walking around, trivia contests, and real *Star Wars* characters available for meet-and-greets (to get in line for autographs, you must get a timed FASTPASS ticket). Since 1997, this annual event has brought costumed enthusiasts from all over.

Then, for one weekend each fall, ABC daytime stars and their fans convene for the **Super Soap Weekend.** Cast members from *All My Children, General Hospital, One Life to Live,* and other shows appear for autographs.

During the winter holidays, the park features the **Osborne Family Spectacle of Lights,** with five million Christmas lights strung on more than 350 miles of wire. This has nothing to do with Donnie and Marie or their brethren—it's the brainchild of Jennings Osborne of Little Rock, Arkansas. There his mania for Christmas lights burdened him with the wrath of his neighbors and $7,000 in attorney fees, but Walt Disney World Resort invited him to relocate his bright idea to the Streets of America city backlots, gussied up for the occasion with the efforts of 66 snow machines. There's no additional fee to see the lights (just regular admission), and each evening features a quick lighting ceremony.

WHAT TO BRING

Comfortable footwear, sunscreen, and multiple cell phones or walkie-talkies will improve the quality of your day. Many attractions at Disney's Hollywood Studios are indoors, so it's a good park to visit on either a blisteringly hot day or a rainy day. The park attractions do not get you nearly as wet as those at Orlando's other theme parks, so changes of clothes are not necessary. Bottled water is also less crucial, as icy-cold water fountains abound in the park. Disney is a stickler about proper attire: Shirt and shoes are required, nothing racy, nothing with obscene slogans.

PRACTICALITIES
Camera Services

The Darkroom on Hollywood Boulevard processes film and stocks film and accessories.

DISNEY PIN TRADING

Walk around the park and you'll see necks encircled by lanyards, weighted heavily by enameled pins. It's genius really, a tradition started all the way back in 1999 as a way for "cast members" and park-goers to engage in conversation. All right, maybe Disney didn't invent it – go to any Girl Scouts overnighter and you'll see a similar phenomenon – girls walking up to other girls and saying shyly, "Wanna SWAP?" With the Girl Scouts it's "Special Whatchamacallits Affectionately Pinned Somewhere," and with Disney it's very expensive enamel pins commemorating Disney characters and special events.

Each park offers a range of collecting pins as a way to remember a favorite attraction, event, or character. There are thousands of different pins, some valuable, some not. Disney cast members wear lanyards or vests or something upon which these pins are pinned, and they are obligated by Disney law to trade with whomever asks. Guests can make up to two trades per lanyard, per cast member, per day. Cast members are also mandated to give away a certain number of pins, so there are freebies to be had if you play your Disney cards right. Cast members wearing green lanyards are supposed to trade only with kids.

Some people collect pins for only one Disney character. Some are more concerned about the rarity of a particular pin – the backs are stamped with information about manufacturing year, limited-edition size, or series number. Some have a grass-is-always-greener approach and just keep 'em circulating.

If you're going to do it, you need a "starter set," which is a lanyard and your first four pins, which you can buy at a souvenir shop at any of the four parks (Tinker Bell was $53.75 recently, Pirates of the Caribbean was a bit more than $60). There are whole websites devoted to Disney pin trading, special pin-trading events, featured pins, "artist proof" pins (the first couple of dozen pins an artist makes, very valuable), retired pins (those no longer made), and further intrigue.

First Aid

First Aid is near Guest Services on Hollywood Boulevard.

Guest Services

The Guest Services office is near the entrance of the park, to the left of the turnstiles. There is also a Guest Services desk just inside the park on your left, as well as at the corner of Hollywood and Sunset. There you will find the lost and found, messages for separated parties, Disney Dollar exchange, foreign currency exchange, and information about services for guests with disabilities and tours. It is also where you make dining reservations and the site of the baby-care feeding and changing station. There are two ATMs at Disney's Hollywood Studios: one beside the package pickup window at the main entrance and one inside Pizza Planet.

Kennels

Pet-care facilities are just outside the park entrance, open one hour before and after the park hours. Call 407/560-4282 to reserve; $10 per pet per day ($13 for overnight if you are a Disney Resort guest). The staff will feed your pet, but you are advised to walk your dog twice during the day. There is no on-site veterinarian. Dogs must have proof of rabies, DHP, parvovirus, and bordetella shots, while cats must have proof of rabies, panleukopenia, rhinotracheitis, and calcivirus shots. All dogs and cats must be at least eight weeks old to be kenneled. No exotic animals are allowed.

Package Pickup

Purchases can be sent to the entrance (the pickup is next to Oscar's Super Service, left of front gates before exiting) and are available for pickup three hours later. They can also be delivered to your Disney hotel. Advise the cashier before buying if you are electing one of these options. Purchases can also be FedExed right from the park.

Rentals

Strollers are available for rent, to the right just inside the park entrance. Single strollers cost $10, doubles are $18.

Wheelchairs are available at the same place, $10 per day rental with no deposit, and motorized ECVs are $35 per day rental with a $5 refundable deposit. Because there are a limited number of wheelchair and ECV rentals, get to the park early to ensure getting one.

Lockers are near Oscar's Classic Car Souvenirs at the main entrance. Cost is $7, $2 of which is a refundable deposit on the key (and if you go to a second park, you can bring your locker receipt and just put down an additional $5 deposit for a locker there).

Shopping

There are two main shopping areas in Disney's Hollywood Studios: Hollywood Boulevard and the central part of Sunset Boulevard. In addition to these two main shopping streets, many rides (Indiana Jones, Muppets, Star Tours, Tower of Terror, Rock 'n Roller Coaster) empty out into ride-specific merchandise stores. Within the Sorcerer Mickey Hat you'll find a large Pin Trading Station and merchandise from the 100 Years of Magic Celebration.

GETTING THERE AND AROUND

Walt Disney World Resort is southwest of Orlando, off I-4, west of Florida's Turnpike. Of the several Walt Disney World exits off I-4, take Exit 64 for Magic Kingdom and Disney's Hollywood Studios.

Disney's Hollywood Studios is accessible by boat from Disney's BoardWalk Inn and Villas Resort, Disney's Yacht Club and Disney's Beach Club Resorts, and the Walt Disney World Swan and Walt Disney World Dolphin Hotels.

Parking

Cost is $10 but free to all Walt Disney World resort hotel guests. If you are park-hopping, your parking receipt will be honored at the other parks. Trams take visitors from the parking lot to the park entrance. There is also wheelchair-accessible parking available for vehicles with a valid Disabled Parking Permit—

follow the blue line or ask at the auto plaza where you pay for parking.

The parking lot is divided into large picture-coded areas (mine was "Stage," with a Mickey on the signs), and rows are numbered on the pavement at the end of each row. Tram guides do a good job of drilling into your head what your area and row numbers are. Should your car poop out while you're visiting, the park offers free AAA towing during park hours.

Park Maps

Pick up free guide maps just inside the park. They are offered in English, Spanish, French, Portuguese, German, and Japanese, as well as in Braille (at Guest Services).

Hollywood Boulevard

Guests enter the turnstiles and immediately find themselves on Hollywood Boulevard. Straight ahead in an open, art deco–inspired plaza is the kiosk where you'll find park maps and show schedules. Most park-goers shuffle around here for several minutes getting their bearings in the morning—in the afternoon it's the locus of much souvenir shopping before departing the park. Straight ahead along the boulevard you'll see the park's icon, an enormous blue **Sorcerer Mickey Hat.** Added to the park in 2001 for the 100 Years of Magic Celebration, the 122-foot-tall hat serves to orient you wherever you are in the park. Adjacent to the hat, you'll find the **guest Information board at Hollywood Junction,** which lists wait times, ride closures, and park tips. A **Guest Relations** booth is also here, along with a **Pin Trading Station** and parade-viewing spots reserved for visitors with disabilities.

THE GREAT MOVIE RIDE

Behind the hat is a replica of Grauman's Chinese Theatre, with the requisite handprints and signatures of celebrities in concrete sidewalk squares. The theater houses this area's only attraction, The Great Movie Ride. One of the park's few remaining original attractions, it's an appropriate entrée into the park, but everyone must agree because it tends to be very busy first thing in the morning. Moving slowly through the preshow queue, you're subjected to a montage of great Hollywood movie moments

---

DISNEY'S HOLLYWOOD STUDIOS RIDE GUIDE

FASTPASS RIDES

Listed in order of importance, these are the rides to FASTPASS:

1. The Twilight Zone Tower of Terror

2. Rock 'n Roller Coaster Starring Aerosmith

3. Star Tours

It's not necessary to FASTPASS the following rides unless it's high season:

4. Indiana Jones Epic Stunt Spectacular!

5. Voyage of the Little Mermaid

RIDE AND ACCESS RESTRICTIONS

- **Star Tours:** Riders must be at least 40 inches tall; people who experience motion sickness should not ride.

- **Rock 'n Roller Coaster Starring Aerosmith:** Riders must be at least 48 inches tall.

- **The Twilight Zone Tower of Terror:** Riders must be at least 40 inches tall; kids find it scary.

On all three attractions, guests in wheelchairs or electronic convenience vehicles (ECVs) will have to transfer to a ride chair.

(I say subjected, because it's too short and repeats four or five times during an average wait). Guests then board slow trams for a 22-minute ride through the movies. It's fairly chronological, starting with Busby Berkeley aquatic spectaculars, moving through James Cagney in *The Public Enemy*, some old John Wayne, *Mary Poppins, Tarzan, Raiders of the Lost Ark,* and *Aliens*. Mostly, scenes from these movies are re-created with animatronic figures, music, and some live actors. There's a very loose plot about a gangster who commandeers your trolley only to be hoisted by his own petard when he tries stealing jewels from the set of *Raiders*. Trolleys have live guides who narrate, some of whom really know their way around a joke.

Tips: It's an all-ages ride (the *Alien* bit and a *Wizard of Oz* room can be scary for young ones), indoors, and fully air-conditioned.

FOOD

Upon entering the park, you'll encounter the park's signature restaurant, **The Hollywood Brown Derby** (entrées $15–29), a tribute to the historic restaurant of the same name at Hollywood and Vine in Los Angeles. This version, like the original, is plastered with caricatures of celebs, and it serves the Cobb salad that was purportedly invented at the original. Fairly pricey, the sit-down, table-service restaurant is open for lunch and dinner. Try the grapefruit cake, as unpromising as that may sound.

SHOPPING

As on Magic Kingdom's Main Street U.S.A., Hollywood Boulevard is host to a mix of enticing souvenir shops and sundries stocking needed merchandise: Find film at **The Darkroom,** a candy bar at **Celebrity 5 and 10,** or a rain poncho from **Crossroads of the World.** Each shop has a fairly distinct theme or motif, but they're all in a glitzy Hollywood-of-the-1930s idiom. **Oscar's Classic Car Souvenirs** sells auto-themed memorabilia. **Sid Caheunga's Antiques and Curiosities** is where to go for vintage movie posters or autographed star photos. **Mickey's of Hollywood** purveys glammy, Mickey-bedecked clothing, **Keystone Clothiers** is a slightly broader-based adult clothing store, and **L.A. Prop Cinema Storage** sells Disney-logo kids' clothing. A little novelty shop called **Cover Story** will put your face on the cover of a magazine. Hollywood Boulevard's **Sweet Success** candy shop seems egregiously overpriced.

Orlando's version of L.A.'s famous Brown Derby

© DISNEY

Echo Lake

The first left at the hat, off Hollywood Boulevard, brings you to Echo Lake. There actually is a small lake here, serving very little purpose, fronted by the permanently docked SS *Down the Hatch* (a snack bar).

INDIANA JONES EPIC STUNT SPECTACULAR!

Continue left past Echo Lake and you'll run into the covered 2,000-seat amphitheater in which Indiana Jones Epic Stunt Spectacular! takes place an average of six times each day (check time guide for schedule). A large handful of audience volunteers are kitted out in appropriately Middle Eastern attire and thrust into the 30-minute action set in the streets of Cairo. Nearly 20 stunt performers demonstrate how the movies create explosions, believable punches, and sword fights, all culminating in that memorable scene from *Raiders* in which Indiana is chased by a giant boulder.

Gertie the Dinosaur welcomes guests to Disney's Hollywood Studios.

Tips: The pyrotechnics and explosions don't seem to perturb even little kids, making this a fun all-ages show. You must be 18 to volunteer; sit at the front to increase your likelihood of being picked.

STAR TOURS

Around the corner from Indiana Jones is Star Tours, which you should FASTPASS. The pre-show outdoor queue is excellent, with an Ewok village and one of those big Storm Trooper AT-AT vehicles to get you in the proper frame of mind. Before boarding a 40-seat intergalactic flight simulator, you'll walk through the hangar area to a brief video on your mission to Endor. Your droid-led star-speeder travels don't go exactly as planned, with some near misses with comets and an inadvertent swerve into a combat zone, all reflected in major tilts and bumps.

Tips: It's a great ride, but a word of caution: I emerged quite nauseous, despite being known as Iron Guts Ace in certain circles. The height requirement is 40 inches. FASTPASS this.

SOUNDS DANGEROUS STARRING DREW CAREY

Sounds Dangerous Starring Drew Carey is across from Star Tours in Echo Lake. Among the lamer attractions at the park, it's worth doing if it's a hot day and you just need to get out of the sun. It's an aurally oriented show—huh, you say? Essentially, it's a silly movie with a hackneyed plot about a detective going undercover to solve a crime—but the picture cuts out early on and you spend much of the 12-minute show in total darkness. Wearing a simple headset, you follow the plot by sound alone—bees buzzing in one ear, knives whooshing by the other.

Just outside the theater in the lobby, a small hands-on **Sound Works** area features a row of sound booths for listening to different nature sounds and for creating sound tracks. Next door to the Sounds Dangerous theater, the ABC-TV Theater sits empty, in front of

© DISNEY

DISNEY'S HOLLYWOOD STUDIOS

which the **Academy of Television Arts and Sciences Hall of Fame Plaza** provides a few worthwhile minutes of ogling the sculptures of TV legends.

Tips: Little kids won't appreciate the pitch black atmosphere of Sounds Dangerous, and the rest of us don't appreciate much else about the experience.

FOOD

The Echo Lake area contains a couple of notable restaurants. The **50's Prime Time Café** (entrées $15–29) will make you feel as if you're back in Mom's kitchen, complete with meat loaf and waitresses prepared to nag you about cleaning your plate. **Hollywood and Vine,** a casual family cafeteria buffet restaurant, offers a Character Breakfast and a Character Lunch suitable for little devotees of *JoJo's Circus* and *The Little Einsteins.* **Backlot Express,** near Star Tours, serves grab-and-go hot dogs, veggie sandwiches, and salads (and beer).

SHOPPING

The area has several small shops that tie into the resident attractions: At the Star Tours exit you'll find **Tatooine Traders** for *Star Wars*-obilia; the **Indy Truck** outside the Stunt Spectacular will help you out with all your Indiana Jones–themed needs; and **Golden Age Souvenirs** has a selection of Disney plush animals.

Streets of America

Due north of Echo Lake is an area called Streets of America, which has three attractions, all well done and attractive to all ages.

◖ LIGHTS, MOTORS, ACTION! EXTREME STUNT SHOW

The top offering here is Lights, Motors, Action! Extreme Stunt Show in the New York Street backlot area (there's a tremendous miracle of "forced perspective" at the exit of the stunt show, in which all of NYC appears to be laid out before you). The show made its debut in May 2005 and is fabulous, set on a huge Parisian street scene with a "fromagerie" and a "tabac" that advertises rolling papers in French, a very un-Disney touch. The 177,000-square-foot facility is the biggest "stage" at Disney and features a show imported from Disneyland Resort Paris.

The conceit here is that a real camera crew is filming a chase scene for a movie out of sequence. Car chases and motorcycle chases ensue, and the whole thing is then played back from different camera angles on an overhead screen. The red "hero" car evades the aggressive maneuvers of a fleet of black bad-guy cars, with stunts up on two wheels, soaring up ramps and over obstacles. It's all good fun, with some amazing driving and cool pyrotechnics. Herbie the Love Bug makes an appearance, cheerfully enduring the indignity of being split squarely down the middle.

Tips: The show is offered three or four times each day, with a preshow of automotive movie trivia to keep people entertained. While the attraction offers FASTPASS, it doesn't seem to benefit guests—standby lines and FASTPASS lines appear to merge at the entrance. There also doesn't seem to be an advantage to getting here early; the waiting queue is an unprotected concrete walkway, punishing on a hot day. Walk in just as the show starts and you'll most often find a spot in the 5,000-seat stadium. The 35-minute show is appropriate for all ages and has no restrictions of any kind.

MUPPET VISION 3-D

Back down the Streets of America, Muppet Vision 3-D is one of Disney's greatest 3-D efforts, combining animatronics, live action, and very few of those annoying 3-D movie tropes (you get squirted with water once). Gonzo is the star of a very funny multiscreen preshow in the holding pen before the audience is let into the 600-seat theater. The show itself is an arch, quick-paced 12 minutes, with an animatronic

Statler and Waldorf (the two crabby old men from *The Muppet Show*) in the balcony heckling, Missy Piggy being suitably divaish, Kermit as the benign problem solver, an animatronic orchestra of penguins, and a visit from a human in a Sweetums costume (he's the really huge, hairy Muppet). Dr. Bunsen Honeydew (the scientist with glasses but no eyes) and Beaker (his lipless assistant) have a cameo and an animatronic Swedish Chef runs the projector. The only unappealing character is a little 3-D animated guy who buzzes around getting into trouble.

HONEY, I SHRUNK THE KIDS MOVIE SET ADVENTURE

The perfect antidote to sitting through a couple of movie-based attractions, Honey, I Shrunk the Kids Movie Set Adventure is more like finding yourself inside the movie, 30-foot-tall blades of grass and all. It's the Disney's Hollywood Studios version of the fly-be-free kids' playground, where all the kids appear to have been victims of Professor Szalinski's electromagnetic shrinking machine.

A small area called **Commissary Lane** leads from Streets of America back to the Sorcerer Mickey Hat. It contains two restaurants and a character greeting area but no attractions.

Tips: The attraction was launched in 1990, but the park has expended a lot of effort keeping the oversize anthills, spiderweb maze, giant sniffing dog nose, and huge Lego bricks looking fresh. It's most appropriate for kids 4–10; adults may sit this one out on the sidelines.

FOOD

In Streets of America, the top restaurant is **❰ Mama Melrose's Ristorante Italiano**

(entrées $15–29), a surprisingly sophisticated Italian trattoria with an open kitchen and blazing pizza oven. From the get-go you'll realize that this place has culinary aspirations: A warm loaf of crusty semolina bread is sent out with a fragrant pesto oil paired with a dab of sun-dried tomato tapenade. A stacked eggplant napoleon brings greaseless fried rounds of eggplant sandwiched with buffalo mozzarella and tomato that tastes like tomato (a rarity in Central Florida). A nice wine list, good flatbread pizzas, and contemporary pastas make this a good choice for lunch or dinner (my top pick for the Fantasmic! Dinner Package).

Two other quick spots in Streets of America serve different interpretations of pizza. **Toy Story Pizza Planet Arcade** serves kid-friendly pizza while **Studio Catering Co. Flatbread Grill's** thin-crust grilled wraps are best for grown-ups.

Commissary Lane

On Commissary Lane, sci-fi fans will need to treat themselves to lunch or dinner at **Sci-Fi Dine-In Theater** (entrées $15–29). The burgers and steaks are just serviceable, but the real allure is the indoor faux drive-in movie experience with a 45-minute loop of old B-movie clips. Just outside the entrance to the Sci-Fi joint is the little **Writer's Stop,** an odd part-bookstore, part-coffee shop concept that has excellent cookies and pastries for a quick snack. The nearby **ABC Commissary** is memorably bad, with a terrible cafeteria ambience and weird menu of Cuban sandwiches, cheeseburgers, and fish-and-chips.

Mickey Avenue

DISNEY'S HOLLYWOOD STUDIOS

Directly behind the hat and Grauman's Chinese Theatre, Mickey Avenue is home to a couple of nice offerings and the "Earffel Tower," a 13-story, 2.5-ton water tower that is the park's old signature icon.

THE DISNEY'S HOLLYWOOD STUDIOS BACKLOT TOUR

The Disney's Hollywood Studios Backlot Tour requires 35 minutes, so plan it around the park's various showtimes. The tour starts with a re-creation of a battle scene from Michael Bay's *Pearl Harbor.* (It's fitting that the four audience volunteers drafted into service provide wooden performances to rival those in the movie.) This live footage is spliced in with prerecorded battle footage and a sound track and then replayed for audiences. Afterward, guests file through a huge props warehouse before boarding a guided tram. It winds past soundstages and a working costume lab with people peering quizzically at fabrics and patterns. A movie vehicle graveyard contains plane replicas for *Pearl Harbor,* the steamroller from *Who Framed Roger Rabbit,* the submersible from *The Life Aquatic,* a truck from *101 Dalmatians,* and other neat mementos. Meanwhile, the tram guide hypes new and upcoming Disney projects and tosses out park trivia: *Ernest Saves Christmas* was the first movie filmed here (a rough beginning), followed by *Passenger 57* and episodes of *Empty Nest* and *The Golden Girls.*

The tram enters Catastrophe Canyon, a Mojave desert set, and there is the eerie feeling something bad is about to happen. Poised on a rickety wooden bridge, the tram endures an earthquake, which in turn causes an oil tanker to burst into flames and then 70,000 gallons of water to pour from somewhere above. Everyone makes it out unscathed, and the tour culminates in a self-guided walk-through of an exhibit titled *Villains: Movie Characters You Love to Hate,* featuring costumes and props from famous movie bad guys.

JOURNEY INTO NARNIA: CREATING THE LION, THE WITCH AND THE WARDROBE

A new addition to the park, at the site of the former Making of the Haunted Mansion, is Journey into Narnia: Creating the Lion, the Witch and the Wardrobe—another skippable attraction. This walk-through of the magical wardrobe and the frozen forest of Narnia is really like an eight-minute trailer for the movie. It's not about the making of the film or a behind-the-scenes tour—it's the movie itself, which most of us saw in the theater with the benefit of popcorn.

TOY STORY MANIA!

A new Pixar-theme "dark ride," Toy Story Mania! is said to be opening in 2008 on Mickey Avenue at the site of the former Who Wants to be a Millionaire-Play It!, but Disney hasn't released a lot of details yet. From what has been leaked thus far, it should resemble Buzz Lightyear's Space Ranger Spin at Magic Kingdom. It's essentially a ride/attraction in which you don 3-D glasses, board a vehicle, and train your toy cannon sights on a series of targets. The ride routes through a colorful midway-type setting and various interactive games will be hosted by *Toy Story* and *Toy Story II* characters. As you score points you reach different levels of play, so that each ride becomes a unique experience.

FOOD

Studio Catering Co. Flatbread Grill is the closest food choice; it's in Streets of America between the Backlot Tour and *Honey, I Shrunk the Kids* Movie Set Adventure. The counter-service restaurant features Mediterranean-style wraps and Greek salads.

SHOPPING

At the exit of the Backlot Tour you'll run into the **AFI Showcase Shop,** stocked with fun movie-related souvenirs.

Animation Courtyard

Continue along Mickey Avenue and you run right into Animation Courtyard, which has two attractions suitable for little kids and one for adults.

VOYAGE OF THE LITTLE MERMAID

Voyage of the Little Mermaid, while it starts strong, is a bit of a disappointment. There's no preshow in the holding pen before guests are let into the theater, which reveals a misty ocean scene surrounded by rough-hewn rock walls. The sound of waves breaking fills the theater before the lights go down and twinkling stars appear overhead. The first number is a black-light puppet extravaganza starring Sebastian singing the crowd-pleaser "Under the Sea." Then we meet Ariel, possessing a spectacular set of pipes and a gorgeous tail, who sings "Part of Your World." Then things begin to fall apart; in the name of expediency, film highlights are shown in what amounts to fast-forward for the remainder of the 17-minute show. A huge Ursula puppet and her creepy hench-eels Flotsam and Jetsam make appearances, and the whole thing wraps up with Ariel's getting a permanent set of legs. The reliance on the film itself is disappointing, as the plot is nearly incoherent in its distilled form. Still, the singing is great, and there are cool laser effects and a neat curtain of rain.

Tips: Ursula can be a little scary for very small children but it's otherwise appropriate for all ages. No height restrictions.

PLAYHOUSE DISNEY—LIVE ON STAGE!

Just across the courtyard is another live show geared toward preschool-age park-goers. While the Little Mermaid show has been around since 1992, Playhouse Disney—Live on Stage! is just a few years old, combining *Bear in the Big Blue House, JoJo's Circus, Stanley,* and *The Book of Pooh* in a live musical review. Slightly saccharine messages about friendship provide the plotline for this 22-minute show in which children are encouraged to twirl, dance, and sing along.

Tips: Since seating is on the floor, the elderly and the pregnant may find it uncomfortable. The show generally runs every 45 minutes, but check the times guide.

THE MAGIC OF DISNEY ANIMATION

Giving Animation Courtyard its name, The Magic of Disney Animation had a major overhaul in 2004 to make it more interactive and appealing to children. The 35-minute guided tour begins with a live animator drawing Mushu, the wisecracking dragon from *Mulan.* There's a short live-action film about animation and a tour of Walt Disney Feature Animation Florida (really, the animators have all worked in California since 2003), after which visitors can try their hand at sound effects, adding color to animated scenes, or creating their own Disney characters. There's also a fun interactive booth in which you answer some questions to find out which Disney character you most resemble.

WALT DISNEY: ONE MAN'S DREAM

While the Backlot Tour is appropriate and fun for all ages, Walt Disney: One Man's Dream may be a little slow for kids. Featuring photos of Walt and early Disney projects, a re-creation of his office, and a slightly gushing 15-minute film tribute to the man behind the mouse, it seems to be the least populated attraction in the park. Both the exhibit and the film tend to accentuate the positive aspects of Disney's life while glossing over any negatives.

SHOPPING

The **Animation Gallery** is at the end of The Magic of Disney Animation tour and sells animation cels, collectibles, and books. Nearby, the **Animation Courtyard Shops** purveys classic Disney film merchandise and costumes, heavy on *The Little Mermaid.*

Sunset Boulevard

Set in a nostalgic re-creation of the Golden Age of Hollywood, some of the park's biggest thrills are packed along Sunset Boulevard. The Twilight Zone Tower of Terror fits right in, housed in its crumbling relic of an old hotel. Rock 'n' Roll Coaster Starring Aerosmith seems a little overly *au courant,* but no one seems to mind that it doesn't blend in with the drop-dead deco shops along the wide avenue (technically it's not a boulevard because it's not lined with trees or a landscaped median).

Suppress your tendency to rush along with the crowds toward the tower, coaster, or the evening's Fantasmic! show, and take a little time to admire all the detailing. A classic five and dime, theater marquees advertising movies that will never play, old filling stations, and period signage all seem scrupulously designed to recall the glorious post-Depression era of Hollywood.

FANTASMIC!

At the very end of Sunset Boulevard, on the right, is the huge waterfront Hollywood Hills Amphitheater in which the nightly Fantasmic! show takes place just before the park closes. The 25-minute show begins with Mickey Mouse conducting from atop a darkened island. Lasers, fireworks, cannon blasts, and music assist in the extravaganza. Animated Disney scenes are projected onto screens made of water, the overarching theme Disney's myriad villains, from Cruella De Vil to Scar. Incongruously, the middle is devoted to a live-action sequence reenacting a battle scene from *Pocahontas*. No matter, it doesn't slow things down much—Mickey battles Maleficent, who has turned into a 40-foot, fire-breathing dragon, the mouse emerges victorious, and everyone celebrates with fireworks.

During the park's busy season, the show is sometimes performed twice (the second time tends to be less crowded). Guests in the front of the amphitheater will get wet from the cannons and the water screens. Small children may be frightened of the loud noises or the giant snake and dragon.

Although it's a great effort, it is overshadowed by the sheer majesty of the evening show at Magic Kingdom. It's not worth what can amount to hours of waiting during peak season. One way to circumnavigate a long wait is to take advantage of the **Fantasmic! Dinner Package** available at the Brown Derby ($43.99 adults, $11.99 children ages 3–9), Mama Melrose's Ristorante Italiano ($32.99 adults, $11.99 children ages 3–9), and Hollywood and Vine ($23.99 adults, $11.99 children ages 3–9). Diners eat dinner first and then get a pass that guarantees them a seat at the Fantasmic! show, circumventing the regular line that can entail waits of up to 90 minutes. Present the Fantasmic! dining voucher 30 minutes before showtime at the Fantasmic! sign on Hollywood Boulevard. During peak season, you can, and should, book up to 180 days in advance; in slower months you can get same-day dinner packages. To reserve, call 407/WDW-DINE (407/929-3463) or visit the restaurant in question.

◖ THE TWILIGHT ZONE TOWER OF TERROR

The Twilight Zone Tower of Terror opened all the way back in 1994 and is still one of the greatest attractions in the park. There are rumors that the 199-foot ride is due for some changes or upgrades, but it lacks nothing in my opinion. Just stand on the sidewalk outside and listen to the screams.

The preshow queue winds through a creepy Hollywood hotel decorated with real *Twilight Zone* props; guests are treated to a short film hosted by Rod Serling. Guests are then led into the hotel's boiler room where the "freight elevator" picks people up. Seated and strapped in, riders zoom up to the 13th floor (never an auspicious number). Before the cable snaps and the elevator "falls," the doors open and close on mysterious hotel floors and ghostly apparitions

© DISNEY

The Twilight Zone¹ Tower of Terror

Terror—FASTPASS one and ride the other. An indoor, "dark ride", the Rock 'n Roller Coaster Starring Aerosmith was rehabbed at the beginning of 2007, adding a single-rider line. After watching Aerosmith working on a studio recording session, guests are invited to a show by Steven Tyler and told to board 24-seat "stretch limos," which then blast off to a pulsating sound track (five speakers for every seat). The coaster goes from 0 to 60 mph in 2.8 seconds with the force of a supersonic F-14, with corkscrews and loops along an imaginary Los Angeles I-5. The initial blastoff is the most intense part of the fairly smooth three-minute, 12-second ride, which is beautifully themed inside and out (love the giant red Fender Stratocaster outside).

Tips: Too intense for the very young, pregnant mothers, and those with bad backs, the ride was responsible for the heart-failure death of a 12-year-old boy in 2006. If you just want to see the preshow, or if you change your mind about riding, you can take advantage of the "chicken exit," which dumps you out into the gift shop. If you do decide to ride, note that there are no storage compartments in the attraction; you may want to stow any loose articles in the lockers near the park entrance. The height requirement is 48 inches. FASTPASS this attraction.

of long-dead hotel guests. After an initial fall, which is faster than free fall, the elevator has several unpredictable shorter falls that are randomly selected (so every ride is somewhat different).

Tips: Young children will be frightened of the dark and the sudden falls—my nine-year-old left a perfect sweat imprint of her hand clutching the arm of the gentleman to her right. This ride can be "child swapped" easily, with the nonriding parent and child sitting through the preshow only before waiting in a holding room for the first riding parent to return. The height requirement is 40 inches. Lines can be very long, so FASTPASS this attraction or take advantage of the Extra Magic Hour program on Tuesdays and Saturdays if you're staying in a Walt Disney World Resort hotel.

◖ ROCK 'N ROLLER COASTER STARRING AEROSMITH

The next-greatest thrill ride in the park is conveniently situated right next door to Tower of

◖ BEAUTY AND THE BEAST–LIVE ON STAGE

If only some of your party consists of inveterate thrill-seekers, the rest can enjoy the nearby Beauty and the Beast—Live on Stage while they whoop and yell on Tower of Terror and Rock 'n Roller Coaster. The best live show at Disney's Hollywood Studios, Beauty and the Beast closely follows the plot of the film—the only animated feature film ever nominated for a Best Picture Academy Award. Belle, Beast, Gaston, Lumiere, Mrs. Potts, Cogsworth, and Chip dance and sing (OK, the teapot is lip-synching to Angela Lansbury), while another dozen cast members in extravagant costumes add their voices and dance stylings. The 30-minute show manages to pack in "Be Our Guest," "Something There," "Beauty

DISNEY'S HOLLYWOOD STUDIOS

---

1   The Twilight Zone is a registered trademark of CBS, Inc. and is used pursuant to a license from CBS, Inc.

and the Beast," and other Howard Ashman and Alan Menken songs with big dance numbers and a dramatic mob scene and fight between Gaston and the Beast. My only complaint is that the Beast, when transformed into the Prince, appears to be wearing a very unfortunate ponytailed wig.

Tips: The lovely, covered Theater of the Stars seats 1,500 guests, but it tends to fill quickly so get there early (usually an entertaining preshow makes waiting not too onerous). There are usually five or six performances each day. Because this show is fairly old (it opened in 1991) there are rumors that it might be replaced soon with a new attraction.

FOOD

Sunset Boulevard has a number of OK grab-and-go spots, from **Fairfax Fries** to **Toluca Legs Turkey Co.** (for those satisfying, yet barbaric, barbecued turkey legs), and **Catalina** **Eddie's** for pizza. For a more sit-down meal, **Starring Rolls Cafe** (entrées $7–10) is fine for breakfast pastries or sandwiches, and **Rosie's All-American Cafe** (entrées $5–10) has veggie burgers and chicken strips.

SHOPPING

For a better array of sweets, many based on Disney characters, head to **Beverly Sunset** on Sunset Boulevard. It is attached to **Villains in Vogue,** a cool store devoted to merchandise sporting the many excellent Disney villains, from Scar to Cruella De Vil. Pooh lovers must head to **Legends of Hollywood** on Sunset Boulevard for Winnie et al-obilia. The **Sunset Club Couture** holds an array of gaudy watches and costume jewelry, much of it emblazoned with Disney logos. Sunset Boulevard is also home to a **Planet Hollywood Superstore,** with a lot of familiar logo merchandise at steep prices.

Entertainment

DISNEY STARS AND MOTOR CARS PARADE

Most of these characters assemble at 3 P.M. daily for a 25-minute celebrity cavalcade that begins at the Star Tours gate, goes down Hollywood Boulevard, and exits near the front of the park at Crossroads. Fifteen custom cars and a handful of motorcycles comprise themed units devoted to *Toy Story, Mary Poppins,* The Muppets, *Star Wars,* and other Disney film and TV projects that tie into attractions at the park. Lightning McQueen, the bright red race car, and Mater, the tow truck, both from *Cars,* are the newest additions to the parade. The grand finale features a 1929 Cadillac stuffed with Mickey, Minnie, and classic Disney characters. While I'm partial to units such as the stretch limo packed with Disney villains such as Cruella De Vil, I still prefer the quirky charms of the afternoon parade at Disney's Animal Kingdom.

The best vantage spots are right at the beginning near the Star Tours gate, or near the end on Hollywood Boulevard near the park entrance. Each day seven park-goers are drafted into parade service, acting as grand marshals or carrying banners.

DISNEY'S ANIMAL KINGDOM

Walt Disney once said, "I have learned from the animal world, and what everyone will learn who studies it is, a renewed sense of kinship with the earth and all its inhabitants." That may be, but Mr. Disney's animal world is populated by creatures less like you'd find on the Discovery Channel and more like you'd find in a psychedelic reverie: a talking mouse wearing impeccable white gloves, pink spotted elephants on parade, long-suffering crabs with heavy Jamaican accents. So what happens when Disney decides to pay tribute to actual, flesh-and-fur animals?

The answer is Disney's Animal Kingdom, Disney's fourth theme park, opened on Earth Day, April 22, 1998. The largest of the Disney parks (at 500 acres, it's five times the size of the Magic Kingdom), it is home to approximately 1,700 real animals, along with fantasy animals of classic Disney invention and other never-on-planet-Earth creatures specific only to the Imagineers who designed this park.

It's a little hard to pin down exactly what it is. Like Busch Gardens in Tampa, it's not a zoo—in fact, "nahtazu" (pronounced "not a zoo") was a fake word used in earlier ad campaigns. It's more zoo-*ish*. Animals are kept in naturalistic habitats without visible bars or barriers to give patrons the illusion of walking among them. And, as in Busch Gardens, animals are interspersed with rides or "adventures." At Animal Kingdom, the adventures are accompanied by somewhat pious conservation messages: Clear-cutting is bad, poaching is bad, extinction happens if we're not careful. It goes Busch Gardens

© DISNEY

HIGHLIGHTS

LOOK FOR ◖ TO FIND RECOMMENDED
SIGHTS, ACTIVITIES, DINING, AND LODGING.

◖ **The Tree of Life:** It's not a ride – it doesn't do anything, sing anything, or catapult you anywhere, but The Tree of Life is still the beating heart of Animal Kingdom. It's 14 stories high, 50 feet wide, with 325 animal carvings swirled into its rough "bark" trunk. It took 10 artists and three Imagineers 18 months to create, topping the whole project off with 103,000 translucent, fluttering artificial leaves (page 129).

◖ *It's Tough to Be a Bug!:* Deep within The Tree of Life you'll settle into long wooden pews for a short screening of a 3-D film inspired by the Disney-Pixar movie *A Bug's Life*. It's loud, raucous, mildly off-color, and fairly frightening for kids under six or so (or anyone afraid of getting a little wet). The animated film is a tongue-in-cheek look at the insect world and mankind's somewhat squeamish relationship to it. There are animatronic creatures that descend from the ceiling, blasts of smells, wiggles in your seat, and a few cooling spritzes of water to coax every sense into the performance (page 129).

◖ **Kilimanjaro Safaris:** Your safari driver points to a gnarled African baobab tree and says, "That tree, sometimes called an upside-down tree, is 1,000 years old." And in a weird way, you believe it – not stopping to think that if Animal Kingdom is only 10 years old, its African flora would be hard-pressed to rack up a millennium, especially in a Florida swamp. It's this carefully coaxed suspension of disbelief that makes the Kilimanjaro Safaris the park's most successful all-ages ride (page 131).

◖ **Expedition Everest:** Opened officially in April 2006 at a reported cost of more than $100 million, this is the number one ride to FASTPASS when you get to the park. Disney Imagineers have built a somewhat scaled-down Mt. Everest (now the tallest mountain in Florida), upon which they have re-created a small Himalayan village (page 133).

◖ **Mickey's Jammin' Jungle Parade:** Every afternoon you begin to see Disney employees squatting down with masking tape to mark off a route for a parkwide, 15-minute parade. It's just about the most exciting part of a visit to Animal Kingdom, worth staking out your territory up to an hour early on the viewing side of the masking tape. Veterans suggest viewing from a spot near the safari entrance in Africa, because the parade makes a big loop, beginning and ending here – double your viewing fun (page 137).

one step further, though, with a few excellent animal-themed shows that draw from Disney blockbusters.

Despite the vast size of the park, it's all doable in a single day. Subtler than some of the other parks, it merits a second day if you're inclined to stop and smell the roses. The lush, tropical garden–like setting is inviting, with hidden Mickeys, barely visible animals, and nuanced architecture to reward the careful observer. Teenagers may think Animal Kingdom doesn't have enough action and all the walking may daunt those with mobility problems, but it's an appealing park for everybody else. Detractors, however, complain that in the hot Florida sun many species seek shady cover, rendering the animal part of the experience akin to a 3-D game of *Where's Waldo?* Thrill seekers tend to be underwhelmed by the g-forces of the park's few hair-raisers.

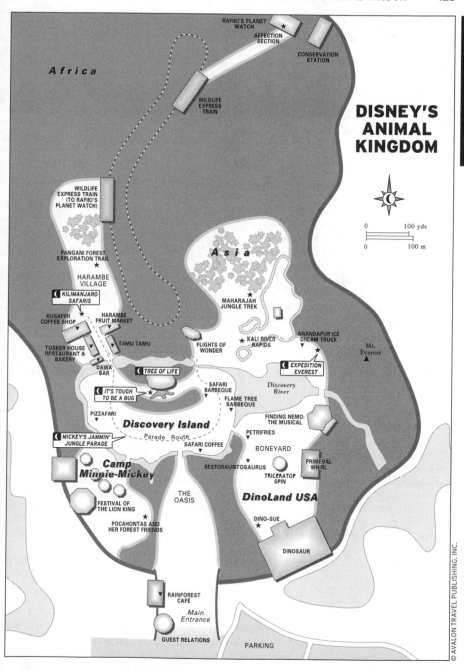

DISNEY'S ANIMAL KINGDOM

Africa

RAFIKI'S PLANET WATCH ★
AFFECTION SECTION
CONSERVATION STATION

WILDLIFE EXPRESS TRAIN

0 — 100 yds
0 — 100 m

Asia

WILDLIFE EXPRESS TRAIN (TO RAFIKI'S PLANET WATCH)

PANGANI FOREST EXPLORATION TRAIL ★

HARAMBE VILLAGE

MAHARAJAH JUNGLE TREK

◖ KILIMANJARO SAFARIS ★

KUSAFIRI COFFEE SHOP ▼   HARAMBE FRUIT MARKET

KALI RIVER RAPIDS ★   ANANDAPUR ICE CREAM TRUCK ▼

TUSKER HOUSE RESTAURANT & BAKERY ▼

TAMU TAMU ▼   FLIGHTS OF WONDER

Mt. Everest ▲

DAWA BAR ▼

◖ TREE OF LIFE

◖ EXPEDITION EVEREST ★

SAFARI BARBEQUE ▼

Discovery River

◖ IT'S TOUGH TO BE A BUG

FLAME TREE BARBEQUE ▼

PIZZAFARI ▼

Discovery Island

FINDING NEMO: THE MUSICAL

◖ MICKEY'S JAMMIN' JUNGLE PARADE

Parade Route

PETRIFRIES ▼

SAFARI COFFEE ▼

BONEYARD

Camp Minnie-Mickey

RESTAURANTOSAURUS ▼

PRIMEVAL WHIRL

TRICERATOP SPIN

THE OASIS

DinoLand USA

FESTIVAL OF THE LION KING ★

POCAHONTAS AND HER FOREST FRIENDS ★

DINO-SUE ★

DINOSAUR

RAINFOREST CAFÉ ▼

Main Entrance

GUEST RELATIONS   PARKING

© AVALON TRAVEL PUBLISHING, INC.

Planning Your Time

The "adventures," along with about 250 animal species, are spread across very authentic-looking jungle, forest, and savanna, thanks to the four million introduced plants and trees. (Plant species that don't manage to thrive in the Florida environment are re-created in plastic and other manufactured materials, but you'd never know it). Animal Kingdom comprises seven discrete theme areas or "lands," some that represent continents and others that are character oriented. **Discovery Island** is at the center of the park, **Africa** is northwest of that, **Rafiki's Planet Watch** is due north, and **Asia** is northeast. To the southwest there's **Camp Minnie-Mickey**, the **Oasis** is due south of Discovery Island, closest to the park entrance, and to the southeast you'll find **DinoLand U.S.A.**

To make reservations at the park's sit-down, table-service restaurant, **Rainforest Café,** or to prebook for the character breakfast at Restaurantosaurus, call 407/939-3463. In September 2007, the Village of Anandapur in Asia opened a new sit-down Asian restaurant, **Yak and Yeti,** run by Landry's Restaurants (which also operates Rainforest Café).

WHEN TO GO

Animal Kingdom is the least frequented of the four parks, so there's a greater degree of flexibility in planning your visit to beat the crowds. Monday and Tuesday tend to be less busy days; weekends are busier. There's a lot of unshaded walking in the sun, so plan your visit for a cooler day, when possible.

Because animals are the central draw, try to get to the park just as it opens in the morning. Animals tend to be more active before the day heats up. If that's not feasible, visit Animal Kingdom in the late afternoon and evening during the extended Extra Magic Hours.

Park Hours

Out of regard for the animals that inhabit Animal Kingdom, this park generally has the shortest hours, changing slightly from month to month. While it's generally 9 A.M. to about 5 or 6 P.M., it is always best to check the website for the calendar of park hours.

WHAT TO BRING

Comfortable footwear is of paramount importance, as are sunscreen and extra water (while you can buy beverages throughout the park, lines can be long and prices are high; refill at water fountains around the park). A backpack or fanny pack is wiser than a purse in terms of keeping your hands free and your valuables firmly attached to your body on the rides. In the Kali River Rapids ride and during the film *It's Tough to Be a Bug!* you will get wet—if this doesn't appeal to you, bring a compact rain poncho or even a disposable garbage bag that you can don during these attractions. Cell phones or walkie-talkies ensure that you'll find each other again if your party splits up.

PRACTICALITIES
First Aid

First Aid is behind Creature Comforts in Discovery Island. It also has a baby station with private rooms for nursing mothers.

Guest Relations

The Guest Relations office is near the entrance of the park, to the left of the turnstiles, in the area called the Oasis. There you will find the lost and found (to report lost items after your departure, call 407/824-4245), be able to exchange money (an ATM, however, is outside the entrance to the park, to the right before the turnstiles, next to the kennel. It accepts Cirrus, Honor, and PLUS systems.), and find out about tours as well as services for visitors with disabilities. It's also where separated parties can leave messages for each other.

Kennels

Pet-care facilities are just outside the park entrance, open one hour before and after park hours. Call 407/938-2100 to reserve; it's $10 per pet per day ($13 for overnight if you are a Disney Resort guest). The staff will feed your pet, but you are advised to walk your dog twice during the day. There is no on-site veterinarian. Dogs must have proof of rabies, DHP, parvovirus, and bordetella shots, while cats must have proof of rabies, panleukopenia, rhinotracheitis, and calcivirus shots. All dogs and cats must be at least eight weeks old to be kenneled. No exotic animals are allowed.

Rentals

Strollers are available for rent at Garden Gate Gifts, to the right just inside the park entrance. Single strollers cost $7 with a Disney Dollar deposit given back when you turn it in; doubles are $13 with a Disney Dollar back.

Wheelchairs are available at the same place, $10 per day rental with no deposit, and motorized ECVs are $35 per day rental with a $5 refundable deposit. If you experience a malfunction of any kind, there are replacement locations at Creature Comforts, Mombasa Marketplace, and the Outpost. Because there are a limited number of wheelchair and ECV rentals, get to the park early to ensure getting one.

Lockers are outside the park entrance and just inside on the left near Guest Relations. The cost is $5, $2 of which is a refundable deposit on the key (and if you go to a second park, you can bring your locker receipt and just put down an additional $2 deposit for a locker there).

GETTING THERE AND AROUND

Walt Disney World Resort is southwest of Orlando, off I-4, west of Florida's Turnpike. Of the several Walt Disney World exits off I-4, take Exit 65. Animal Kingdom is at the end of the Osceola Parkway on the western end of the property, between Blizzard Beach and the Disney All Star resorts.

Parking

The cost is $7, but it's free to all Walt Disney World resort hotel guests. If you are parkhopping, your parking receipt will be honored at the other parks. Trams take visitors from the parking lot to the park entrance. There is also wheelchair-accessible parking available for vehicles with a valid Disabled Parking Permit.

Park Maps

Pick up free guide maps just inside the park.

ANIMAL KINGDOM RIDE GUIDE

FASTPASS RIDES

Listed in order of importance, these are the rides to FASTPASS:

1. Expedition Everest

2. Kilimanjaro Safaris

3. Dinosaur

It's not necessary to FASTPASS the following rides and show unless it's high season:

4. Kali River Rapids

5. Primeval Whirl

6. It's Tough to Be a Bug!

RIDE RESTRICTIONS

- **Dinosaur:** Riders must be at least 40 inches tall; children under age six might find it scary.

- **Expedition Everest:** Riders must be at least 44 inches tall.

- **Kali River Rapids:** Riders must be at least 38 inches tall.

- **Primeval Whirl:** Riders must be at least 48 inches tall.

- **It's Tough to Be a Bug!:** While there are no height restrictions, it may be too scary for children under age six.

On the first four of these rides, guests must transfer from a wheelchair or electronic convenience vehicles (ECV).

They are offered in English, Spanish, French, Portuguese, German, and Japanese, as well as in Braille (at Guest Relations).

Tours

All tours should be booked in advance by calling 407/939-8687. The first two require that tour-goers are 16 years old and fit enough to do substantial walking. There is a 48-hour cancellation policy for a full refund.

Backstage Safaris (three hours, $65 per person) gives guests a sense of how intensely the keepers are devoted to the hundreds of species at the park. Visit the Animal Nutrition Center, Veterinary Hospital, and other backstage housing areas while getting a heavy dose of wildlife conservation ethics. Interesting fact: It takes about four tons of food per day to feed all the animals in the park.

Want to learn more about the park's design? **Wild by Design** (three hours, $58 per person) is a walking tour in which you learn how Disney Imagineers integrate native art, cultural artifacts, and history into this fantasy world of animals. It's a way to appreciate the park's subtle storytelling and attention to detail—things that can be lost in a whirlwind romp through the park. Everyone on the tour is equipped with wireless headsets to facilitate hearing everything and the tour includes a nice breakfast at Tusker House in Africa.

And then there's the over-the-top **VIP Tour Services** ($125 per hour with a six-hour minimum, so at least $750). Your personal handler will plan the day's itinerary, whisk you to the fronts of the lines and the best seats, and generally make you feel superspecial.

The Oasis

Guests take trams from the vast parking lot (areas are identified by an animal and your row, so you may be chanting "Dinosaur 32" during the course of the day as a reminder) to the entrance, where you will find strollers, wheelchairs, bathrooms, ATMs, lockers, and other necessities to gird your loins for the day ahead. From here there is only one choice: Walk through the Oasis, a luscious tropical garden shot through with dappled streams and rushing waterfalls. A fair number of visitors rush through this area, squinting at their park maps and strategizing, which is a real shame. Technically the Oasis is not a "land"—there's nothing to do here except walk and observe the African spoonbills, giant anteaters, muntjacs, swamp wallabies, and other animals tucked under the dense foliage on either side of the winding paths (they all interconnect, so wander a bit). Disney animal handlers are stationed throughout, one perhaps with a tarantula, another with a sassy, yet articulate, macaw.

FOOD

With an erupting volcano, animatronic trumpeting elephants and peevish gorillas, bird calls, and inclement weather (the dining room endures periodic thunderstorms), the **Rainforest Café** (lunch and dinner, $15–29) is among the more frenetic restaurants you're likely to visit. Add to that the very long lines with lots of tired and hungry small people and it's enough to cut into your enjoyment of its enormous and fairly well-made pizzas, pastas, and salads.

The Rainforest Café is at the entrance of the Oasis, with a second entrance from outside the park. If you want to forgo the experience in Animal Kingdom, there's another Rainforest Café at Downtown Disney that, while busy, seems less frenzied.

SHOPPING

Many people appear to be doing their souvenir shopping at **Garden Gate Gifts,** just inside the entrance to the park. While this may be true, it's also where people retrieve their packages that they bought elsewhere in the park, and photographs taken by Disney photographers around the park, before departing for the day.

Discovery Island

The Animal Kingdom's seven themed lands are all connected through a central hub, Discovery Island. It's surrounded by Discovery River, so access to each of the lands is over a bridge. Discovery Island is also where you'll find the park's tip board, the place to look for showtimes, park maps, and the approximate wait time at the park's biggest draws. It is the locus of much of the dining and shopping activity in the park, which makes it a good place to pause midday or at the end of the day before you head back through the Oasis to the park's exit.

(THE TREE OF LIFE

All paths from the Oasis lead to Discovery Island, but just as the former empties into the latter sits one of the park's greatest photo ops—a magnificent view of the The Tree of Life, the perfect backdrop for your smiling crew. (Much like Epcot's giant golf ball, the Tree of Life is used as a photo op and a navigational tool.) The central attraction in this land, the tree is visible from various vantage points around the Discovery Island Trails, on which you'll encounter cotton-top tamarins, giant Galapagos tortoises, capybaras (now that's a *big* rodent), and other creatures in naturalistic settings.

The Tree of Life®

(*IT'S TOUGH TO BE A BUG!*

Deep within the hollow center of The Tree of Life, 400 humans at a time don goofy "bug eyes" (3-D glasses) and settle into long rows to watch *It's Tough to Be a Bug!*, an animated movie loosely based on Pixar's *A Bug's Life*. Mostly animated, with just a bit of yucky live-action bugs, it's narrated by sweet Flik, with guest appearances from the evil Hopper and a handful of other thespians from the bug world.

Tips: Special effects and animatronic things jumping out make it scary for kids under six.

DISCOVERY ISLAND TRAILS

What used to be called The Tree of Life Gardens, Discovery Island Trails is an underappreciated part of the park. Paths and trails wind around the root structure of The Tree of Life, providing chance encounters with wildlife, from lemurs to a giant Galapagos tortoise to a capybara. Some of the animals are in naturalistic enclosures, while others are accompanied by a handler who can also answer any of your questions.

FOOD

Discovery Island is home to several quick-service dining spots. **Flame Tree Barbeque** offers counter-service smoked ribs and chicken as well as competent salads that you eat in a lovely outdoor pavilion overlooking Discovery River. For the caveman-turned-theme-park experience of gnawing on a turkey leg, head to **Safari Barbecue.** On the other side of Discovery Island you'll find **Pizzafari,** with individual pizzas and sandwiches, and pep-up coffee drinks at **Safari Coffee.**

SHOPPING

Discovery Island has the greatest concentration of shops, with clothing and souvenirs at **Beastly Bazaar** and **Disney Outfitters,** trading pins and supplies at **Island Mercantile,** and the animal-theme toys at **Creature Comforts.**

Camp Minnie-Mickey

With the architectural idiom of a summer camp in the Adirondacks, Camp Minnie-Mickey is first and foremost the site of Animal Kingdom's big shows: **Festival of the Lion King** and **Pocahontas and Her Forest Friends.** In the southwest corner of the park, it also boasts the greatest concentration of Disney character greetings and autograph signings along what is known as the **Greeting Trails.**

FESTIVAL OF THE LION KING

Some of the creatures and floats used in Mickey's Jammin' Jungle Parade appear in this live show about Simba, Timon, Pumbaa, and the gang. The 30-minute spectacular is held in a wood-beamed theater-in-the-round, with gymnastics, audience participation, some slapstick humor, and truly wonderful voices, at least in the case of the four stars. It's Cirque du Soleil-meets-African tribal dance, with an aerial ballet, fire jugglers, trampoline acrobatics, and stilt walkers. The enclosed air-conditioned amphitheater seats more than 1,000 people on long benches.

Tips: Arrive 30 minutes before showtime to get a seat, but be warned that the line area outside is unshaded and can be somewhat sweltering. Showtimes change during the course of the year, but it is usually performed seven or so times each day. A weekly times guide for shows is inserted in park maps, or you can check the tip board on Discovery Island.

POCAHONTAS AND HER FOREST FRIENDS

Pocahontas and Her Forest Friends is geared for little kids (in fact, the first three rows are reserved for children). Pocahontas and her animatronic mentor, Grandmother Willow, introduce the crowd to a big snake, a porcupine, possum, raccoon, and skunk in a 12-minute outdoor show in the 400-seat Grandmother Willow's Grove. The show is scheduled about eight times a day, but it's less sweltering if you see it earlier in the day. Once a day there is an animal training session that demonstrates how the animals learn to behave properly with Pocahontas on stage.

Tips: The Pocahontas show is sweet, with a one-note environmental message, but it is not nearly as spectacular as Festival of the Lion King, so if you intend to see only one show, skip this one.

CHARACTER GREETING TRAILS

In Camp Minnie-Mickey, along what is called the Character Greeting Trails, Mickey, Minnie, and other characters such as Pluto, Goofy, Rafiki, Pooh, and Tigger hang around for photos, autographs, and a little one-on-one. Each trail is marked with the characters that appear—a good activity before or after seeing the Pocahontas or Lion King shows, or even while you wait in line. (There are also daily scheduled character greeting times in Discovery Island and Rafiki's Planet Watch; times are indicated on your times guide.)

FOOD

There's a nice little ice-cream stand, **Camp Soft Serve,** for refreshments while you wait in line along the greeting trails.

Africa

The single greatest allure in the land of Africa, Kilimanjaro Safaris, is also the biggest. The rest of Africa is given over to dining and shopping options.

◖ KILIMANJARO SAFARIS

Kilimanjaro Safaris takes up 100 acres of Animal Kingdom, making this ride the size of the entire Magic Kingdom. An actor, deep in character as an African safari guide, loads you into a dusty jeep and sets off on a "two-week" adventure on the Harambe Reserve. The scripted narration is based on a story about poachers and a couple of at-risk elephants, but the animals don't necessarily play along. The lions, giraffes, timid bongos, elephants, rhinos, Thomson's gazelles, mandrills, and others cavort and preen, wander in front of the jeep, and generally behave like wild animals. More than 30 other species roam free (the lions and cheetahs are craftily penned in such a way that it preserves the illusion that they're loose) while your safari jeep bumps and slides along "rutted" dirt roads in the carefully constructed reserve.

HIDDEN MICKEYS

It started as a joke. Disney Imagineers entertained themselves, and each other, through the years by slyly introducing tributes to the big-eared mascot of Disney's 47-square-mile kingdom. You know the shape: It's a big ball topped on either side by two smaller balls, signifying Mickey's head and ears in silhouette. In murals, queue areas, on new attractions, in golf course sand traps, in hotel lobbies, in snack bars – the shape is everywhere, sometimes understated, sometimes flagrant.

Millions of annual guests couldn't care less. But for some, sussing out these "Hidden Mickeys" has become a hobby verging on obsession. There are whole websites devoted to the sport (www.hiddenmickeys.org, www.hiddenmickeysguide.com). It's a bit like avid birders who "collect" bird sightings in a life list; Hidden Mickey hunters catalog their finds, sometimes arguing over whether something is the genuine article or just wishful thinking. People use magnifying glasses and binoculars, documenting their finds photographically.

If you want to get in on the action, here are just a handful of Hidden Mickeys at each park to get you started.

MAGIC KINGDOM

The **Haunted Mansion** boasts "999 Happy Haunts," but you can also find one mouse, formed by an arrangement of dishes on the table in the attraction's banquet scene. Ride **Splash Mountain** at night and you will fleetingly see that the burning cabin on Tom Sawyer's Island off to the right is burning in the shape of Mickey's head.

EPCOT

At Spaceship Earth in **Future World,** Mickey is hidden in a constellation of stars just beyond the attraction's loading area. In the France area of **World Showcase,** there's a mock garden of Versailles in which one of the shrubs is shaped like Mickey's head.

DISNEY-MGM STUDIOS

At **Rock 'n Roller Coaster Starring Aerosmith,** you'll find two Hidden Mickeys in the tile floor of the attraction's rotunda area. The balconies in the lobby of **The Twilight Zone Tower of Terror** are shaped like Mickey heads.

DISNEY'S ANIMAL KINGDOM

At the woolly mammoth dig site in **DinoLand U.S.A.**'s Boneyard, Mickey has been formed with a fan and two hard hats. And there are more than 25 Hidden Mickeys at **Rafiki's Planet Watch,** mostly in the lush mural of animals at the entrance.

The open-sided vehicles give a front-row view of everything (little ones are encouraged sternly to keep their bottoms in their seats, so situate them with maximum viewing in mind). Great care has been taken to introduce native African plants to the environment, complete with 20-foot-high fake termite mounds for verisimilitude. There's also a tiny island inhabited by pink flamingoes that insiders reveal is in the shape of a "hidden Mickey."

The tour-guide drivers (some actually from Africa) are exceptionally well versed in the animals on view, tossing in interesting facts and anecdotes as they see fit. To heighten your experience, use the species chart above your head in the safari vehicles to identify what you're seeing.

Tips: The 20-minute attraction is appropriate for all ages. Most veteran park-goers suggest going here just as the park opens to preempt the long lines and to see the animals at their most active. If lines are long right from the beginning, FASTPASS the safari and spend your waiting period walking through the Pangani Forest Exploration Trail.

PANGANI FOREST EXPLORATION TRAIL
It was originally called the Gorilla Falls Exploration Trail, and gorillas are indeed the central attraction of this area. But curious meercats, creepy naked mole rats, little dik-diks, gerenuks (like a giraffe morphed with a gazelle), and nearly 40 other species are spread through eight exhibit areas along the trail.

FOOD
In Africa, the top eats are to be had at **Tusker House Restaurant and Bakery** (breakfast, lunch, and dinner, under $14). To the right of the order counter are a crowd of burnished chickens roasting slowly on spits, which should inform your menu selection, but the pan-seared salmon and the chicken salad are also very nicely done. Enjoy either in a cool, African-theme cafeteria. While Tusker House serves beer, you'll need to head to Africa's **Dawa Bar** for a cocktail. Grab a piece of fruit from the picturesque **Harambe Fruit Market,** but forgo the sweets at the **Kusafiri Coffee Shop** or **Tamu Tamu** ice cream.

SHOPPING
Mombasa Marketplace purveys safari clothing and African handicrafts.

Rafiki's Planet Watch

Rafiki's Planet Watch is not technically a "land." Rather, it's an area wedged between Africa and Asia, loosely connected by an overarching theme of conservation and animal well-being.

Because there are no large-scale "adventures" in this area, many people think it's the weakest link at the park and there has been talk that this area might undergo significant changes. Pleasant discovery trails and a slower pace make it appealing for young kids, however, and signs and interactive exhibits render it fairly educational. To get there, board a **Wildlife Express Train** at the edge of Africa;

trains leave every 5–7 minutes. For park-goers interested in discovering hidden Mickeys around the park, the entrance mural to this area is said to be packed with them. **Out of the Wild** offers a nice array of conservation-themed books and toys.

WILDLIFE EXPRESS TRAIN
Its roof packed to capacity with fake luggage, this old-timey wooden train takes guests from Africa to Rafiki's Planet Watch. Along the way, you can rest your feet and glimpse behind the scenes of some of the park's animal housing areas. The five-minute ride is

appropriate for all ages, with outward-facing seats and a cheery narration that points out notable sights along the way. There are a couple of trains that run continuously, so lines are seldom long.

HABITAT HABITAT!

A walk-through animal trail, Habitat Habitat! allows for viewing endangered cotton-top tamarins.

CONSERVATION STATION AND AFFECTION SECTION

Rafiki's Planet Watch is the only place in the Animal Kingdom where, in the petting zoo–like Affection Section, you can actually touch animals. The Conservation Station provides a behind-the-scenes look at animal care at the park. You'll watch animals feed and see veterinary examinations through glass windows, with most activity taking place during morning hours.

Asia

The most lovely of the lands, the architecture and attention to detail merit a walk all the way to the end, to Expedition Everest, even if you have no intention of meeting the fierce Yeti from the vulnerable position of a runaway train. Some Imagineers spent as long as three months in Nepal taking notes and collecting 2,000 handcrafted artifacts and Nepalese doodads. Park-goers wander through the village, fingering weathered crampons and Sherpa trekking gear while Tibetan prayer flags flap gently in the breeze.

◖ EXPEDITION EVEREST

Upon reaching the entrance to Expedition Everest, standby riders head one way, FAST-PASSers another. Either way, the waiting period is ameliorated by a winding walk through what amounts to a small mountain-climbing museum and exhibit devoted to the Yeti, or Abominable Snowman.

You will be steeped in Yeti lore as you board a simulated steam train (two seats per row, 17 rows) on the way to the base camp of Mt. Everest, which adds to the tingly anticipation of meeting said mythical monster. Everest is a must for thrill-seekers, with a story line that takes would-be trekkers through a Himalayan village before boarding a train/coaster through the "forbidden mountain" guarded by the Yeti. In a fit of pique, the monster has torn up the tracks, causing the coaster to swoop backward through an ice cavern. Still, it's not a thrill ride exactly, despite the coaster's 80-foot drop and some miscellaneous hairpin turns, but the shortcut through the "forbidden mountain" does put you face to face with a truly heart-pounding audioanimatronic Abominable Snowman.

Tips: A smooth ride and speeds of up to only 50 mph make it an appropriate ride for young and old, as long as you're taller than 44 inches. However, being stalked by an angry Yeti can be frightening for kids under eight. Still it's very fun, especially if you can get in the first row (the last row purportedly blocks riders' view of the ripped-up tracks). At just longer than three minutes, it's the ride to FASTPASS.

KALI RIVER RAPIDS

The next most appealing ride in this land is Kali River Rapids. The 12-passenger white-water rafting experience down the Chakranadi River lasts only a little more than four minutes and gets you fairly drenched, but it is still a hoot. After queuing through a slide show on unscrupulous logging practices, board your raft to begin traveling through an Asian rainforest. Halfway through your trip you'll spot the smoking remains of a logging-gutted section of forest. Rafts spin and bob, go over a small waterfall, and are the target of water-gun marksmen along the banks.

Tips: Bring a plastic bag for anything that shouldn't get wet; the little storage spot at the center of each raft isn't watertight. The ride is appropriate for all ages, but the height requirement is 38 inches.

FLIGHTS OF WONDER

In the Caravan Stage in Anandapur at the entrance to Asia, Flights of Wonder is an appealing bird show. Bald eagles, hawks, vultures, and parrots swoop, squawk, eat, and preen for an audience in 20-minute shows usually scheduled five times each day. Like all the Disney shows, it has a story line; this one is rather self-referential and postmodern about a goofy trainee bird handler and a bird-phobic tour guide. Again, the overarching theme is conservation, preservation of habitat, and the glories of the natural world. Nearly 30 species, including vultures, hawks, macaws, cranes, ibis, and bald eagles, swoop in and strut in this outdoor amphitheater (the birds aren't really doing tricks but rather just being birds).

Tips: The handlers bring some of the birds to the seats nearest the stage, so arrive early to grab these premium spots. Be advised that birds do swoop right overhead; this is appropriate for all ages.

MAHARAJAH JUNGLE TREK

Before leaving Asia, walk the trails of Maharajah Jungle Trek to see tapirs, tigers, Komodo dragons, and giant fruit bats. All are tucked into a lush jungle setting amid Thai palace ruins and ornate structures of Nepalese, Indian, and Indonesian design.

FOOD

Wait until you get into Asia to satisfy your sweet tooth. Here you can sample the wares

Maharajah Jungle Trek®

© DISNEY

at the gorgeously decorated **Anandapur Ice Cream Truck,** where the soft serve and the root-beer floats are worth the wait in line.

SHOPPING

The newest shop, **Serka Zong,** is just at the entrance to Expedition Everest in Asia. I'm not sure what the name means, but the shop is largely devoted to books and memorabilia on the Yeti and Himalayan trekking. Also in Asia, **Mandala Gifts** showcases Asian knickknacks and tiger-themed clothing.

DinoLand U.S.A.

DinoLand is, by design, the most generic, all-American state fair–inspired part of the park. It's supposed to induce nostalgia for the old-timey roadside fair or traveling carnival, which in some ways seems antithetical to the whole Disney experience. Whack-a-mole and ring toss games (in a subarea called **Dino-Rama!**) are all fine and good, but they don't jibe with the fully realized, totally mediated, and story-lined "adventure" that one expects of Disney. The area is underwritten by McDonald's and has a loose dinosaur theme. There used to be paleontologists working on the real skeleton of a big *T. rex* found in South Dakota. Now the real bones are in the Chicago's Field Museum, so DinoLand has a replica called Dino-Suc.

In November 2006, Animal Kingdom launched a new musical in DinoLand U.S.A., **Finding Nemo.** It tells the story of the Pixar film with songs, animated backdrops, and oversize puppets.

DINOSAUR

The biggest draw in DinoLand is Dinosaur. The story line travels back 65 million years to the Cretaceous period to rescue a stray dinosaur from a hungry predator and an approaching meteor (a heavy message about extinction). It's really a bumpy, three-minute ride on a 12-seat "time rover" through the dark until emerging in a prehistoric forest with animatronic dinosaurs.

Tips: Kids under six may find the ride scary and dark; others may find it too jarring. The height restriction is 40 inches.

FINDING NEMO - THE MUSICAL

Talk about a big fish story. Finding Nemo - The Musical opened in November 2006, the first Disney musical created from a nonmusical feature. The 30-minute performance takes place in the newly constructed Theater in the

Dinosaurs live again at Dinosaur at DinoLand U.S.A.

DISNEY'S ANIMAL KINGDOM

© DISNEY

Primeval Whirl®

CHESTER AND HESTER'S DINO-RAMA!

Another really whiplash-inducing ride here is **Primeval Whirl** (must be 48 inches to ride), a spinning, small-scale roller coaster that jerks and dips past cardboard cutouts of space creatures, asteroids, and dinosaurs. Very skippable, it's in a subarea of Dino-Land U.S.A. called Chester and Hester's Dino-Rama!, which also contains the family-friendly **TriceraTop Spin,** a hub-and-spokes-style ride in which you zip around in four-person dino vehicles that rotate and lift up and down—a classic state fair kiddie ride. Chester and Hester's Dinosaur Treasures also sells dinosaur-theme items.

THE BONEYARD

The rest of DinoLand is geared toward young children, especially The Boneyard, a fossil-filled, dino-themed playground with tunnels, slides, and a fake "archaeological dig." It's a nice place to give the little ones a little freedom while adults rest their feet.

FOOD

DinoLand U.S.A. is underwritten (or co-produced) by McDonald's, so there's a lot of golden arch activity in this area. **Restaurantosaurus** is essentially a scaled-down McDonald's (hamburgers, fries, a salad) for lunch and dinner, but for breakfast it is the home of **Donald's Prehistoric Breakfastosaurus** ($15–29 per person), where you can mug, hug, and get autographs from Donald or his pals Mickey, Goofy, and Pluto. The breakfast buffet is generally scheduled close to when the park opens (8 or 9 A.M.); ask for exact times when prebooking. The multiroom restaurant has a fun paleontology and dinosaur memorabilia theme. Also in DinoLand U.S.A. is a **PetriFries** stall with some mighty fine examples of fresh-from-the-fryer McDonald's fries.

Wild, with live actors, oversize puppets, and original songs by Avenue Q composer Bobby Lopez. Like Voyage of the Little Mermaid at Disney's Hollywood Studios, it's a black-light show with humans operating bright puppets that shine in the ultraviolet light. You can actually see the people operating the puppets, but somehow it doesn't destroy the illusion of Nemo, Dory, et al frolicking under the sea.

The plot follows the film's story line fairly closely, with about 20 performers on stage and a bubblelike projection screens as an animated backdrop. It incorporates aerialists (now commonplace in Disney shows, thanks to the popularity of Cirque du Soleil), dancers, and a lively sound track.

Tips: Since the show is new, the 1,500-seat theater is packed every time—get there early. This is appropriate for all ages, but younger kids will enjoy it the most.

Entertainment

◖ MICKEY'S JAMMIN' JUNGLE PARADE

There's no doubt that the parade at Magic Kingdom is iconic, seminal—"off the hook." But it's easy to prefer the afternoon parade at Animal Kingdom, which starts at the Tusker House in Africa and swirls around Discovery Island, Asia, and back to Africa. The roughly 15-minute parade started in 2001 and runs every afternoon, often in the neighborhood of 4 P.M. (it depends on the closing time of the park). Industrious Disney employees tape off the parade route, while spectators assemble on the other side of the demure white line. Rafiki, Mickey and Minnie Mouse, Donald, and Goofy get their own floats (mounted on safari vehicles) and corresponding songs, but the real stars are the wildly inventive stilt walkers and enormous African-inspired animal puppets. Designed by Michael Curry, whose company created the puppets for *The Lion King* on Broadway, each puppet is operated by a single person with ropes and levers—nothing high-tech—to create the illusion of a leaping eight-foot-tall frog or lizard. Disney characters ride on floatlike character jeeps while more than 60 "cast members" run through choreographed numbers. The music is first rate, rendered all the more fun by stupendous African-inspired puppets. It's one of the park's greatest photo ops, as the characters will come right over and give a hug or mug for the camera.

MORE DISNEY ATTRACTIONS

Disney is no one-trick pony. It's got the theme parks, the resort hotels in which to house the theme park–goers, and a shopping, dining, and nightlife complex in which to entertain and feed them all. But the hits just keep on coming. Disney has also masterminded two water parks—Typhoon Lagoon and Blizzard Beach—that get their guests in the water, and a cruise line that heads them out on the open sea. In the mood for something entirely different? Tramp around on a Disney-owned wilderness preserve or catch a ballgame at Disney's Wide World of Sports complex.

All of these disparate attractions are linked by what Disney does best. With characteristic knack, all have been orchestrated to appeal across a wide age range and to entertain several generations of the same family all at the same time. The water parks can be added on to any Disney theme park ticket, while the wilderness preserve, cruises, and sports complex are all separately ticketed.

© DISNEY

Disney's Water Parks

Disney owns two water parks not far from the rest of its theme parks, both within walking distance of several of the Disney hotel properties. So, if you have only one day for a water park, which is better? Thrill seekers prefer **Blizzard Beach,** while families tend to enjoy the little-kid offerings at **Typhoon Lagoon.** The theme is more over the top at Blizzard Beach. Typhoon Lagoon is more relaxing with a better beach area. Both water parks will induce swimsuit wedgies with regularity.

Each is a full-day activity to be added onto a multiday Magic Your Way ticket or offered as a single-day stand-alone ticket. Typhoon Lagoon and Blizzard Beach are both $36 per day for ages 10 and up, $30 for ages 3–9, younger than three free. Both parks are open most of the year, often closing for some weeks during the winter for park refurbishment. Hours vary by season, but they both tend to open at 9 A.M. and close between 6 P.M. and 9 P.M. To buy tickets, call 407/824-4321 or visit www.disneyworld.com.

Unfortunately, there is no water-park hopping, so entrance into Typhoon Lagoon does not gain you admittance to Blizzard Beach. However, many of the multipark Disney tickets entitle entrance to the water parks. Buses run every 20 minutes from all Disney Resort hotels and theme parks to both water parks. (Note that the bus from Downtown Disney to the water parks no longer runs.) There are no parking fees at either park, but the parking lots do fill up on busy days and there are no trams that run from the parking lot to the park entrances.

Practicalities

One cooler is allowed per family at both water parks—no glass bottles or alcohol. Small and

MORE DISNEY ATTRACTIONS

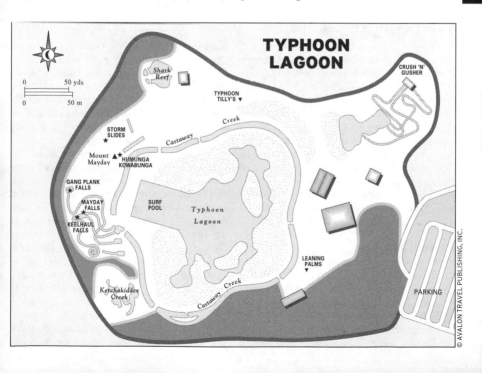

© AVALON TRAVEL PUBLISHING, INC.

large lockers are available for rent ($10 small, $12 large), as are towels ($1). Wear water shoes or sandals at both parks—walking over hot concrete all day is a drag. Do not wear a bathing suit with a belt, rivets, or anything that could puncture the sides of the rides (and leave your jewelry at home). Bring a disposable camera and waterproof sunscreen with an SPF of 30. The most important thing: Drink lots of water. There have been serious illnesses and even deaths reported at the water parks in the past couple of years. Being in and out of water all day may mask the symptoms of heat prostration and hyperthermia. Make sure you and your children stay hydrated and take time to get out of the sun.

While many of the parks' attractions are wheelchair-accessible, most attractions require guests to transfer from wheelchairs to the attraction either by themselves or with the assistance of a member of their party. Wave pools permit wheelchairs, but only in the very shallow end.

TYPHOON LAGOON

The 61-acre Typhoon Lagoon is the older park, opened in 1989 (a third, older park, Disney's River Country, is now closed; however, there is a non-Disney water park called Wet 'n Wild —see the sidebar in the *International Drive* chapter for details). As with all things Disney, there's an overarching "theme" story about a typhoon that caused havoc in a formerly pristine tropical paradise (not too charming in light of the 2004 tsunami). At the center of the park, near Downtown Disney West Side, is *Miss Tilly,* a shrimp boat left high and dry atop 95-foot Mt. Mayday (which erupts with a 50-foot geyser every half hour).

Attractions

Typhoon Lagoon's major attractions include **Crush 'n' Gusher,** a new raft-driven water coaster thrill ride; eight twisty water slides down from Mt. Mayday (including three enclosed 30-mph "speed" Humunga Kowabunga slides, for which the height requirement is 48 inches; or the Rudder Buster, Stern Burner, and the Jib

Jammer, with a height requirement of 60 inches on all three); and a 2.5-acre wave-making **Surf Pool** lagoon with surfing-size waves.

Because of the height restrictions on this first bunch of thrill rides, younger kids are essentially shut out (as are those who have a fear of heights). Unfortunately, while there's no height limit on the surf pool, the waves are substantial enough that this gets pretty hairy for younger kids. They should be supervised at all times (and, yes, there are lots of lifeguards) and spend the bulk of their time at the shallow end of the zero-entry surf pool. The deep end is six feet, with robust waves.

One cool feature of the surf pool is the 2.5-hour surf lessons offered by **Craig Carroll's Surf School.** Students must be at least eight years old and surfboards are provided. The cost is $140 per person and lessons take place before the park is open to regular guests. Group size is limited. Call 407/939-7529 to book; the price does not include general entry to Typhoon Lagoon.

There are three rafting-style rides: the "white-water" **Mayday Falls,** the twisty **Keelhaul Falls,** which takes you through caves, and **Gang Plank Falls** with three- to five-passenger rafts that enable families to ride together. Circling the lagoon is **Castaway Creek** (children must be supervised), a 2,100-foot stream on which guests ride inner tubes at a drifting, leisurely pace through a misty rainforest and a hidden grotto.

Guests can also snorkel in the 362,000-gallon saltwater **Shark Reef** stocked with tropical fish. Pick up a face mask, snorkel, and life vest at the counter (no extra charge) and then sit on the ledge at the entry point while a park employee gives you basic guidance on how to use the mask and snorkel. Tip over into the fairly chilly water (much colder than elsewhere in the park) and swim through the reef gazing at vibrant little tropical fish and a few small sharks. It's appropriate for all ages, assuming you have basic swimming skills, but children under 10 must be accompanied by an adult. You can also document your swim with a $10 photo. If you don't want immersion, you can watch the goings on from the portholes of an upside-down, immersed freighter.

If snorkeling was just too darned fun, the park offers an "S.A.S. Adventure" (that's Surface Air Snorkeling) class, using a small pony tank and regulator. It's really an introduction to scuba, $20 per half hour. You must be at least five years old; sign up near the entrance to Shark Reef.

For younger children, **Ketchakiddee Creek** is a water playground with slides and fountains geared to toddlers up to about kindergarten (must be 48 inches tall or shorter). The **Bay Slides** are also geared specifically for the young (must be under 60 inches), with a gentle slide that lands swimmers in the shallow end of the surf pool.

Food and Practicalities

Food at the park is entirely of the fast-snack variety: **Typhoon Tilly's** serves sandwiches, salads, and beer; **Leaning Palms** doles out hamburgers and pizza; there's a little ice-cream stand near Leaning Palms and another one called **Lowtide Lou's Snacks** near the raft slides.

The park has ladies' and men's changing areas, lockers, and showers, and there's a fairly large picnic area.

BLIZZARD BEACH

Just north of Disney's All-Star Resorts, the 66-acre Blizzard Beach opened in 1995, with an entirely different Disney "legend" at work: A freak snowstorm led one misled entrepreneur

MORE DISNEY ATTRACTIONS

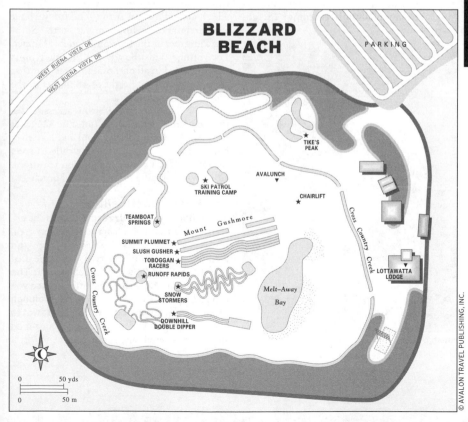

© AVALON TRAVEL PUBLISHING, INC.

MORE DISNEY ATTRACTIONS

to build Florida's first ski resort, complete with chairlifts and ski jumps. The snow, as one might predict, didn't stick and the 220-foot Mt. Gushmore has been given over to the flumes and slides resulting from the melt. The biggest rides off the mountain all have a fairly stringent height requirements, so younger kids may be frustrated by the offerings at Blizzard Beach. Teens and tweens may be more excited to spend a day here. Some guests anticipate that this outdoor park will be icy cold… wouldn't that be a major feat during a Florida summer? Don't worry. The water is 80°F, with the exception of the melting snow in the ice cave of Cross Country Creek.

Attractions

The major rides are off the mountain, including the 55-mph **Summit Plummet** (height

© DISNEY

Slush Gusher

requirement 48 inches), the nation's tallest, fastest free-fall speed slide; the **Downhill Double Dipper** (height requirement 48 inches), side-by-side racing water slides that stand 50 feet high and 200 feet long; the **Slush Gusher** (height requirement 48 inches) speed slide that drops guests through a snowbanked mountain gully; and three "slalom" flumes (no height requirement) called the **Snow Stormers.** There are six-passenger white-water rafts at **Teamboat Springs** (no height requirement), an eight-lane **Toboggan Racers** (no height requirement), and inner tube **Runoff Rapids** (no height requirement).

The Summit Plummet is the biggest thrill rush, verging on really scary for the speed alone (the height is dizzying, too). The more timid may want to stick to the slalom flumes, which are still twisty, turny good fun without the vertiginous feeling you get on the Summit Plummet or the Downhill Double Dipper. For younger kids, be advised that they must be supervised in all of the adult areas, but that there's a *maximum* height of 48 inches in the kiddie **Tike's Peak** area.

Below the mountain, which is accessible via the wooden-bench chairlift (must be 32 inches to ride), you'll find a wave pool and lazy river à la Typhoon Lagoon, this one called **Cross Country Creek** (adult supervision required), along with a kiddie splash area and beach.

Food and Practicalities

The **Village at the Blizzard Beach** is the entrance area that contains a tube pickup area, towel rentals, lockers, first aid, a shop, and a couple of the dining options—a bar called **Frostbite Freddie's** and light snacks at **The Cooling Hut.** Near the chairlift entrance you can pick up snacks and sandwiches at **Avalunch** or desserts at **Sled Dogger.** The **Lottawatta Lodge** is a big, casual counter-service, fast-food spot with covered outdoor seating.

Downtown Disney

The 120-acre Downtown Disney, at the intersection of Buena Vista Drive and Hotel Plaza Boulevard, is a shopping and dining complex comprising the **Marketplace, Pleasure Island,** and the 66-acre **West Side.** The restaurants tend to be outposts of major chains and the shopping is more souvenirs, luxury goods, and zany impulse buys. I have made some excellent purchases here, such as a chili-cheese dog refrigerator magnet (very lifelike) and one can of Flarp!, described euphemistically as "noise-making goop." If one were so inclined, one could also buy just-dipped candy apples, a magic trick spinning sphere that appears to hover in space, a battery-operated hamster that runs incessantly inside a clear plastic ball, or a premium cigar.

Parking is free at Downtown Disney; buses do not run from the theme parks, but Disney resort properties offer transportation here. Shops generally open at 9:30 A.M. in the Marketplace and at 10:30 A.M. in West Side; all close at 11 P.M. Pleasure Island clubs are open 7 P.M.–2 A.M. Call 407/WDW-2NITE (407/939-2648) for more Downtown Disney information.

WEST SIDE

The largest of the three Downtown Disney areas, West Side boasts 344,000 square feet of buildings and a 9,500-square-foot open area for events and entertainment.

Entertainment
DISNEYQUEST

DisneyQuest (one-day ticket $38.34 for ages 10 and up, $31.95 for ages 3–9, children younger than three free) is another allure for families pre- or postdinner. Billed as a 100,000-square-foot "family entertainment environment," this five-story arcade and virtual-game hall is broken into four zones: the Explore Zone, an exotic virtual adventure land; the Score Zone, a superhero game-playing competition area; the Create Zone, for more artistic self-expression; and the Replay Zone, for nostalgic old-timey games and rides. Many of the games are actually based on Disney rides and attractions (Aladdin's Magic Carpet Ride, Pirates of the Caribbean—Battle for Buccaneer Gold), so there's crafty cross-marketing going on. DisneyQuest also has a small souvenir shop and a café.

Nearby, an enormous **AMC 24 Theatres** offers all the blockbusters, heavy on the family films.

LA NOUBA

The major entertainment splurge in West Side is Cirque du Soleil's La Nouba, which many visitors say is the best $112 (gulp!) you can spend in Orlando at one fell swoop—that's for the top-tier tickets; children get in for less, but there are category 2 and 3 tickets that range $97–50. The circus troupe runs through its signature range of humor, dance, aerial fancies, juggling, and

a LEGO dinosaur at Downtown Disney
© LEGO

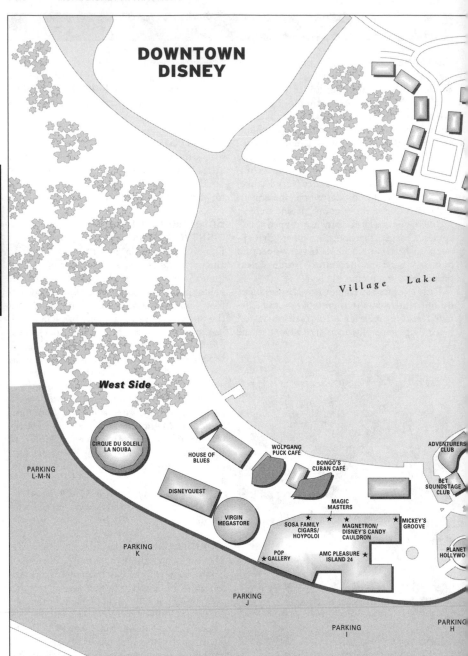

DOWNTOWN DISNEY

Village Lake

West Side

PARKING L-M-N

CIRQUE DU SOLEIL/ LA NOUBA

HOUSE OF BLUES

WOLFGANG PUCK CAFÉ

BONGO'S CUBAN CAFÉ

ADVENTURERS CLUB

BET SOUNDSTAGE CLUB

DISNEYQUEST

VIRGIN MEGASTORE

MAGIC MASTERS

★ SOSA FAMILY CIGARS/ HOYPOLOI

★ MAGNETRON/ DISNEY'S CANDY CAULDRON

★ MICKEY'S GROOVE

PARKING K

★ POP GALLERY

★ AMC PLEASURE ISLAND 24

PLANET HOLLYWO

PARKING J

PARKING I

PARKING H

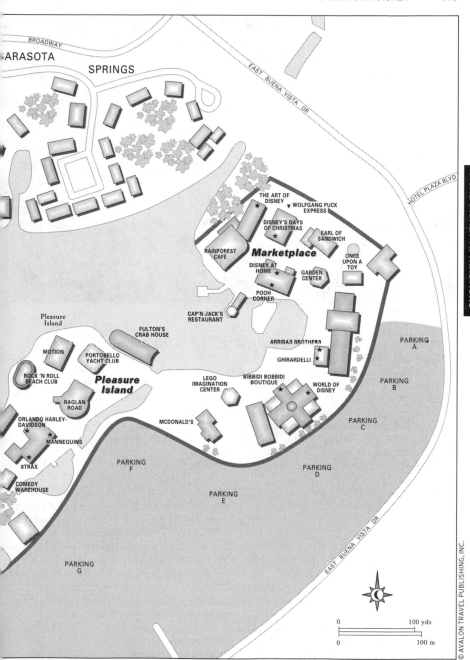

BROADWAY

ARASOTA

SPRINGS

EAST BUENA VISTA DR

HOTEL PLAZA BLVD

THE ART OF
DISNEY

WOLFGANG PUCK
EXPRESS

DISNEY'S DAYS
OF CHRISTMAS

EARL OF
SANDWICH

RAINFOREST
CAFÉ

Marketplace

ONCE
UPON A
TOY

DISNEY AT
HOME

GARDEN
CENTER

POOH
CORNER

CAP'N JACK'S
RESTAURANT

Pleasure
Island

FULTON'S
CRAB HOUSE

PARKING
A

MOTION

PORTOBELLO
YACHT CLUB

ARRIBAS BROTHERS

GHIRARDELLI

PARKING
B

ROCK 'N ROLL
BEACH CLUB

*Pleasure
Island*

LEGO
IMAGINATION
CENTER

BIBBIDI BOBBIDI
BOUTIQUE

WORLD OF
DISNEY

RAGLAN
ROAD

ORLANDO HARLEY-
DAVIDSON

MANNEQUINS

MCDONALD'S

PARKING
C

8TRAX

PARKING
F

PARKING
D

COMEDY
WAREHOUSE

PARKING
E

PARKING
G

EAST BUENA VISTA DR

0   100 yds

0   100 m

© AVALON TRAVEL PUBLISHING, INC.

La Nouba show at Cirque du Soleil®

LA NOUBA BY CIRQUE DU SOLEIL®

acrobatics in a permanent structure built especially for the show. Cirque aficionados claim this show rivals the permanent shows in Vegas (O, Zumanity, Ka, Mystere, and that new Beatles tribute, Love). As with all Cirque shows, it has a loose plotline: Two groups of characters are in conflict, the wacky, colorful Cirques and the monochromatic "Urbains." Think *West Side Story* but with more contortionists and acrobatics. Performances are held at 6 P.M. and 9 P.M. Tuesday–Saturday. Tickets range $63–112 for ages 10 and up and $50–90 for ages 3–9. Call 407/939-7600 to book.

Food

The single best offering on West Side is **Wolfgang Puck Café** (407/938-9653, 11:30 A.M.–11 P.M. daily, until 11:30 P.M. Fri.–Sat.). It offers a rather inexpensive café menu ($6.95–17.95) downstairs and on the patio of this stylish eatery and a much more expensive dinner menu (entrées $16–35) upstairs. Either way, the large restaurant runs like a well-oiled machine, with a careful hand in the kitchen

with salads and its signature pizzas. The bartenders also mix a mean cocktail.

House of Blues (407/934-2583, 10:30 A.M.–11 P.M. daily, entrées $10–25) doesn't necessarily proffer authentic renditions of Mississippi Delta cuisine, but it's a fun and affordable place, especially for its Gospel brunches. The music venue side of the property holds 2,000 people, so it gets mighty busy here when a good band is in town. A huge, Death Star-looking **Planet Hollywood** (407/827-7827, 11 A.M.–2 A.M. daily, entrées $9–20) serves a familiar American menu along with its movie memorabilia decor and theme merchandise.

The single most reprehensibly bad restaurant in West Side is **Bongos Cuban Café** (407/828-0999, 11 A.M.–2 A.M. daily, entrées $10–25), a huge 500-seater purportedly owned by Gloria Estefan. Loud and cavernous with inelegant and ersatz Cuban food served by indifferent and unskilled servers, it's best avoided.

Shopping

Magnetron is the aforementioned source of quality refrigerator magnets. **Candy Cauldron** provides the candy apples; its open kitchen does all kinds of alluring candy making in the window to draw the masses in. Visit **Sosa Family Cigars** for quality smokes and **Magic Masters** for that magic trick I mentioned. The store is supposed to look like Harry Houdini's personal library, and it has magic demonstrations all the time. The **Virgin Megastore** encourages you to while away the hours trying out the various featured albums on headsets. **Hoypoloi** carries (mostly ugly) decorative arts, and there's lots of sculpture at the **Pop Gallery**. **Mickey's Groove** stocks Disney clothing and souvenirs, and there's also a sunglasses shop and a place to buy huge pretzels.

PLEASURE ISLAND

Pleasure Island's 72,000 square feet of themed nightclubs are meant to go head to head with Universal's CityWalk. I'd opt for the latter if I wanted to tear it up at night. Neither is an organically grown constellation of clubs and bars and both have a prefab "boozy theme park for adults" quality to them, but CityWalk is more sophisticated and varied in its offerings.

Entertainment

Pleasure Island is free to walk through, but you must pay cover charges to enter anywhere ($20.95 plus tax for multiclub admission). Music offerings include **8Trax** for the '70s disco-ball-and-Grand-Funk-Railroad crowd (although on Thursday nights the era inches up into the 1980s). **Mannequins Dance Palace** gets the action hopping with strobes, lasers, smoke, bubbles, a rotating dance floor, and droning techno trance. Although it's a strictly over-21 club (except for this and BET SoundStage Club, the others admit people 18 and older), the age seems to go down a bit at Mannequins—not as many folks in their 30s and 40s. Generally, Mannequins has the best dancers of all the nightspots in Pleasure Island or nearby clubs. **BET SoundStage Club** showcases rhythm and blues, reggae, and soul; despite its affiliation with Black Entertainment Television, the club casts a wide net with partiers of all ethnicities and age groups.

If you want to relax and catch some oldies or a little live music, stop into the three-level, tropical-themed **Rock 'n Roll Beach Club.** The club admits underage folks if they are accompanied by adults, so you'll see a lot of teenagers adopting studied nonchalance as a first-time clubbing experience with Mom and Dad. There are tables, so you needn't stand the whole time as at several of the other clubs. Music videos on huge screens at **Motion** are mostly top-40 and predictable; it's better to spend the evening at the hilarious **Adventurers Club** with its masks, shrunken heads, and safari motif. A 1930s-style radio murder mystery is part of the entertainment, with performing waiters and lots of high jinks. For more traditional improvisation and showcase comedy, **The Comedy Warehouse** (shows 8 P.M., 9:05 P.M., 10:15 P.M., and 11:45 P.M. Sun.–Wed., 8 P.M., 9:05 P.M., 10:15 P.M., 11:45 P.M., and 12:45 A.M. Thurs.–Sat.) draws from audience suggestions. And the **Pleasure Island Jazz Company** is a haven for jazz and blues fans (although I didn't see anything too impressive during a couple of tries).

At all Pleasure Island clubs, the lines stretch out a little during spring break and the summer (15–45 minutes on a busy night), but the wait is ameliorated by the fact that waiters offer cocktails while you're in line. Lines for the Comedy Warehouse and Mannequins are the longest. If you look under 30, have your ID handy—the clubs do card with regularity.

Food

There is one really excellent restaurant, **Raglan Road Irish Pub and Restaurant** (407/938-0300, 11 A.M.–11 P.M. daily, entrées $15–25), an Irish pub with great beers and a refined, contemporary Irish American menu. Although it's right next door to Raglan, **Portobello Yacht Club** (407/934-8888, entrées $17.95–36.95) is considered to be in the Marketplace. Chef Massimo Fedozzi serves up straight-ahead regional Italian dishes with lovely patio dining in view of Lake Buena Vista.

Shopping

The Orlando **Harley-Davidson** store (9:30 A.M.–11:00 P.M. Sun.–Thurs., until 11:30

MORE DISNEY ATTRACTIONS

MORE DISNEY ATTRACTIONS

Fri.–Sat.) supplies clothes and collectibles for aficionados. Note: Pleasure Island closed most of its shops in the middle of 2006.

MARKETPLACE

The former Lake Buena Vista Shopping Center is now Marketplace, an outdoor mall at one end of Downtown Disney. It has 20 or so shops and a large handful of restaurants, with occasional live entertainment at the Dock Stage. At its centerpiece is the **World of Disney,** a huge Disney-theme store divided into theme rooms, with a much-heralded new salon in the Princess Room at the **Bibbidi Bobbidi Boutique.** Little princesses (ages three and up) can have their hair, makeup, and nails done while their brothers hang out in the Adventure Room, wondering why their sisters get to burn $35 on hair and makeup. (The "Castle Package" is even more—$175 for the works plus a princess costume and accessories of their choice).

Food

The Marketplace's top offering for full-service destination restaurants is the riverboat **Fulton's Crab House** (407/934-2628, entrées $20.95–38.95), serving a seafood-heavy array of New American dishes with a luxurious continental hand at saucing. **Portobello Yacht Club** (407/934-8888, entrées $17.95–36.95) offers serviceable regional Italian, and at **Rainforest Café** (407/827-8500, entrées $12.99–39.99), you can eat pricey but reasonably healthy American cuisine in an often mobbed jungle setting. There's also a gift shop that exerts a tremendous pull on the wallet.

The quick offerings include oysters and clam chowder at **Cap'n Jack's Restaurant** (407/828-3870, entrées $16–24), a very expertly made sandwich from an outpost of the chain **Earl of Sandwich** (407/938-1762, $8–10), and the same professionalism shown with the pizzas and sandwiches at **Wolfgang Puck Express** (407/828-0107, $8–12).

A new offering, **T-Rex: A Prehistoric Family Adventure, A Place to Eat, Shop, Explore and Discover** will open in 2008. The second of its kind (the first is in Kansas City),

riverboat dining at Fulton's Crab House

© DISNEY

this casual restaurant boasts animated dinosaurs and a mock fossil dig along with accessible American food.

All restaurants are open 11 A.M.–11 P.M. daily.

Shopping

The overarching theme here is Disney, with **Disney Tails,** a Disney-oriented pet-product place; a **Disney's Days of Christmas** collectibles store; **Wonderful World of Memories,** a Disney scrapbooking store; a **Disney's Pin Traders** open-air kiosk; a major Disney-and-Hasbro toy store called **Once upon a Toy;** and a **LEGO Imagination Center.** For adults the shopping is less enticing and includes a glassware shop called **Arribas Brothers,** a Disney animation and collectibles store called **The Art of Disney,** a fragrant lotions-and-potions store called **Basin, Goofy's Candy Company,** a **Ghirardelli Soda Fountain,** and **Summer Sands** swimwear shop.

Disney Adventures

DISNEY WILDERNESS PRESERVE

Fifteen miles south of Walt Disney World lies the Disney Wilderness Preserve. The what, you say? In 1993, The Walt Disney Company entered into a partnership with the Florida Department of Environmental Regulation (DER), The Nature Conservancy, and five other agencies to establish 12,000 acres of preserved land. The preserve, now managed by The Nature Conservancy, is home to hundreds of wildlife species that find their homes in a diversity of habitats—from pine flatwoods to oak scrub and wetlands.

For the visitor, there is a three-mile hiking trail along pristine Lake Russell and Reedy Creek Swamp and two-hour Sunday buggy tours that explore just a part of the preserve, which lies within the headwaters of the Kissimmee Chain of Lakes, which in turn feeds the Kissimmee River, Lake Okeechobee, and the Everglades system.

To get there from I-4, exit onto Highway 535 and head south. Follow Highway 535 to Poinciana Boulevard. Turn right (south) onto Poinciana Boulevard. Follow it for about 15 miles until you reach the intersection of Poinciana Boulevard and Pleasant Hill Road. Turn right onto Pleasant Hill Road. Continue into Poinciana to the first stoplight, which is Dover Plum. Turn left onto Dover Plum and continue until you come to the second stop sign, at the end of Dover Plum. Turn right and shortly thereafter turn left at the first left onto Scrub Jay Trail and follow it into the preserve to the parking lot.

The preserve is open 9 A.M.–5 P.M. Monday–Friday; buggy tours are noon–4 P.M. Sunday October 1–May 31. Admission is $3 adults, $2 ages 6–17; tours are $10 adults, $5 ages 6–17. A small conservation center contains educational exhibits and shaded picnic tables are situated at several points. To make a reservation, call 407/935-0002.

DISNEY'S WIDE WORLD OF SPORTS

Most theme park–goers pass by signs for it again and again and scratch their heads, but sports enthusiasts seem to find a variety of reasons to head over. Disney's Wide World of Sports is a 220-acre, 9,500-seat facility that holds more than 180 amateur and professional events annually. Some of this is endurance running competitions (marathons, Iron Mans, the works), but there are dodgeball tournaments and even the world footbag championships (no, I have no idea either).

The **Atlanta Braves** hold their spring training in the ballpark in late February and late March. The **Tampa Bay Devil Rays** also play several regular-season games here. The complex contains four other professional baseball fields and a practice infield. Then there are six fields for fast pitch softball, slow pitch softball, and

MORE DISNEY ATTRACTIONS

© DISNEY

Disney's Wide World of Sports®

youth baseball. Smaller venues such as the **Milk House** hold basketball, volleyball, wrestling, martial arts, and inline hockey events; and the **Hess Sports Fields'** eight fields host football, baseball, softball, fastball, soccer, rugby, lacrosse, field hockey, archery, and windball cricket. A large track and field complex, another one for tennis, and a large cross-country course draw athletic groups from all over.

Visitors can tour the complex ($11.25 ages 10 and older, $8.50 ages 3–9), but special events are all separately ticketed. Atlanta Braves spring training single tickets range from $14 general admission to $22.50 for lower level reserved seats. For tickets, call 407/839-3900 or visit www.ticketmaster.com. The complex is at 800 Victory Way, Lake Buena Vista. For information, call 407/939-1500. Bus transportation runs from Disney's Hollywood Studios and the Downtown Disney area.

DISNEY CRUISES

Owned by the Walt Disney Company, Disney Cruise Line was launched in 1995 and is headquartered in Celebration. As at the theme parks, what Disney seems to do best is orchestrate environments in which families can have fun together. On the Disney Cruise Line, this is accomplished through a range of programs and shows. Shown in the 977-seat Walt Disney Theatre, evening shows include *The Golden Mickeys,* a song-and-dance salute to Walt Disney and his legacy; *Disney Dreams,* a bedtime story featuring Peter Pan, Belle, Aladdin, Cinderella, Ariel, and others; *Hercules—The Muse-ical,* a musical comedy in which the brawny hero teams up with a goofy Greek goddess villain; and *Twice Charmed: An Original Twist on the Cinderella Story.* Also on each cruise, there's a pirate-themed dinner and deck party, first-run movies, and three themed restaurants.

Whereas the Disney theme parks entail all-day family interaction and herding of small people through throngs, the cruise ships have hit upon a formula of some together time/some apart time. This is achieved through zoning: Each ship contains areas that are especially designed for toddlers, young children, teens, and adults. Then, each age group has its own "club" onboard: the Oceaneer Club (ages 3–7) themed to Peter Pan's Never Land with a Captain Hook's pirate ship, where you can dance with Snow White or sit in for an animation workshop; Oceaneer Lab (ages 8–12), with a video wall and flat-screen computers, where you can build your own volcano or produce wacky radio commercials; and The Stack or Aloft (teens only), with a dance floor, Internet café, and lounge with big-screen plasma TVs. Adults get their own special club: onboard spa and fitness, nightclub, wine tastings, and adult pools.

Obviously, the biggest customer base is nuclear families in search of a memorable vacation. That said, honeymooners, singles, multigenerational travelers, and special-needs travelers are accommodated with Disney's characteristic aplomb.

For more information about Disney Cruise Line, visit disneycruise.com or call 888/325-2500.

Cost

Disney cruises are not cheap. For instance, a three-night Bahamian cruise for one person in a standard inside stateroom will cost about $946 during the cheapest parts of the year, whereas an 11-night Mediterranean cruise for a family of four in a deluxe family stateroom with a veranda will run $15,440. The range of prices is vast, contingent upon where in the ship you are (a three-night Bahamian cruise in June for a standard inside stateroom is about $1,200; a deluxe stateroom with veranda will run $2,861), but also when in the year you go (in May that same deluxe stateroom with veranda is $1,811; in September it's $1,200). If you want to go on a cruise but are flexible about dates, there's a lot of financial wiggle room. And whether you elect a budget-oriented interior room or a windowed room on the outside of the ship depends upon your comfort level with small spaces—interior rooms are very tight. Price your cruise with and without airfare included. From certain airports it may make more sense to buy airfare separately.

Schedule

Disney cruises travel to the Bahamas for three or four nights and to the eastern and western Caribbean for seven nights. In addition, there are special cruises that include 10- and 11-night Caribbean cruises, 10- and 11-night Mediterranean cruises throughout Europe, and 14-night eastbound and westbound transatlantic cruises. All cruises include days at sea onboard the *Disney Magic* or *Disney Wonder,* two 875-stateroom ships that are virtually identical, as well as stops and excursions at ports of call as follows:

- **Eastern Caribbean ports:** St. Maarten, St. Thomas/St. John, and Castaway Cay (which is Disney's private island in the Bahamas, with pirate ships, teen beaches, adults-only areas, and family activities)

- **Western Caribbean ports:** Key West, Florida; Grand Cayman, British West Indies; Cozumel, Mexico; and Castaway Cay

- **Mediterranean ports:** Barcelona, Spain; Palermo, Sicily; Naples, Italy; Olbia, Sardinia; Civitavecchia, Italy; La Spezia, Italy; Marseilles, France; and Villefranche, France

- **Transatlantic ports:** Tenerife, Spain; Cadiz, Spain; Gibraltar, U.K.; Barcelona, Spain; and Castaway Cay

In 2008, the *Disney Magic* sails to Los Angeles for 12 consecutive seven-night cruises from Los Angeles to the ports of Cabo San Lucas, Mazatlán, and Puerto Vallarta. Except for this last cruise, the departure point for Disney cruises is from Port Canaveral, Florida (the closest deep-water port, about 45 minutes east of Orlando International Airport).

ORLANDO

© 2007 UNIVERSAL ORLANDO. ALL RIGHTS RESERVED.

UNIVERSAL ORLANDO RESORT

Universal has kept bulking up since its original opening such that it now ably competes with Disney as a multiday destination. After the launch of its first park, Universal Studios Florida in 1990, Islands of Adventure was unveiled in 1999, and around the same time came CityWalk. This means the whole 444-acre complex now contains two dramatically different theme parks, one next to the other, a 30-acre dining, shopping, club, and live-entertainment area called CityWalk, and three on-site hotel properties, all serviced by two huge parking structures. What this means is that you can pull into the garage and never leave the property for several days of varied fun and games.

Universal Studios Florida competes directly with Disney's Hollywood Studios—they are both motion picture and television theme parks that contain working film and TV production facilities. The idea is, ostensibly, that you may visit these parks and catch a glimpse of movie-making magic in action. This seldom happens, but you're slightly more likely to see camera crews at work in a Universal back lot. So, which to patronize? Each has its merits (Disney's Hollywood's Tower of Terror is reason enough for a visit), but Universal Studios is bigger, with more rides and attractions.

Islands of Adventure, on the other hand, doesn't really have a close competitor. If you're attentive, you'll note it's been patterned a bit on the Magic Kingdom in terms of areas, theming, and kinds of rides, but its closest relative is probably Busch Gardens in Tampa. Islands of Adventure is best appreciated by teens and

© 2007 UNIVERSAL ORLANDO. ALL RIGHTS RESERVED.

HIGHLIGHTS

LOOK FOR █ TO FIND RECOMMENDED SIGHTS, ACTIVITIES, DINING, AND LODGING.

█ **Revenge of the Mummy:** Brendan Fraser's dough-faced earnestness may lull you into a false confidence as you enter Universal Studios's newest "dark ride." What starts as a visit to the set of a mummy flick ends up a wild coaster ride as you're chased by soul-sucking mummy warriors, swarms of scarab beetles, and plumes of fire (page 160).

█ **Men in Black Alien Attack:** An MIB agent trainee, your goal is to zap 120 different alien species as you career through the streets of New York. The ride's outcome depends on your team's score – a natural attraction to re-visit, if only for a new ending (page 162).

█ **Incredible Hulk Coaster:** This stunning Bolliger and Mabillard roller coaster in Islands of Adventure is often voted tops in

Orlando, partly for its incredible launch lift hill and partly for its smooth ride and seven inversions. It also makes a cool Hulklike roaring noise (page 168).

█ **The Amazing Adventures of Spider-Man:** A long, meandering walk through the *Daily Bugle's* offices pays off when you board this ride in Islands of Adventure. A combination of moving vehicles and 3-D film puts you right into Spidey's world as he battles Doc Ock, Electro, Hobgoblin, Hydro Man, and Scream (page 168).

█ **Caro-Seuss-el:** Every regular carousel will seem humdrum after a gander at Theodor Geisel's kooky creatures spinning around in Islands of Adventure's Seuss Landing. You don't need to ride to be enthralled by a Cowfish or one of the other 53 mounts (page 172).

veteran thrill-riders: The focus is on big, thrilling rides likely to induce whoops, screams, and on unfortunate occasions, vomit. CityWalk is Universal's answer to Downtown Disney's Pleasure Island. Billed as an adult playground, it's mostly a collection of restaurants that amp up the volume late at night once the kids have gone home.

HISTORY

Once upon a time, MCA owned Universal Studios, which unveiled Universal Studios Florida in 1990. In 1991, Matsushita Electronics bought MCA, but attractions at the Studios kept chugging along unfazed. In 1993, Universal Studios Florida announced plans to open Universal's Islands of Adventure and Universal CityWalk. In 1995, the Seagram Company bought MCA, and then the next year MCA was renamed Universal Studios. New rides kept getting unveiled all the same (Barney, Terminator 2: 3D, Twister... Ride It Out). In 1999, Universal's Islands of Adventure and Universal CityWalk opened to the public, and the Loews Portofino Bay Hotel opened as the first on-site hotel. The next year, the Black-

stone Group acquired a 50 percent interest in Universal Orlando and Vivendi merged with Seagram (which included its interest in Universal Studios), creating the new Vivendi Universal. Rides kept opening. In 2001, the Loews Hard Rock Hotel opened, and the next year the Loews Royal Pacific Resort opened as the second and third on-site hotels. Rides kept opening (Jimmy Neutron's Nicktoon Blast, Shrek 4-D, Revenge of the Mummy). In 2004, General Electric acquired Vivendi Universal's interest in Vivendi Universal Entertainment and merged the company with NBC to become NBC-Universal. And the rides kept opening (Fear Factor Live, the Seuss Trolley Train).

The moral of the story: What's in a name? A coaster by any name would sell its seats.

PLANNING YOUR TIME

How much time each park requires is entirely contingent upon when you visit. During peak season, it will be difficult to see everything Universal Studios offers in a single day. During the quietest times of the year, you may be able to tour both Universal Studios and Islands of Adventure in one day—it all depends on line lengths and how many people are shuffling along in the streets. With a few exceptions, lines tend to be shorter at Universal Studios because so many of the attractions are 3-D movies and large audience shows, as opposed to Islands of Adventure, where each individual rider is strapped in before being catapulted on some new voyage.

When planning a visit, the makeup of your posse may determine your priorities. Traveling with several generations, including little kids? There may be more for everyone to do at Universal Studios. Or are you an adrenaline junky? Visit Islands of Adventure first.

Somewhat unlike the Disney parks, Universal is a tough place to spend the whole day together as a family. Height requirements and health/safety concerns on many rides mean little kids and the elderly won't be able to go on everything teens and tweens are eager to try. It may sound like an admission of defeat, but it could save strain and frustration to agree to split up into two smaller groups, one aimed at the little-kid adventures and the other heading for the monster rides. For smaller children, time the indoor shows to coincide with nap time.

It may pay to do your homework, charting out your day at each park online before your visit, and allowing each family member to pick his or her most important attractions. The prevailing wisdom of park veterans is to arrive early and immediately head for the back of the park and work your way forward against the tide of park-goers.

Orientation

Universal Studios and Islands of Adventure (mailing address: 1000 Universal Studios Plaza, 407/363-8000, www.universalorlando.com) are about 10 minutes northeast of Walt Disney World along I-4, just north of SeaWorld. After parking in one of the two large garages, enter the resort near CityWalk. Due north is Universal Studios and due south is Islands of Adventure. The two parks are next to each other but require separate admission and have separate entrances, although there are tickets that allow admission to both parks on the same day.

When to Go

The least busy months at Universal Orlando Resort seem to be September, November, and January. If you can plan your visit during one of these months, wait time on rides is cut dramatically, and the weather is lovely in the fall. While during spring break (Mar.–Apr.) and summer vacation (June–Aug.), some wait times are upward of 90 minutes—especially on water rides on a hot day—in November you may just walk on to the blockbuster rides. This means that it is possible to cover everything in both parks in two days.

Park Hours

Operating hours at both parks normally begin at 9 A.M. Closing times vary throughout the course of the year, usually between 6 P.M. and 9 P.M. Universal CityWalk hours are 11 A.M.–2 A.M. Universal Orlando is open 365 days a year.

Special Events

Universal Orlando puts on some top-notch events during the course of the year, so timing a visit to coincide with one of its parties is a nice way to enrich your experience. On Saturday nights in February, March, and April, Universal Studios celebrates the spirit of New Orleans with the annual **Mardi Gras celebration,** bringing in nationally known bands along with beads, floats, and high spirits. Mid-February, **Reggae Fest at Universal CityWalk** honors the history and music of Jamaican culture. Maybe the biggest event of the year happens every October, with **Halloween Horror Nights at Universal Orlando** transforming the parks into everyone's worst nightmare. Universal erects specially designed haunted houses and truly heart-pounding scare zones, and it brings in hundreds of street performers. This is a "hard ticket" event that does not include regular admission to the parks. And then during the holiday season, the parks feature special holiday-themed entertainment, decorations, and food, culminating in a huge **New Year's Eve at Universal CityWalk.**

What to Bring

As with all the theme parks, comfortable shoes are a must. This does not mean flip-flops, which can fly off into the stratosphere on the more aggressive rides. Shoes and shirts must be worn at all times at both parks. Swimwear is wise if you're spending time in Islands of Adventure (lots of water rides), and bring Ziplock bags for your wallet, camera, and other valuables. Sunscreen is a must; hats and sunglasses are helpful but are just that many more belongings to whisk in and out of lockers all day. You may bring snacks and drinks in a backpack or shoulder bag (no coolers), which helps to defray your in-park expenses. If you want to bring a cooler and keep it in the car, you may exit the park and have a tailgate lunch before reentering.

Bringing multiple cell phones helps keep track of wandering teens. For smaller children, it's wise to pin your cell number on their sleeve, or even write it on their arm with washable ink; if they get lost, park employees know what to do.

Tickets

A **two-park, one-day ticket** to both Universal Studios and Universal's Islands of Adventure is $73 online for adults ($77 at the gate) and $63 online for children 3–9 ($67 at the gate). The **two-park unlimited admission ticket** is $85 for all ages, offered online only. It entitles guests to admission for up to seven consecutive days to Universal Studios and Universal's Islands of Adventure, including all-club access to Universal CityWalk. Floridians get a special deal: Florida residents who buy a **one-park,**

one-day ticket online for $67 adults, $56 children, receive a free second day and second park ticket. Parking is an additional $10. These are nontransferable, nonrefundable tickets.

Guests are welcome to leave and return to the park the same day. Get your hand stamped at the exit and keep your ticket as a precaution.

Multipark Tickets

To compete with multiday Disney packages, several of the other theme parks have banded together to offer ticket packages. A **Five-Park Orlando Flex Ticket** gives you unlimited admission to Universal Studios, Universal's Islands of Adventure, SeaWorld, Wet 'n Wild (see sidebar in the *International Drive* chapter), and Busch Gardens Tampa Bay for up to 14 consecutive days; adults $234.95, children 3–9 $199.95. A four-park ticket (no Busch Gardens) is $189.95 adults, $155.95 children.

Express Plus

Most of the attractions at Universal Studios offer a second line for Express Plus cardholders, so I have not specifically singled them out. There are a couple of ways to bypass the longer lines and opt instead for the short "Express Plus" lines. When you stay at one of the on-site hotels (Royal Pacific, Hard Rock, or Portofino), your room key doubles as an Express Plus card, a major incentive to stay in the park during high season. Or you can buy an Express Plus Pass, which is in addition to your park admission ticket. It's a whopper of a fee: $40 additional (the price changes a bit seasonally) for one-day, one-park Express Plus, and it's valid for only one entry per attraction.

Universal Studios

Universal Studios opened in 1990, but it is in a constant state of evolution as it parlays the public's enthusiasm for Hollywood blockbuster films and hit television shows into motion-simulators, 3-D movies, shows, and interactive attractions. This park is less about monster coaster, animals, or character meet-and-greets than many of Orlando's other parks. Instead, it is a celebration of Universal Pictures through the years, letting visitors "Ride the Movies."

Virtually everything at Universal Studios is some kind of interactive ride/movie/show, which lends the park a certain homogeneity. Too many attractions are essentially movies viewed from seats that bump and wiggle—it can get monotonous. Between these attractions, much of the park is designed to look like back lots at movie studios, with fake building facades interspersed with real buildings, clustered in areas to look like New York or San Francisco or Hollywood. Guests spend a great deal of their day walking past these facades—lovely, but not much to do. And because a fake Tiffany store facade may house a Universal Studio souvenir shop, it is sometimes difficult to find what you're looking for. A riot of fake and real advertisements, billboards, admonishments, and directions render it very difficult to find your way around the park.

UNIVERSAL ORLANDO RESORT

UNIVERSAL STUDIOS RIDE GUIDE

Some rides and attractions require special considerations of height, maturity, or fitness. Visitors with health restrictions, mothers-to-be, and those with heart conditions or mobility problems are strongly urged to stay away from most of the attractions with height requirements.

UNIVERSAL STUDIOS
Minimum Height Requirements:

* Back to the Future the Ride: 40 inches

* Jimmy Neutron: 40 inches (stationary seating available for shorter riders)

* Men in Black Alien Attack: 42 inches

* Revenge of the Mummy: 48 inches

* Woody Woodpecker's Nuthouse Coaster: 36 inches

"Parental Discretion" Rides:

* Beetlejuice's Graveyard Revue

* Jaws

* Terminator 2: 3-D

* Twister... Ride It Out

* Universal Horror Make-Up Show

ISLANDS OF ADVENTURE
Minimum Height Requirements:

* Doctor Doom's Fearfall: 52 inches

* Dudley Do-Right's Ripsaw Falls: 44 inches

* Dueling Dragons: 54 inches

* Flying Unicorn: 36 inches

* High in the Sky Seuss Trolley Train Ride: 34 inches

* Incredible Hulk Coaster: 54 inches

* Jurassic Park River Adventure: 42 inches

* Popeye and Bluto's Bilge-Rat Barges: 42 inches

* Pteranodon Flyers: minimum 36 inches, maximum 56 inches (unless accompanied by child)

* The Amazing Adventures of Spider-Man: 40 inches

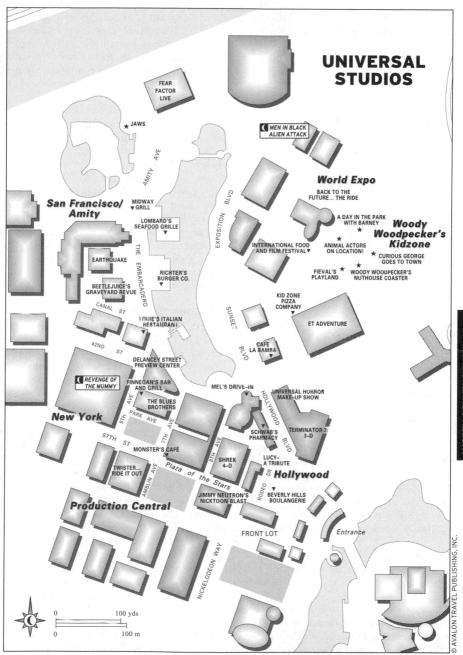

UNIVERSAL STUDIOS

FEAR FACTOR LIVE

★ JAWS

MEN IN BLACK ALIEN ATTACK

San Francisco/ Amity

MIDWAY GRILL ▼

LOMBARD'S SEAFOOD GRILLE ▼

EARTHQUAKE

BEETLEJUICE'S GRAVEYARD REVUE

RICHTER'S BURGER CO. ▼

CANAL ST

LOUIE'S ITALIAN RESTAURANT ▼

42ND ST

DELANCEY STREET PREVIEW CENTER

REVENGE OF THE MUMMY

FINNEGAN'S BAR AND GRILL

THE BLUES BROTHERS

New York

5TH AVE
PARK AVE
7TH AVE

57TH ST

MONSTER'S CAFÉ

TWISTER... RIDE IT OUT

8TH AVE

AMBLIN AVE

Plaza of the Stars

SHREK 4–D

JIMMY NEUTRON'S NICKTOON BLAST

Production Central

NICKELODEON WAY

AMITY AVE

THE EMBARCADERO

EXPOSITION BLVD

SUNSET BLVD

World Expo

BACK TO THE FUTURE... THE RIDE

A DAY IN THE PARK WITH BARNEY ★

Woody Woodpecker's Kidzone

INTERNATIONAL FOOD AND FILM FESTIVAL ▼

ANIMAL ACTORS ON LOCATION! ★

★ CURIOUS GEORGE GOES TO TOWN

FIEVAL'S PLAYLAND ★

★ WOODY WOODPECKER'S NUTHOUSE COASTER

KID ZONE PIZZA COMPANY

ET ADVENTURE

CAFE LA BAMBA ▼

MEL'S DRIVE–IN

UNIVERSAL HORROR MAKE-UP SHOW

HOLLYWOOD BLVD

SCHWAB'S PHARMACY

TERMINATOR 2: 3–D

LUCY– A TRIBUTE

RODEO DR

Hollywood

BEVERLY HILLS BOULANGERIE

FRONT LOT

Entrance

0   100 yds
0   100 m

© AVALON TRAVEL PUBLISHING, INC.

UNIVERSAL ORLANDO RESORT

Because movie and television audiences are fickle, the park is compelled to retire rides and introduce new ones at a fairly rapid clip—rumor has it several rides will be retired. I've indicated these, but don't be surprised if one or two others has undergone a dramatic makeover by the time you visit.

PRODUCTION CENTRAL

Right through the front gates of Universal Studios is a nondescript area called Production Central that's supposed to look like a real working TV and film studio. A little skimpy on rides and attractions, it's where you'll find locker, wheelchair, and stroller rentals; the lost and found (at the Studio Audience Center); guest services; and a handful of souvenir shops and quick-eats stands.

Jimmy Neutron's Nicktoon Blast

A fairly tame place to start your day at the park, this simulator ride is based on Nickelodeon's movie and TV show, *Jimmy Neutron*. You board a "rocket" and follow Jimmy and his friend Carl to catch the evil Ooblar the Yokian, who has stolen Jimmy's prized rocket, the *Mark IV*. Along the way you meet other Nick characters on the screen—the Rugrats, SpongeBob SquarePants, the Fairly OddParents—while your "rocket" yanks and jerks you. If you don't meet the height requirement or you experience motion sickness, you can snag one of the stationary seats at the front (there's a separate line for these seats, which moves more quickly than the regular line). The ride exits into an interactive "control room" area and gift shop (where a guy in a SpongeBob suit awaits your camera).

Tips: The height requirement is 40 inches.

Shrek 4-D

A 3-D movie that will be mostly familiar territory for the seasoned theme parker, it does the classics—you don 3-D "OgreVision" glasses, water squirts at you when someone sneezes, and your seat bumps and shimmies while Shrek and Donkey slide through some fairly amusing patter as they battle a ghost Lord Farquaad. The plot line is a little thin for this 12-minute animated movie (the ghost Farquaad wants Fiona back, everyone goes over a waterfall, the dragon saves the day), but the preshow is a pretty funny few minutes of exchange between a live announcer and an animatronic Pinocchio.

Tips: Characters Shrek and Donkey appear across from the exit at Ye Olde Souvenir Shop to sign autographs and smile for the camera.

NEW YORK

Continuing straight on Plaza of the Stars, which becomes 57th Street, you'll enter the area called New York. Buildings are suitably NYC-ish, with replicas of the New York Public Library, the Palace Theater, and other landmarks. In this area are two of the park's biggest rides, Twister and Revenge of the Mummy, and there are a respectable Irish pub and Irish shop (why, in New York?).

◖ Revenge of the Mummy

The park's only coaster opened in 2004 and lent a little muscle with great effects. Set entirely indoors, in the space that used to house Kongfrontation, the ride whisks you through the dark, past fireballs and a cool flaming ceiling, fierce-looking animatronic warrior mummies, and beetles pouring toward you via CGI animation. The storyline is introduced on a big screen: Your mission is to stop the Mummy's curse, a curse that has affected the making of the latest *Mummy* flick. All in all, it's a very fun ride on 16-passenger single-car vehicles, although the coaster has no inversions and reaches only the tame speed of 45 mph.

Tips: The height requirement is 48 inches; it's not appropriate for children who spook easily. You must put all loose belongings in a locker before riding. Lines can be very long in high season, but the preride lead-up takes riders through an enjoyable Museum of Antiquities and around a burial chamber and archaeological dig.

Twister... Ride It Out

This attraction baffles me. The waiting line

takes 2,400 people at a time through Wakita, Oklahoma—tornado alley—and then a furrowed-brow Bill Paxton and Helen Hunt appear on side-by-side screens to tell us how scary it was making the film *Twister,* and how it was hard for them to tell reality from the filming. They finish up with lots of platitudes about the awesome forces of nature. After this, the crowd is ushered through a re-creation of the ruined house of Aunt Meg's from the movie before reaching the final chamber. For the best effect, stand in the first row. It's an empty Wakita Street, with a couple of parked cars and a drive-in Galaxy movie theater showing a horror double feature. The wind picks up, it begins to rain, and then you see a funnel in the distance. It approaches, the wind becomes fierce, and cars, signs, and one hapless cow, visibly on strings, are propelled by Mother Nature's fury around the stage. A towering funnel of smoke swirls center stage, then retreats. Winds die down and the show is over. You feel as if you've been watching the Weather Channel.

The Blues Brothers

Jake and Elwood put on one of the park's only live shows, drawn from that classic 1980 comedy. Set outdoors on Delancey Street, the show begins with a sizzling saxophonist, and then Mabel comes out and sings an Aretha-style "Respect," before Jake and Elwood, black suits, sunglasses, and white socks just right, dance and sing their way through "Shake Your Tailfeather" and others. It's goofy fun, with room for dancing along. Showtimes vary, but it generally plays 5–6 times daily.

Delancey Street Preview Center

Universal Studios visitors get to preview and rate new television shows under consideration by the networks. Allow at least 30 minutes if you decide to participate. It's open seasonally.

UNIVERSAL ORLANDO RESORT

SOUNDSTAGES

Florida is the third-largest film-production state in the country, and so much of the activity occurs in Orlando that it has been dubbed "Hollywood East." The Central Florida area has recently been featured in *The Punisher,* starring John Travolta, and *The Waterboy,* with Adam Sandler. Go back a bit further, and this area was the filming location of *Fried Green Tomatoes, Lethal Weapon 3,* and Ron Howard's *Cocoon;* back further still, it was the locale of Esther Williams's underwater extravaganzas in the 1950s. Some of this activity is due to the area's year-round climate and lush tropical foliage, but some of it can also be attributed to the top-notch soundstages situated here, along with dozens of support companies for postproduction, hair and makeup, and other movie-related needs.

Universal Studios Florida is home to nine soundstages, the largest with 22,000 feet of space. Soundstage 24 has a huge expanse of hardscape for car racing, while Soundstages 18 and 19 used to house Nickelodeon Studios,

before it pulled out in 2005, filming game shows such as *Get the Picture, Family Double Dare,* and *Legends of the Hidden Temple.* Scenes from the movie *Parenthood* were filmed here, as were parts of *Psycho IV: The Beginning* (all right, nothing to brag about). The studios have hosted *Wheel of Fortune, Fear Factor,* and *The Ellen DeGeneres Show,* as well as tons of World Championship Wrestling, including Total Nonstop Action Wrestling's *Impact.*

These days, park visitors can be a part of the live studio audience for *iVillage Live,* a one-hour talk show that broadcasts live at noon Monday–Friday and airs on NBC (call 866/448-5360 or send an email request to iVillageLivetickets@nbcuni.com at least one day in advance). Topics include health, food, beauty, style, parenting, and pregnancy and are covered on the website, also called iVillage.com. If you want to get on the show, you can't be wearing logo clothing or hats. The recommended minimum age is 10.

SAN FRANCISCO/AMITY

East on South Street, which becomes The Embarcadero, guests enter an area that is devoted both to San Francisco and the fictional setting of the 1975 Spielberg film *Jaws* (pretty odd, because Amity was supposed to be an island off Maine, not particularly near Northern California). It's an area that features some old and some new, with a little more attraction diversity than elsewhere in the park (also some of Universal Studios's better dining options).

Beetlejuice's Graveyard Revue

The only live show in this area, it's just undergone a revamp with new music and costuming. Still, it maintains a slightly crude and risqué humor that is fitting for the show's namesake film. Dancing monsters, pyrotechnics, a mummy's crypt, and one wisecracking Beetlejuice are all accompanied by a loud and somewhat incongruous pop-music score. Audience participation is solicited, especially from the first few rows—plan your seating accordingly. Showtimes vary, but it usually takes place 2–3 times each day.

Tips: Parent discretion advised.

Earthquake

Board a BART (Bay Area Rapid Transit) train compartment, and dang if things don't go terribly awry, with crumbling walls, live wires snaking around, and explosions. But that's public transportation for you. Supposedly the mock quake you experience on this ride is equivalent to quake that measures an 8.3 on the Richter scale, but first riders slog through a very lengthy preshow about special effects in the movies. Nothing about this is particularly fresh or exciting, as so many attractions jiggle you around, spray you with a little water, and (especially at Universal) create fireballs complete with notable blasts of heat. Longtimers say this attraction used to be more thrilling, when the earthquake part had not been curtailed in favor of the special-effects edutainment.

Fear Factor Live

Your age determines your appreciation for this interactive attraction. It's based on the popular reality television show, and the premise is fairly low-tech: Park guests compete against each other in an array of extreme stunts such as drinking an earthworm shake. If your first thought is, "Why would I want to drink an earthworm shake or watch someone else do this?" you are too old for Fear Factor Live. Bridging the gap between a live broadcast and an in-the-can show, park guests' competitions are rendered a little more slick and professional with state-of-the-art video, audio, and lighting accompaniment. Also, the competitors seem to be super hotties of all sorts, sometimes scantily clad. Shows take place several times each day, and casting occurs 75 minutes before each show at the kiosk in front of the stadium.

Jaws

Wisecracking Captain Jake takes you on a boat tour of Amity Harbor. While you wait to board, TV monitors broadcast local news about creepy events going on in Amity, despite the fact that that menacing great white was killed way back in 1974. As you head out into open water, a crackly radio transmission alerts the captain to impending danger before you see a telltale dorsal fin break the surface. The big guy comes out of the water, jaws agape, on the left-hand side of the boat, before the boat heads into a "safe" boathouse. Unperturbed, the great white busts into the boathouse, and the chase is on. It goes on like this—a fun, all-ages water ride.

Tips: Jaws is best experienced from an outside seat, especially on the left-hand side. All riders will get robustly moistened during the ride, so plan it for the hottest part of the day.

WORLD EXPO

The smallest area, at the easternmost edge of the park, World Expo offers only two attractions and their associated memorabilia stores.

◖ Men in Black Alien Attack

I love this attraction, but one question: If riders board "MIB training vehicles" that careen through a huge New York City street set, why is this ride not in the area of the park called New

York? Not to be picky, because it's a hoot—part ride, part interactive video game. The queue leads riders through a re-created MIB headquarters before they board their vehicles and gear up to kick some alien butt. More than 120 animatronic aliens pop up and you zap them with your "laser gun" as your car spins and dips. Depending on your team's score, the ride has a series of different endings, making it a wonderful attraction to revisit. Disney has a similar Buzz Lightyear–themed ride, but this still seems very novel.

Tips: The minimum height is 42 inches.

Back to the Future... the Ride

At this point lots of kids have never seen the 1985 movie on which this attraction is based, and the ride itself opened back in the dark ages of 1991. There's some talk that it is soon to be replaced by a new simulator ride, but for now you board an eight-seater DeLorean (complete with those pull-down doors), and you're off on a bumpy simulated adventure across the space-time continuum, documented on a 70-foot IMAX screen above you. The waiting rooms have replicas of gadgets from the three movies, and parked outside sits the real DeLorean from the films.

Tips: The height requirement is 40 inches.

WOODY WOODPECKER'S KIDZONE

Stop a six-year-old in this area and ask him who Woody Woodpecker is. He doesn't have a clue. That doesn't stop this from being the concentrated area in Universal Studios appealing to littler kids. A series of sweet live shows and interactive playgrounds make this the place that the height-challenged and their attendant parent go when the other, taller family members are enjoying the big rides at Universal Studios.

E. T. Adventure

This used to be the signature for the park, with guests mounting bicycles and soaring with E. T. toward the luminous moon. It's still nostalgic and lovely, except that park-goers get onto bikes glued to an eight-person platform to save E. T.'s dying planet (the ride at Uni-

versal Studios Hollywood is closed altogether, so I'm not complaining). The front row is the place to be and the preride queue is a verdant forest, cooling on a hot day. The goofiest part is that you get an "interstellar passport" with your name, so that at ride's end E. T. gives you a personal thanks—only he doesn't exactly know who is who and his pronunciation leaves something to be desired.

Woody Woodpecker's Nuthouse Coaster

Accompanied by Woody's signature laugh, parents and children can enjoy a training-wheels coaster. It's a single fire-engine-red minitrain with eight cars, two people across, and reaches a maximum speed of just over 20 mph.

Tips: If the line is long, consider skipping it because it's over in the blink of an eye. The height requirement is 36 inches.

Animal Actors on Location!

Animal Planet Live! closed and five days later this new show opened in its place. How'd they do it so quickly? It's mostly because it's a similar show, heavy on the humor, with live animals, a little audience participation, and some reliance on video in a brief, 20-minute show. The show is performed five or more times each day.

Tips: Outside, near E. T. Adventure, animals sometimes hang out with their trainers for a photo op.

Water Play Areas

Two discrete water playgrounds make this the place to cool off for the little ones. Bathing suits are essential. **Curious George Goes to Town** is a colorful, goofy town shaped in a C (with only one, narrow exit area so parents don't lose anyone). Alive with little geysers and fountains, the area occasionally gets doused with 500 gallons of water (a bell goes off just before, so skedaddle if you don't want to get wet). This area also has a "ball factory" with foam balls, tubing, and cannons. (Park employees say this part of the park is haunted at night with the laughter of children.) The playground area called **Fievel's Playland** is

UNIVERSAL ORLANDO RESORT

WHAT'S NEW

In June 2007, Universal Orlando Resort launched a show meant to compete with the likes of Cirque du Soleil's La Nouba at Downtown Disney. The **Blue Man Group** will take up residence in a new facility accessible from both Universal CityWalk and Universal Studios. The building that once housed Nickelodeon Studios has been totally redesigned as a 1,000-seat theater in which to showcase the Blue Man Group's charms. What those are exactly is a little hard to say.

What started as a street act in the 1980s by three friends, Chris Wink, Matt Goldman, and Phil Stanton, has blossomed into a multicity performance art event that incorporates rock music, comedy, and multimedia artistry. The show always features three guys in skull caps, gooey blue facial paint, and black suits. Beyond that, the act involves paper, food substances, paint, and other things that get sprayed from the stage (the front rows receive courtesy ponchos). Their brand of goofy props, audience participation, and sly social commentary will all be customized for a super family-friendly show in Orlando. For tickets, call 888/340-5476 or visit www.universalorlando.com.

It's not exactly new, but **Universal 360: A Cinesphere Spectacular** will be returning summer 2007, from June 30 to August 18, at Universal Studios. It was unveiled during summer 2006 and is being refurbished so that the four 30-foot-tall globes will once again be used to internally project clips from more than 150 famous Hollywood films. It's the Saturday night grand finale – each three-story-tall ball is mounted onto a floating barge in the center of the park's lagoon and projects a montage of familiar movie bits on 360-degree screens, all set to music in a 16-minute show. Add some fireworks and a mighty laser display and it's a thrilling way to end your day at the park (too bad the residential neighbors nearby don't seem to agree).

And in May 2007, Universal unveiled a plan to do a whole part of the park in a Harry Potter theme, to be unveiled in 2009.

---

sometimes preferred because it has a water slide and a maze, but it's really just a fancified neighborhood playground. The conceit here is that it's a mouse's-eye view of the big world, so everything is very oversize. The best part is the Mouse Climb rope tunnel.

A Day in the Park with Barney

This is my worst nightmare, complete with an endless loop of the song. But, hey, some people love the purple dinosaur. It's actually a fairly innocuous 25-minute sing-along show, with B. J., Baby Bop, and the other guys. Barney shows up for a meet-and-greet in Barney's Backyard playground after the show.

HOLLYWOOD

The final area in the park before you reach the exit, this is the most entertaining to walk through—back-lot stage sets are lovingly recreated along Hollywood Boulevard and Rodeo Drive, complete with stars on the pavement.

Universal Horror Make-Up Show

Running each day 8–9 times, this is an educational show about what goes into creating the blood and gore for the movies. Dark humor, a trick knife, and creepy monsters make it inappropriate for young children. Outside the theater in the lobby you'll see props and set pieces from horror films, along with a behind-the-scenes video from *Van Helsing*.

Terminator 2: 3-D

Just as inappropriate for little kids (loud and somewhat violent), this is a 12-minute 3-D movie showcasing the California governor's wilder side and, um, a different approach to border patrols. It also includes live-action stunts and special effects, as well as a gorgeous Harley Fat Boy. Shows run continuously all day.

Tips: Stationary seating is also available (seats that don't buck and wiggle to simulate the action on screen).

Lucy–A Tribute

One of the only bones the park throws at older generations, this reads like an *I Love Lucy* memorabilia shop with glass cases containing costumes, scripts, and continuously running videos.

Tips: It's usually empty and very air-conditioned, making it a nice place for a bit of calm regrouping.

FOOD AND SHOPPING

Each of the park's six areas offers a range of dining options. The park also offers a meal deal whereby adults can eat all day at Louie's Italian Restaurant, Mel's Drive-In, or International Food and Film Festival for $18.99 (children nine and younger, $9.99). Since you'll probably eat breakfast before arriving at the park at 9 A.M. and probably eat dinner elsewhere when the park closes at 6 P.M., it doesn't seem to be a good deal.

By and large, shopping in each area corresponds to the attractions therein. For example, ride the Men in Black Alien Attack, and you'll find the MIB store located handily at the ride's end. Almost all of the larger rides have an affiliated gift shop, sometimes unavoidable just as you hop off the ride.

Character Dining

On Fridays and Saturdays during high season **Finnegan's Bar and Grill** presents a "character" breakfast buffet (reservations 407/224-3613, $15.95 adults, $9.95 children nine and under). Guests meet Shaggy and Scooby Doo, Dora the Explorer, Jimmy Neutron, and others.

Production Central

Visit **Monsters Café** for counter-service rotisserie chicken, pizza, pasta, and salads.

You'll find the all-encompassing **Universal Studios Store** of souvenirs and apparel, conveniently located for pre-park-exit purchases and package pickup. There's a large **Nickstuff** toy store with SpongeBob SquarePants-, Jimmy Neutron-, and Dora the Explorerobilia, as well as a smaller **Nick Kiosk** of Nickelodeon characters. Shrek 4-D also has its own **Shrek Souvenir Shoppe** across from the attraction exit.

New York

Choose between **Louie's Italian Restaurant's** counter-service pizza, pasta, and salads, or **Finnegan's Bar and Grill** ($9.95–21.95) for full-service fish 'n' chips, corned beef and cabbage, or Guinness beef stew. The latter has a full bar.

Shopping in New York is uncharacteristically limited, with an **Aftermath** store of Twister attraction apparel and collectibles, **Sahara Traders** featuring Revenge of the Mummy apparel and souvenirs, and a small Irish shop called **Rosie's.**

San Francisco/Amity

This area of the park has the greatest concentration of real restaurants, from the park's fanciest, **Lombard's Seafood Grille** ($10–20) serving seafood, chowder, and pastas, to the very respectable counter-service burgers of **Richter's Burger Co.** There's also **Midway Grill** for Nathan's hot dogs and fries.

Travel from New York to San Francisco, where you can peruse the delicious wares at the eye-popping **San Francisco Candy Factory,** buy some shades at the **OakleyT,** or a little beach attire from **Quint's Surf Shack.**

World Expo

As the name might suggest, World Expo's **International Food and Film Festival** adopts a world-beat approach with cafeteria-style Asian, Italian, and American standbys.

As would be expected, World Expo shopping is restricted to doodads from the **MIB Gear** shop or **Back to the Future the Store.**

Woody Woodpecker's KidZone

Woody's only offer here is counter-service pizza and chicken fingers at **Kid Zone Pizza Company.**

Woody's KidZone caters to its demographic with **The Barney Store, E. T.'s Toy Closet and Photo Spot,** and the **Cartoon Store** filled with stuffed animals one might be coerced into buying.

UNIVERSAL ORLANDO RESORT

UNIVERSAL ORLANDO RESORT

Hollywood

Hollywood has a number of quick-eats. **Beverly Hills Boulangerie** serves breakfast croissants, soups and sandwiches, and cheesecake from the Cheesecake Factory. **Schwab's Pharmacy** offers hot-fudge sundaes and milkshakes. For counter-service burgers and shakes, head to **Mel's Drive-In,** or try **Cafe La Bamba** for counter-service rotisserie chicken, ribs, burgers, and tortilla salads.

In Hollywood, the shopping ops are shared between **Cyber Image,** which features Terminator and No Fear gifts and apparel, and **Silver Screen Collectibles** of Hollywood apparel and memorabilia.

Islands of Adventure

Islands of Adventure opened in 1999 with Steven Spielberg as creative consultant. This 110-acre theme park is all about muscular monster rides, the kind that take grit and wherewithal—oh, and height. Divided into five themed "islands" connected by footbridges around a central lagoon, Islands of Adventure is geared to older school-age kids, teenagers, and young adults. The pregnant, those with disabilities, and the just plain short will spend the bulk of their time standing on the ground and waiting for their thrill-seeking family members to return. Seuss Landing is the "island" in the park devoted to younger kids, and it will keep people happily occupied for a couple of hours.

Music is used aggressively in this park, with one loud song segueing to the next as visitors walk along from attraction to attraction. The rides, shows, and attractions here are much more varied than at Universal Studios, making for a better overall experience. Park-goers can amble from Orlando's best coaster, the Incredible Hulk, over to one of Orlando's top 3-D experiences at The Amazing Adventures of Spider-Man; each complements the other. The theming and storytelling is also exceptionally

© 2007 UNIVERSAL ORLANDO. ALL RIGHTS RESERVED.

Incredible Hulk Coaster, a favorite attraction at Islands of Adventure

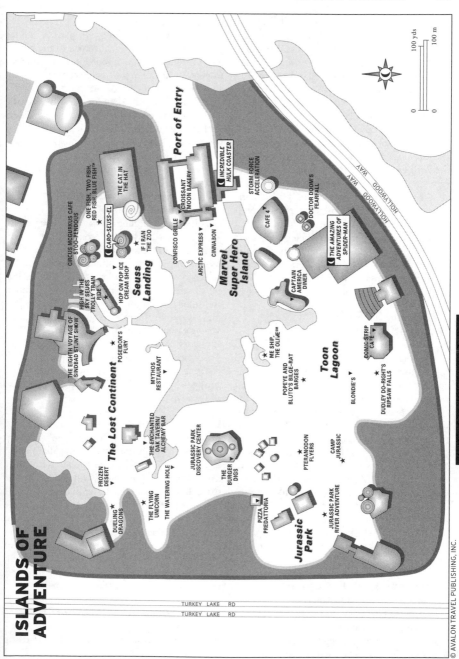

ISLANDS OF ADVENTURE

Port of Entry

Seuss Landing
- CIRCUS MCGURKUS CAFE STOO-PENDOUS
- ONE FISH, TWO FISH, RED FISH, BLUE FISH
- THE CAT IN THE HAT
- CARO-SEUSS-EL
- IF I RAN THE ZOO
- HOP ON POP ICE CREAM SHOP
- HIGH IN THE SKY SEUSS TROLLY TRAIN RIDE

Marvel Super Hero Island
- INCREDIBLE HULK COASTER
- CROISSANT MOON BAKERY
- CONFISCO GRILLE
- ARCTIC EXPRESS
- CINNABON
- STORM FORCE ACCELERATION
- CAFE 4
- DOCTOR DOOM'S FEARFALL
- THE AMAZING ADVENTURES OF SPIDER-MAN
- CAPTAIN AMERICA DINER

Toon Lagoon
- ME SHIP, THE OLIVE
- POPEYE AND BLUTO'S BILGE-RAT BARGES
- COMIC STRIP CAFE
- BLONDIE'S
- DUDLEY DO-RIGHT'S RIPSAW FALLS

The Lost Continent
- THE EIGHTH VOYAGE OF SINDBAD STUNT SHOW
- POSEIDON'S FURY
- MYTHOS RESTAURANT
- THE ENCHANTED OAK TAVERN/ALCHEMY BAR
- FROZEN DESERT
- DUELING DRAGONS
- THE FLYING UNICORN
- THE WATERING HOLE

Jurassic Park
- JURASSIC PARK DISCOVERY CENTER
- THE BURGER DIGS
- PTERANODON FLYERS
- CAMP JURASSIC
- PIZZA PREDATTORIA
- JURASSIC PARK RIVER ADVENTURE

HOLLYWOOD WAY

TURKEY LAKE RD
TURKEY LAKE RD

100 yds
100 m

UNIVERSAL ORLANDO RESORT

© AVALON TRAVEL PUBLISHING, INC.

UNIVERSAL ORLANDO RESORT

good, making it easy to suspend disbelief and immerse oneself in the adventure at hand.

One caution: On a couple of visits, I encountered very pushy salespeople trying to entice me into time-share purchases and something involving laundry soap.

PORT OF ENTRY

As with Production Central in Universal Studios, the Port of Entry is the get-your-bearings-and-eat-a-snack area of the park, just north of the park entrance. Part Arabian bazaar, part New England seaside town, the theming in this area is dramatic and attractive, if a bit confused. Spend your time here charting a plan of attack with the park map while snarfing a pastry from Croissant Moon Bakery. Do your shopping here before departing the park in the afternoon. You'll also find locker, wheelchair, and stroller rentals as well as guest services (407/224-4233) here.

MARVEL SUPER HERO ISLAND

Just to the west of the Port of Entry, this island is all about monster rides inspired by Marvel superheroes and villains. The main drag of this comic book city is Stan Lee Boulevard, named for the Marvel cocreator. Generally, this is the first area people visit in the park—perfect for the thrill-ride enthusiast, but with precious little for younger children to do. When traveling with kids of varying ages, it might behoove some of your crowd to head west from the park entrance, toward Marvel, and some to head due east, toward Seuss Landing. You're likely to see masked avengers ambling around in tights on the hour, and Spidey appears nearly all day long at the Marvel Alterniverse Store for photo ops. This island has four main rides, listed here from most awesome to least.

◖ Incredible Hulk Coaster

My favorite coaster in Orlando, it's more than two minutes long and stunningly smooth, but with so many inversions, camelbacks, and corkscrews that not even the biggest adrenaline junkie feels shortchanged. The queue is somewhat bare

bones, with lots of fence and pipes painted Hulk-green to herd people along. No matter, as once you reach the ride you realize you didn't need a lot of careful theming about Dr. Bruce Banner to get you in the mood. I don't mean to spoil any surprises, but the ride turns a classic coaster cliché on its ear—the slow "tick-tick-tick" of the initial long ascent is done away with, so riders are launched upward 150 feet at top speed. Top speeds of 67 mph, two subterranean trenches, fog, freefall—this ride has it all.

Tips: The height requirement is 54 inches.

◖ The Amazing Adventures of Spider-Man

Get off the Hulk feeling a little rubber-legged and waddle west to Spidey, the second-best attraction in the park. At more than 1.5 acres, this dark ride is essentially a souped-up simulator that uses a 12-passenger spinning "news van," 3-D glasses, dozens of screens, and a barrage of fireballs, water, and smoke to tell this superhero's tale. The pre-show is one of the more enjoyable and follows the quotidian woes of the *Daily Bugle,* and the 100-story "drop" off the top of a New York City skyscraper is utterly memorable.

Tips: The height requirement is 40 inches; younger kids may be frightened by the noise and visuals.

Doctor Doom's Fearfall

Dr. Doom's plan: Suck the fear from your very marrow. To oblige the enterprising villain, strap in and zoom 185 feet into the air with more thrust than a 747 jet engine and faster than the space shuttle. Then drop faster than gravity. The height requirement is 52 inches. The downside is that lines can be long and the ride itself is very, very short. The upside is that the views from the top are wonderful, if fleeting. There are two 200-foot towers side by side to cut down on wait times (their height makes them good landmarks when you're navigating the park).

Storm Force Acceleration

A teacup ride on steroids, this one's theming is about Storm from the X-Men, battling Magneto.

© 2007 UNIVERSAL ORLANDO. ALL RIGHTS RESERVED.

Doctor Doom's Fearfall

TOON LAGOON

Walk due north from Marvel to Toon Lagoon, the water-centric part of Islands of Adventure and with a careful veneer of the Sunday funny pages. More than 150 cartoon cutouts of Popeye, Beetle Bailey, and Betty Boop, along with sometimes cryptic, sometimes charming dialogue bubbles, lend this area a more nostalgic feel than elsewhere in the park. Its crowd density is entirely contingent upon the weather—on a warm day this is the busiest part of the park; on a cool day, every ride is walk-on.

Dudley Do-Right's Ripsaw Falls

As usual, Dudley Do-Right has to save Nell from the emphatically mustachioed Snidely Whiplash, and we're along for the ride—only it's over the falls in a log. Seasoned flume riders won't see anything new here, but it's a nice way to get wet on a hot day, with a healthy 75-foot drop.

Tips: The height requirement is 44 inches.

Popeye and Bluto's Bilge-Rat Barges

A 12-seater white-water raft much like Kali

River Rapids at Walt Disney World's Animal Kingdom and Congo River Rapids at Busch Gardens, this ride isn't reinventing the wheel, but on a hot day who needs a new wheel? The theming is about the conflict between Popeye and Bluto for Olive Oyl's affections, but it's essentially bumps, drifts, and dips on a water course and guaranteed to get you soaked.

Tips: Bring a poncho or garbage bag to wear if you don't relish being wet. The height requirement is 42 inches.

Me Ship, the *Olive*

People not tall enough to go on the other two rides in this area can exact their revenge: Water cannons can be fired from this interactive three-level play ship to hit the unsuspecting folks riding Popeye and Bluto's white-water rafts. Beyond this payback, the area boasts slides, crawl spaces, musical instruments, and net climbs. Benches make it a reasonable place for a break.

JURASSIC PARK

Walk due east from Toon Lagoon and you'll enter Jurassic Park, the largest of the five islands at more than 21 acres and the most overrated part of Islands of Adventure. There just isn't that much to do here, and the best ride is really not too different from what you've experienced in Toon Lagoon. The conceit here is that, as in the movies of the same name, dinosaurs come back to life on a tropical island and you get to wander among them, if you dare. The landscaping is lovely and dense, so it's pleasant to walk around—I just kept looking for something to do.

Jurassic Park River Adventure

Starting as a leisurely ride that gets steadily more hair-raising, this is another boat/flume ride that's gussied up with animatronic velociraptors and one formidable *T. rex,* along with an excellent 85-foot drop at the end. If you've just exited the Toon Lagoon water rides, this will seem redundant unless you're fond of having ever-sodden underpants.

Tips: Wear a poncho or bring dry clothes to change into. The height requirement is 42 inches.

© 2007 UNIVERSAL ORLANDO. ALL RIGHTS RESERVED.

UNIVERSAL ORLANDO RESORT

The Lost Continent

Pteranodon Flyers

Two single-person swings, which look like pterodactyl skeletons, are attached to a skyway-style tram on which you and a buddy zoom overhead in Jurassic Park. For just a quick bird's-eye view, the ride is crazy-short.

Tips: The ride is designed for children 36–56 inches tall, and if you are over the height limit you may ride only accompanying a child. The big problem is that the wait is often the very longest in the park. You may wait in line for an hour, only to ride your flyer for less than a minute.

Jurassic Park Discovery Center

Billed as a hands-on interactive area, it's not much more than a hamburger restaurant and gift shop. You'll find some dinosaur skeleton replicas, a game "sequencer" that pretends to combine your DNA with that of a dinosaur, fake dinosaur births, and a few other interactive games, all set in a vast building that is supposed to look like the visitors center in the film. All that said, during a summer thundershower it's the place to kill time.

Camp Jurassic

A very well-executed, multilevel children's play area, Camp Jurassic features dark "amber mines," net climbing and rope bridges, water guns, and twisty passages. It's easy to get a little lost, so younger children shouldn't be allowed to roam free. The best part is a series of dinosaur footprints, which you step on to hear that particular dinosaur's noise, emanating creepily from the woods nearby.

THE LOST CONTINENT

Completely across the park from Marvel Super Hero Island, this is the other locus of major thrill rides. As you come due east from Jurassic Park, you'll first encounter Merlin Woods, then Sindbad Village, and finally Lost City—all in a mystical/magical Ye Olde Renaissance Faire idiom interspersed with colossal ruins. There are a couple of good places to eat here (Mythos Restaurant and The Enchanted Oak), along with a bar that does a robust happy-hour business, and rides that represent the greatest breadth of any of the five islands in the park.

© 2007 UNIVERSAL ORLANDO. ALL RIGHTS RESERVED.

Dueling Dragons pits park-goers on dueling coasters.

UNIVERSAL ORLANDO RESORT

Dueling Dragons

This is a truly great idea, whereby riders are presented with a choice of two coasters and then pitted against each other; they swirl and spin around each other through five inversions and corkscrews and come within a foot of each other a few times. (The full trains are weighed to synch the timing of the near-collision points, thwarted by a camelback roll, a double helix, and compound inversion.) I found myself hairy-eyeballing the riders on Fire when I was on Ice and then doing the same to the Ice crew when I was with the Fire posse. There's nothing wrong with a little park-goer rivalry if it includes a great coaster ride. Not quite as smooth or long as the Hulk, it's still a thrilling ride (although Fire goes a little faster than Ice). A theming story goes with this—something about two battling dragons named Pyrrock and Blizzrock laying waste to an unsuspecting castle—but this might get lost in riders' enthusiasm to hop aboard.

Tips: The height requirement is 54 inches.

Lines can be long, with even longer lines for the front row.

Poseidon's Fury

Poseidon's Temple is hard to miss, its interior cooling and dark. But now what? It's a 20-minute walk-through with a tour guide/archaeologist, exploring creepy undersea chambers, some filled with treasures and warrior bones, another with a 42-foot spinning vortex of 17,500 gallons of water (you stay dry). What starts as an archaeological expedition soon segues to a story line involving an epic battle between Poseidon and the evil Darkenon, with park-goers in the crossfire, complete with explosions and fireballs.

Tips: One of the park's only live shows, it's exciting but not appropriate for kids under six. During peak season, lines can be untenably long.

The Eighth Voyage of Sindbad Stunt Show

A 1,700-seat open-air amphitheater live-action

UNIVERSAL ORLANDO RESORT

stunt show meant to compete with Disney's Indiana Jones show, it plays at least a couple of times each day. The plotline is goofy and clichéd (Sindbad and his zany sidekick Shish Kabob try to rescue princess Amoura from the evil witch, Miseria), but the stunts are pretty good. There are big water explosions, a flaming high dive in which a stunt person is set on fire and dives into a watery pit, and some almost-plausible fight scenes. The theater itself is well conceived, with drippy blue stalagmites and ghostly shipwrecks. There are two splash zones, one at the front right and the other near the ship prow that extends into the seating area. After the show, toss a coin into the **Mystic Fountain** outside.

The Flying Unicorn

A simple training-wheels coaster, it reaches speeds of 28 mph and has a 30-foot drop. The height requirement is 36 inches.

SEUSS LANDING

Under no circumstances should visitors think of Seuss Landing as the little-kid ghetto. The most gorgeous part of the park, it will take your breath away with its sheer imagination and whimsy, especially if you are among the legions who have logged innumerable hours reading *Go, Dog. Go!* and *The Cat in the Hat.* Closest to the exit, on the right-hand side of the park, this "island" is something of a grand finale. Even the lampposts, signage, music, and concessions are Seuss-inspired, with not a straight line in evidence anywhere.

(Caro-Seuss-el

At the core of it all is a stunning all-Seuss-character interactive, 47-foot-diameter merry-go-round. While the kids hop on board one of 54 magical creatures, adults will be naming as many as they can: "That's a Cowfish from *McElligot's Pool,* and that's a Dog-a-lope from *If I Ran the Zoo.*" Going a regular carousel one better, most of the mounts have special features: Pull the collar and the head might move; pull a lever and its eyes blink or the nose wiggles.

Tips: This is especially nice for those in a wheelchair, as the ride has a special wheelchair platform that raises and lowers.

The Cat in the Hat

This is another exceptionally themed ride, but I hesitate to hype this one quite as much because on two separate visits something on the ride busted, once causing all of us to disembark and wander back through the tunnel to the exit. Guests load onto moving six-person couches, very colorful and Seusslike, only to enter the world of that mischievous cat, the long-suffering fish, and Thing 1 and Thing 2 (you can buy excellent "Thing" T-shirts in one of the gift shops). It's a dark ride, just slightly creepy at times, rushing past more than a dozen scenes with animatronic characters and projected animation to tell the tale of just what happened "all that cold, cold, wet day."

Tips: The couch twirls and races with a spoken Seuss soundtrack—it's appropriate for everyone, but little kids might get nervous at points.

One Fish Two Fish Red Fish Blue Fish

Again, the theming is gorgeously executed on this somewhat familiar ride in which guests steer a three-person fish through an obstacle course with squirting fountains. At first a rhyming song gives riders guidance about when to ascend and when to descend to avoid the squirts, but by the end you're on your own. Wet but not soaked, everyone has fun on this one.

If I Ran the Zoo

Set the kids loose in this Seuss-styled interactive play area. It may provide some of the best photo ops of the day, with three sections—Hedges, Water, and the New Zoo—and lots of things to do and see. There's also a lovely little maze.

High in the Sky Seuss Trolley Train Ride

One of the park's newest additions, it's an absolute must for Seussophiles. About six years in the making, it was unveiled in 2006. On two separate tracks, riders board and get a 20-feet-up, bird's-eye view of all of Seuss Landing, even traveling on the trolley right through Circus McGurkus Café Stoo-pendous. The theming here is heavy on the Sneeches, but other Seuss creatures crop up.

Tips: The height requirement is 34 inches; children 34–48 inches must be accompanied by an adult.

FOOD AND SHOPPING

Each of the park's "islands" offers a range of dining options. As at Universal Studios, the park offers a meal deal whereby adults can eat all day at Circus McGurkas Café Stoo-pendous, Comic Strip Café, or Captain America Diner for $18.99, children nine and younger eat for $8.99—it's not particularly economical if you intend to eat breakfast and dinner elsewhere.

Character Dining

Like Universal Studios, the park hosts a "character" breakfast buffet Thursday–Sunday mornings at **Confisco Grille** (reservations 407/224-4012, $15.95 adults, $9.95 children nine and younger). You'll meet Spider-Man and The Cat in the Hat—strange dining companions. Wonder what they have to talk about?

Port of Entry

The **Confisco Grille** ($8.95–17.95) offers table-service sandwiches and burgers, salads, fajitas, a low-carb menu, and a full bar, while **Croissant Moon Bakery** offers counter-service *paninis,* pastries, and cheesecakes. **Cinnabon's** sugary confections are as big as your head and **Arctic Express** purveys ice creams and funnel cakes.

Get all of your photography needs met at **De Foto's Expedition Photography,** including photo pick-up (plus two-way radio rentals). The **Port of Entry Christmas Shoppe** features ornaments, decorations, and assorted holiday cheer. **Island Market and Export Candy**

Shoppe is your go-to spot for fudge and other sugary decadence. Logo clothing and merchandise can be found at **Port Provisions** and **Islands of Adventure Trading Company.**

Marvel Super Hero Island

Here you'll find **Cafe 4** for counter-service pizza, pasta, and Caesar salads. The **Captain America Diner** sends out counter-service cheeseburgers, chicken sandwiches, chicken fingers, and chicken salads.

Got webs? For all your Spider-Man accoutrements, head to the **Spider-Man Shop.** For other Marvel comics collectibles and apparel, hit **Marvel Alterniverse Store.** There's also a comic book shop called the, um, **Comic Book Shop** and an **Oakley** store for cool shades both for superheroes and mere mortals.

Toon Lagoon

Because of its location, Toon Lagoon ends up being where lots of people choose to eat lunch. **Comic Strip Café** dishes out cafeteria-style Chinese, Italian, New England, and Mexican staples, **Wimpy's** serves burgers (duh) and chicken wraps, **Blondie's** does fat Dagwood sandwiches (double duh), and **Cathy's Ice Cream** does ice cream (except it's Ben and Jerry's).

At **Gasoline Alley** you'll pick up kids' games and cartoons. There's a **Betty Boop Store** for the diehard fan, and another, more general interest accessories and apparel shop called **Toon Extra.**

Jurassic Park

The hungry will find pizza at **Pizza Predattoria,** ribs and chicken at **Thunder Falls Terrace,** burgers at **The Burger Digs,** and frozen froufrou drinks at **The Watering Hole.** All venues are counter service.

Dinosaur-related merchandise is convened at **Dinostore,** and suitable dino-hunting attire can be acquired at **Jurassic Outfitters.**

The Lost Continent

The Lost Continent has the park's best sit-down place with hip and contemporary

Mythos Restaurant (reservations accepted, 407/224-4012, $12.95–18.95), as well as nicely done ribs, chicken, and turkey legs at **The Enchanted Oak Tavern** ($5.95–12.95). When you feel like a drink, head for the **Alchemy Bar,** for sundaes try the **Frozen Desert,** and for gyros, hot dogs, or chicken fingers, head to **Fire Eater's Grill.**

Get a psychic reading or a henna tattoo at **Star Souls,** the most interesting shopping in the park. Buy dragon doodads at **The Dragon's Keep,** watch glass being blown at **Chimera Glass,** or pick up a coat of arms while doing a little genealogy research at **Historic Families - Heraldry.** If that all seems too out there, there are tame snow globes and souvenirs at **Treasures of Poseidon.**

Seuss Landing

Kids seem to enjoy the familiar offerings at **Circus McGurkus Café Stoo-pendous,** but they are quite terrified of the green egg-and-ham sandwiches from **Green Eggs and Ham Cafe** (but the burgers are less menacing). Ice cream is the finale at **Hop on Pop Ice Cream Shop,** but the pious might opt instead for a fruit cup from **Moose Juice Goose Juice.**

Cat in the Hat hats (along with Thing One and Thing Two T-shirts) can be picked up at **Cats, Hats & Things.** All the Dr. Seuss books are assembled at **All The Books You Can Read.** There's also a **Snookers & Snookers Sweet Candy Cookers** candy shop, and **Mulberry Street Store** sells other Seuss merchandise and creatures.

CityWalk

There's something very Vegas about CityWalk. To that, some of you may say, "Yee-haw," while others raise a concerned eyebrow. Orlando is the number two convention site in the country, second only to that playground in Nevada. And like Sin City, Orlando manages to entertain people with more than mouse ears, which means on any given night, Universal's 30-acre adult playground of restaurants, nightclubs, and music venues is chockablock with thousands of pharmaceutical salesmen, orthopedists, certified public accountants, and Sysco managers who have been cooped up in meetings all day and just want to play. Not that Orlando will adopt the "what happens in Orlando, stays in Orlando" credo anytime soon, but CityWalk may harbor its share of secrets, or at least hazy memories.

Opened in 1999, CityWalk keeps retooling and rethinking its concepts, so there is constantly something buzz-worthy along its length. It's right at the entrance to both Universal Studios and Islands of Adventure, with a gorgeous 20-screen AMC movie theater and a real range of dining and imbibing possibilities open along a two-tiered promenade. Guests can buy a party pass for $9.95 for unlimited admission to the clubs for one evening (reasonable only if you arrive after 9 or 10 P.M. when restaurants and clubs start charging cover). For $19.95, guests can enjoy dinner at one of the restaurants followed by a movie. Some might prefer just ambling along, enjoying a cocktail here, an appetizer there, a bit of jazz somewhere else. Parking is free in the two multilevel parking structures after 6 P.M., defraying the cost of an evening on the town. For more information about CityWalk, call guest services at 407/224-5500.

ENTERTAINMENT

Most of these nightclubs also serve food, but it's my impression that the following are more about evening entertainment than comestibles. Most have a $7 cover charge; for more information, call 407/224-3663.

Added to CityWalk in 2006, **The Red Coconut Club** (6 P.M.–2 A.M. daily) has a lovely all-ages vibe, live music or DJ, two stories and a long bar, capacious martinis, and good appetizer specials during happy hour, 6–8 P.M. For a bad behavior–inducing Hurricane, try **Pat O'Brien's** (4 P.M.–2 A.M. daily, $7.95–15.95) with its dueling pianos and "flaming fountain" patio. **CityJazz** (8 P.M.–1 A.M. Sun.–Thurs., until 2 A.M. Fri. and Sat.) features live jazz with a slightly more mature/staid atmosphere (comedy Thurs.–Sun. nights). When you feel like shaking it to '70s and '80s dance tunes, head on over to **The Groove** (9 P.M.–2 A.M. daily). Of course, being a girl of the 1980s, for me this entails wiggling my arms in the air and whooping occasionally—20th-century dance behavior that is fully sanctioned here.

SHOPPING

Shopping at CityWalk mostly comprises impulse-buy souvenir shops, with nothing particularly upscale or notable. You'll find character apparel and memorabilia at **Cartooniversal,** the obvious incendiary delights of **Cigarz at CityWalk,** and an **Endangered Species Store** worth a few minutes of idle exploration. For new duds, check out **The Island Clothing Store** for Tommy Bahama and Lilly Pulitzer beachwear, **Quiet Flight Surf Shop** for surf duds, and bright cotton clothing for the whole family at **Fresh Produce. Fossil** sells watches and other apparel and accessories.

FOOD
Casual Dining

Just at the complex's entrance, **Pastamoré** (5 P.M.–midnight daily, 407/363-8000, $8–20) is a comfortable family-style Italian eatery, serving all the usual suspects in a sit-down environment or to-go all day at the Marketplace Cafe. Added to the complex in July 2006, the equally comfortable **The Bubba Gump Shrimp Co. Restaurant and Market** (11:30 A.M.–midnight daily, 407/903-0044, $10–18) is a tribute to shrimp first, Forrest Gump second. The decor is a signature blend of flotsam, jetsam, and memorabilia (the first theme restaurant inspired by a film, very appropriate for Universal), and the waitstaff is aggressively perky.

With live entertainment nightly, often of the Jimmy Buffett variety, **Margaritaville** (11:30 A.M.–2 A.M. daily, $5 cover after 10 P.M., free with theme park ticket stub for that day, priority seating, 407/224-2155, $14–25) is the

UNIVERSAL ORLANDO RESORT

© 2007 UNIVERSAL ORLANDO. ALL RIGHTS RESERVED.

Emeril's Restaurant Orlando – BAM!

local Parrothead paradise, with three bars and accessible Floribbean cuisine, heavy on the lime and tequila. The Lone Palm Airport is the restaurant's newest lounge; drinks are served in Jimmy Buffett's very own grounded seaplane, the *Hemisphere Dancer.*

Rendered islands-mellow from a run-in with a cheeseburger in paradise, head to **Bob Marley–A Tribute to Freedom** (4 P.M.–2 A.M. daily, 407/224-3663, $7 cover after 8 P.M., $9–20) for a bit of reggae, mon. It has a hip open-air veranda and courtyard, and the restaurant (a re-creation of Marley's home in Kingston, Jamaica) features photos, artifacts, and video highlight clips from his musical career.

Set off to one side is the biggest **Hard Rock Cafe** (11 A.M.–2 A.M. daily, 407/351-7625, $11–24) in the world—a veritable "Roman Colosseum of rock," replete with memorabilia from Kiss, Elvis, The Beatles, and Bob Dylan, along with an all-American menu of burgers, ribs, and salads. In its second incarnation, **NASCAR Sports Grille** (formerly NASCAR Café, 11 A.M.–midnight, 407/224-7223, $11–22) is brand new on the scene as of winter 2007, with table-side plasma screens, simulator games, and an outdoor "Tailgating Experience." The menu is familiar ribs, pasta,

and sandwiches. Similar in style, but with another all-American idiom at work, **NBA City** (11 A.M.–10:30 P.M. Sun.–Thurs., until 11:30 P.M. Fri. and Sat, 407/363-5919, $15–22) gives you exclusive NBA-created programming along with a familiar menu of pizzas, pastas, burgers, and salads, more expertly crafted than they have to be.

The **Latin Quarter** (4–10 P.M. daily, 407/224-3663, $8–20), on the other hand, is a bit of a disappointment in its interpretations of Latin American/Caribbean fare, but the live music and dancing compensate for it.

You'll also find a big **Starbucks,** a big **Cinnabon,** and a big **TCBY,** all ready to satisfy big cravings.

Fine Dining
Kick it up a notch (wait, was that Emeril or that other loud guy?) and head to 【 **Emeril's Restaurant Orlando** (11:30 A.M.–2 P.M. and 5:30 P.M.–10 P.M. daily, an hour later on Fri. and Sat., 407/224-2424, $25–50) for Emeril Lagasse upscale spins on Louisiana-style oyster stew, duck, and rib eye. The cocktails are good, but the 12,000-bottle wine list merits some robust consideration. A notable cigar bar and all-prime beef makes for an expense-account paradise.

Accommodations

ON-SITE HOTELS
Three hotels are on the property, each with its own flavor and price point. Each is within walking distance of Universal Studios, Islands of Adventure, and CityWalk, and guests get "Universal Express" preferred access to theme park rides and attractions, along with priority seating at most on-site restaurants and shows. Other features are courtesy water taxi and bus transportation between the resort and park, free package delivery of in-park purchases to guest rooms, and you can use your resort ID to charge purchases throughout Universal Orlando.

The following on-site properties are listed

here from least expensive to most. For reservations at any of the on-site hotel restaurants, call 407/503-3463.

Royal Pacific Resort
The Loews Royal Pacific Resort (6300 Hollywood Way, 407/503-3000, rates from $129) has a South Pacific vibe, complete with luscious tropical landscaping and lagoons on a 53-acre property. It's big, with 1,000 rooms and 85,000 square feet of meeting space, so you'll see a preponderance of business and convention travelers here, swirling around the central fountain of the lobby's Orchid Court or the ac-

© 2007 UNIVERSAL ORLANDO, ALL RIGHTS RESERVED.

Vacation like a rock star at the Hard Rock Hotel.

tive lobby bar. Rooms are attractive, with standard rooms and suites in a vaguely Indonesian/ Dutch colonial style. The huge Lagoon Pool is family friendly (water play area, kiddie pool), and you'll find a putting green, stage area for shows, and several worthwhile restaurants, including Emeril Lagasse's Tchoup Chop.

RESTAURANTS
Emeril's Tchoup Chop (pronounced "chop-chop", 11:30 A.M.–2:30 P.M. and 5:30–10 P.M. daily, until 11 P.M. Fri.–Sat., $20–30) is an upscale, imaginative pan-Pacific culinary romp in a stunning dining room. **The Islands Dining Room** (7 A.M.–2:30 P.M., 5–10 P.M. daily; breakfast $16.50 adults, $7.75 children 3–12; dinner $32.95 adults, $17.95 children 3–12) is a more straight-ahead hotel restaurant, serving three meals a day with buffets on some nights. Then there's the **Wantilan Luau** buffet (6 P.M. Sat., Fri. nights May 11–Aug. 31, $49.50 adults, $29 children under 12) every Saturday evening in the Royal Garden, complete with fire eaters and hula dancers; two bars, **Jake's American**

Bar and **Bula Bar and Grille,** next to the pool, admirably slake your thirst.

Hard Rock Hotel
For when you want to spend a little time up close with one of Elvis's rhinestone jumpsuits or a little footwear from Elton John's closet, head straight for the Hard Rock Hotel (5800 Universal Blvd., 407/503-7625, rates from $149), designed in a hip California mission style with 650 rooms. As with other Hard Rocks, the public spaces are chockablock with rock memorabilia, and huge video screens run concert footage. Some rooms face the gardens, others the pool area; a club level has rooms with large-screen TVs and other amenities such as fax machine, cordless phones, and breakfast and evening hors d'oeuvres (no extra charge). One particularly family-friendly feature of the Hard Rock, opened in 2001, is its kids' suites, featuring a main room equipped with a king and an adjoining room with two single beds and a small table and chair set. Be sure to request a wake-up call: You can choose your favorite rocker to whisper sweet nothings to you each morning. This Loews property is pet friendly. You'll find a nice on-site retail store for Hard Rock merchandise, a beach pool with a white sand beach and beach volleyball, and a handful of fun restaurants.

RESTAURANTS
The top offering at the Hard Rock Hotel is **The Palm Restaurant** (5–10 P.M. daily, $20–32), sister to the fabled New York City steak house, with walls covered with caricatures of celebrities. **The Kitchen** (7 A.M.–11 P.M. daily, $14–26) is more lighthearted, eclectic fun, whether you're enjoying Sammy Hagar's seared sea scallops or Dee Snyder's braised short ribs. Poolside, stop into the **Beach Club** for sandwiches and salads, or maybe try a cocktail in the hip lobby's **Velvet Bar.**

Portofino Bay Hotel
The 🅒 **Portofino Bay Hotel** (5601 Universal Blvd., 407/503-1000, rates from $159) aims for Mediterranean luxury. Opened in 1999, the

Portofino Bay Hotel

© 2007 UNIVERSAL ORLANDO. ALL RIGHTS RESERVED.

hotel features 750 rooms in a kind of Italian seaside village environment. It's won awards such as the AAA Four Diamond Award and a place in *Travel and Leisure Magazine*'s "Top 500 Hotels in the World," mostly for its lovely rooms with garden or bay views and its wide array of amenities (integrated entertainment centers with bells and whistles, high-speed Internet access for $9.95/day). A Loews hotel, it's pet friendly with a well-run Campo Portofino supervised children's activity program that takes advantage of the property's three themed pools. Restaurants on-site vary from upscale to family-friendly Italian, an ice-cream shop, a deli, and a couple of bars. The Portofino Bay also boasts the full-service Mandara Spa and more than 42,000 square feet of meeting space, with a 15,040-square-foot Tuscan Ballroom.

RESTAURANTS

Portofino Bay has a number of worthwhile options in an Italian idiom. The very gastronomically forward special-occasion **(Bice Ristorante** (5:30–10 P.M. daily, $30–50) wins regularly for best local Italian. The fanciest restaurant on the property, it also offers a great view of Portofino Harbor. For everyday occasions, try the more family-oriented **Mama Della's Ristorante** (5–10 P.M. daily, $22–34). **Trattoria del Porto** (7 A.M.–3 P.M. daily, 5 P.M.–11 P.M. Thurs.–Mon.) serves breakfast, lunch, and dinner with an extensive buffet (dinner buffet $29.95 adults, $12.95 children). You can buy quick bites at **Sal's Market Deli** (11 A.M.–11 P.M. daily) or poolside at **Splendido Pizzeria** or a cocktail from **Thirsty Fish** (6 P.M.–2 A.M. Mon.–Fri., noon–2 A.M. Sat., noon–midnight Sun.).

UNIVERSAL PARTNER HOTELS

The official partner hotels offer super-shuttle service to the parks and CityWalk, a passport of savings coupons, a Destination Universal Desk for tickets and information, and, in many cases, golf reservations and free transportation to select area courses.

Under $100
Fairfield Inn and Suites near Universal Orlando (5614 Vineland Rd., 407/581-5600, rates from $89) is close to Universal (less than two miles), with 96 rooms on six floors. It offers free continental breakfast and high-speed Internet access. Also, guests can play golf at Windermere Country Club. Another **Fairfield Inn and Suites by Marriott** (7495 Canada Ave., 407/351-7000, rates from $85) is within one mile of Universal, with all of the same features and a nice heated pool.

$100-150
LaQuinta Inn and Suites Orlando Convention Center (8504 Universal Blvd., 407/345-1365, rates from $109) is within two miles of Universal, with 184 rooms on seven floors, a serviceable pool, and includes high-speed Internet access and breakfast.

Close enough to walk to, **Doubletree Hotel at the Entrance to Universal** (5780 Major Blvd., 407/351-1000, rates from $107) is a 19-floor high-rise with 742 rooms with exceptionally cushy beds and those signature chocolate chip cookies. Also within a mile of Universal, **Holiday Inn at the Entrance to Universal** (5905 Kirkman Road, 407/351-3333, rates from $119) is another large budget-minded hotel with nearly 400 rooms, 134 of which are

family-size suites with your choice of one- or two-bedroom floor plans, complete with full kitchens. The on-site restaurant is T.G.I. Friday's (7 A.M.–10 P.M. daily).

Geared a little more for the business traveler, **Embassy Suites International Drive/ Jamaican Court** (8250 Jamaican Ct., 800/327-9797, rates from $155) is close to Universal and the Orlando Convention Center, with 246 two-room suites, cooked-to-order breakfast, and wireless high-speed Internet access throughout the hotel.

For something special, book at the 【 **Rosen Shingle Creek** (9939 Universal Blvd., 866/996-9939, rates from $109), a sister property to the Rosen Plaza Hotel and a variety of other Rosen properties in Orlando. Opened in September 2006, it's set on 230 acres of lush landscape (with a David Harman–designed championship golf course and the on-site Brad Brewer Golf Academy) along Shingle Creek, the headwaters for the Florida Everglades. Drawing on "Real Florida" history, notably Patrick Smith's *A Land Remembered,* the huge luxury property has pools, restaurants, and amenities that make it ideal for family travel, but with 445,000 square feet of meeting space (including the country's biggest column-free ballroom) it competes with the convention center and Kissimmee's Gaylord Palms for large-scale special events.

Practicalities

INFORMATION AND SERVICES
Child Swap
Sounds tempting sometimes, doesn't it? Really, what this means is that one parent or older member of the family watches over a small child while everyone else rides the ride, and then there's a line-free option for the waiting adult to hop on afterward. Ask the ride attendant about where to stand.

Guest Services
Guest services are within the entrance to each

park, each offering first aid. In addition, the main health services station is on Canal Street right across from Beetlejuice's Graveyard Revue at Universal Studios, and in Sindbad's Village within The Lost Continent in Islands of Adventure. Companion restrooms are at first-aid locations.

Kennels
Guests can board their pets for the day (no overnight boarding) at the kennel in the parking structure (ask the toll-plaza attendant for directions). Cost is $10 per pet per day, and

guests must provide food and return periodically to walk their pets. The kennel closes two hours after the last park closes.

Lockers

Lockers are available within each park for $8 per day, with family-size lockers available at Universal Studios for $10. Additional lockers are available at Islands of Adventure for $2 per hour, with a $14 per day maximum. These lockers are available at the entrance of the Incredible Hulk Coaster, Dueling Dragons, and Jurassic Park River Adventure.

A number of the rides require that you put your loose belongings in a locker, banks of which are provided just outside each ride. The first hour is free, so it costs nothing to move your purse and camera around the park from locker to locker. On the other hand, the locker system is a nightmare—terminals, offered in multiple languages, walk you through identifying a locker and using a thumbprint identification for unlocking it. It is imperative that you remember your locker number—no small feat after you've had five or six different ones around the park—and the thumbprint technology sometimes malfunctions. I saw countless people in near tears as they (a) tried to find their locker and (b) tried to open it.

Rentals

Guests can rent strollers ($10 single, $16 double), wheelchairs ($12, plus $50 deposit), and electric convenience vehicles (ECV, $40, plus $50 deposit) upon entrance to either park, to the left side of each entrance. Manual wheelchairs are also available at the rotunda area of the parking structure. Because of limited supply, make reservations for ECV rentals (407/224-4233).

Special Needs

Most shows at the parks offer assisted-listening devices and several of the larger shows offer sign language interpretation. For expectant mothers, those in wheelchairs or with disabilities, and the elderly, it's a rough day at the park—many of the rides and attractions, especially at Islands of Adventure, warn you off with strident signage. A day at Universal Studios entails a lot more sightseeing, making it the better choice for those in wheelchairs or with mobility issues.

GETTING THERE AND AROUND

Universal Orlando is north of the International Drive resort area, framed by I-4 to the south, Highway 435 (Kirkman Road) to the east, Vineland Road to the north, and Turkey Lake Road to the west. From I-4 eastbound, take Exit 75A. From I-4 westbound, take Exit 74B. From there, follow the signs to Universal Orlando's main parking garage or to one of the three resort hotels.

Parking

Two very well-designed multilevel enclosed parking garages service both parks and City-Walk, accessible by moving sidewalks, escalators, and elevators. Parking is $10 for cars, vans, and motorcycles, $11 for RVs and trailers. Valet parking is available for cars and vans for $16; follow the signs for Valet Parking. Vehicles can leave and return the same day by stopping at the toll plaza upon reentry and presenting their parking ticket. After 6 P.M., parking is free in the garage, except on designated special-event nights.

Shuttle Service

From the on-site hotels there is free transportation to theme parks and CityWalk via water taxis and walkways throughout the resort; from partner hotels there are free shuttles.

Park Maps

Park maps are offered just inside the entrance to each park in English, French, Japanese, Spanish, Portuguese, and German. Take a couple, because they get wet and rumpled during the course of the day.

SEAWORLD ORLANDO

Orlando's 200-acre marine park has hosted more than 80 million visitors clamoring to see Shamu. The star of the park was in fact was born at SeaWorld Orlando on September 26, 1985, the first killer whale successfully born and raised in a zoological environment. Since then, the park has been blessed with the birth of 13 killer whales, the most recent, named "Trua" (Icelandic for "believe"), was born on Thanksgiving in 2005. It is the park's commitment to conservation, animal rescue and husbandry, and education that lifts SeaWorld Orlando so far above any other aquarium, zoo, or marine park.

While SeaWorld Orlando boasts the largest killer whale breeding program of any park, those orcas have a lot of competition for audience enthusiasm. Dolphins, sea lions, stingrays, penguins, sharks, and countless other aquatic creatures are on view in gorgeous walk-through exhibits, live shows, even up-close meet-and-greets. Add to these a few state-of-the-art thrill rides, and SeaWorld Orlando competes very ably with any of the Disney parks or Universal. And the sheer diversity of activities renders it an appropriate park for visitors of all ages, from very small children to the very elderly. Oh, and not to burst anyone's bubble, but there is more than one Shamu—it's really the stage name for all adult orcas in performances at SeaWorld parks.

HISTORY

SeaWorld Orlando has sister marine mammal parks in San Diego, California, and San Antonio, Texas (until 2001 there was another

COURTESY OF SEAWORLD ORLANDO

HIGHLIGHTS

LOOK FOR ◖ TO FIND RECOMMENDED SIGHTS, ACTIVITIES, DINING, AND LODGING.

◖ **Blue Horizons:** This new dolphin show is a study in more-is-more aesthetics. Dolphins compete with Cirque-like acrobats and divers, flocks of colorful birds, a stunning blue set of fake waves, and a stirring musical score for audience attention. The dolphins, with their powerful spirals and somersaults, handily win the competition (page 186).

◖ **Clyde and Seamore Take Pirate Island:** The swashbuckling adventure is really an excuse for first mate Clyde, the sea lion, to upstage his animal trainer/straight man. Two sea lions, an otter, and an impressively toothy walrus exhibit perfect comic timing in this pirate-themed family show (page 186).

◖ **Penguin Encounter:** More than 200 birds, all dressed up and with no place to go, inhabit this gorgeous, icy habitat. Time your visit for 1 P.M., when an aviculturist hosts a question-and-answer session with the audience. Answer the questions correctly and you may even get your own behind-the-scenes penguin encounter (page 188).

◖ **Shark Encounter:** Foreboding music and an artificial tropical reef studded with creepy, undulating moray eels gets you in the mood for SeaWorld Orlando's most impressively scary exhibit. Visitors glide on a moving walkway through a 124-foot acrylic tunnel, as sawtooth, nurse, brown, bull, and sandpiper sharks swim in a balletic swirl around you (page 190).

◖ **Kraken:** If you're a coaster junkie (and more than 54 inches tall), this is the park's headlining ride. The trains lack floors or sides as they climb 140 feet above the Serpent's lagoon only to plunge down a 14-story drop, through seven disorienting inversions, ultimately reaching speeds of 65 mph. (page 191).

in Cleveland, Ohio), all owned by Anheuser-Busch Company. Launched in 1964, the San Diego location was the first, the brainchild of four friends from UCLA. SeaWorld Orlando opened in 1973 and was purchased by Harcourt Brace Jovanovich, primarily a textbook publisher, in 1976. When the parks ran into a bit of financial hardship, Anheuser-Busch offered to buy the SeaWorld parks, eventually agreeing to buy all of HBJ's six theme parks (it also owned Cypress Gardens in Winter Haven and Boardwalk and Baseball in Baseball City). Then Anheuser-Busch sold off Cypress Gardens and closed Boardwalk and Baseball, focusing its attention on revitalizing the SeaWorld brand. The park has seen marked growth in recent years, with new stadium shows, thrill rides, and revitalized animal habitats, all with an overarching wildlife conservation theme. Although some animal-rights groups object to certain practices (SeaWorld parks own more than half of the killer whales in captivity), the Anheuser-Busch Adventure Parks are major supporters of wildlife conservation and research and education efforts at home and around the world.

PLANNING YOUR TIME

The entire park can be toured in a single day. However, if you have your heart set on seeing all of the major shows, they are timed such that it's tricky to catch all six of them on the same day. Build your itinerary around showtimes, which are printed daily on the back of the park map you receive at the park entrance. By zipping out a few minutes early here, missing a couple of minutes of another, you can hit all the high points.

Orientation

There are no thematic "lands" or discrete areas in SeaWorld Orlando, and there are no huge landmarks to orient you in the park (à la Epcot's giant golf ball or Magic Kingdom's castle), making it among the more difficult parks to navigate. And because visitors tend to organize their day around particular showtimes, people find themselves crisscrossing and backtracking

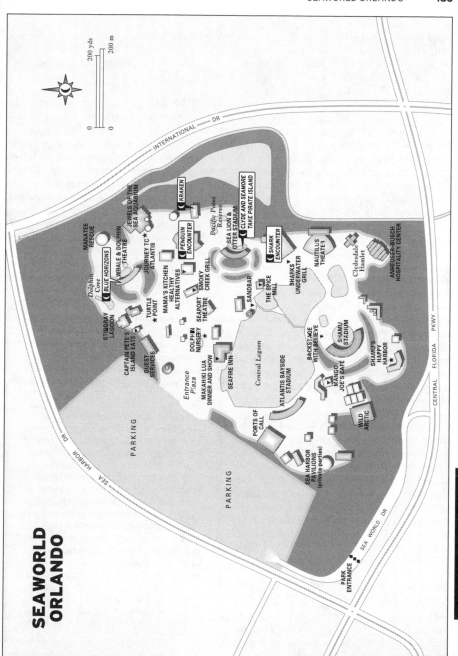

SEAWORLD ORLANDO

© AVALON TRAVEL PUBLISHING, INC.

to an annoying degree. Roughly at the center of the park is a 17-acre lagoon; to the northeast of that is Shamu Stadium; to the northwest of the lagoon is the Sea Lion and Otter Stadium; and due west is the Whale and Dolphin Theatre. The park's three biggest shows take place in these locales. One approach is to plan your day around how best to hit these three shows. On the other hand, one might simply start to the left of the entrance and travel clockwise around the park during the day, which will stagger seeing the various shows, ending with the last performance of Believe at Shamu Stadium in the early evening.

For general park information, call 800/327-2424 or visit the website at www.seaworld.com (a separate educational website worthy of a visit is at www.seaworld.org).

When to Go

Many people come to Orlando for a week and their first thought is Disney. For this reason, parks such as SeaWorld Orlando tend to be less crowded early in the week. It's Thursday through Sunday that often draw the crowds here, after visitors have spent several days touring the Disney offerings. On the other hand, it's a mellower experience than the Disney parks or Universal, so it may be good sandwiched between days with a more breakneck pace.

About two-thirds of the activities at SeaWorld Orlando are outdoors—this means that in January and February it's a fairly chilly time to visit, while summers can be punishingly hot. Unlike in the Disney parks, less effort has been expended to create shade areas for park-goers, so waiting in lines is slightly more arduous. On the other hand, this park's greatest attractions consist of large arena shows and walk-through exhibits (as opposed to seated rides), so there are fewer lines in which to stand.

Park Hours

SeaWorld Orlando is open every day of the year. The park's opening time is always 9 A.M., but the closing hour changes throughout the year. For much of January it is 6 P.M., February and March is 7 or 8 P.M., in April it's as late

as 10 P.M., May is mostly until 7 P.M., June–August the hours are until 9 or 10 P.M., September and October it's mostly until 7 P.M., and much of November and December it's open until 6 P.M.

What to Bring

Bring a waterproof camera so you can take photos of shows even if you find yourself in the soak zone. Because getting wet is part of the fun, consider bringing a change of clothes, bathing suits, or a jacket or sweater for when the day cools off. As at all the theme parks, bring sunscreen, sunglasses, hats, comfortable shoes, and water and snacks in a backpack. Young kids may want to bring a notepad or autograph book to collect the signatures of animal experts, water-skiers, and costumed characters.

AQUATICA

In the middle of 2006, SeaWorld Orlando announced plans to add a new water park to its complex, plans that were approved by Orange County in August 2006. Those plan are now in motion. Parent company Anheuser-Busch is scheduled to open the new water park in spring 2008. Aquatica, designed to compete with Disney's Lagoon and Blizzard Beaches and Universal's Wet 'n Wild, will be across the street from the main park, on the east side of International Drive and south of Sea Harbor Drive between the existing SeaWorld park and the Williamsburg residential subdivision. The 58-acre park will offer 36 water slides, six pools and lagoons, and an 80,000-square-foot beach. Visitors will come in close contact with marine life via a series of clear, acrylic flume slides that will jet folks through a lagoon containing South American dolphins. Said to be more upscale than SeaWorld Orlando, Aquatica will be one-third the size of the original park and twice the size of the oh-so-exclusive Discovery Cove – its calling-card a mix of aquatic thrill rides nestled in naturalistic settings.

Tickets

A **Single-Day Admission** to Seaworld Orlando is $61.95 adults, $49.95 children ages 3–9, free for those younger than three. Discounts are available for guests with disabilities, senior citizens (there are special discounts and one-hour symposiums on Tuesdays for seniors), military personnel, and AAA members. For Florida residents there is a special "twofer" deal for which you choose any two days, anytime in the calendar, for the price of one, $61.95 adult, $49.95 child. There is an additional savings if you buy tickets online, rolling adult admission back to $49.95, but purchases must be made seven days in advance.

If you plan to visit SeaWorld Orlando repeatedly, it makes sense to opt for one of the passport memberships. The **Fun Card** is unlimited general admission for the calendar year, for $66.95 adults, $54.95 children. A **Silver Passport** adds free parking, discounts on in-park purchases, and a monthly payment option for $94.94 adults, $84.95 children and seniors. The **Gold Passport** gives you unlimited access for 24 months with all the benefits of the Silver, for $144.95 adults, $134.95 children and seniors. For a sizable additional fee, Busch Gardens Tampa Bay and Adventure Island admission can be added to your passport tickets.

Shows

All shows are included in your regular ticket price, and most are offered several times each day with plenty of seating. Some venues close their doors at the beginning of the shows, so arrive on time. Also, many offer entertaining preshows for which arriving early is merited.

BELIEVE

The park's newest show, billed as the most ambitious project in the brand's 41-year history, was nearly four years in the making, replacing the old Shamu show in Shamu Stadium in May 2006. Yes, it's visually stunning and the killer whales never fail to inspire awe, but the heavy-handed "message" takes a lot of fun out of the experience.

Four 20-foot LED screens (one of them looking a little shabby already) work independently and then pull together to broadcast the story line: A young boy is obsessed with killer whales, carving their elegant fan-shaped tail fluke out of wood and racing his kayak out into the water to commune with these graceful animals. Fast-forward maybe 20 years and that same boy, all grown up but wearing the wooden whale fluke as a necklace, runs out to greet the audience in front of Shamu Stadium's gorgeous semicircular pool. A grave voice-over says something like, "There comes a time when you stop wondering and begin to believe...."

What follows is an amazing show of the trainers' deep connection with the park's group of killer whales, taking them through some 60 learned behaviors. Trainer and whale burst up out of the water, the trainer balanced on the whale's nose and costumed in black and white to look like a little biped orca. You'll see whale cuddling and dancing, and deep underwater balletic choreography between whale and trainer, visible through the glass front wall of the tank. The killer whales splash those in the "soak zone" (the first 20 rows) mischievously, the trainers "surf" the whales at breakneck speed. It's all good fun until a trainer comes out and delivers a philosophical rant about the privilege of working with these animals and "becoming one" with the killer whales. That much interspecies enthusiasm is meant to get you misty eyed but ends up making many visitors merely eye rolling.

Believe has a preshow movie short about penguins that's just plain silly, and then there's a very stirring tribute to American armed forces that precedes the show. During each show a child is picked out of the audience to get his or her own whale fluke necklace and to meet

Shamu up close—a nice touch, but with too much saccharine voice-over about the whales "helping us to believe in ourselves." Above- and below-water cameras project the action onto the big LED screens, and 100 speakers around the stadium broadcast a swelling original score performed by the Prague National Symphony Orchestra. While the stadium seats more than 5,000 people, try to arrive 30 minutes before showtime during peak season to ensure a seat.

(BLUE HORIZONS

Another new show, Blue Horizons may initially seem to be a kitchen-sink approach to putting on a show—there's so much going on at any given time that you run the risk of whiplash with all that neck swiveling. Still, it's a truly wonderful show, full of inventive approaches to staging a dolphin and false killer whale performance. The Whale and Dolphin Theatre has industrial-looking blue metal scaffolding 40 feet above a large front pool and several "back-stage" pools. Blue metal waves and iridescent bubbles complete the aquatic decor.

The theming for this half-hour show is loose, the back story a simple tale of a young girl, Marina, with a vivid imagination and an affection for the creatures of the wide open sea and the blue sky above. Trainers leap onto the stage dressed in costumes reminiscent of superhero garb, inspiring Marina to dive right in, meet a dolphin (he's chatty, with lots of trilling squeaks), and begin to commune with this intelligent species. The dolphin swimming is more impressive than that at the killer whale show, partly because there are more dolphins in the pool at one time, and partly because they swim at such dizzying speeds and with such agility. They spin, wave tails, zoom and twist with the trainers underwater, and shoot straight up out of the pool.

But there's much more going on: A fleet of blue and gold macaws jet over the heads of the crowd, a flock of sun conures zoom by later, and an Andean condor swoops low, its immense wingspan startling against the blue of the pool. Echoing the beautiful plumes and

PHOTO BY CHRIS GOTSHALL/COURTESY OF SEAWORLD ORLANDO

Blue Horizons unites dolphins and false killer whales with performers and exotic birds.

colors of these birds, a troupe of aerialists/divers struts out, bedecked with feathers, and begins diving with stupendous choreographed spins and flips (much like the Cirque du Soleil *O* show at the Bellagio in Vegas). Two sturdy guys in somber black feather hats come out and perform a bungee/swing aerial act, diving as one into the pool far below.

It goes on in this manner. At the end, flags are waved, birds are swooping all over, dolphins are whizzing around, and pageantry is at a manic level. The applause is commensurate. The show is usually performed four or five times each day; arrive 30 minutes before showtime to grab a seat. The soak zone is a little smaller than at Shamu Stadium, but the first dozen rows get wet.

(CLYDE AND SEAMORE TAKE PIRATE ISLAND

This is my favorite show, hands down, in large measure because it's light and funny in the wake of too many heavy, knitted-brow conservation and "sea creatures are endangered" messages at SeaWorld Orlando's other attractions and shows. This show is a romp, the Sea Lion and Otter Stadium given over to a big pirate ship fronted by a central pool. The daytime show gets my vote, with Captain Squid and Slappy, two hapless seafarers, mostly at the mercy of a couple of sea lions, Clyde and Seamore, and a wily otter. It's a story line that doesn't really merit a big recap (lost loot, treasure map that goes missing), but the jokes are funny and the sea lions' tricks right on cue. The best part is a skit about stealing fish—you wouldn't think sea lions' faces could convey studied innocence, but they can. If you see the daytime Clyde and Seamore show, the evening version will be slightly redundant, with many of the same tricks, but the overarching story line in the evening is that the sea lions and their human straight men perform a parody of the other shows at the park. The half-hour daytime show is performed four or five times a day; get there early to catch the funny preshow with the sadistic mime (think audience participation).

PETS AHOY!

Also with a lighter, more humorous touch, Pets Ahoy! showcases the talents of garden-variety dogs, cats, ducks, doves, parrots, rats, skunks, potbellied pigs, and other animals, many of which have been rescued from animal shelters. After spending much of the day watching the antics of sea creatures, it's a change of pace to observe goofy tricks and skits involving the furred and the feathered in the Seaport Theatre, squarely in the middle of the park. Kids enjoy the show—high-wire walking, musical numbers, flips, and aspiring canine Evel Knievels. The 25-minute show takes place four or five times each day; arrive on time, partly because the theater is small and partly because the doors close at showtime. The cast and their trainers are pretty friendly, and are eager to meet the audience at show's end.

ODYSSEA

This is a Cirque du Soleil–style circus, but with an underwater fantasy theme. Again, the 30-minute show at the Nautilus Theater closes its doors at showtime, so get there early. The mostly silent performers are put through some tremendous feats—a contortionist in a clamshell who can balance and twist on one hand, aerialists in an "underwater" coral reef twirling on ropes and suspended metal rings—but somehow it fails to hold many children's interests (the music can be a bit ponderous, too). The funniest bits are worth enduring the slower ones. Especially compelling are the acrobats in penguin suits who tumble on a trampoline-enhanced floor while making penguin-ish squawks and the multicolored accordioned tubular sea worms jiggling through a funny dance. Longtime SeaWorld Orlando fans lament that this show supplanted the beloved Cirque de la Mer show of old.

MISTIFY

Strictly a nighttime show, Mistify gets mixed reviews. Some say it's a rip-off, or tribute to, the Fantasmic show at MGM Studios; others find it utterly magical. SeaWorld Orlando's central lagoon is the stage for a light-and-water show that features 100-foot fountains, waterfalls, flames, fireworks, and—most unusually—60-foot projection screens made out of water mist. The 20-minute show is the grand finale to the day during peak summer season only, with underwater explosions and larger-than-life marine creatures projected onto the wall of mist, all set to a musical score performed by the Seattle Symphony Orchestra and several choruses. Restaurants in the Waterfront harbor's little seaport village offer outdoor seating from which to watch the show.

FUSION

Another show offered only during the warmest months, both during the day and at night, it's a stunt show set at the waterfront Atlantis Bayside Stadium. Stunt kites perform an aerial ballet, water skis and other watercraft zig and zag, bathing-suited beauties dance and dive off a scary-high platform, all set to the park's most rock/pop score. It doesn't hurt that the whole cast of this 30-minute show comprises extremely attractive young athletes.

SEAWORLD ORLANDO

Animal Attractions

Animal shows, walk-through animal-viewing areas, and animal encounters are what Sea-World Orlando does best. More dynamic than a zoo or aquarium, the animal environments are transporting and magical, and often the animals themselves are very close to visitors. From the left of the entrance, here are the animal attractions clockwise around the park.

DOLPHIN NURSERY

Home to new dolphin mothers and their calves, the small, shaded outdoor pool is a good place to stand and get oriented with your park map while you wait for a glimpse of adorable baby dolphins swimming by in tight formation with their moms.

TURTLE POINT

In an area called Key West (loosely grouping warmer-water animals), a low-frills, natural-looking lagoon surrounded by sand houses green, loggerhead, and hawksbill turtles. As one might expect, the pace at Turtle Point is somewhat slow—these guys don't exactly put on a show—but it's nice to know that Sea-World Orlando has rescued more than 300 sea turtles, many of them endangered species. As with most animal attractions at the park, things get more interesting, and certainly more educational, when a staffer is on hand to answer questions.

STINGRAY LAGOON

Also in the area called Key West, where Jimmy Buffett is piped in with reckless abandon, a 40,000-gallon habitat is devoted exclusively to stingrays and guitarfish. Under a shade roof, guests can feed and reach in and touch them as they swim by in the shallow main pool, with nearly 200 of them roiling the water. A second "nursery" pool in one corner holds the young rays. Paper trays of fish are offered for $4, but often the stingrays seem oblivious to the chunks of fish raining down upon them—you're better off just watching.

DOLPHIN COVE

While ponying up the dough for stingray snacks may not be worth it, it's absolutely essential to stand in the long line to pay $4 for a tray of smelt-like little fish (offered only at designated feeding times) for the dolphins in Dolphin Cove, also in the Key West section of the park. Enthusiastic eaters, the dolphins aren't shy if they think you're holding fish. It's a great photo op, you nose to nose with a bevy of hopeful Atlantic bottlenoses at the edge of this gorgeous, 700,000-gallon lagoon. Staff photographers are also snapping pictures that are available for purchase. Keep your possessions away from water's edge—a staffer in a kayak is positioned to make sure visitors aren't risking the dolphins' well-being with cameras, glasses, or other loose, dangling articles. Dolphin Cove's underwater viewing area gives you a below-the-surface view of the dolphins frolicking.

MANATEE RESCUE

Another above-the-water-and-below-the-water attraction, this one features the endangered West Indian manatee. Florida has a dense concentration of the gentle sea cows that retreat during the winters to the warmer waters of Gulf Coast rivers that feed into the Gulf of Mexico. These lumbering mammals often encounter speedboat propellers and other man-made hazards, and SeaWorld Orlando has made it its business to rescue and rehabilitate the animals in a "halfway house" lagoon before releasing them back into the wild.

❰ PENGUIN ENCOUNTER

The most delightful of all the animal attractions, this is a little piece of Antarctica, kept a frosty 30°F behind thick glass with 6,000 pounds of snow falling daily. Many species of penguin—Rockhopper, Gentoo, King, Chinstrap, and Emperor, the stalwart birds made film stars by *March of the Penguins*—frolic and cavort, slipping in and out of the water. Eye level is right at the watermark, so it's easy to keep track of what's going on above and

DISCOVERY COVE

Discovery Cove is SeaWorld's superexclusive, superluxurious, reservations-only, 30-acre, Caribbean-theme water park. Only 1,000 guests are admitted each day (and only 150 each evening during the summer for a "Twilight Discovery") for a very up-close experience with dolphins and other exotic marine life. Guests arrive in what looks like a swanky hotel lobby and are shepherded through donning wet suits and snorkels.

Nature paths lead guests around the gorgeously landscaped property – past the coral reef where visitors snorkel with schools of tropical fish (barracuda and sharks add a thrill, but they're tucked behind clear acrylic walls); lovely beaches, pools, and a meandering tropical river; a free-flight aviary with 250 exotic birds; and a quiet ray lagoon where people frolic with hundreds of southern and cownose rays.

It's all artificial but done with enough style and attention to detail – mature palms, whooshing waterfalls, craggy rock ledges – that one almost feels transported to the Caribbean.

Guests spend the day snorkeling, lying in the sand, and floating down the river, but the centerpiece is the Dolphin Lagoon. Participating guests (you can opt out and your ticket price goes down to $179 in high season) are assigned a time to convene for a preswim orientation and short film. Briefed, guests enter the shallows of the Dolphin Lagoon in groups of about six. A trainer and a designated dolphin (one of about 30 on property) are assigned to you.

I forgot my dolphin's name, but she was clearly a supergenius, very friendly and affectionate and with the smoothest gray, rubbery skin. I rubbed her belly, I kissed her, and then the interspecies party started. Holding fiercely to her dorsal fin, I whooped and grinned as she sliced through the water of the lagoon, our combined bodies making a low wake on either side. It was over in less than a minute, and it was spectacular.

My heart gradually slowing to normal, I exited the shallows and had to do some final mathematical calculations.

A one-day dolphin-encounter ticket is $279 per person during high season; there is no reduced price for children or seniors. For a family of four, that's $1,116 for the day, including food, parking, locker, wet suit, snorkel, and mask. But what if your family of four eats breakfast elsewhere (add $35) and then goes out to dinner (add $100) before returning to the hotel for the evening (add $160). That's a $1,411 day. Now, if your annual household income is $60,000, then this particular day just cost more than 2 percent of your annual income. If, on the other hand, you earn $200,000 a year, then the day is only 0.7 percent of that. A mere pittance.

Not often thought of as fiscally prudent, I feel squeamish approaching SeaWorld's Discovery Cove this way. However, when the cash extraction is so aggressive, it's tempting to evaluate an experience like this mathematically.

I went to Discovery Cove, I had a dolphin encounter. Full disclosure: I did not spend $279; I was a guest. But I had at least $211 worth of fun, most of it concentrated during my dolphin swim, which was essentially half an hour. So, if $100 of my fun were concentrated then (more than $3 per minute), that means the rest of my 6.5 hours rang in at only $0.28 a minute.

All snide parsimony aside, it's a very different, very memorable day at the park, and admission includes a seven-day pass to SeaWorld Orlando or Busch Gardens Tampa Bay. Guests must be six years old to enjoy the dolphin swim or the special "trainer for a day" program ($429 per person).

To get there, take I-4, then Exit 71 (SeaWorld exit). Discovery Cove is on Central Florida Parkway, just past the sign for SeaWorld Orlando. Reservations should be made by calling 877/434-7268 or by visiting the website (www.discoverycove.com).

SEAWORLD ORLANDO

below. Visitors enter the building and bear to the right to be herded onto a 120-foot moving walkway—if you'd rather stay a while and watch, move to the left, where you can stand behind the people mover and you won't get shuffled through so quickly. Rock formations and drifts of snow make it a naturalistic backdrop in which the penguins conduct their daily business. The building that houses the exhibit is a little bare bones, incongruously sponsored by Southwest Airlines with some flagrant advertising near the exit.

A smaller habitat in the same building showcases alcids, a group of birds that includes puffins and murres—similar to the penguin exhibit, except these little dudes fly, too.

The Penguin Encounter is a great place to cool off for a bit on a hot day, and its proximity to Kraken makes it the ideal place to wait for those in your party who want to experience that thrill ride.

PACIFIC POINT PRESERVE

A re-creation of California's blustery Pacific Coast, the two-acre lagoon can be viewed from vantage points around its entire circumference, waves crashing for extra verisimilitude. From wherever you look, harbor seals and sea lions bask in the sun, scuffle, bark, sleep, flirt, and beg for food. Again, park-goers can buy paper containers of little smelt to toss out to the sea lions that bellow and exhort at top volume from the water or strategically positioned rocky outcroppings. Just as strategically positioned, though, are dozens of great blue herons, snowy egrets, ibis, and other Florida birds eager to grab your fish. Sea lions are irate when their rightful due gets snaked by a bird, so you may find yourself shelling out more dough to appease their wounded egos. Precious little shade makes this an attraction to visit in the cooler parts of the day.

◖ SHARK ENCOUNTER

Billed as the world's largest underwater acrylic tunnel, the Shark Encounter is one of the most impressive parts of the park. Visitors board a moving walkway through a glass tunnel, and seemingly all around sharks slither past, over, and around, while an eerie soundtrack of submarine noises sets the mood. Smaller exhibits of eels, barracuda, and other fish are well marked with identification plaques of all the fish species—a huge scorpionfish tank and another of delicate leafy seadragons nearly steal the show, were it not for the gnashing multiple rows of teeth and cold stares of all those sharks.

The signage in this exhibit is the most careful and stylish in the park, with a cool pop art/comic approach that works with all age groups. Outdoors another pool allows you to feed small sharks, again removing another $4 from your wallet for a little tray of fish. And the entire shark tank comes tableside if you choose to dine in the park's fanciest restaurant, Sharks Underwater Grill.

CLYDESDALE HAMLET

Tucked off in a quiet part of the park near the Anheuser-Busch Hospitality Center, the Budweiser Clydesdales seem somewhat out of place here. You can visit during daily posing and petting sessions, but often these beefy, heavy-footed giants are off entertaining the crowds elsewhere in the park. Still, they are beautiful animals, very well groomed, even if they don't fit seamlessly with their more aquatic park mates.

The Anheuser-Busch Hospitality Center is where visitors are treated to free beer and a little hops education at the **Brewmaster's Club** show held several times each day (reservations recommended). You'll often see dads sneak off here while their families are engaged elsewhere in the park, the building being a pleasant place to pick up Anheuser-Busch souvenirs, a sandwich from the on-site deli, or to just sit and enjoy a beer along with the view of a pretty lake and wide, sprawling lawns.

Rides

◖ KRAKEN

SeaWorld Orlando has historically been an animal-focused park, but the opening of Kraken in 2000 tipped it a little closer to a thrill-ride destination. The attraction is loosely based on the ancient myth of gigantic sea monsters the size of islands, who lurked off the coasts of Norway and Iceland. Unlike a lot of Disney rides, the theming of Kraken isn't over the top with nuance and details, but it's a very fun ride (for coaster junkies, it's a highly regarded effort from Switzerland's Bolliger and Mabillard). With three trains, eight cars per train, four people across, it's an open-sided floorless coaster. So riders strap in, legs swinging, to ascend 140 feet. The initial drop is delicious weightlessness, and the heart continues to get pumping at a dive loop, a fine corkscrew, and three subterranean dives. On most floorless coasters, riders are suspended from the track above, but Kraken features a neat pedestal-style seat that leaves rides feeling suspended in space by nothing but a shoulder restraint.

With speeds of up to 65 mph, it's a smooth ride all the way through more than three minutes, with good use of water features: In the last tunnel, riders on the left side get a little misted from the waterfalls, and bystanders to the ride get the occasional plume of spray from the passing trains. Riders must be 54 inches or taller.

JOURNEY TO ATLANTIS

A step down from Kraken in terms of thrills, Journey to Atlantis is a combination log flume and roller coaster, appropriate for most everybody in the family, as long as you don't mind getting extremely wet. The course for the ride, which opened in 1998, winds around a just-beginning-to-look-tired, four-acre recreation of the mythical underwater world of Atlantis. Each boat holds eight guests in four rows.

COURTESY OF SEAWORLD ORLANDO

Thrill seekers enjoy a spin on Kraken, SeaWorld Orlando's "floorless" roller coaster.

SEAWORLD ORLANDO

SEAWORLD ORLANDO

Riders bob along gently at first in regular flume fashion, making it surprising when all of a sudden roller-coaster tracks are perceptible and the boats begin to gain speed, passing through the fog and darkness.

The park's first thrill ride, the five-minute ride is best scheduled for the warmest part of the day: A final 60-foot drop at ride's end gets everybody damp, especially the feet of those in the first row and the backs of those in the fourth row. Because most people have this same great idea, lines can be long. Still, it's pleasant enough queuing up in the little Greek fishing village in which you learn a somewhat confusing and garbled tale of Atlantis emerging from the depths, then a friendly pet sea horse accompanies you on your journey and saves you from a vengeful Siren/Medusa creature. Keep your cameras off the ride or safely sealed in plastic self-sealing bags. Riders must be 42 inches tall.

WILD ARCTIC

Ironically, the bumpiest and most turbulent ride at SeaWorld Orlando is a motion simulator in a jet helicopter adventure to research Base Station Wild Arctic. A good bet for a cooling respite in the hottest part of the day, the fairly intimate attraction features a panoramic movie that is quite spectacular, with excellent Arctic animal footage and an awe-inspiring avalanche. Lines can be up to 30 minutes, and the seats do jolt more than some visitors like, but most folks think the walk-through at the ride's end makes up for it: Doors open at movie's end and visitors walk through an Arctic expedition base camp with above-water and below-water wildlife-observation areas that include polar bears, walruses, harbor seals, and beluga whales. For some reason, the walruses feel very comfortable going eye-to-eye close to the glass, and occasionally you'll be privy to the balletic grace of polar bears Klondike and Snow as they swim.

You exit into the gift shop, from which you can view the ride lurching in full motion. If you like your films with fewer bumps, you can bypass the ride, see the movie in a nonmotion environment, and still see the live Arctic animal area. Riders must be 42 inches tall. Don't time a visit here for right after you've gotten wet elsewhere in the park or you'll be uncomfortably cold, and try to avoid hitting this right after a show has finished at Shamu Stadium, when it's likely to get mobbed instantly.

SHAMU'S HAPPY HARBOR

Not really a ride, Shamu's Happy Harbor is the whoop-it-up, five-acre play area for little kids, centered around a four-story, L-shaped structure of nets, tunnels, slides, and water features. Key West–style bright pastels and flamingos dominate the area, which has recently expanded to include the **Shamu Express** kiddie-coaster, a garden-variety (but spout-themed) teacup ride, and some other small-scale midway rides. It's a slam dunk in the hottest part of the day, with Pete's Water Maze the most cooling area, and an under-42-inch-only area called Dolly Dolphin's Playground for toddlers and preschoolers to romp unperturbed by their older colleagues.

Only the most intrepid adults will appreciate the area's greatest charms: Within the oversize play structure you'll find tire swings, tight crawl tubes, and cargo netting along which to climb. Outside of this central structure there are the now-ubiquitous climbing walls, bouncy rooms (limited to 54-inch visitors or shorter), and "ball crawls" à la Chuck E. Cheese's.

The downside of this area is the added expenditures that seem fairly mercenary on top of your regular admission price: Remote-controlled cars and tugboats can be taken out for a quick spin with $1 tokens, water balloons can be slung at your designated nemesis, two buckets for $5—it all adds up. Refocus kids' attention instead on exploring the child-size schooner or climbing on the models of Shamu and Baby Shamu.

Accommodations

If your aim is to spend the majority of your Orlando stay at SeaWorld, it makes sense to take advantage of the park's association with participating Orlando Marriott and Renaissance Hotels and Resorts. Kids nine and younger stay free with a minimum two-night stay, but there are loads of other perks. The packages offered include deluxe accommodations, one admission to SeaWorld Orlando for children nine and younger with each paid adult admission (maximum two per package), a SeaWorld Orlando Guest Value Booklet of ride-again passes and dining discounts, an Adventure Pak Shamu bag per child upon arrival (it's got a stuffed Shamu, activity book, tattoos, and stickers). Some of the participating hotels also offer free breakfast for kids nine and younger, and/or scheduled transportation to SeaWorld Orlando. The Marriott package also includes a "Length of Stay" ticket, which means for the price of a single-day ticket at the park, Marriott guests receive SeaWorld Orlando tickets good for the entire length of their stay.

All nine of the participating hotels are within a few miles of the park, also very close to Universal Orlando Resort, Wet 'n Wild, and International Drive.

$100-150

The **Residence Inn Orlando SeaWorld/ International Center** (11000 Westwood Blvd., 407/313-3600, rates from $109) is six stories in a Floribbean motif, with 350 rooms and one- and two-bedrooms suites with fully equipped kitchens. There's a very nice hot breakfast buffet that is thrown in, with waffles, pancakes, and all the fixings, which you can eat out by the pool. It's a great family hotel, entertaining the kids with a big heated pool, playground, game arcade, and sports courts.

Courtyard Orlando International Drive (8600 Austrian Ct., 407/351-2244, rates from $118) is a newly renovated business-travelers' hotel just a mile from the Orange County Convention Center. The rooms contain fastidious bedding and free high-speed Internet. There are a small fitness center, pool, and whirlpool bath, and an on-site market for late-night needs.

Marriott's Grande Vista (5925 Avenida Vista, 407/238-7676, rates from $120) is six floors, 1,526 rooms, of one-, two-, and three-bedroom villas. It's part of Marriott Timeshare Vacation Villas, and each unit has living and dining areas, full kitchens, washer/dryer, and a master suite with oversize soaking tub. On-site is Faldo Golf Institute by Marriott. Its Sea-World Orlando package starts at $457 and is for three- or four-night stays, including Sea-World tickets for the length of your stay.

Horizons by Marriott Vacation Club Orlando (7102 Grand Horizons Blvd., 407/465-6100, rates from $135) is a hoot, especially for families, with an on-site 22,000-square-foot miniature golf course, an on-site water playground called WaterWorks, and a pirate-themed pool complete with water slide and water cannons. The two-bedroom and two-bath villas feature full kitchens, living/dining areas, screened balcony, and utility room with washer and dryer.

The Fairfield Inn and Suites by Marriott is another partner hotel (see the *Universal Orlando Resort* chapter).

$150-200

The **℃ Renaissance Orlando Resort at SeaWorld** (6677 Sea Harbor Dr., 407/351-5555, rates from $179) is directly across from SeaWorld Orlando, Discovery Cove, and one mile from Orlando's Orange County Convention Center. The hotel boasts 185,000 square feet of meeting and event space with a 10-story atrium (full of waterfalls, exotic birds, and goldfish ponds), 18-hole championship golf course, three lighted tennis courts, and an Olympic-size swimming pool. The 778 rooms have recently been renovated, along with 64 suites. All rooms feature 32-inch flat-panel televisions, king beds with a sleep sofa or double queen-size beds. The continental restaurant, Atlantis, is well regarded locally.

Marriott's Cypress Harbour (11251 Harbour Villa Rd., 407/238-1300, rates from $174) is another Marriott Timeshare Vacation Villa, with two-bedroom/two-bath villas that come with screened balconies or porches and a full kitchen. It's just had a major renovation of its main pool and bar area, with a nice marina and outdoor play areas. You'll find the same thing with the **Marriott's Royal Palms** (8404 Vacation Way, 407/238-6200, rates from $204), with two-bedroom/two-bath villas, but right next to the convention center. A very similar property is the **Marriott's Sabal Palms** (8805 World Center Dr., 407/238-6200, rates from $255), also near the convention center.

OVER $200

Orlando World Center Marriott (8701 World Center Dr., 407/239-4200, rates from $239) is a gorgeous property built on 200 acres of lush tropical landscaping. The property is the largest Marriott in the world, with 2,000 rooms and suites, a full-service spa, the 18-hole championship Hawk's Landing Golf Club, 214,000 square feet of meeting space, and 10 restaurants and lounges, including Ristorante Tuscany,

Hawk's Landing Steakhouse, and Mikado Japanese Steakhouse. It's a little bit farther away from SeaWorld Orlando (six miles), but it's a lovely property with six pools and six hot tubs, sand volleyball and four lighted tennis courts, and nice kids' activities.

Two miles east of SeaWorld Orlando, **Grande Lakes Orlando** (4040 Central Florida Pkwy., Ritz-Carlton 800/682-3665, JW Marriott 800/682-9956, rates from $350) is actually a luxury property that comprises two hotels, set on 500 lush acres at the headwaters of the Florida Everglades. The Ritz-Carlton Orlando, Grande Lakes, boasts 584 guest rooms, including 64 suites, and 56 Ritz-Carlton Club Level rooms and suites. JW Marriott Orlando, Grande Lakes, contains 100,800 square feet of meeting space and 1,000 guest rooms and suites, with a unique "lazy-river" outdoor heated pool. The on-site Ritz-Carlton Golf Club is an 18-hole, par-72 Greg Norman signature golf course, with a Golf Caddie Concierge program. There's also The Ritz-Carlton Spa, Orlando, Grande Lakes, with 40 treatment rooms, a 4,000-square-foot lap pool, and a 6,000-square-foot fitness center.

Food and Shopping

The park has nine dining options, several of which rival the best of the Disney character meals; the rest are easy grab-and-go spots. For some reason, crowd movement through food lines isn't nearly as effective as it is at Disney parks. In several visits, the longest lines I endured were for an ice-cream cone or a bit of lunch. Because the park's parent company is Anheuser-Busch, beer is widely available all over the park (wine drinkers will have to rough it).

CHARACTER DINING
Makahiki Luau Dinner and Show

This is the big daily dinner event at SeaWorld Orlando, held at the Seafire Inn as the sun begins its colorful descent over the Waterfront harbor. It is by reservation only (in high season

there are two seatings at 5:30 and 8:15 P.M., the rest of the year dinner is at 6:30 P.M., $45.95 adults, $29.95 children 3–9, younger than three free). It is almost as good as Disney's Spirit of Aloha Show at Disney's Polynesian Resort and better than the Wantilan Luau at the Royal Pacific Resort at Universal. The best part: Diners don't have to pay for park admission or parking. Make dinner reservations and you'll get a confirmation number that gets you into the park an hour before dinner. You can explore the park for an hour, have dinner, and then wander the park until it closes (only feasible during the extended summer or holiday hours, when the park stays open until 9 or 10 P.M.). The dinner price includes one cocktail and unlimited sodas, and a choice of mahimahi with piña colada sauce, sweet and sour chicken, or Polynesian-style spareribs; for children there are also the standard chicken tenders and hot dogs. Sides include a perfunctory vegetable medley and a workhorse fried rice. In all, the food is very serviceable.

The evening's entertainment brings ashore a colorfully attired "tribe" of Pacific Island dancers. Coaxed into wonderful dancing by the evening's excellent band (some Islands-inspired music, some crowd-pleasing rock), it's a combination of hula and stomping around, heavy on the drums. The performance includes fire, bubbles, smoke, and other effects to achieve its particular brand of island magic. Young kids may not find it nearly as interesting as the more animal-oriented dining options.

The Seafire Inn also hosts a weekend **Shamu and Crew Character Breakfast** (9–10 A.M., $14.95 adults, $9.95 children 3–9,) with everyone's favorite killer whale and his aquatic friends. French toast, pancakes, scrambled eggs, cereal, and other standard breakfast offerings are enlivened by costumed characters.

Backstage with Believe

Dining poolside with killer whales in Shamu Stadium, guests are treated to a training session with Shamu and opportunities to chat with the trainers. While the Makahiki Luau features a limited menu and table service, Believe's one-hour, all-you-can-eat buffet ($37 adults, $19 children 3–9, younger than three free) includes beef bourguignonne, seafood Creole, pasta primavera, oven-roasted chicken, and lots of it. Seating time varies according to park hours, but it's sometimes the ungodly-early hour of 4:15 P.M. Again, reservations are required and can be made by calling 800/327-2424 or by visiting the park's information counter at the front gate. For your money, this is more of a one-of-a-kind experience than the luau.

Sharks Underwater Grill

SeaWorld Orlando goes fancy-pants at **Sharks Underwater Grill** (open 11 A.M. to one hour before park close, entrées $18–25). There's a very commendable à la carte menu

COURTESY OF SEAWORLD ORLANDO

Dine amid the underwater scenery at Sharks Underwater Grill.

SEAWORLD ORLANDO

of Floribbean dishes—sushi-grade tuna with tropical slaw, Caribbean conch chowder, jumbo lump crab cakes with Key lime mustard mayonnaise—served in an elegant, "underwater" dining room. Not really, but the enormous walls of shark tanks are truly compelling if dinner conversation lapses. It's first-come, first-served, but you can put your name in for priority seating and come back at a designated time.

PARK DINING

SeaWorld Orlando has had a recent push to offer more healthful dining options. A recently added quick-service restaurant, near the Penguin Encounter, **Mama's Kitchen Healthy Alternatives,** serves whole-wheat bread and whole-grain pastas, stamping out foods with those dreaded trans fats and preservatives. Still, there are miles to go.

In general, the park's snacks and quick-service spots are a little cheaper than the Disney parks but also just slightly inferior in quality. The best of the bunch for lunch is **Sharks Underwater Grill at the Waterfront,** with a pasta bar and competent pizza—inexplicably served with fries—and the greatest number of kids' options (which come in a souvenir Shamu lunch box that you must then schlep around the park all afternoon). Nearby, at the base of the Sky Tower (additional charge of $3 to guests), the **SandBar** is where to stop in for a hot dog or snack, whereas **Captain Pete's Island Eats** in Key West is the place to go when you feel an inexorable pull for the arterial double whammy of funnel cakes and chicken nuggets. Also not far from the Penguin Encounter, **Smoky Creek Grill** purveys competent Texas-style barbecue ribs, chicken, and smoked brisket (not quite as good as the barbecue at the sister park, Busch Gardens in Tampa), which diners devour at pleasant patio tables. Near Shamu Stadium and Wild Arctic, **Mango Joe's Café** offers beef and chicken fajitas, fried chicken fingers, and garden wraps. At the **Anheuser-Busch Hospitality Center** you are entitled a bit of Anheuser-Busch product taste-testing, assuming you're 21. A pleasant deli turns out sandwiches. Lo-

cated in the Waterfront area, **Voyagers Wood Fired Pizza** ($6–10) offers cafeteria-style pizzas from a big wood-fired oven, pastas, fresh salads, kid's meals, and even baby food, with two lines to keep things moving even when the park is busy.

The only place in the park serving what one might call "ethnic" cuisine is **The Spice Mill,** not far from the paddleboats. Unfortunately, the jerk chicken sandwiches and Cajun jambalaya are not going to win any gastronomic awards, but it's a nice place to sit and watch the Mistify show on a summer's evening.

The rest of the park is dotted with spots to get fudge, fruit smoothies, soft serve, snowcones, and beverages (but there are not nearly enough places to get water). The park serves Gerber baby food and 2 percent milk at all restaurants, and kosher meals are available at Sharks Underwater Grill.

SHOPPING

Shamu souvenirs and Anheuser-Busch merchandise are the big draws at SeaWorld Orlando. A cluster of gift shops near the entrance and a long row of them along the Waterfront provide a number of shopping options.

Opened in 2003, the Waterfront area is a five-acre dining, entertainment, and shopping area that looks vaguely like a historic harbor town. Stores flow one into the other, so you'll find a **Visiting Artists** store of international arts and crafts, then a sea-life fantasy store called **Allura's Treasure Trove** of dolls, dress-ups, and jewelry, a housewares and resort wear shop called **Tropica Trading Company,** and a kitchen and home shop called **Under the Sun.** Much of the merchandise in these shops bears a subtle or overt sea-life theme, heavy on figurines and small sculptures, some of them big-ticket items. And a percentage of your purchase price goes to rescue stranded sea mammals.

Beer enthusiasts will find a **Anheuser-Busch Trading Company** of beer-brand merchandise in the Waterfront area, and at the Anheuser-Busch Hospitality Center you'll find the **Label Shop** for beer-logo clothing and memorabilia.

One of the more interesting shops at Sea-

World Orlando is the **Oyster's Secret.** Guests watch through an underwater window as divers swim around looking for pearl-containing oysters. It's a gamble, but you can buy an oyster, unopened, in the hopes of a pearl. If you get lucky, you can then have the pearl placed in a custom jewelry setting.

Several shops right at the park entrance contain the expected logo merchandise, plush stuffed Shamus, and souvenirs of your visit.

Practicalities

INFORMATION AND SERVICES
Diaper-changing and baby-nursing areas, foreign-currency exchange, 24-hour automated teller machine, taxi, and bus parking may be found on-site.

First Aid
First aid facilities are behind Stingray Lagoon in Key West and in Shamu's Happy Harbor, near the Air Bounce. Both are staffed by registered nurses and emergency medical technicians.

Guest Relations
Guest Services is next to the information counter outside the park entrance and dispenses a variety of general information about tickets and schedules, as well as services for guests with disabilities. Within the park, the Guest Assistance Center, behind Voyagers Wood Fired Pizza between Sea Lion and Otter Stadium and the Smoky Creek Grill, can provide guidance during park hours about directions, show updates, ride information, and ticket information. The center is also equipped with a nursing mother's room.

Rentals
Strollers, wheelchairs, and electronic convenience vehicles (ECVs) can be rented at the park or reserved online or by calling 888/800-5447. To change or cancel your reservation, call by noon of your reservation date; after that it's nonrefundable. Single strollers are $9.39 for the day, doubles are $16.90, and both come with a storage shelf, sunshade, and safety straps. Wheelchair rentals are $10 per day, ECV rentals are $35. Lockers are available ($1 small, $1.50 large) and indoor, climate-controlled pet kennels are available for $6 per cat or dog per day.

Special Needs
Wheelchair seating is available at all facilities, and all restaurants and gift shops are accessible. For the hearing impaired, assistive listening devices are available at Guest Services with a same-day, refundable deposit, which can be used at almost all the shows. American Sign Language interpretation is also free and can be provided at live shows with a minimum of one week's notice. Call 407/363-2414 for reservations.

GETTING THERE AND AROUND
From Orlando, take Exit 72 off I-4; from Tampa, take Exit 71 off I-4. The entrance is near I-4, between Highway 528 (the Beachline Expressway, formerly the Bee Line Expressway) to the north and Central Florida Parkway to the south. It is approximately 15 minutes south of downtown Orlando and 20 minutes from Orlando International Airport.

Parking
Parking at SeaWorld Orlando is $10 per day for cars, vans, and motorcycles; $12 for RVs and trailers; and $15 for a preferred parking spot. Lots here aren't enormous. It's feasible to walk to the park's entrance from your parking spot, but there are also trams that carry guests to the entrance. Parking sections are marked by a letter and a number, but signs are designed so they are very difficult to read from far away.

SEAWORLD ORLANDO

Shuttle Service

SeaWorld Orlando offers a shuttle service to its sister park, Busch Gardens in Tampa. For $10 round-trip, you can leave the ugly 1.5-hour drive along I-4 and I-75 to a bus driver. There are five pickup locations around Orlando. Call 800/221-1339 for locations and make reservations one day in advance.

Park Maps

A single-page map is available right inside the entrance to the park. The day's schedule of shows is printed daily on the back, as are a list of attractions and restaurants and a number of helpful hints. The map is an essential tool in navigating the park, so you may want to grab a couple in case one gets wet in a soak zone.

Tours

The top-of-the-line SeaWorld Orlando tour, **Adventure Express Tour** (800/406-2244) is a six-hour tour that includes front-of-the-line access to the park's rides; reserved seating at two select shows; a behind-the-scenes visit with a penguin; dolphins, sea lions, and stingrays feeding; and lunch. At $89 for adults and $79 children 3–9 (this does not include park admission), it makes sense only during peak season when circumventing lines is important.

The park also offers hour-long "behind the scenes" tours (800/406-2244, $16 adults, $12 children 3–9). On the **Polar Expedition Tour,** explore the backstage areas of Wild Arctic and touch a penguin. **Explore Predators Tour** allows guests to touch a small shark and peer down into the 600,000-gallon Shark Encounter and visit backstage at Shamu Stadium. Visit rescue and rehabilitation facilities where endangered manatees and sea turtles receive medical treatment and hand-feed exotic birds in the free-flight aviary during the **Saving a Species Tour** ($1 of your tour admission is donated to the SeaWorld and Busch Gardens Conservation Fund).

SeaWorld Orlando hosts sleepovers for birthday parties or other groups (Boy Scouts, church groups), as well as offering a few special interactive programs for individuals, such as the **Beluga Interaction Program,** the **Marine Mammal Keeper** program, or the **Sharks Deep Dive.** For more information about these tours, call 800/327-2424.

DOWNTOWN ORLANDO AND WINTER PARK

They call it the City Beautiful. Well, those who know it exists. If you hop off a plane at Orlando International Airport and drive west to the theme parks, you may catch a glimpse of it if you crane your neck out the side of your car toward those sleek skyscrapers off in the distance. The truth is, Orlando is a real place that has experienced a massive renaissance in recent years. Since the beginning of this millennium countless lavish construction projects have gotten under way: new resort hotels, an ambitious new arts complex, restaurants, theaters, and condominiums are sprouting like so many mushrooms. Spurred by tourism dollars and the low cost of Central Florida real estate, it's a boomtown these days, all centered around Lake Eola.

Though the lake really started as a lowly sinkhole, Downtown Orlando is decidedly sophisticated, with an array of cultural allures that ably compete with the theme parks for visitors' attention. Surrounding the lake and its signature UFO-shaped fountain, 43-acre Lake Eola Park anchors Downtown's cultural district. A small, eight-block historic district holds buildings that date to the 1880s, but for the most part the Downtown has a slick, 21st-century feel to it. Thornton Park is the Downtown's highly desirable urban residential neighborhood, with lofts and loads of renovated Craftsman-style bungalows along with a superabundance of excellent restaurants. College Park is another hot residential area, just to the northwest of Downtown. Its Edgewater Drive is a long stretch of lovely homes and carefully maintained turn-of-the-20th-century

COURTESY OF ORLANDO/ORANGE COUNTY CONVENTION & VISITORS BUREAU, INC.

HIGHLIGHTS

⟪ Orlando Museum of Art: Founded in 1924, OMA welcomes high-profile traveling exhibits such as *The Art of the Motorcycle* and *Gee's Bend: The Architecture of the Quilt*. The museum also has a very respectable permanent collection of American art, African art, and art of the ancient Americas (page 202).

⟪ Cornell Fine Arts Museum at Rollins College: Perhaps it's because the first paintings were bequeathed more than a century ago and it's just kept up a steady pace since, but the recently reopened Cornell has a permanent collection of more than 6,000 works – one of the largest collections in Florida. Only a fraction is on display at any time, coupled with dramatic and ambitious traveling exhibits (page 210).

⟪ Charles Hosmer Morse Museum of American Art: Many of the contents of Louis Comfort Tiffany's 84-room dreamhouse have made their way to this stunning Winter Park museum now exhibiting Tiffany jewelry, lamps, pottery, paintings, art glass, leaded-glass windows, and the chapel designed for the 1893 World's Columbian Exposition in Chicago (page 210).

⟪ Winter Park Scenic Boat Tour: Take a 12-mile, narrated trip on this zippy pontoon boat as it winds through the canals connecting Winter Park's many lakeside mansions and historic homes (page 211).

LOOK FOR ⟪ TO FIND RECOMMENDED SIGHTS, ACTIVITIES, DINING, AND LODGING.

bungalows. Winter Park, to the northeast of Downtown, offers many draws to the visitor.

HISTORY

Orlando got its name from a word carved into a tree. Around 1866, sugar-mill owner Orlando Reeves etched his mark into a sapling on a whim. This signature, assumed to be his gravesite, lent the surrounding area the name of "Orlando's grave." The population was fairly sparse through the Third Seminole War in the 1850s. And all the way through the Civil War, it was given over mostly to hardy cattle ranchers and their intrepid families. The citrus boom in the 1870s saw Or-

lando's incorporation and nurtured a growing population, until a freeze in 1894–1895 put many of the small citrus farmers out of business. Brief real-estate flurries in the 1920s and the 1950s brought greater numbers, although the city's big break came in 1965 when Walt Disney chose Orlando over Miami or Tampa as the site of his next theme park venture.

All of this construction was mercifully far from Downtown and Winter Park. Certainly buoyed by tourist dollars, growth could continue organically, yielding sophisticated, cosmopolitan communities without any of the artificiality that marks the tourist area to the southwest.

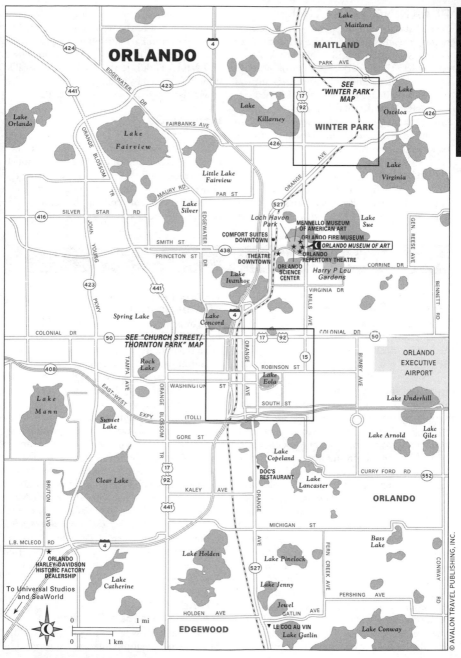

© AVALON TRAVEL PUBLISHING, INC.

PLANNING YOUR TIME

Several days could be spent seeing the museums, theaters, and historic attractions of Downtown Orlando and Winter Park. As an add-on to a theme park trip, a day of museum going provides some countervailing cultural ballast. The increasing number of luxury accommodations also makes Downtown an alluring place to stay, but be aware that it can take more than a half hour to reach the theme parks to the southwest on I-4.

Orientation

I-4 takes you right to the Downtown, with exits at Anderson, Robinson, and Colonial. The Orlando Centroplex, with all of its cul-tural venues, and Downtown's central business district are just to the north and west of Lake Eola. Thornton Park surrounds the park to the south and east. College Park is to the northwest and Winter Park is to the northeast, accessible from Downtown by Orange Avenue. The town of Maitland is northwest of Winter Park.

When to Go

High season and low season roughly correspond to those at Orlando's theme parks, but Downtown Orlando and Winter Park are much more year-round. Business travelers make the Downtown bustle all year, while "snowbirds" and winter residents bulk up the winter population of Winter Park.

Downtown Orlando

SIGHTS

◖ Orlando Museum of Art

The Orlando Museum of Art (2416 N. Mills Ave., from I-4, take the Princeton Street Exit 85, 407/896-4231, www.omart.org, 10 A.M.–4 P.M. Tues.–Fri., noon–4 P.M. Sat. and Sun., $8 adults, $7 seniors, $5 students 6–18, five and younger free) is a jewel, founded in 1924 in beautiful Orlando Loch Haven Park. Originally skeptical of this whole Downtown Orlando thing, I popped in to see *The Art of the Motorcycle,* a Guggenheim Museum traveling exhibition. Gleaming hogs of all vintages were arrayed in a lovely space, and a thoughtful audio tour accompanied the whole thing. I went back again for a *Paths to Impressionism* exhibit and then a *Gee's Bend: The Architecture of the Quilt.* They were all good, all amazingly curated, and arrayed in a stunning museum space. In addition to the thoughtfully chosen traveling shows, the museum has a lovely permanent collection that varies from Aztec to Zapotec ancient art of the Americas, a small collection of contemporary American art, and American portraits and landscapes that include the work of Benjamin West, Thomas Moran, and Rembrandt Peale.

Mennello Museum of American Art

Nearby is another local treasure. The Mennello Museum of American Art (900 E. Princeton St., 407/246-4278, www.mennello museum.org, 10:30 A.M.–4:30 P.M. Tues.–Sat., noon–4:30 P.M. Sun., $8 adults, $7 seniors, $5 students, 11 and younger free) is a small but tremendous collection of "outsider" art—folk art by amateur artists—anchored by a collection of works by Earl Cunningham. Donated by Marilyn and Michael Mennello in 1998, the collection has a kind of naive painterly style, married with an almost psychedelic, fantastical approach that visitors of all ages can appreciate. In addition, the Mennello hosts traveling exhibits such as the recent *American Masterworks from the Mitchell Museum,* a lovely assemblage of late 19th- and early 20th-century American paintings, from Thomas Eakins to Mary Cassatt and John Singer Sargent.

Orange County Regional History Center

This has been a work in progress for a while, but recent developments are exciting: The

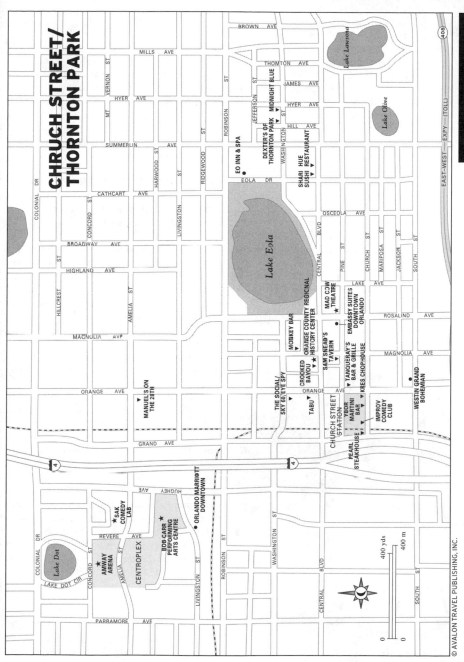

CHRUCH STREET/ THORNTON PARK

© AVALON TRAVEL PUBLISHING, INC.

Orange County Regional History Center (65 E. Central Blvd., 407/836-8500, www.the historycenter.org, 10 A.M.–5 P.M. Mon.–Sat., noon–5 P.M. Sun., $10 adults, $6.50 students and seniors, $3.50 children 3–12) was recently accepted as an affiliate of the Smithsonian Institution, which means it has begun incorporating aspects of the Smithsonian's collections into its permanent and seasonal exhibits, starting with a wonderful Civil War exhibit in 2007 that features one of the 48 original copies of the Emancipation Proclamation signed by Abraham Lincoln.

The bulk of the five-story museum is taken up with exploring the state's history: the Native Americans' first encounter with the Spanish, the Seminole Wars, and Central Florida's early pioneers, the Big Freeze in the 1890s and then in the 20th century, the Orlando Air Base during World War II, and on to Walt Disney. It's not as interactive as many history museums these days, but there's a replica of a WWII B-17 bomber and a restored 1927 courtroom to capture kids' interest.

COURTESY OF ORLANDO/ORANGE COUNTY CONVENTION & VISITORS BUREAU, INC.

Lake Eola Park

Orlando Fire Museum

What used to be part of the Orlando Historical Society, the Orlando Fire Museum (814 E. Rollins Ave., 407/898-3138, 9 A.M.–1 P.M. Mon.–Fri., free admission and parking) is another similar historical museum, with a small fire station restored to its 1926 glory, complete with old fire trucks and a 1911 horse-driven steam engine. It's a quickie, most appropriate if you have a firefighting enthusiast in your entourage. It offers short tours.

Orlando Science Center

An ideal rainy-day alternative to the theme parks, the Orlando Science Center (777 E. Princeton St., 407/514-2000, 10 A.M.–6 P.M. Sun.–Thurs., until 11 P.M. Fri. and Sat, $25 adults, $23 seniors and students, $20 children 3–11, two and younger free) is one of a growing number of large-scale, hands-on science museums in Florida. This one seems aimed at slightly older kids—but maybe I have that sense because my visit coincided with the controversial traveling *Bodies* exhibit. There's a nicely corresponding permanent exhibit, BodyZone 3-D, which is a 15-seat 3-D digital theater where guests journey through the circulatory system from the point of view of a red blood cell. The rest of the BodyZone exhibit contains interactive areas in which you find out what food does to the body (and vice versa), put a skeleton together, and listen to some slightly pious messages about nutrition and the evils of smoking. A "Measure Me" area is very little-kid appropriate, with exhibits that measure your size, strength, flexibility, agility, and sensory abilities. There are a huge exhibit on Florida's ecosystems, daily demonstrations of its scanning electron microscope, and what the museum claims is the world's largest Iwerks domed theater and Digistar II planetarium, with 28,000 watts of digital sound, that screens familiar IMAX films and a nighttime star show.

Bob Carr Performing Arts Centre

A clearinghouse for Orlando's lively arts directly across from the Expo Centre in the

Downtown Orlando Centroplex, the Bob Carr Performing Arts Centre plays host to the **Orlando Opera** (407/426-1700, www.orlando opera.org), the Orlando Philharmonic Orchestra (407/896-6700, www.orlandophil.org), the excellent **Orlando Ballet** (407/426-1733, www.orlandoballet.org), and the **SunTrust Broadway in Orlando** (407/950-4647, broadwayacrossamerica.com) lineup of traveling Broadway shows. The Orlando Centroplex is owned by the City of Orlando, but the city has just approved the construction of a huge new $1.05 billion performance art complex Downtown, so the 2,518-seat Bob Carr's role in the future will be less primary.

The Orlando Ballet has been especially high profile in recent years. In fact, the ballet company in its current state is fairly new, having changed its named to Orlando Ballet as recently as 2002 under the direction of international star Fernando Bujones. After the unexpected death of Bujones in 2005, ballet great Bruce Marks stepped in as artistic director. These days, the company of 28 international professional dancers, four apprentices, and 13 female trainees is Central Florida's only professional resident ballet company and one of the few ballet companies of its size performing the full-length classical ballets (recently of note: a gorgeous *Midsummer Night's Dream*). Its associated ballet school also continues to expand, with 1,000 students in four locations, including the Tampa Bay Performing Arts Center.

Harry P. Leu Gardens

Mr. Leu spent a quarter of a century cultivating plants in his Central Florida gardens, traveling the world collecting seeds, before turning the whole kit and caboodle over to the city in 1961. The 50 acres of botanical gardens (1920 N. Forest Ave., 407/246-2620, www.leu gardens.org, gardens 9 A.M.–5 P.M. daily, house 10 A.M.–4 P.M. daily but closed in July, tours every 30 minutes on the hour and half hour, $5 adults, $3 children 6–18, five and younger free) are heavy on the camellias—supposedly more than 2,000 specimens—with the state's largest formal rose garden (250 varieties). There are

COURTESY OF HARRY P. LEU GARDENS ORLANDO

Leu House Museum

also a tremendous cold-hardy palm collection, incredible bamboo, orchids, a tropical stream garden, and a butterfly garden. Despite being on the National Register of Historic Places, tours of the Leu House Museum are ho-hum; for another $7 (make reservations), you can take a guided 1.5-hour tour of the garden that is extremely educational for the rookie or even seasoned gardener. Camellias are at their peak between October and March.

Orlando Magic at the Amway Arena

It's one of those vexing sports facilities that occasionally experiences a name change and throws everyone temporarily into confusion. The former TD Waterhouse Centre was actually born as the Orlando Arena; it's now the Amway Arena (One Magic Place, 600 W. Amelia, 407/896-2442) and is part of the Orlando Centroplex Downtown along with the Bob Carr and other venues. The arena is home to the NBA's Orlando Magic, to the AFL's Orlando Predators, and to a variety of sporting and entertainment events. Having attended exactly one Magic game here, I thought it was an intimate, wonderful venue in which to see professional basketball. Evidently I'm in the minority—it's ranked near the bottom of the NBA in terms of capacity and luxury suites. The City of Orlando has come to an agreement with the Magic to allocate $480 million for a new arena. Construction is set to begin in 2008 with the Magic eventually moving to a new venue by 2011.

ENTERTAINMENT AND SHOPPING
Theater

Sarasota may reign supreme in Florida when it comes to sheer number of theater options, but Orlando supports a remarkable number of companies doing work that varies from the avant-garde to crowd-pleasing musicals. **Orlando Repertory Theatre** (1001 E. Princeton St., 407/896-7365, www.orlandorep.com) is a professional company that works in partnership with University of Central Florida to

stage family-appropriate classics and riffs on kids' lit. It has the regular main stage season, an "American Classics" series that honors U.S. playwrights, and a youth academy for aspiring young actors. The **Orlando-UCF Shakespeare Festival** (812 E. Rollins St., 407/447-1700, www.shakespearefest.org) is another partnership with UCF, the results of which are largely adult oriented. It's a misnomer, really, as it's not a festival, nor does it exclusively stage Shakespeare or his ilk. The company performs in three theaters, two in the John and Rita Lowndes Shakespeare Center adjacent to the Orlando Museum of Art, and one at the Lake Eola Amphitheater Downtown (that's usually Shakespeare, usually in the summer). Plays vary from heavy stuff such as *Crime and Punishment* or *Into the Woods* to family-friendly shows such as *Really Rosie*.

Mad Cow Theatre (105 S. Magnolia Ave., 407/297-8788, www.madcowtheatre.com) is an excellent small theater, with Equity and non-Equity performers in a 10-play season. It has moved locations a couple of times, but the Downtown theater, with two separate stages, is intimate and adequate for its modestly staged productions. The quality of the acting is excellent—I saw a staging of *Sweeney Todd* and it was the greatest, and creepiest, demon barber of Fleet Street I ever saw. The theater also hosts an annual Orlando Cabaret Festival and The Orlando Puppet Festival. After performances on Thursday and Sunday evenings the cast and production team does an onstage "talkback" with the audience.

Just a couple of blocks from the Loch Haven Park complex (Orlando Museum of Art, Orlando-UCF Shakespeare Festival), **Theatre Downtown** (2113 N. Orange Ave., 407/841-0083, www.theatredowntown.net) has been staging several shows a year since its first, David Mamet's *American Buffalo* in 1989. Recent seasons have included productions of A. R. Gurney's *Sylvia* and Tennessee Williams's *Cat on a Hot Tin Roof*. **Orlando Youth Theatre** (407/254-4930) also puts on some fun, family shows at local high school and churches, and **People's Theatre** (511 W South St., 407/426-

0545, wwwpeoplestheatre.org) stages shows that deal largely with multiculturalism, ethnicity, or the minority experience.

Nightlife
The Church Street area was until recently anchored by Club Paris, but the huge nightclub closed down in August 2007. As of this writing, the other venues in the adult-entertainment complex are still open, but call ahead to make sure.

Expert martinis can be had at either **Ybor Martini Bar** (41 W. Church St., 407/316-8006, 4 P.M.–2 A.M. Mon.–Sat.) or **Monkey Bar** (26 Wall St., 407/481-1030, 4–11 P.M. daily, bar 4 P.M.–2 A.M.). **Tabu** (46 N. Orange Ave., 407/648-8363, www.tabunightclub.com) and **The Social** (54 N. Orange Ave, 407/246-1419, www.thesocial.org) are both worth a whirl, with live music at The Social. **Sky 60** (54 N. Orange Ave., 407/246-1599, 5 P.M.–2 A.M. Mon.–Fri., 8 A.M.–2 A.M. Sat.), located between the two, has a lovely tree-lined rooftop deck with cabana seating, very South Beach. **Eye Spy** (54 N. Orange Ave., 407/246-1599, 9 P.M.–2 A.M. Mon.–Fri., 10 P.M.–2 A.M. Sat.), its sister nightspot in the same location, is a chill hangout marked cryptically by a British telephone booth.

There are two comedy clubs: **Improv Comedy Club and Restaurant** (129 W. Church St., 321/281-8000, www.orlando improv.com) in Church Street Station, and **SAK Comedy Lab** (380 W. Amelia St., 407/648-0001, www.sak.com). Call to confirm SAK Comedy Lab events; rumor has it that it might be going out of business.

Shopping
While rich in restaurants and nightlife, Downtown's shopping hasn't quite caught up. There's a pleasant **Antique Row** on Orange Avenue Downtown, stretching from Colonial Drive/Highway 50 to Lake Ivanhoe, but it's not going to knock anyone's socks off. Church Street has a smattering of shopping, but for something that will get your pulse racing a little, spend a little time at the **Orlando Harley-Davidson**

Historic Factory Dealership (I-4 near Conroy Rd. Exit 78, 3770 37th St., 407/423-0346). It rents fatboys for just $99 a day.

ACCOMMODATIONS
Luxury hotels are coming fast and furious Downtown, but it's all of recent vintage.

$100-150
The Eõ Inn and Spa (227 N. Eola Dr., 407/481-8485, rates from $139) boasts 17 suites tucked into a 1923-era building overlooking Lake Eola Park and the Downtown skyline. A rooftop terrace with whirlpool, a day spa, and an in-house Panera restaurant make it an extremely pleasant stay.

For a middle-of-the-road, all-suites hotel within walking distance of the Amway Arena and Church Street Station, the **Embassy Suites Downtown Orlando** (191 E. Pine St., 407/841-1000, rates from $149) offers all suites, with private bedrooms and spacious living rooms, two televisions, two telephones, but only one refrigerator (two would be excessive, right?).

In a similar vein, **Orlando Marriott Downtown** (400 W. Livingston St., 407/481-0555, rates from $129) is 290 rooms right across from the Bob Carr Performing Arts Center and the Amway Arena. It's a very business-oriented hotel with good workout facilities and a pleasant steak house called Zinfandels. **Comfort Suites Downtown** (2416 N. Orange Ave., 407/996-0523, rates from $107) is right across the street from Florida Hospital Orlando, with 122 guest rooms, some with kitchenettes, all with high-speed wireless Internet access included.

Over $150
Hotelier Richard Kessler opened the AAA four-diamond **C Westin Grand Bohemian** (325 S. Orange Ave., 407/313-9000, rates from $249) in 2001 and people thought he was a little touched. The laugh's on them, because the hotel has been a hit among business travelers, its 250 guest rooms gorgeously kitted out with velvet drapes, plush leather headboards, and crisp white bed linens on pillow-top beds.

The hotel's Boheme Restaurant consistently wins kudos from food magazines, its luxurious menu featuring dishes such as seared foie gras with fig bread pudding and a warm huckleberry sauce, and surprising Asian fillips as in the sushi bento box for two or the Thai spiced duck breast with black bean sauce. A Sunday jazz brunch draws a huge following, and the Bösendorfer Lounge (with one of only two Imperial Grand Bösendorfer pianos in the world) features nightly jazz.

FOOD
Church Street Station

Historically, Church Street Station was a Downtown dining-and-nightlife mecca that did well for a while and then fell on hard times. Now it's back, with a spate of new restaurants and clubs that really rival those in the greater Orlando area. The jury's out on whether the area will really make a successful go of things, but for the visitor it's a lively evening on the town. Among the newer entries is **Pearl Steakhouse** (125 W. Church St., 407/581-8865, 5–10 P.M. Mon.–Wed., until 11 P.M. Thurs.–Sat., $24–39) for prime beef superseared at 1,800°F with all the fixings, such as creamed spinach or crispy fried onions.

The folks at Hue (see below) are responsible for the swanky steaks-and-chops **Kres Chophouse** (17 W. Church St., 407/447-7950, 11:30 A.M.–midnight Mon.–Fri., 5 P.M.–midnight Sat., $20–35).

Thornton Park

In the greater Downtown area just east of Lake Eola Park, there are a couple of hot beds of hipster dining activity along Washington Street, Summerlin Avenue, and Central Boulevard. The epicenter of this might be **(Hue Restaurant** (629 E. Central Blvd., 407/849-1800, 3–11 P.M. Sun.–Wed., until midnight Thurs.–Sat., $23–32), opened in 2002 but already ensconced as the "original" Downtown see-and-be-seener. The interior is posh, although the menu isn't pushing any envelopes: It's familiar but expertly crafted wood-grilled

New York strip with red wine demi-glace or oven-roasted Chilean seabass with salty/tangy asiago tapenade.

Shari Sushi (621 E. Central Blvd., 407/420-9420, 11:30 A.M.–2 P.M. Mon.–Sat., 6–10 P.M. Mon.–Wed., until 11 P.M. Thurs.–Sat., $12–20) in the same block features an attractive interior and very apt renderings of traditional sushi, *nigiri,* and sashimi, and a bunch of fun signature rolls.

In place of the former Rocco's, **(Midnight Blue** (900 E. Washington St., 407/999-9012, 6 P.M.–midnight Tues.–Sat., brunch 11 A.M.–3 P.M. Sat. and Sun., $13–20) serves exceptional 21st-century small plates overseen by local superstar chef Jephanie Foster. It's comfort food you can feel hip wallowing in, from the sliders to the chicken-fried chicken.

For a less ironic and more caloric meal, the hoagies at **Dexter's of Thornton Park** (808 E. Washington St., 407/648-2777, 11 A.M.–10 P.M. Mon.–Thurs., until 11 P.M. Fri. and Sat., 10 A.M.–10 P.M. Sun., $16–25) are casual and fun. There are fancier entrées such as a laudable pressed-duck sandwich, mostly to satisfy its rock stars-in-their-own-minds crowd.

Downtown

Fairly new on the scene, **Doc's Restaurant** (1315 S. Orange Ave., 407/839-3627, 11 A.M.–2:30 P.M. Mon.–Fri., 5–9 P.M. Wed. and Thurs., until 10 P.M. Fri. and Sat., $18–34) is straight-ahead steaks and seafood, with noteworthy crab cakes and clam chowder.

The very fanciest of the Downtown offerings is clearly **Manuel's on the 28th** (390 N. Orange Ave., 28th Floor Bank of America Bldg., 407/246-6580, 6–10 P.M. Tues.–Sat., $26–36), a traditional special-occasion menu trotted out in a floor-to-ceiling-windows room on the 28th floor of a Downtown building.

The playing field is so densely packed Downtown that a number of other restaurants are worth a quick word: You'll find **Sam Snead's Tavern at Lake Eola** (301 E. Pine St., 407/999-0109, 11 A.M.–10 P.M. Mon.–Thurs., until 2 A.M. Fri.–Sat., $12–22) for

DOWNTOWN ORLANDO

American food in a golf-themed atmosphere; fancy French food at **Le Coq Au Vin** (4800 S. Orange Ave., 407/851-6980, 5:30–10 P.M. Tues.–Sat., 5–9 P.M. Sun., $17.50–29); suave cocktails in a former bank vault at **Tanqueray's Bar and Grille** (100 S. Orange Ave., 407/649-8540, 11 A.M.–2:30 A.M. Mon.–Fri., 6 P.M.–2:30 A.M. Sat.–Sun.); and New Orleans–inflected cocktails and nibbles at **Crooked Bayou** (50 E. Central Blvd., 407/839-5852, 11 A.M.–2 A.M. Mon.–Sat., 7 P.M.–2 A.M. Sun., $7–10).

Just northeast of Downtown along Colonial Drive and Mills Avenue is a stretch of Vietnamese, Korean, Thai, and Chinese restaurants to support the growing population of Southeast Asian residents.

Winter Park

Most residents at some point squeeze in the fact that Winter Park once had the greatest per capita wealth of anyplace in the country. As Muhammad Ali said, it ain't braggin' if it's true. If you doubt the claim, just stroll past Park Avenue's collection of shops and restaurants, visit the handful of exceptional small museums, or drive around gawking through the eight square miles of posh residential neighborhoods. Then visit the boat ramp and all the fancy accoutrements of Rollins College, and you'll be convinced. Unlike most of Central Florida, Winter

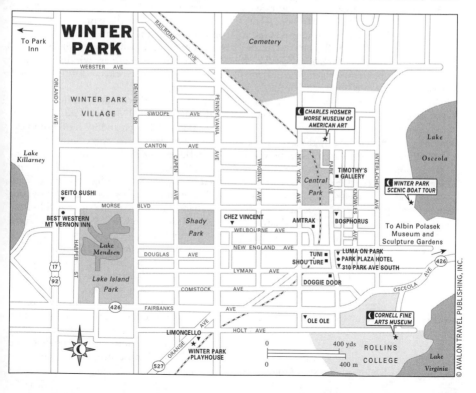

© AVALON TRAVEL PUBLISHING, INC.

Park has palpable history, a sense of place. Built on a system of canals connecting little lakes, houses are wide-set and gracious, with sweeping water views and shaded by 100-year-old live oaks draped with Spanish moss.

The city was chartered in 1887 and populated at first by wealthy northerners escaping New England winters. A veritable who's who of business tycoons, magnates, and assorted robber barons made up the original residents. Not surprisingly, cultural amenities were quick to follow. These days, the city swells by 250,000 visitors each mid-March for the annual Winter Park Sidewalk Art Festival, but it's worthy of a visit anytime.

SIGHTS
◖ Cornell Fine Arts Museum at Rollins College

Considered one of the country's top college art museums, the Cornell (1000 Holt Ave., 407/646-2526, 10 A.M.–5 P.M. Tues.–Sat., 1–5 P.M. Sun., $5) is a jewel, its permanent collection and thoughtfully curated shows bound to engender quiet contemplation as well as lively debate. Newly renovated, the museum reopened at the beginning of 2006. An early exhibit is a fair example of the museum's ambition: Obliquely concerned with environmental issues, *Revising Arcadia: The Landscape in Contemporary Art* was curated by the dynamic E. Luanne McKinnon, drawing together powerful works by some of America's leading contemporary artists expressed through photography, painting, and mixed media. Many of the works featured dystopian views of contemporary life, but each was curiously beautiful and surprising in its depiction. In early 2007, the museum showcased four of Chicago-based artist Nick Cave's celebrated *Soundsuits,* another stunning exhibit with impact that far exceeds the museum's small size.

Rollins College is the oldest college in Florida, established in 1885 by New England Congregationalists as a bastion of liberal arts education. Today it's thought of as one of the premier liberal arts colleges in the country, having produced Rhodes, Fulbright, Goldwater,

and Truman scholars and even Nobel laureates through the years. It's teensy, with only 1,700 undergraduates on a stunning 70-acre campus. Visitors are welcome to walk the Spanish Mediterranean–style grounds and peek at the unbelievably swanky 75,000-square-foot Alfond Sports Center and at the Cornell Campus Center.

◖ Charles Hosmer Morse Museum of American Art

Having waxed so rhapsodic about the Cornell, darned if I'm not going to do it again with the Morse (445 N. Park Ave., 407/645-5311, 9:30 A.M.–4 P.M. Tues.–Thurs. and Sat., until 8 P.M. Fri., 1–4 P.M. Sun., $3 adults, $1 students, children 12 and younger free). Right on Park Avenue, Winter Park's main drag, this half-day museum contains the world's most comprehensive collection of the works of Louis Comfort Tiffany. I hesitate to describe it as a "decorative arts" museum, which somehow has come to seem slightly pejorative. Let's say it's a fine art museum in which much of the art resembles lamps, leaded-glass windows, china, and miscellaneous crockery of the 19th and 20th century.

Stand before the chapel interior Tiffany designed for the 1893 World's Columbian Exposition in Chicago and it's hard not to experience awe. It's a sacred space, luminous with light reflected off thousands of tiny pieces of glass. The rest of the museum contains dozens of Tiffany windows and objects from Tiffany Studios (enamels, lamps, art glass, pottery) but that chapel interior is a showstopper. The museum lent more than 250 of its Tiffany items to the Metropolitan Museum of Art in New York for an exhibition called *Louis Comfort Tiffany and Laurelton Hall: An Artist's Country Estate* through May 2007, at which point it all returned home to Winter Park.

The museum has a truly impressive collection of Rookwood art pottery and Arts and Crafts pieces and a nice permanent collection of American paintings, primarily of the 19th and early 20th centuries and heavy on Florida artists.

EATONVILLE AND MAITLAND

Six miles north of Orlando, Eatonville was incorporated in 1883 and placed on the National Register of Historic Places in 1998. It's the oldest all-black town in the United States, formed after the Emancipation Proclamation in 1863. Its most famous former resident is Harlem Renaissance author and folklorist Zora Neale Hurston, who spent her childhood in Eatonville and writes about her time there in *Their Eyes Were Watching God* and *Dust Tracks on a Road*. Huston is credited as being the first to collect and publish African American and Afro Caribbean folklore, which she published in her book *Mules and Men*. Her love of Florida (she once wrote, "I've got the map of Florida on my tongue") is matched by Florida's love of her. Every January the town puts on a raucous weeklong **Zora Neale Hurston Festival of the Arts and Humanities** (www.zoraneale hurstonfestival.com) and the small **Zora Neale Hurston National Museum of Fine Arts** (227 E. Kennedy Blvd., 407/647-3307,

9 A.M.-4 P.M. Mon.-Fri., free admission but donations encouraged) pays tribute to her by showcasing the work of artists of African descent. The small museum takes about 20 minutes to tour, after which you can grab a walking tour brochure and visit some of the remaining historic structures in the small town (her house, however, is gone).

Artist Jules Andre Smith did a series of paintings depicting life in Eatonville in the 1930s and '40s, some of which you can see in the nearby **Maitland Art Center** (231 W. Packwood Ave., Maitland, 407/539-2181, 9 A.M.-4:30 P.M. Mon.-Fri., noon-4:30 Sat. and Sun., admission $3), which was founded in 1938 by Smith as an art colony. These days it's an exhibit space and venue for art classes, but it merits attention for its architecture, which is described as "fantasy architecture." It features Mayan/Aztec motifs and includes 23 structures linked by gardens and courtyards. Smith did much of the intricate carving and painting on the building himself.

Albin Polasek Museum and Sculpture Gardens

A much more idiosyncratic array of works, the Polasek (633 Osceola Ave., 407/647-6294, 10 A.M.–4 P.M. Tues.–Sat., 1–4 P.M. Sun., $5 adults, $4 seniors, $3 students, younger than 12 free) features the work of the Czech sculptor arrayed in his slightly weird house (he designed the no-frills cinderblock home himself). In addition to Polasek's finished pieces, small-scale maquettes (studies), and drawings, the museum houses artworks by other people that Polasek collected throughout his life (lots of Czechs and Poles represented). A lakeside garden contains liturgical, mythological, and classical sculptures by Polasek and others. The museum can be viewed in an hour; children aren't wild about it.

Central Park

Just outside the Morse Museum on Park Avenue is the large park known as Central Park.

Charles Hosmer Morse himself deeded the park to the city. These days, it's the site of countless park-bench picnics and regular arts and crafts festivals. Take a break from shopping along Park Avenue to explore the walking paths of this lovely urban park.

◖ Winter Park Scenic Boat Tour

My very favorite thing to do in Winter Park has been a local treasure for half a century. The Winter Park Scenic Boat Tour (312 E. Morse Blvd., 407/644-4056, www.scenicboattours .com/home.htm, 10 A.M.–4 P.M. daily, $10 adults, $5 children 2–11, younger than two free, no credit cards) takes you on an 18-person, hour-long pontoon boat ride through the historic canals and past the lakefront mansions of Winter Park. The boat captain/narrator is a wealth of information on botany, animals, and history, with some good puns and cheap jokes thrown into the mix. You're likely to see anhingas and great blue herons stalking their prey; unbelievable manses with manicured gardens; sailboats and speedboats gleaming at lakes' edge; mullet jumping out of the water; and pampered Rollins students sculling or enjoying the sun on their lakeside campus.

ENTERTAINMENT AND SHOPPING

The **Winter Park Playhouse** (711-B Orange Ave., 407/645-0145) is the only local professional theater, staging several shows each year in a mix of family-friendly shows, musicals, and dramas.

If your visit happens to be in February the annual **Bach Festival Society of Winter Park** (407/646-2182) has staged a two-week festival of world-class lecturers, soloists, and ensembles for the past 75 years. While most of the hoopla is about the work of Johann Sebastian Bach, other great composers get a little attention, too. In March, the annual **Winter Park Sidewalk Art Festival** (407/672-6390, www.wpsaf.org) draws art lovers to the area by the thousands.

Park Avenue is home to 10 blocks of shops and galleries interspersed with restaurants, from Swoope Avenue south to Fairbanks Avenue. You'll see Williams-Sonoma, Pottery Barn, Restoration Hardware, Ann Taylor, and some other ubiquitous names, but independent shops abound, from clothing boutiques including trendy **Tuni** (301 S. Park Ave., 407/628-1609, 10 A.M.–7 P.M. Mon.–Wed. and Sat., until 8 P.M. Thurs.–Fri., noon–6 P.M. Sun.) or **Shou'Ture** (339 S. Park Ave., 407/647-9372, 10 A.M.–6 P.M. Mon.–Wed. and Sat., until 7 P.M. Thurs.–Fri., noon–5 P.M. Sun.) for fashion-forward shoes and a quick pedicure to boot. **Timothy's Gallery** (236 N. Park Ave., 407/629-0707, 10 A.M.–5:30 P.M. Mon.–Sat., 1–5 P.M. Sun.) sells ceramics, jewelry, and home accessories. Even **Doggie Door** (356 S. Park Ave. 407/644-2969, 10 A.M.–6 P.M. Mon.–Wed., until 7 P.M. Thurs.–Sat., noon–5 P.M. Sun.) provides treats for the canine back home.

Winter Park Village (500 N. Orlando Ave., 407/571-2502) is a nearby small shopping center with retail shops, about a dozen restaurants, a great chocolate shop, and a 20-plex movie theater.

ACCOMMODATIONS

Park Plaza Hotel (307 S. Park Ave., 407/647-1072, rates from $120) is right in the thick of Downtown. It's a small independent hotel with 27 smallish rooms kitted out with antiques, many with balconies that overlook Park Avenue. Street noise and thin walls can be a problem. For a clean, simple, old-style, low-rise motel, **Park Inn** (951 N. Wymore Rd., 407/539-1955, rates from $62) may fit the bill. The **Best Western Mt. Vernon Inn** (110 S. Orlando Ave., 407/647-1166, rates from $104) is a little nicer, with 144 rooms, meeting facilities, a lovely small pool; it's about a mile to Park Avenue.

FOOD

Orlando is a serious food city, where restaurants engage in fierce competition for the approbation of the sophisticated, worldly locals. **(Luma on Park** (290 S. Park Ave., 407/599-4111, 5:30–11 P.M. Mon.–Thurs., until midnight Fri. and Sat., 11 A.M.–3 P.M. Sun., $25–40) gets top honors for its incredible array of wines by the glass as well as contemporary dishes such as Gulf red snapper with corn and local chanterelles or pizzas such as the Copper River sockeye salmon with fennel salad, olives, and saffron. At the corner of Park and New England Avenues, it's in a perfect corner spot in the recently remodeled Bank of America building, with a striking two-story illuminated wine vault.

The number two spot is a hard call. Some people favor the comfortable **310 Park Ave. South** (310 S. Park Ave., 407/647-7277, 11 A.M.–10 P.M. Mon.–Wed., until 11 P.M. Thurs.–Sat., 10 A.M.–10 P.M. Sun., $15–30) for herb-crusted salmon or a simple pork chop. But the family-owned Mediterranean **Limoncello** (702 Orange Ave., 407/539-0900, 5:30–10 P.M. Tues.–Sun., $14–22) also does a brisk business with familiar Italian pastas.

Other top contenders include **Bosphorus** (108 S. Park Ave., 407/644-8609, 11 A.M.–

10 P.M. Sun.–Thurs., 11 A.M.–midnight Fri. and Sat., $9.50–24.95), which gets high marks for its authentic Turkish cuisine. **Seito Sushi Japanese Restaurant** (510 N. Orlando Ave., 407/644-5050, 5–10 P.M. Mon., 11:30 A.M.–2:30 P.M. and 5–10 P.M. Tues.–Sat., $6–15) gets the nod for sushi. **Chez Vincent** (533 W.

New England Ave., 407/599-2929, 11:30 A.M.–2:30 P.M. and 5–10 P.M. daily, $16.95–25.95) seems to be a favorite for classic French bistro fare. **Ole Ole** (601 S. New York Ave., 407/673-1653, 11 A.M.–10 P.M. Mon.–Thurs., until midnight Fri. and Sat., noon–9 P.M. Sun., $7–25) is the place to go for tapas.

Practicalities

INFORMATION AND SERVICES

In an emergency, dial 911; for nonemergencies, the Orlando Police Department is at 100 South Hughey Avenue and can be reached at 407/246-2414. In case of a medical emergency, Florida Hospital Orlando (601 East Rollins St., 407/303-6611) offers full emergency-room services.

GETTING THERE AND AROUND
By Car

Major interstates—I-95, I-75, and I-10—provide access into Florida from the north, with connections directly into the area via I-4, Florida's Turnpike, and U.S. Highway 192.

I-4 takes you directly Downtown. To get to Winter Park, take Orange Avenue to the northeast, or take East Colonial and make a left on Semoran Boulevard.

By Air

The area is serviced by major airlines and charter services at the **Orlando International Airport** (1 Airport Blvd., 407/825-2001), 10 minutes away. All major rental-car companies are available from the airport.

By Train

Amtrak has a major train station Downtown (1400 Sligh Blvd., 800/872-7245, 10 A.M.–6:30 P.M. daily).

INTERNATIONAL DRIVE

International Drive, often called I-Drive, is not so much a destination as it is an inevitable route for navigating Orlando's theme parks and attractions. The whole of I-Drive is 15 minutes southwest of downtown Orlando and 15 minutes northeast of Walt Disney World, and, roughly speaking, the length of I-Drive parallels I-4, just a touch to its east. With more than 100 hotels, 150 restaurants, and a generous handful of half-day or several-hour attractions, the boulevard exerts the kind of magnetic pull that assures every visitor spends a little time along its length, if only in the name of dinner. The Orange County Convention Center (the country's second largest) and the bulk of Orlando's high-end and outlet mall shopping are also to be found here—in fact, the north end of I-Drive ends in a cul-de-sac at the Prime Outlets Orlando and its south end is another cul-de-sac at Orlando Premium Outlets.

PLANNING YOUR TIME

International Drive's location makes it an ideal place to stay if the bulk of your time in Orlando will be spent at Universal Orlando Resort, SeaWorld Orlando, or the Orange County Convention Center. It makes less sense if your locus of activity will be around Walt Disney World Resort—that's too much time sitting in traffic.

Orientation

The north end of I-Drive (near Universal Orlando Resort) can be reached by Exit 75A and 75B off I-4; the southern end (near SeaWorld Orlando) can be reached by Exit 71 off I-4.

COURTESY OF ORLANDO/ORANGE COUNTY CONVENTION & VISITORS BUREAU, INC.

HIGHLIGHTS

◖ **I-Ride Trolley Service:** Hop aboard one of 15 trolleys as they shoot up and down I-Drive, obviating the need for driving in one of Central Florida's most congested tourist hubs. The trolley stops at most hotels, the theme parks, malls, and attractions along its length (page 217).

◖ **Wonder Works:** A perfect rainy-day alternative to the theme parks, this amusement park/science museum features more than 100 educational but fun hands-on exhibits, all housed in a photo-worthy upside-down building (page 218).

◖ **SkyVenture:** A rookie skydiver's first jump is often spent harnessed to an instructor. Unless, of course, you try Orlando's indoor skydiving free-fall wind tunnel. Splurge a little and get a hilarious keepsake DVD recording of your flight experience (page 221).

◖ **Outlet Malls:** Supposedly as many people come to Orlando to shop as to visit Walt Disney World Resort. The reason? It boasts major outlet malls. Prime Outlets Orlando and Orlando Premium Outlets entice bargain shoppers with deep discounts at hundreds of stores (page 224).

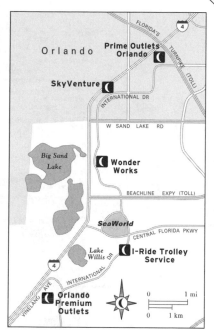

LOOK FOR ◖ TO FIND RECOMMENDED SIGHTS, ACTIVITIES, DINING, AND LODGING.

Like much of greater Orlando, I-Drive seems constantly to be a work in progress. Begun in the 1960s by Martin Marietta, the first bit was the stretch just north of Sand Lake Road, now among the most congested and trafficky spots in the area. Souvenir shacks, T-shirt shops, chain restaurants, and a number of attractions vie for attention on this part of I-Drive, which is harrowing to navigate on foot (too many curb cuts and disoriented tourists cutting them). Also, because there is no median or center turn lane in this section, gridlock is a common occurrence during busy traffic periods.

I-Drive is two lanes in either direction from Pointe Plaza Drive and north, and three lanes in either direction south of that. The farther south you go, toward Highway 528 (formerly the Bee Line Expressway, now the Beachline Expressway) and past the convention center, it gets a bit more spread out, upscale, and pedestrian friendly.

Universal Boulevard

To circumnavigate some of the densest traffic along I-Drive, consider using Universal Boulevard, which runs roughly parallel to it on its east from the Pointe Orlando shopping center to just north of Carrier Drive (at Wet 'n Wild), where Universal and I-Drive cross. North of this, Universal crosses I-4 and runs into Universal Orlando Resort. In the south, around the Pointe Orlando, Universal Boulevard splits from I-Drive and heads east and south to connect with the Beachline Expressway.

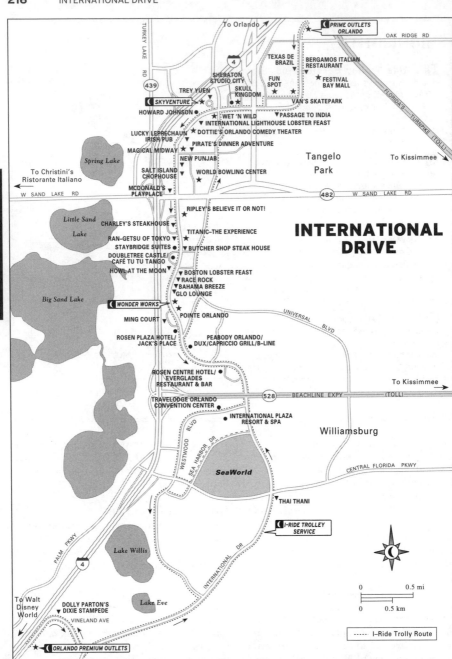

COURTESY OF ORLANDO/ORANGE COUNTY CONVENTION & VISITORS BUREAU, INC.

The I-Ride Trolley eases I-Drive traffic congestion.

Although recent growth on Universal Boulevard is every bit as robust as I-Drive, it's newer and with fewer major attractions dotting its length—consequently, it's a less congested drive. Universal Boulevard is six lanes from Vineland Road south to International Drive, and then four lanes farther south to Pointe Plaza Boulevard, and then six lanes again to the Beachline Expressway.

◖ I-Ride Trolley Service

No one would say that International Drive is best explored on foot. At the same time, driving it can prove stressful, especially in high season around dinnertime. For visitors staying or playing along I-Drive, the I-Ride Trolley Service is a wonderful way to traverse Central Florida's densest tourist corridor. Since it started service in 1997, more than 14 million rides have been logged, with 15 trolleys shooting up and down the boulevard 8 A.M.–10:30 P.M. daily. On the Main Line route you can expect a trolley every

20 minutes; the Green Line route is more like every 30.

The Main Line route follows International Drive from Prime Outlets to SeaWorld and continues to the South International Drive corridor, ending at the Orlando Premium Outlets. The Green Line route travels from Wet 'n Wild to the Orange County Convention Center and ends at SeaWorld. The total trolley route distance one-way is 14 miles.

Servicing hundreds of I-Drive destinations with around 100 trolley stops, the system involves oversize color-coded numbered signs on either side of the boulevard that correspond to numbers on the trolley route map. Trolleys are air-conditioned and conductors tend to be helpful guides to the area.

A single adult fare is $1, seniors $0.25, children 12 and younger ride free. Unlimited ride passes are $3 for one day, $5 for three, and $9 for seven. Each trolley has two wheelchair positions and an ADA-specified hydraulic lift system.

Sights and Recreation

For those spending multiple days touring Orlando's theme parks, I strongly recommend breaking it up with at least a day of seeing the sights and goofing off along International Drive. Several of the half-day or several-hour attractions here are a breath of fresh air—fun, affordable, air-conditioned, and not entailing miles of walking. Many of them might also be treated as a postdinner activity or a rainy-day alternative to the big parks. Several regularly offer discount coupons in tourism brochures to the area, and many extend online ticket discounts.

◖ WONDER WORKS

It's hard to miss. You'll be driving along I-Drive when it appears you're passing a building that has had the grave misfortune of being dropped, upside-down, from some height. The regal white edifice, its Corinthian columns somewhat the worse for wear, is like a turtle on its back, audibly groaning and creaking. Why, you ask? Wonder Works (9067 International Dr., 407/351-8800, 9 A.M.–midnight daily, Wonder Works admission $19.95 adults, $14.95 seniors and children 4–12; one game lazer tag $4.95; The Outta Control Dinner Show $21.95 adults, $14.95 seniors and children 4–12; with combo prices to do two or three of the above; park at the Pointe Orlando parking structure) is somehow the victim of a freak tornado, we're told, which has wrenched it from the Bermuda Triangle to Orlando.

After going through a spinning, black-light entrance tunnel, all is right-side up. But the traditional perspective is hardly a disappointment: More than 100 interactive exhibits render it somewhere between an amusement park and a science museum—worth about two hours of time, it's more educational than the former, less pious than the latter. Simulators allow you to fly a fighter jet or land the space shuttle (boy, is it hard to put that puppy down gently). I spent ages in the bubble corner, blowing enormous and elastic bubble loops big enough to step into and extend like a transparent column above me. You can try out a bed of nails (not comfy, but not puncturing either), take quizzes about earthquakes and other natural phenomena, or design your own roller coaster. While I've heard from other visitors that exhibits frequently go on the fritz, all was in working order during my visit.

The basement is given over to laser tag in a big way, with 10,000 feet of space devoted to people zapping each other. And in the evenings, at 6 and 8 P.M., Wonder Works is home to one of Orlando's best, and most affordable, dinner shows. Unlimited pizza, popcorn, beer, wine, and soft drinks are snarfed while watching a show that is heavy on the improv comedy (lots of audience participation) and some really notable magic. Reservations recommended.

RIPLEY'S BELIEVE IT OR NOT! ORLANDO ODDITORIUM

Right down the street from Wonder Works, Ripley's (8201 International Dr., 407/363-4418, 9 A.M.–1 A.M. daily, $18.95 adults, $11.95 children 4–12, free parking) makes for a great evening activity with its late hours. Like Wonder Works, it's housed in a building that desperately needs the attention of one of the perky teams at HGTV—it appears to be sinking into the ground. Robert Ripley, obsessive collector of the peculiar (a Mona Lisa made out of toast) and downright gross (preserved two-headed animals), has his collection spread throughout 27 museums in 10 countries now, each one containing mostly unique items. This particular museum arrays the collection in 16 galleries of miscellaneous flotsam and jetsam, requiring 90 minutes or so to explore (children younger than seven might find some items impressively lurid). There are shrunken heads, freakishly big and little people exhibits, a Rolls-Royce made out of matchsticks, a billiard room with a skewed table on which you can test your trick shots, torture implements, and brain teasers (different from torture implements).

TIME-SHARE SCARE

A single day at Universal Orlando Resort, with admission to both parks, is $77. SeaWorld Orlando is $61.95. Walt Disney World Resort is $67 for a one-day, one-park ticket. There's gotta be a better way, I said to myself. It was going to be five of us for an impromptu day at the park, and full-price tickets were strikingly unpalatable. There must be cheaper tickets out there, and I began to search the Internet.

Yes, there are. Kind of. Most of the parks offer several dollars off if you buy your tickets online, but key in the words "half price tickets" and "Disney" and you'll find a whole other thing entirely. The websites won't indicate this anywhere, not even the fine print, but these sites are luring you in for a time-share pitch.

Orlando is awash in time-share options, and the competition is fierce to attract us saps, I mean potential owners. How bad could it be? I signed up. I won't name any names, but my guess is that most of these experiences run something like this:

My mother and I arrived just as the sun was lifting free of the horizon, bathing Universal Drive in the warm first light. Checking in, we were interrogated at length by a woman behind a counter. Income, marital status, practically our shoe size. We were then retrieved by our fresh-faced "associate," who led us into a huge, balloon- and banner-strewn room with '80s pop blaring at top volume. All around us, similarly fresh-faced associates were getting their game faces on, honestly saying "It's show time!" before retrieving their own first customers. Our associate must have been newly minted from sales school because his relentless insertion of our first names in sentences played like an unfortunate tic (I could imagine the manual with "insert name here" in each script). For emphasis, he would yell, "Guys!!" to call our attention to something particularly amazing.

Basically, he was offering us the right to occupy a vacation property during a single week each year, a Saturday to a Saturday. We could exchange our interval with intervals in comparable facilities in other parts of the world, or we could add additional intervals for a deeply discounted price. This comes with an actual deed that is salable and transferable to my lucky progeny upon my death. All of this was conveyed with props and a great number of pictograms jotted on a legal pad.

The cost? $13,000. Amortizing that over a bunch of years, that's still a pretty pricey week. And what if I don't always want to stay for a week in Orlando? And what if I don't like any of the sister properties, or they're not available? And I've heard that time-share values don't go up the way regular property does, so it's not really an "investment." In fact, I've heard resales of time-shares often go for about half of the initial price. And who's to say the management company will take great care of the place through time?

Our associate was getting discouraged. I was clearly the bad cop; my mother's role was to sit and look blankly. We waited him out, a 90-minute game of chicken. And then he brought in the big guns, the Closers. Billed as "his managers," these were tougher-looking guys with peculiarly sculpted facial hair. They leaned in. They said things such as, "What, you don't like vacations?" "Um, I'm fine with vacations, I just don't want to buy this time-share." "What would it take to make you change your mind?" "Nothing on god's green earth could make me change my mind."

I won. We emerged blinking in the 10 A.M. sun, a little sweaty, a little disheveled. And we had vouchers for five half-price tickets to Walt Disney World Resort. Was it worth it? Depends on how tough you are.

Much of the contents will seem vaguely familiar if you've been to other outposts, but here's something to consider: Ripley's now calls Orlando its corporate headquarters, so somewhere nearby in Orlando is a vast closed-to-the-public warehouse space stuffed to the gills with things such as a Lincoln Town Car decorated compulsively with gold coins, the world's biggest rocking chair, and an absolute smorgasbord of human skulls.

TITANIC–THE EXPERIENCE

Practically within view of Ripley's is the world's only permanent *Titanic* exhibit. Titanic—The Experience (8445 International Dr., 407/248-1166, 9 A.M.–9 P.M. daily, $19.95 adults, $12.95 children 4–12, three and younger free, free parking) does re-create many of the *Titanic*'s most famous rooms, with re-creations of the Grand Staircase, a first-class suite, and the Promenade Deck. Actors in period dress take visitors on a one-hour guided tour, culminating in the Underwater Room, which houses 200 artifacts from the ship.

I've seen a couple of really spectacular *Titanic* exhibits in recent years, and this one fails to get my blood boiling. There's an eight-foot replica of the submerged wreck that doesn't manage to excite the imagination, and children don't see much compelling about some silverware sets and historic deck chairs. It seems a pricey hour's entertainment.

SKULL KINGDOM

Maybe it's because construction costs are fairly low in Florida, or maybe it's a form of one-upmanship, but Orlando has more weird-looking themed buildings than anywhere I can think of. I like to drive by Skull Kingdom (5933 American Way, just off I-Drive at Kirkman Rd., 407/354-1564, $8.99 day show, $14.04 evening show, $19.75 adult ticket for dinner show, $15.97 children dinner show) and speculate about what will be done with the skull-festooned fake castle once this attraction has ebbed away. Turn it into a haunted 7-Eleven? MRI clinic?

Between 10 A.M. and 5 P.M., Skull King-dom is an all-ages haunted maze, explored by flashlight and with a wise-cracking guide. It's spooky, but it's not going to make anyone sleep with the lights on. In the evening, the cast is elaborately and ghoulishly costumed, the show is more interactive, and it does get pretty spine-tingling. The dinner show is a spooky/funny magic show, accompanied by bare-bones (card table chairs, paper plates, and Styrofoam cups) pizza and drinks. Fun, but for my money I'd hit the magic show at Wonder Works.

For the really spooky stuff, Universal wins, hands down, with its Halloween Horror Nights every year. But by the time this is published, Orlando will have another entry in the bone-chilling permanent horror attractions. **Terror in Orlando** (7316 International Dr., 407/351-4164, noon–10 P.M. Mon.–Thurs., until midnight Fri.–Sat., $12 adults, $10 children 12 and younger, combo ticket $17 adults, $15 children 12 and younger) will feature two different themed walk-through haunted houses—one purportedly called Mayhem Manor and the other a 3-D fun house.

HELICOPTER TOURS

If your appetite for flight goes unslaked at SkyVenture, **Helicopters International** (8990 International Dr., 407/354-1400, 10 A.M.–7 P.M. Sun.–Thurs., 10 A.M.–8 P.M. Fri. and Sat., $20–350, reservations not necessary, weight limit 280 pounds) offers nine different pilot-narrated tours of Orlando in Robinson R44 helicopters, from a quickie $20 tour just up and around SeaWorld and the convention center, to a $350 hop around all the theme parks with a jaunt around lovely Lake Apopka, the third largest in Florida.

Before or after a helicopter outing, check out the on-site **Train Land International** ($8 adults, $6 seniors and children), one of the country's largest indoor model G-gauge railroad trains. In 4,000 square feet, the little museum features 14 model railroad trains with 12-foot-tall mountains, three waterfalls, and more than 30 trestles and tunnels. Kids will especially enjoy the scavenger hunt checklist sheets. Outside, visitors can catch a quick ride on a replica of an 1880s California Victorian–style half-open/half-closed trolley.

THE HOLY LAND EXPERIENCE

The Holy Land Experience (4655 Vineland Rd., just north of the end of I-Drive, 866/872-4659, 10 A.M.–6 P.M. Mon.–Sat., $35 adults, $30 seniors, $23 children 6–12, five and younger free, tickets good for return visits for seven days, $5 parking) is touted as Orlando's only Christian amusement park. It's really more museum than rides, navigable in a single day, with an 18,000-square-foot Scriptorium that houses a vast collection of biblical artifacts, a replica of the Garden Tomb where Jesus was purportedly buried, a replica of the Qumran Caves where the Dead Sea Scrolls were discovered, and a model of Jerusalem. Kids may be more enthusiastic about the laser show that's set to a chanted prayer soundtrack or about the musical theater shows of stories from the Old Testament and the ministry of Jesus.

While some say the biblical stories are presented from an evenhanded historical perspective, others say the attraction reflects a Protestant bias. Everyone agrees that the gift shop provides some unusual offerings (prayer shawls, ram's horns), and that the on-site café, albeit small, is a welcome respite from standard theme-park food, offering healthy Middle Eastern dishes. Time your visit around Easter or Christmas to enjoy a range of special holiday programs.

◖ SKYVENTURE

Not far west of Orlando, the sleepy burg of Zephyrhills is known the world over as a preeminent "drop zone," drawing rookie and veteran skydivers from all over. If you want to experience a little of the thrill without actually leaping out of an aircraft, SkyVenture (6805 Visitor Circle, off International Dr. near Wet 'n Wild, 407/903-1150, 2 P.M.–11:30 P.M. weekdays, noon–11:30 P.M. weekends, $39.95–94.95, reservations suggested) is Orlando's indoor skydiving free-fall wind tunnel. The basic package is a one-hour

COURTESY OF ORLANDO/ORANGE COUNTY CONVENTION & VISITORS BUREAU, NC.

The Holy Land Experience

training session (15 minutes of instructor training and a five-minute video) with gear rental (a cool flight suit, pads, and goggles) and two one-minute flight rotations. The observation deck makes a great spot from which to wait your turn while boning up on effective techniques or merely mocking the arm flailings of the free-fall challenged.

A recent equipment overhaul has improved the experience, with five 125-horsepower electric motors replaced with 200-horsepower units, making for wind speeds of 150 mph (they also have the ability to change speeds more quickly now, a boon to more advanced divers who train here). The staging area and padded flight chamber have been gussied up as well to add to the exhilarating illusion of free-fall. Guests don't jump into the chamber; instead it's all about leaning into the wind flow until you are "flying."

The experience has an upper weight limit of 250 pounds, 230 pounds if you're under six feet tall. While SkyVenture allows children as young as three to "fly," all participants under 18 must have a waiver filled out by parent or legal guardian.

MINIGOLF AND GO-CARTS

It is possible that Kissimmee's U.S. Highway 192 is the minigolf capital of the world, but

WET 'N WILD

Drive up International Drive and you'll see hundreds of people walking in bathing suits, hair slicked, damp towel over a shoulder. By and large, they look relaxed and cheery. They have just come from Wet 'n Wild (6200 International Dr., 407/351-1800, www.wetnwildorlando.com, general hours 10 A.M.–7 P.M. daily, $36.95 adults, $30.95 ages 3–9, younger than three free, $29.95 Florida residents, $49.95 for return visits during length of stay). It opened in 1977 and is purported to be the country's first water park. It may be the grande dame of water thrills, but like the other theme parks in Orlando, Wet 'n Wild is constantly in a state of evolution. Several key rides closed in summer 2006 to make way for the new.

The park was founded by George Millay, the SeaWorld founder, but sold to Universal in 1998. Its vibe is similar to Universal's Islands of Adventure: very PG-rated with lots of teens in skimpy suits. While magazines keep bestowing Wet 'n Wild with the honor of America's number one water park, it lacks the extended theming conceit of Disney's water parks – which it makes up for in sheer high-energy, corkscrewy slides and hair-raising flumes.

It seems to be an all-day attraction for teens and tweens but just a half-day amusement for littler kids and adults. I kept seeing adults dragging their waterlogged teens away, while elementary-age kids kept whining, "When are we going to leave?"

The 30 acres contain the standard array of fake beach, wave pools, a lazy river upon which you tube, and then a smorgasbord of slides (many with height restrictions that preclude kids under age eight). The **Black Hole** sends a two-person raft twisting through the dark. Then there's the long multipassenger tube **Surge,** a six-story free-fall speed slide, simulated knee-boarding and wake-boarding rides as well as simulated white-water rafting, and a kiddie area with tamer versions of many of these attractions. For adults, the coolest area may be **Disco H2O,** which made its debut in 2005; it's a four-person raft blasted through an enclosed flume of disco tunes and mirrored disco balls.

Pools are heated seasonally and the park is open year-round. Rides are renovated and overhauled between September and March, however, so the offerings are more limited, as are the hours.

Guests can bring a cooler with lunch (no glass bottles) or visit one of the on-site food courts. There are on-site life guards, lockers, towels, life vests, tube rentals, and shower facilities. Appropriate bathing suits are required: no shorts, cutoffs, or suits with metal fasteners, rivets, zippers, or buckles.

I-Drive gives it a run for its money. And because the competition is fairly stiff, each minigolf outpost features a glitzy motif or elaborate theme to tempt the putting hoards. **Congo River Golf Orlando** has two I-Drive courses (5901 International Dr., near Universal, 407/248-9181, and 6312 International Dr., 407/352-0042, 10 A.M.–11 P.M. Sun.–Thurs., until midnight Fri. and Sat., $10.45 adults one course, $14.50 both courses, $2 discount for children younger than 10, one child younger than five free with each paid admission), each with craggy mountains, waterfalls, and caves through which 36 holes meander. To add a little drama, a pen of 25 gators jostles for meaty snacks that guests feed them from poles. Each course also boasts an air-conditioned video arcade.

Steel drums, a 50-foot volcano spewing lava, more waterfalls, and tiki torches complete the Hawaiian theme of **Hawaiian Rumble Adventure Golf** (8969 International Dr., 407/351-7733, 9 A.M.–11:30 P.M. Sun.–Thurs., until midnight Fri. and Sat., $9.95 adults one course, $14.95 both courses, $7.95 children 4–10 one course, $11.95 both courses). Two 18-hole courses challenge players with putt-through logs, hills, waterfalls, and tunnels. The on-site caf' serves suitably tropical drinks; it's also a pleasant place from which to check email with high-speed Internet.

Indoor, black-light, glow-in-the-dark minigolf? Orlando's got it, at **Putting Edge Glow-in-the-Dark Mini Golf** (5250 International Dr., Festival Bay Mall, 407/248-0700, 11 A.M.–9 P.M. Mon.–Thurs., until 10:30 P.M. Fri. and Sat., 11 A.M.–7:30 P.M. Sun., $8.50 adults, $6 seniors, $7.50 children 7–12, $6 children 5–6). Eighteen holes, loud pop music, and everyone's teeth looking supernaturally white—what could be better?

For go-carting, I-Drive has two highly enticing possibilities: **Fun Spot Action Park** (5551 Del Verde Way, off International Dr. at Kirkman Rd., 407/363-3867, 10 A.M.–midnight daily, $29.95 adults, $14.95 children)

and **Magical Midway** (7001 International Dr., 407/370-5353, 11 A.M.–11 P.M. daily, $15.95–27.95). Both are carny/midway attractions within a couple of blocks of Wet 'n Wild, the former with four multilevel go-cart tracks, a huge game arcade, a 100-foot Ferris wheel, bumper cars and bumper boats, and lots of little kids' rides. The latter has more of the same, but with a few crazy-extreme rides such as the new StarFlyer (individual chair swings on a central pole that gets these babies 230 feet in the air going 54 mph) or the 180-foot-tall major-G-force Space Blast Tower.

SKATEBOARDING

Vans Skatepark (5220 International Dr., near Prime Outlets Orlando, 407/351-3881, 10 A.M.–11 P.M. daily, $12 two-hour sessions weekdays, $15 weekends, $5 safety equipment rental, $5 skateboard rental) is said to be the second-largest indoor skateboard park in the world. With a 25,000-square-foot indoor wood street course and another 15,000-square-foot outdoor concrete street course (both with obstacles, handrails, quarter pipes, ledges, and a "hubba"), a "Dough Boy" pool-like bowl, a serious vert ramp, and two miniramps, the park is a skater's dream, regardless of skill level. Part of a nationwide chain, the park requires safety gear for all skaters. Beginning skaters may have the most fun hanging out on the elevated walkway and just watching the harrowing feats going on below. There's also a video arcade.

BOWLING

Surreal murals of bowlers (astronauts, or bowling atop Mt. Rushmore) add a little pizzazz to the all-American 32-lane **World Bowling Center** (7540 Canada Ave., just off I-Drive at Sand Lake Rd., 407/352-2695, noon–11 P.M. daily, with special late-night bowling until 2 A.M. on Tues., Fri., and Sat., $4 adults, $3 children 12 and younger, $3 shoe rental). Late-night it's techno music and disco lights, but the rest of the time it's family-friendly 10-pin in suitably goofy rented shoes.

Entertainment and Shopping

NIGHTLIFE

Close to I-Drive, Universal's CityWalk is one-stop-shopping for nightlife of all sorts, as is Downtown Disney's Pleasure Island. Still, along I-Drive there are a handful of nighttime venues.

Dottie's Orlando Comedy Theater (7052 International Dr., 407/226-3680, two daily shows, $16.95 adults, $10.95 children) opened in 2006, offering the *All Star Comedy and Variety Show* suitable for ages 12 and older, and a second evening show for those 18 and older. It may be *I Love You, Now Shut Up,* starring Tommy Blaze, or an ensemble comedy show called *He Said, She Said.*

A creamy smooth Guinness and a few choruses of Danny Boy at **Lucky Leprechaun Irish Pub** (7032 International Dr., 407/352-7031) and you'll be pining for old County Cork, even if you're not Irish. It's I-Drive's only Irish-owned pub, so count on a rollicking good time with all your Blarney Stone–kissing cronies. There are a killer black and tan, a warming Irish coffee, and a fair representation of Irish staples, from rib-sticking, mashed-potatoey shepherd's pie to respectable fish-and-chips. The bar is home to the official Glasgow Celtic Supporters Club of Orlando.

Two Yamaha baby grands are at the center of all the festivities at **Howl at the Moon** (8815 International Dr., 407/354-5999, 6 P.M.–2 A.M. nightly). The staff is quick to break into song, which doesn't diminish the sense of barely contained conviviality at this watering hole. The cuisine is largely pleasant and forgettable, but the drinks are stiff and the crowd is anything but. The mostly 20s and 30s revelers are locals and out-of-towners with a song in their hearts.

Two blocks north of the convention center, **GLO Lounge Orlando** (8967 International Dr., 407/351-0361, 9 P.M.–2 A.M. Tues.–Sat., men must be 21 but—get this—girls can be 18) is where people go to shake it. Music genre varies by theme night ('80s on Tuesday "hospitality night," techno on Thursday "European night," top 40 on Saturdays). The club features bil-liard tables, four 50-inch plasma TVs, and VIP lounges with bottle service.

SHOPPING

Orlando is a retail smorgasbord, with 52 million square feet of shopping, 485 stores and outlets, and nine notable malls in the greater Orlando area. Much of this shopping is along the I-Drive corridor.

(Outlet Malls

The two biggies are Prime Outlets Orlando (formerly Belz Outlets) at the northern tip of I-Drive and Orlando Premium Outlets at the southern tip of I-Drive. Orlando's largest, **Prime Outlets Orlando** (5401 W. Oak Ridge Rd., 407/352-9600, www.primeoutlets.com, 10 A.M.–9 P.M. Mon.–Sat., until 7 P.M. Sun.) is in the midst of a huge $150 million renovation (to be completed July 2008) that will render it more of an outdoor pedestrian mall. One of the two adjacent centers was closed, but there are still more than 200 outlet stores clustered in Mall 1, Annex 4, and Designer Outlet Centre, including Adidas, Ann Taylor, Banana Republic, Gap Outlet, Liz Claiborne, Nautica, Samsonite, Timberland, Tommy Hilfiger, Universal Studios Outlet, and other familiar names.

Orlando Premium Outlets (8200 Vineland Ave., 407/238-7787, www.premiumoutlets.com/orlando, 10 A.M.–11 P.M. Mon.–Sat., until 9 P.M. Sun.) has 110 stores. Newer entries include an Ann Taylor Factory Store, Dior, Lucky Brand Blue Jeans, and Diesel. In addition, you'll find Barneys New York Outlet, DKNY, Coach, Burberry, Escada, Fendi, Kenneth Cole, BCBG Max Azria, Fendi, Giorgio Armani, Hugo Boss, and Kenneth Cole. The outlet mall also offers free shuttles to participating hotels in the greater Walt Disney World Resort area.

I-Drive Malls

Festival Bay Mall at International Drive (5250 International Dr., 407/351-7718, shopfestivalbaymall.com, 10 A.M.–9 P.M. Mon.–

Sat., 11 A.M.–7 P.M. Sun.) is right in the thick of I-Drive, with a young hipster bent and lots to do. There are 60 specialty stores in an unusual lineup that includes Bass Pro Shops Outdoor World, Sheplers Western Wear, Steve and Barry's University Sportswear, United World Soccer, PacSun, Journey's, Nine West Outlet, Kasper Outlet, Jones New York Outlet, and a 15,000-square-foot Ron Jon Surf Shop, featuring the world's first wave-pool facility built specifically for surfing and bodyboarding. It will feature three surf pools, the biggest of which, the Pro Surf Pool, will create up to six saltwater waves per minute, up to eight feet high and with ride lengths 60–100 yards. You can't do that at every mall.

Beyond shopping, Festival Bay features 11 restaurants, a Cinemark 20 movie theater, Putting Edge minigolf, and Vans Skatepark.

The **Pointe Orlando** (9101 International Dr., 407/248-2838, www.pointeorlando.com, 10 A.M.–10 P.M. Mon.–Sat., 11 A.M.–9 P.M. Sun.) features more traditional mall stores in a recently renovated complex right across from the convention center. This mall underperformed in its former configuration, so a new interior courtyard surrounded by more upscale shops and restaurants has been added in the hopes of drawing in the right demographics. The Capital Grille opened in 2006, Tommy Bahama Café opened in 2007, with B. B. King Blues Club, and Emporium, and the Oceanaire Seafood Room soon to follow.

Stores include some familiar names (Sunglass Hut, Chico's, Bath and Body Works, FootLocker, Express, and B. Dalton), as do the more longstanding food venues (Johnny Rockets, Starbucks, Hooters), but the complex also includes Maggie Moo's ice cream and the Muvico Pointe 21 Theaters.

Near I-Drive

Two of the area's other big malls are within minutes of I-Drive. **The Mall at Millenia** (4200 Conroy Rd., 407/363-3555, www.mall atmillenia.com, 10 A.M.–9 P.M. Mon.–Sat., noon–7 P.M. Sun.) is just northeast of the end of I-Drive. This swanky, two-level complex is anchored by Bloomingdale's, Macy's, and Neiman Marcus. The 150 smaller stores include some really elite boutiques such as Jimmy Choo and Louis Vuitton, and the mall is set to open an IKEA store in fall 2007. While you'll see some familiar names, more than 80 of the featured stores are unduplicated in the Orlando market.

The **Florida Mall** (8001 S. Orange Blossom Tr., at Sand Lake Rd., 407/851-6255, 10 A.M.–9 P.M. Mon.–Sat., noon–6 P.M. Sun.) is just a bit farther away, due east of I-Drive. Featuring a little more standard fare, it's anchored by Dillard's, JCPenney, Macy's, Nordstrom, Saks Fifth Avenue, and Sears, with more than 250 other specialty stores. There are a few interesting tenants, such as the red-hot Club Libby Lu "princess" store for girls.

Accommodations

UNDER $100

Clustered around the convention center are the kind of low-frills, utilitarian hotels and motels that come in handy when your aim is to spend all day at a convention (or a theme park) before falling, exhausted, into bed. **Howard Johnson** (6603 International Dr., 407/351-2900, $50–60) is such a place, offering standard double queen rooms including refrigerators, a continental breakfast

featuring hot biscuits and a make-your-own waffle bar, small fitness center and game room, ample parking, and shuttle service to Disney, Universal, and SeaWorld. The same goes for the three-story **Travelodge Orlando Convention Center** (6263 Westwood Blvd., off I-Drive, 407/345-8000, $55–99). Basic but clean, all rooms come with two double beds, children 17 and younger stay free in their parents' room. Built in 1984, it had a

GOING TO THE DOGS

People travel with their pets more and more, and canine accommodations have kept pace. The International Drive resort area boasts a number of properties that cater to the four-legged. Be sure to ask about extra charges for pets and rules for leaving your pet unattended in the room. All pets should be wearing collars with your name and cell phone (not your home phone) clearly visible. Most accommodations require proof of inoculation.

La Quinta Inns: All three inns on I-Drive allow pets up to 80 pounds. Locations are La Quinta at Universal, La Quinta Inn and Suites Orlando Convention Center, and La Quinta Inn Orlando International Drive.

Loews Hotels at Universal Orlando Resort: Unleashing its "Loews Loves Pets" program at the Portofino Bay Hotel, the Royal Pacific Resort, and the Hard Rock Hotel in 2000, the hotels provide pets their own special mat, food and water bowl, toys, and treats. A room-service menu is available for pets and a property map indicates pet-friendly walking areas. There is no weight limit and a deposit is not required. Proof of inoculations a must.

Masters Inn: It's happy to check in pets up to 20 pounds, but pets must be placed in kennels in the room when they are left alone.

Quality Inns: The Quality Inn Plaza, a block from the Orange County Convention Center, and the Quality Inn International both welcome pets weighing up to 50 pounds.

Residence Inns: Residence Inn SeaWorld International Center, Residence Inn Convention Center, and Residence Inn by Marriott Orlando I-Drive all accept pets up to 30 pounds.

Sheraton World Resort: Pets up to 60 pounds are welcome, and there's a special designated pet-walking area. The hotel provides a special bed and a bowl for food and water.

Wyndham Orlando Resort: The Wyndham allows up to two pets with a 50-pound weight limit per pet. Proof of current inoculations is required.

renovation several years ago but is looking just a bit tired. Still, you'll find high-speed Internet (no extra charge) in public areas, two outdoor pools, a small business center and fitness center, and continental breakfast, included in the rate, as is shuttle service to the parks.

What used to be called the Sheraton World Resort is now the **International Plaza Resort and Spa** (10100 International Dr., 407/352-1100, $99–149), a tremendous bargain very close to SeaWorld. The 1,102 guest rooms and suites are lovely, especially those in the "corporate tower" (the older low-rise motel-style rooms tend to be a little less impressive, but a renovation was planned). It's a great family hotel, with 28 acres of landscaping and a huge lagoon pool with waterfalls, two smaller children's pools, a game room, playground, and minigolf greens. For adults, there are a multilevel lounge with live entertainment and L'Espirit Day Spa. Rates include a shuttle to Walt Disney World Resort.

$100–200

An all-suites environment, **Staybridge Suites, International Drive** (8480 International Dr., 407/352-2400, $100–176) was renovated in 2005, with five stories and 146 one-bedroom or two-bedroom/two-bath suites. Right on I-Drive, the hotel has a heated outdoor pool, a children's pool, whirlpool tub, video game room, and laundry facilities.

Hardly a surprise in the city of the Magic Kingdom, **The DoubleTree Castle Hotel** (8629 International Dr., 407/345-1511, $99–169) is deeply committed to a medieval castle theme complete with towering spires, rooftop gardens, and dancing fountains. For when you need to feel like a prince or princess, the 216 spacious rooms come with pillow-top mattresses (no pea hidden beneath), three telephones, a stereo system, and high-speed Internet access. There are the signature Doubletree chocolate chip cookies upon registration, a nice outdoor circular pool with fountains and a bar, and several laudable on-site restaurants. Rates include shuttle service to the parks.

The 21-story art-deco **Sheraton Studio City** (5905 International Dr., 407/351-2100, $95–229) is near Universal and, in keeping, celebrates classic Hollywood movies in its decor. There are 301 rooms, nicely kitted out with Sweet Sleeper beds, cable, high-speed Internet access, voice mail, and data ports. Fronted by majestic palms and topped with glamorous spotlights, the hotel has a lovely outdoor heated Palm Springs swimming pool and patio bar, and a playroom for kids. Rates include shuttle service to the parks.

If you're coming to Orlando with kids in tow, you almost have to check out the first-of-its-kind **Nickelodeon Family Suites** (14500 Continental Gateway, off I-Drive, 407/387-5437, $149–200), a Holiday Inn property. The family suites are fine, garnished liberally with Nick cartoons, but the allures lie elsewhere: The complex of swimming pools includes slides, flumes, climbing nets, water jets, and a 400-gallon "water dump." There's a kids' spa with manicures, pedicures, hair wraps, and temporary tattoos for your young ones. Or hang out in Studio Nick, a million-dollar, state-of-the-art theater, or maybe play the nine-hole minigolf course, or visit the 3,000-square-foot game room. You get the idea. Rates include shuttle service to the parks.

OVER $200

Harris Rosen is the largest independent hotel owner in Orlando, and there are good reasons to patronize his businesses: He has championed local causes, from sending underprivileged kids to school (on his dime) to funding the Rosen College of Hospitality. He has created thousands of jobs in the city, adheres to forward-thinking labor practices, and seems to have some kind of war going on with the *Orlando Sentinel*. The **Rosen Plaza Hotel** (9700 International Dr., 407/996-9700, $200–275) is adjacent to the convention center, with 800 guest rooms and 32 suites with high-speed Internet access and data ports, in-room movies, and voice mail. The hotel

features a nice heated swimming pool and spa, a fitness center with "Life Fitness" machines, and worthy restaurants (Jack's Place and Café Matisse). Guests can arrange tee times at Rosen Shingle Creek Golf Club (a sister property; see the *Universal Orlando Resort* chapter), and the hotel offers airport shuttle service and a new baggage airline service. Basically within a stone's throw is his **Rosen Centre Hotel** (9840 International Dr., 407/996-9840, $195–400), which acts as a spillover for the convention center, with 100,000 square feet of on-site meeting space and more than 1,300 rooms and suites. It's huge, with a real business orientation—an on-site destination management team, top-notch service, and suites and rooms that do double duty as small meeting spaces. The property also has a large swimming grotto, lighted tennis courts, and the Body and Sol Spa. Eateries include Everglades Restaurant and Café Gauguin.

(**The Peabody Orlando** (9801 International Dr., 407/352-4000, $260–405) is the grande dame of I-Drive luxury hotels, opened all the way back in 1986. It remains at the top of the heap as one of only two Mobil four-star, AAA four-diamond hotels in Orlando. Some of this is the luxurious rooms (with fancy "dream beds" by Simmons Beautyrest, gorgeous fabrics, and the latest technological bells and whistles), but a lot of it is the palpable service orientation of everyone on staff. Oh, and the ducks who live in the hotel's fountain that, on queue, march through the lobby each evening to much fanfare. Near the convention center, The Peabody does a rollicking meeting and convention business (57,000 square feet of flexible function space), but it also adeptly serves vacationers. The hotel boasts a heated Olympic-style lap pool, four lighted tennis courts, access to several of the local championship golf courses, and a certified Nautilus training center and spa. Dux, Capriccio Grill, and the B-Line Diner, the on-property restaurants, all have a following in the local community.

Part of my admiration for the hotel has

nothing to do with the facility: The hotel has been instrumental in the launching of the Orlando Peabody Alliance for Arts and Culture (OPAAC), which has served since 1996 to raise awareness of the arts organizations in Orlando. The Orlando Ballet, museums such as the Charles Hosmer Morse Museum of American Art and Cornell Fine Arts Museum, the Orlando Opera Company, and other outstanding arts organizations sometimes suffer in the mouse-shaped shadow of Walt Disney World Resort. The organization effectively promotes and celebrates the arts, drawing locals and visitors alike.

Food

I-Drive has the densest concentration of restaurants in the area. Many are the usual array of chain restaurants (clustered in the north end), but some of the region's high-end destination restaurants are also here (in the midsection or southern end of I-Drive).

AMERICAN

A huge category, this might go on for pages with familiar chain concepts and even independent ventures. Each of the shopping centers in the area is home to several slick American eateries. For example, The Pointe Orlando (9101 International Dr.) boasts an elegant **Tommy Bahama's Tropical Café** (321/281-5888, 11 A.M.–11 P.M., Sun.–Thurs., until midnight Fri. and Sat., $26–35), as well as an outpost of ubiquitous steak-and-chop **The Capital Grille** (407/370-4392, 11:30 A.M.–3 P.M., 5–10 P.M. Sun.–Thurs., until 11 Fri.–Sat., $22–41). Following are just a few more of I-Drive's more notable (and sometimes peculiar) choices.

Race Rock (8986 International Dr., 407/248-9876, 11:30 A.M.–11 P.M. daily, $7.45–22.95) is a 20,000-square-foot motor sports–themed restaurant decked out with rare racing memorabilia from all forms of motor racing. Interactive simulators, huge video screens, and exhibits of driving gear and vehicles (such as Big Foot, the largest monster truck in the world) give the huge space a frenetic party atmosphere. The culinary aesthetic is more-is-more: a huge menu of enormous dishes. Safest bets are the burgers.

In the Rosen Centre Hotel, **Everglades Restaurant and Bar** (9840 International Dr.,

407/996-2385, 5:30–9:30 P.M. daily, $22–39) is notable because it pays tribute to the Florida Everglades, both in its decor and its menu. The former boasts murals of dense Everglade foliage and a huge sculpture of a manatee; the latter features alligator chowder, mango-crusted Florida grouper, and the archetypal Key lime pie. A part of the restaurant's profits are donated to the Everglades Trust for Preservation.

ASIAN

A vast restaurant within walking distance of the convention center, **(Ming Court** (9188 International Dr., 407/351-9988, 11 A.M.–2:30 P.M. and 4:30–11:30 P.M. daily, $10–40) is among I-Drive's most longstanding and well-known dining attractions, dating all the way back to 1989 (practically the Paleolithic era by Orlando standards). From the koi pond out front to the stunning painting in the lobby called *Joyous Dragon,* the restaurant has the opulent feel of someplace that might have existed in the Ming Dynasty. It's got 1,000-gallon fish tanks, terraces surrounding an interior courtyard, numerous private dining rooms, a gazebo, and a slick sushi bar. The menu is suitably gigantic, spanning the cuisines of Canton, Hunan, Szechwan, and even a few places that aren't in China (a little Taiwanese, some Japanese). As one might expect with such a broad menu, the kitchen doesn't hit it out of the park on every try, but the dim sum dumplings are quite good and the kitchen makes admirable use of seasonal Chinese vegetables. Traditionalists will also find all their favorite Chinese-American dishes.

Trey Yuen Restaurant (6800 Visitors Circle, 407/352-6822, 11 A.M.–midnight daily, $8–15) is another grande dame of Chinese cooking around here, near Wet 'n Wild and SkyVenture. It's affordable, familiar, with very competent dim sum offered 11 A.M.–3 P.M. daily (pan-fried pot-stickers, taro puff, *siu mei*). Unlike Ming Court, there's nothing "special occasion" about Trey Yuen, and the clientele encompasses a reassuring number of Chinese.

For some reason, I-Drive and the touristy parts of Orlando are awash in Japanese steak houses. Maybe this is because of the pageantry and "dinner show" qualities of all that flipping shrimp and onion-volcano construction. Kanpai of Tokyo, several outposts of Kobe Japanese, Shogun Japanese, and others deliver competent, Western-friendly gather-round-the-flattop grilling of beef, chicken, or shrimp, flavored with soy sauce and not much else. **Ran-Getsu of Tokyo** (8400 International Dr., 407/345-0044, 5–11:30 P.M. daily, $12–98 for complete meals) is much better for its range of authentic hands-on dishes such as sizzling su-kiyaki meat and veggies made tableside, or the onomatopoetic "shabu-shabu" of veggies and meats waggled in broth. Sure, it's a party for the whole family (there's even Japanese drumming on the weekend), but the food is bright, clean, and expertly flavored. Dinners can be pricey, but dishes such as the *yosenabe* (Japanese bouillabaisse) or the house sashimi are worth it.

Highest Thai honors go to **Thai Thani** (11025 International Dr., 407/239-9733, $8–20), a huge, ornate outpost of familiar Thai cooking, with goofy Chinese dishes thrown in like so many red herrings. Pad thai, papaya salad, tom ka gai, and fried whole fish are expertly spiced with the distinctive Thai balance of spicy, sweet, salty, and herbal.

CARIBBEAN

Both a meet-and-greet nightlife hot spot and island-inflected eatery, **Bahama Breeze** (8849 International Dr., 407/248-2499, 11 A.M.–1 A.M.–Sun.–Thurs., until 1:30 A.M. Fri. and Sat., $9–24) is one branch of a successful chain that doesn't sweat the verisimilitude. The

COURTESY OF ORLANDO/ORANGE COUNTY CONVENTION & VISITORS BUREAU, INC.

INTERNATIONAL DRIVE

Bahama Breeze

menu is Caribbeanish, from coconut shrimp to Spanish paella to artichoke-spinach dip. Great happy-hour specials, a wide outdoor deck with live reggae music, and a vivacious young crowd make it loads of fun, even if the islands accent is a little forced, mon.

DINNER SHOWS

An area just above I-Drive along Dr. Phillips Boulevard and Sand Lake Road is justifiably called "Restaurant Row." Several of Orlando's fabled "dinner shows" are along this strip. All feature a mostly-edible multicourse meal including booze, served while you watch a themed arena show.

One of the newest is a real rootin'-tootin' crowd pleaser. **Dolly Parton's Dixie Stampede Dinner and Show** (8251 Vineland Ave., 407/238-4455, www.dixiestampede.com, 5:30 daily, with a second show at 8 P.M. Sat., $48.99 adults, $21.99 children 4–11) takes place in a new $28 million, 128,000-square-foot facility christened by Dolly herself in 2003. It, too, is a fast-paced show of thrilling horsemanship, but with a Southern accent. It starts with a number called "Stampede of the Buffalos," a heart-swelling story of America, and ends with the patriotic finale "Color Me America" written by Dolly Parton herself. In between, there is trick riding, kooky ostrich and pig races, singing and dancing, and (as is imperative with all dinner adventures) a punitive amount of audience participation. Dinner is a cover-the-law all-American feast of barbecued pork, rotisserie chicken, corn on the cob, roasted potatoes, apple pastry, and free-flowing beer, wine, tea, coffee, or Pepsi.

The best time to go to Dixie Stampede is during the Christmas holiday season, when the huge arena is transformed into a wonderland of snow, wreathes, garlands, and twinkly lights. Snow and ice skaters complete the illusion, with a horseback "living carousel" and a visit from Santa.

My favorite may be the **Pirate's Dinner Adventure** (6400 Carrier Dr., 407/248-0590, www.piratesdinneradventure.com, 8:30 P.M. daily, with an additional show on Sat. at 6 P.M., $51.95 adults, $31.95 children 3–11). It's another one where you get a colored swath of crepe paper (a neckerchief? a headband?) and a color-designated pirate—and you root for this pirate as hard as you can. And they're pretty good. It's a real story, with the luscious Princess Anita and her attendees being held hostage by the dastardly Sebastian the Black. You'll see plundering and pillaging along with some fairly expert swordsmanship. Production quality is very high, the pirate-ship sets are first rate. The biggest drawback? The food hovers at the margin of edibility.

FAST FOOD

Not a subject anyone needs much guidance on nor one worthy of lavish gastronomic scrutiny, but I-Drive bears the distinction of housing the world's largest **McDonald's Playplace** (6875 Sand Lake Rd., just west of I-Drive, 407/351-2185, open 24 hours daily). You know the menu, but the 15,000-square-foot playground is like the Promised Land for kids, with all the usual tubes and slides plus a full video arcade. In fact, the area is chockablock with themed McDonald's outposts, mostly owned by Oerther Foods—from an Ancient Ruins branch to a Motorcycle McDonald's to a Club Safari McDonald's with an Animatronic toucan and African masks.

FINE DINING

This category is mostly the purview of the fancier hotels along I-Drive. Each seems to have its signature pull-out-all-the-stops joint. The Peabody may win top honors with ⟨ **Dux** (9801 International Dr., 407/345-4550, 6–10 P.M. Tues.–Thurs., Fri. and Sat. until 11 P.M., $32–39), a destination restaurant for visitors and locals alike, and with good reason. Like the hotel, its fanciest restaurant manages to be sophisticated and warm simultaneously, with a weekly changing menu that allows for serious splurges (osetra with all the accoutrements, a fat veal chop with tomato caper relish) but also reflects a focus on the seasonal and the artisanal (heirloom tomato salad with arugula). The name, although spelled idiosyncratically,

COOKING UP CHEFS

With more than 120,000 hotel rooms, 4,000 restaurants, and 75 theme parks and attractions, each with its own food-service venues, Orlando needs more executive chefs, line cooks, prep cooks, expediters, general managers, food and beverage directors, sommeliers, and waiters than the average town. Harris Rosen, local hotelier and entrepreneur, was aware of this when he set the wheels in motion to build the state-of-the-art **Rosen College of Hospitality,** part of the University of Central Florida. The facility opened in January 2004 with the educational mission of providing students with the knowledge, skills, and ability to identify opportunities and challenges in management roles in the hospitality industry.

Taking advantage of the largest learning laboratory in the world – studying the tastes and needs of more than 42 million annual visitors – students hone their chops in classrooms and through experiential learning in the Orlando business community. The college grants Bachelor of Science degrees in hospitality management, event management, and restaurant and food service management; offers a master's program in hospitality and tourism management; and a PhD program in hospitality education.

More than $200,000 in scholarships have been awarded to worthy students each year, much of it by Rosen himself. But this surely is not a strictly philanthropic effort: Half a million people in the state of Florida are employed in the hospitality industry, a fair percentage of those required right here in Central Florida. The city and its theme parks are desperately in need of educated, qualified hospitality professionals, many recruited directly from the Rosen College through job fairs and externships. It's this kind of back-and-forth and cross-pollination that raises the bar for the whole industry, a phenomenon that only benefits the visiting public.

The Rosen College campus is at 9907 Universal Boulevard at the junction with Beachline Expressway. Campus tours are offered at 1 P.M. every Monday and Friday. For more information, call 407/903-8000.

honors the family of ducks that live in the hotel's central fountain and parade through the lobby at a designated time each afternoon. The Peabody also has an Italian-inflected steak house called **Capriccio Grill** (901/529-4199, 6:30 A.M.–10 P.M. daily, entrées $31–50) and a pleasant diner called the **B-Line** (open 24 hours daily, entrées $8–20).

The nearby Rosen Plaza Hotel contains the notable special-occasion restaurant **Jack's Place** (9700 International Dr., 407/996-9700, 5:30–9:30 P.M. daily, $19.95–38.95). The menu features familiar steaks, chops, and expense-account froufrou (pan-seared filet mignon and crab cake with tarragon hollandaise), all elevated by the presence of hundreds of autographed celebrity caricatures sketched by Mr. Rosen's father when he worked at New York's Waldorf-Astoria.

Jeffery's Restaurant and Piano Bar (7533 W. Sand Lake Rd., 407/996-9292,

www.jefferysrestaurant.com, 5 P.M.–midnight Sun.–Thurs., 5 P.M.–2 A.M. Fri.–Sat., entrées $18–34), opened in early 2007 replacing Anaelle and Hugo which sadly closed in 2006. Jeffery's features include a private room, full bar, and live entertainment Tuesday through Saturday. Menu items range from pasta to chops and seafood.

INDIAN

Passage to India (5532 International Dr., 407/351-3456, 11 A.M.–10 P.M. daily, $12.95–15.95) gets the nod for its array of fragrant stuffed naan and breadth of vegetarian offerings. There's nothing too out of the ordinary here, but very freshly made Northern Indian served in a simple but pleasant environment. **New Punjab** (7451 International Dr., 407/352-7887, 11:30 A.M.–11 P.M. Tues.–Sat., 5–11 P.M. Sun. and Mon., $7.95–12.95) is another long-time local favorite, with excellent biryani rice specials and laudable Northern Indian tandoori chicken and kebabs. Local Indian food aficionados point to **Memories of India** (7625 Turkey Lake Rd., Bay Hill Plaza, 407/370-3277, 11:30 A.M.–2:30 P.M. and 5:30–9:30 P.M. daily, entrées $8–15) and **Kohinoor** (249 W. Hwy. 436, Altamonte Springs, 407/788-6004, 11:30 A.M.–2:30 P.M. Tues.–Sun., 5–10 P.M. Tues.–Thurs. and Sun., until 11 P.M. Fri. and Sat., $8–14) as the best in the Orlando area, but both are a real hike for visitors staying in the touristy areas.

ITALIAN

Bergamos Italian Restaurant (Festival Bay Mall, 5250 International Dr., 407/352-3805, 5 P.M.–10 P.M. daily, entrées $16–28) has been one of I-Drive's top Italian restaurants, largely because of the opera-singing waiters. The food is more serious than the singing gimmick would imply, and the wine list has always been notable for its unusual bottlings.

For a splurge Italian dinner, head to **◖ Christini's Ristorante Italiano** (7600 Dr. Phillips Blvd., near I-Drive, 407/345-8770, 6 P.M.–midnight daily, dressy, $25–40), recipient of the *Wine Spectator's* coveted best of award of excellence. The kitchen follows suit, with careful renderings of veal scaloppine with morels, rack of lamb with a vivacious Sardinian sauce, and velvety housemade pastas.

LATIN/SOUTH AMERICAN

Part of a small regional chain, **The Samba Room** (7468 W. Sand Lake Rd., 407/226-0550, 11:30 A.M.–10 P.M. Mon.–Thurs., until 2 A.M. Fri. and Sat., 4–11 P.M. Sun., $12–25) purveys sophisticated Latin fusion fare in a hip environment. It's mojito time, with generous happy-hour specials and live music and salsa lessons on the weekend. Sweet corn arepas, an empanada sampler, and crispy Florida red snapper gussied up with mango are all worthy of investigation.

Leaf through any in-flight magazine these days and you're led to believe that every city in the land is stocked to capacity with Brazilian *churrascarias* (that's shoo-HOSS-ka-REE-

ahs). You know the photos: Attractive Latin men standing tableside, wielding absurdly long skewers dense with rolls of beef in one hand and a sword in the other. **Texas de Brazil** (5259 International Dr., 407/355-0355, 5–10 P.M. Mon.–Thurs., 5–11 P.M. Fri., noon–11 P.M. Sat., noon–9:30 P.M. Sun., $42.99, children 7–12 half price, six and younger free, drinks and dessert are separate, as are tax and tip) is one of the more successful chains, marrying the allures of the gauchos and the cowboys, both out there on the range cooking big hunks of meat over an open fire. This is a major splurge restaurant, fiscally prudent only for the superbig appetite. The menu is prix fixe, an all-you-can-eat meat smorgasbord carved tableside with vegetables and other distractions easy enough to ignore.

Decidedly more peninsular Spanish than Latin American, **Café Tu Tu Tango** (8625 International Dr., in Doubletree Castle Hotel, 407/248-2222, 11:30 A.M.–11 P.M. Sun.–Thurs., until 1 A.M. Fri. and Sat., $5–11) attempts to recreate a bohemian Barcelona artist's garret vibe, with lots of low couches and velvet pillows. Live music, flamenco, art exhibits, belly dancers, and tarot readers keep the atmosphere suitably boho, and the menu is an array of traditional tapas (antipasti of Serrano ham, chorizo, manchego, and olives; black bean soup) and not-so-Spanish small plates (shrimp spring rolls, kimchee-glazed ribs).

SEAFOOD

The stadium-size, all-you-can-eat seafood house is definitely overrepresented in Orlando, with a couple of the biggies on I-Drive. Some diners give the nod to **International Lighthouse Lobster Feast** (6400 International Dr., 407/355 3750, noon–10:30 P.M. daily, $29.95 adult lunch, $14.95 children lunch, $34.95 adult dinner, $16.95 children dinner) for its Maine lobster and Alaskan crab legs, served along with ribs, salmon, and grouper. Others favor **Boston Lobster Feast**'s (8731 International Dr., 407/248-8606, 4–10 P.M. Sun.–Thurs., until 11 P.M. Fri. and Sat., $34.95 4–6 P.M., $39.95 after that, children 4–11 $14.95, three and younger free) lobster, oysters, steamers, crab legs, and salad bar.

For me, the lack of decor and institutional nature of these kinds of places is off-putting, and I never manage to pack away enough food to make it seem financially efficacious. I'd opt for the à la carte approach of **Salt Island Chophouse and Fish Market** (7500 International Dr., 407/996-7258, 5–11 P.M. daily, $12.95–26.95), a hip, newish, 14,000-square-foot surf-'n-turf emporium. The Wave Bar is gorgeously kitted out in blue couches, waterfalls, and blown-glass jellyfish, there's the outdoor Sand Bar with nightly entertainment, and the main dining room is attractive if a little loud. The kitchen has a fairly straightforward approach to wood-fire grilled finfish, which you can judiciously pair with a luxurious crabmeat béarnaise or a gorgonzola dill sauce. Salt Island also has a laudable number of usual wine options by the glass (many that hover around $12, so it ain't cheap), and a small list of specialty cigars.

STEAK HOUSES

Charley's Steak House, Butcher Shop Steak House, and Vito's Chop House are all near each other and all have devoted fans among visitors and locals. **Charley's Steak House** (8255 International Dr., 407/363-0228, 5–10:30 P.M. Sun.–Thurs., until 11 P.M. Fri. and Sat., $13–37) is a small regional chain with several outposts that specialize in USDA Prime and Choice aged steaks cooked in a 1,100°F hardwood pit, married with an award-winning wine list suitably weighty in the cabernets and bordeaux. It's pricey and the portions are huge.

With a familiar menu of steaks and accoutrements (creamed spinach, asparagus with hollandaise—all sides à la carte), the **Butcher Shop Steak House** (8445 S. International Dr., 407/363-9727, 5–10 P.M. Sun.–Thurs., until 11 P.M. Fri. and Sat., $25–35) is the kind of place that brings the meat to your table to earnestly discuss your cut of aged Midwestern grain-fed beef. Porterhouse and prime rib seem to reign supreme here.

Vito's Chop House (8633 International Dr., in Doubletree Castle Hotel, 407/354-2467, 5–10:30 P.M. Sun.–Thurs., until 11 P.M. Fri. and Sat., $25–40), with its red leather booths and suave waiter, brings an Italian spin to the steak house. In addition to the usual suspects, you'll find cedar plank–roasted salmon, lobster fra Diablo, and a range of veal scaloppine dishes.

INTERNATIONAL DRIVE

Practicalities

INFORMATION AND SERVICES

Begin a visit with a stop for maps and literature at the **Official Visitor Center** (8723 International Dr., Suite 101, 407/363-5872, 8 A.M.–7 P.M. daily). You can also visit www.orlandoinfo.com or www.InternationalDrive Orlando.com for a copy of the International Drive Resort Area Official Visitors Guide along with maps and booklets of discount coupons.

The Visitor Center also sells tickets to the major Orlando attractions, offering a slight discount over the front-gate prices at each park (except for one- and two-day Disney passes, which are not discounted). Before buying these, compare the prices to the discounts offered on the parks' own websites. The center also offers the Orlando Preferred Visitor Magicard, free to visitors, with savings on a variety of area attractions, accommodations, restaurants, and shops. The card can also be downloaded at www.orlandoinfo.com.

Orange County Convention Center

The vast Orange County Convention Center (407/685-9800, www.occc.net) complex has a North Building (9400 Universal Blvd.), a West

COURTESY OF ORLANDO/ORANGE COUNTY CONVENTION & VISITORS BUREAU, INC.

Orange County Convention Center

Building (9800 International Dr.), and a South Building (9899 International Dr.). If you're in town for a convention, enter north on International Drive and access the West Building parking lot by turning left at either Convention Way (south entrance) or Exhibit Way (north entrance). From Westwood Boulevard, the west entrance is accessible via West Entrance Drive. The North/South Building parking lot is accessible by turning right at the South Concourse sign or continuing north on International Drive and turning right onto Convention Way, following that to Universal Boulevard, and turning right onto Universal Boulevard.

Police and Emergencies

In an emergency, dial 911. If you find yourself in need of a hospital, Orlando Regional Sand Lake Hospital (9400 Turkey Lake Rd., 407/351-8500) offers full emergency-room services. For a doctor's visit during regular business hours, MainStreet Physicians (8723 International Dr., 407/370-4881) accepts walk-in appointments. For your pharmacy

needs, there are five Walgreens Drug Stores that dot the length of I-Drive.

GETTING THERE AND AROUND

The north end of I-Drive (near Universal Orlando Resort) can be reached by Exit 75A and 75B off I-4; the southern end (near SeaWorld Orlando) can be reached by Exit 71 off I-4. I-Drive runs essentially north-south, just east of I-4. It is bisected by east-west roads (listed from north to south): Oak Ridge Road, Kirkman Road (Exit 75A off I-4), Universal Boulevard (Exit 74B off I-4), Carrier Drive, Sand Lake Road (Exit 74A off I-4), Beachline Expressway (Exit 72 off I-4), and Central Florida Parkway (Exit 71 off I-4). Take Beachline Expressway (also called Hwy. 528) east to the airport. Universal Boulevard is a slightly less congested road that parallels I-Drive to the east.

Parking

Most hotels offer on-site self-parking at no extra charge (usually with a hang tag that fits over your rearview mirror to identify you as a guest) in addition to pricey by-the-day valet parking. The convention center has vast pay-by-the-hour parking lots, and malls offer free parking. Beyond this, each small strip mall on I-Drive contains parking, but don't think you can park indefinitely at a spot for a restaurant or dry cleaner, say, as your car may be towed during a lengthy absence on your part.

Shuttle Service

In addition to the I-Ride Trolley, many hotels on International Drive run shuttles to Walt Disney World Resort, SeaWorld Orlando, Universal Orlando Resort, Wet 'n Wild, and the malls. Ask at the hotel's front desk for shuttle schedules.

INTERNATIONAL DRIVE

KISSIMMEE AND VICINITY

Eighteen miles due south of Downtown Orlando, Kissimmee is actually just a few miles east from Walt Disney World Resort's main gate, making it a convenient (and, for the most part, inexpensive) place for park-goers to stay. A number of Kissimmee's attractions are worth a half-day investigation, all of them providing a more natural, unmediated experience than the theme parks to the west and north. Bass fishing on Lake Toho, a swamp buggy ride through a working cattle ranch, a staring contest with the mighty reptiles at Gatorland—as it was with the cattle ranchers of the last century, it's more a place for rodeos than ballet. Historic downtown Kissimmee, with the oldest courthouse in continual use in Florida, has a sweet old-time charm that makes one instantly nostalgic, though it's seen more flush times.

The area to the south of Kissimmee in Polk County is deliciously rural and small-town feeling, with lakes and wide pastures that are a welcome surprise after the hubbub of Orlando's tourist corridor and Walt Disney World Resort. The town of Winter Haven (30 miles southwest of Kissimmee) has several claims to fame. Called the "Chain of Lakes City" because of its 50 linked freshwater lakes, it is home to historic Cypress Gardens amusement park and was the site of the first Publix supermarket in the 1930s. Lake Wales (about 30 miles due south of Kissimmee) boasts Historic Bok Sanctuary and legendary Spook Hill (an optical illusion whereby a car in neutral appears to be traveling uphill).

Farther north, tucked just between Kissimmee and Walt Disney World Resort to the west,

COURTESY OF KISSIMMEE CONVENTION & VISITORS BUREAU

HIGHLIGHTS

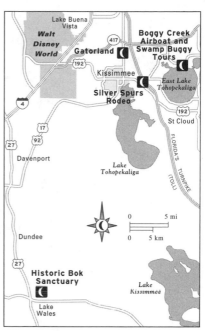

Gatorland: Touted as Orlando's best half-day attraction, Gatorland leaves nothing to smoke and mirrors or high-tech crowd management. It's you, your family, a handful of hot dog chunks, and a few hundred mercurial alligators, crocodiles, and their literal hangers-on (page 240).

Historic Bok Sanctuary: Live carillon-bell performances ring out over the lush landscapes of Frederick Law Olmsted Jr.'s garden designs from the top of a 205-foot Gothic and art deco tower (page 243).

Boggy Creek Airboat and Swamp Buggy Tours: Glide through a twisty natural canal before putting the pedal to the metal and speeding through the swamps of Central Florida past alligators, tall wading birds, and other indigenous – and indignant – local fauna (page 245).

Silver Spurs Rodeo: Get the Stetson out of mothballs and two-step it to the legendary rodeo. It comes only twice a year; the rest of the time it's a strictly homegrown affair Friday nights at the KSA Rodeo. Either way, the bull riding and calf roping are a window into Kissimmee's rugged "cow hunter" history (page 248).

LOOK FOR ◖ TO FIND RECOMMENDED SIGHTS, ACTIVITIES, DINING, AND LODGING.

the town of Celebration is worth several hours of exploration. Patterned after Walt Disney's utopian visions of communities of the future, the Disney-master-planned town was founded in 1994. Using a similar model, Ginn Reunion Resort is a town-size private resort built around three signature golf courses.

A few cavils: Kissimmee isn't altogether pretty. The main drag, U.S. Highway 192, seems in a perpetual state of construction. Once fully constructed, it's probably going to be one long sprawl of utilitarian, low-rise commerce—one Jiffy Lube after another Outback Steakhouse. And traffic can be bad, with not nearly enough left-hand turn arrows or four-way stops to accommodate the many curb cuts. Still, even in high season it takes a mere 15 minutes to reach Walt Disney World Resort from Kissimmee (versus 25 minutes from some hotels on International Drive or up to 45 minutes from Downtown Orlando).

HISTORY

Middle school students in Florida read the 1984 classic, Patrick Smith's *A Land Remembered*, a tale of 100 years of hardscrabble life for a single intrepid family in the wilds of Kissimmee (and that's pronounced "ki-SI-mee," with the accent on the second syllable).

When they reached the source of the St. Johns in a lake that seemed to mesh into an impenetrable swamp, they camped there for a month, fishing with crude hooks

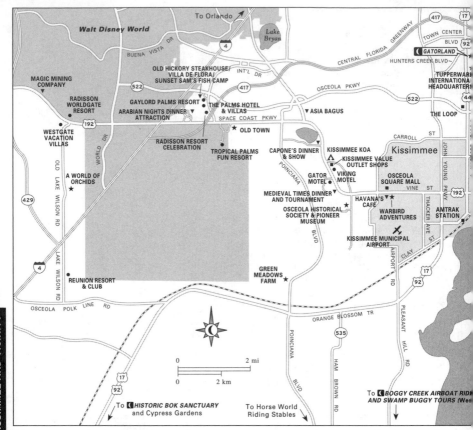

they made from thorn bushes, and killing coons and rabbits with the whip. Then they turned inland and wandered again, finally coming to a dense hammock along the bank of the Kissimmee.

Tobias knew at once that this isolated place was what he was looking for. There were no other homesteads nearby, and the nearest trading post was at Fort Capron, fifty miles to the east.... Spring had passed into early summer, and the woods were alive with the sounds of chattering birds and rambling animals. Squirrels barked and great blue herons squawked loudly as they glided along the nearby river.

It was here that the MacIvey family settled in 1866, spending the bulk of the next century rounding up cattle (cattle they called "yellowhammers" but most folks call "Cracker cattle") on miles of open land and herding them west to Punta Rassa, where they were sold and shipped off to Cuba. And they were not alone. Hardy and independent-minded entrepreneurs drove cattle through, cracking whips to round up the recalcitrant dogie. Like their counterparts in the Wild West, they were men of big hats and few words. They were men who liked the rodeo, the ballet not so much.

Vestiges of this cattle-ranching history are still apparent, and while tourism is the number one industry in Osceola County, there's still a fair

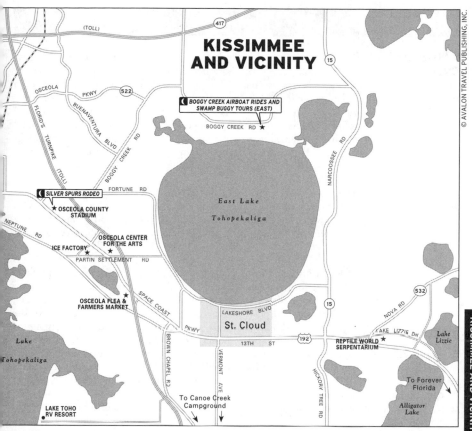

© AVALON TRAVEL PUBLISHING, INC.

KISSIMMEE AND VICINITY

amount of cattle ranching. Before Disney set up shop in the town next door, Kissimmee made a robust go at citrus farming, sugarcane farming, and river steamboating, but the "cow hunter" history is what resonates with many visitors.

PLANNING YOUR TIME

Man cannot live by theme park alone. Kissimmee's more homespun attractions make for several half-days of respite from the big-name parks. If you stay in Kissimmee, it's a 10–20 minute commute to Walt Disney World, another 20 minutes to SeaWorld and Universal.

Walt Disney World, the other theme parks, and the greater Orlando area are a year-round draw, with the peak times during spring break in March and April, all summer long, and then a flurry of activity around the December holidays. Summer in Central Florida is spectacularly hot and humid, so pack accordingly and bring plenty of sunscreen. If your primary aim is to spend time exploring Kissimmee itself, time a visit for when the **Silver Spurs Rodeo** comes to town (February and October); anglers may opt instead for a visit during the Bassmaster Classic (also in February).

Sights

AMUSEMENT PARKS
Cypress Gardens

Many of the Orlando theme parks maintain a rigid devotion to their theme of choice—the movies, the future, whatever. Cypress Gardens Adventure Park (6000 Cypress Gardens Blvd., Winter Haven, southwest of Kissimmee off U.S. Hwy. 27 S, 863/324-2111, hours vary by season but roughly 10 A.M.–6 P.M., later in summer, closed Jan.–Mar., $39.95 adults, $34.95 seniors and children 3–9, children two and younger free) is a breath of fresh air. It's an old-school theme park in which the theme is somewhat ambiguous. Waterskiing? Nature? Nostalgia? Who can say, really?

Cypress Gardens was Central Florida's first theme park, opened in 1943 by Dick and Julie Pope. It was the birthplace of performance waterskiing when Dick Pope, his sister Adrienne, and their friends put on a little show for visiting servicemen. Today they still do those skiing pyramids, jump off ramps, and ride funny hydrofoil skis that seem to make skiers hover over the water (a 91-year-old skier named Banana George Blair, the Guinness World Record holder for oldest barefoot water-skier, uses these). It's just one of the wholesome, old-timey shows that make Cypress Gardens different.

Clearly the mix of attractions hasn't always been a hit. Women in antebellum hoop skirts; vegetable, rose, and butterfly gardens; fairly tame thrill rides—it just didn't seem to measure up to the cutting-edge entertainment of Disney et al. So in 2003, in the wake of low post-9/11 tourism, Cypress Gardens closed its doors. New ownership and a cash infusion got it back up and running in November 2004, but there are still rumors that closure might again be on the horizon.

It makes for a less crowded, less frenetic day than most of the other theme parks. Popular music of the 1950s is piped in to cement the mood as folks wander from the Sunshine Sky Adventure (one of only three in the world, it's a platform at the end of a huge arm that lifts you up and spins slowly for a panoramic view) to water rides such as the Storm Surge or the Wave Runner (both essential activities on a hot day). A bit like Busch Gardens in Tampa—Cypress Gardens was once also owned by Anheuser Busch—there are zoolike animal attractions and shows, giving it a something-for-everyone appeal, appropriate for an intergenerational day out.

Old Town

Another classic "midway" experience, Old Town (5770 W. Irlo Bronson Memorial Hwy./U.S. Hwy. 192, 407/396-4888, www.old-town.com, 10 A.M.–11 P.M. daily, tickets $1, all-day ride pass $20, Sun. noon–6 P.M., $12) is an affordable place to take the whole family, even if it's just for a couple of hours after dinner. Target your visit for a Saturday when the area is swarmed with classic cars for the weekly impromptu car cruise (Friday nights newer models come to cruise, and Thursday evenings bring motorcycles). Sunday nights usually feature a rumba band or other Latin music to entertain Kissimmee's large Latin American community.

The amusement rides include a fairly enormous Ferris wheel, a 365-foot bungee catapult, a go-cart track, and lots of teacuplike rides for young visitors. There are stores such as the Sock Exchange, a puppet store, and somewhere to get your hair wrapped with bright twine, and booths to satisfy many sybaritic culinary urges (places devoted to popcorn, daiquiris, pizza, and ice cream).

◖ GATORLAND

Gatorland (14501 S. Orange Blossom Tr., 407/855-5496, www.gatorland.com, 9 A.M.–6 P.M. daily, $19.95 adults, $12.95 children 3–12, younger than three free) is the archetypal Kissimmee attraction, even if it's technically just over the border in Orlando. It's as "Old Florida" or "Real Florida" as you'll find, with a low-tech charm that is at once whole-

COURTESY OF GATORLAND

Gatorland

reptiles' backs until enterprising ibis and snowy egrets pluck them off. If you want to see the beasts in action, you have a few choices: The Gator Jumparoo Show brings gators leaping out of the depths to grab a snack; the Gator Wrestling Show pits young animal keepers against the snapping jaws and foul breath of big gators; but the best, for an additional $10, is the Adventure Tour in which park guests go behind a big fence and actually hand-feed the gators. Chicken thighs and other mysterious hunks of meat are heaved straight at the assembled crowd of gators, who are not above a little friendly jostling for position. It's truly heart-thumping. Showtimes vary by season, but all are offered three times daily.

Beyond the gators, Gatorland has a lovely aviary and bird rookery, a fine collection of snakes, a boardwalk "swamp" walk and observation tower, and a sweet train ride that takes visitors through the jungle crocs and breeding marsh areas. Pearl's barbecue is fairly good and the gift shop is *de rigueur* for gator tchotchkes.

In April 2007, Gatorland opened **Gator Gully Splash Park,** a $1 million water park expansion. The new attraction features an animal theme, including giant egrets spilling water, water guns mounted on giant alligators, and Grandma's Wet Shack. New characters known as the Gator Gully Gang are the symbols of the splash park. The water attraction is geared toward children and is included in the regular park admission price.

TUPPERWARE INTERNATIONAL HEADQUARTERS

There's another attraction next door to Gatorland that you owe it to yourself to see, largely for the deeply satisfying juxtaposition. Take a left out of the Gatorland parking lot and the next building you will see, the sprawling one-story with all the international flags flying and the huge fountain outside, is the Tupperware International Headquarters (14901 S. Orange Blossom Tr., 407/826-5050, www .tupperware.com, 9 A.M.–5 P.M. Mon.–Fri., free admission).

some and campy. It was opened as a roadside attraction in 1949 by Owen Godwin Sr., an enterprising butcher and postmaster. Godwin tinkered with the idea of an alligator attraction, calling it first the Florida Wildlife Institute (too serious), and then Snake Village and Alligator Farm (too pedestrian), before settling on Gatorland. His first attractions, a 13-footer named Cannibal Jake and a 15-foot croc called Bone Crusher, drew thousands of road-tripping tourists with strategically placed highway billboards.

Today, people come to the 110-acre theme park and wildlife preserve as an antidote to the glitz and marketing slickness of nearby Disney. A fire at the end of 2006 closed it briefly (one dwarf crocodile, two pythons, and two baby gators died in the blaze), but the upshot was that the gift shop and other structures have been recently rebuilt. Unperturbed, hundreds of gators and crocs still bask in the sun while good folks bean them with hot dog chunks as an exhortation to move. Mostly the hot dog chunks go unnoticed, collecting on the mighty

KISSIMMEE AND VICINITY

COMPANY TOWN

Walt Disney had a dream. It was for an utterly new utopian community in Florida, what he called the Experimental Prototype Community of Tomorrow. Of it he said he "would like to be part of building a model community, a City of Tomorrow.... This might become a pilot operation for the teaching age – to go across the country and across the world." The upshot? EPCOT. It's not exactly what he had in mind, but it's a lovely day at the theme park. Some of Walt's interests in technology and the future were explored, but all thoughts of a residential community got tossed along the way.

So, with some of the land Walt bought in the early 1960s, the master-planned community of **Celebration** was founded in 1994. There are eight regimented developments within Celebration – North Village, South Village, East Village, West Village, Celebration Village, Lake Evalyn, Roseville Corner, and Artisan Park – with homes built in a number of preapproved styles. But at the core of the whole thing is the idea of New Urbanism, a mixture of residential and commercial space organized around common green space (for more info about New Urbanism, pick up a copy

of Andres Duany, Elizabeth Plater-Zyberk, and Jeff Speck's excellent *Suburban Nation: The Rise of Sprawl and the Decline of the American Dream*). Detractors say it's just Disney for grown-ups, an ersatz version of a simpler time, but there's something entirely forward-thinking about a compact, walkable, mixed-use town. If you live or stay in Celebration, you can park your car and be done with it for a while. Sidewalks are generous and inviting, nothing's too far to walk (for the lazy there are cool Segway two-wheel vehicles and little electric cars called NEVs). Regular festivals and community events get things jumping downtown and an 18-hole golf course winds through it all.

It's not all sweetness and light. There's a little Stepford weirdness. Owners face restrictive homeowners' covenants, and for a long time there were no elected officials – a company called The Celebration Company ran the town with an iron fist, exhibiting a penchant for choices in favor of tourist-friendly gift shops and against unsightly additions such as a gas station.

It's worth checking out – a quick drive

In 1951, Earl Tupper bought 1,000 acres of cow pasture in sleepy Kissimmee and set about building the headquarters for Tupperware Home Parties Inc. Tupper's plastic products revolutionized food storage, but more important, the company's direct-sale "party" strategy enabled countless women in the 1950s to effectively enter the workforce. Forget Rosie the Riveter—all hail "the bowl that burps."

The headquarters is largely an office complex with a single small room that functions as a museum, displaying the innovative designs and storage solutions that have kept Tupperware viable and winning design awards all these years. The receptionist even gives visitors little Tupperware key chains upon departure.

Two important Tupperware asides for the

enthusiast: Dave Barry and his band the Urban Professionals have a wonderful tribute song called "The Tupperware Blues." And while there was a fairly good documentary on the company released in 2004, the best film on Tupperware, hands down, is *Lifetime Guarantee*, which chronicles Jewish lesbian folksinger Phranc's success as a Tupperware lady, culminating in her triumph at the annual Tupperware Jubilee right here in Kissimmee.

REPTILE WORLD SERPENTARIUM

If cold-blooded creatures really get your blood boiling, there are more to view at Reptile World Serpentarium (5705 E. Irlo Bronson Memorial Hwy./U.S. Hwy. 192, St. Cloud, 407/892-6905, 9 a.m.–5:30 p.m. Tues.–Sun., $5.75 adults, $4.75 children 6–17, $3.75 chil-

through and maybe a stop for lunch or dinner along the two main streets, Market and Front.

ACCOMMODATIONS

Wanna experience Celebration whole-hog, hook, line, 'n sinker? Book a room at the **Celebration Hotel** (700 Bloom St., 407/566-6000, $189-389) at the end of Celebration's main street. In a neoplantation style, the 115 guest rooms and suites have a gracious, old-time feel to them, with lots of dark wood, rattan furniture, and big four-posters with fancy sheets. There are the usual modern conveniences (such as high-speed Internet), but the lakeside setting complete with nature trails feels like a retreat from all the commercial bustle of Walt Disney World a mere five minutes away. Golfers will appreciate the Robert Trent Jones Sr.- and Jr.-designed Celebration Golf Club.

FOOD

Celebration has a handful of very respectable restaurants along Front Street, worthy of a detour if you're staying on the U.S. Highway 192 strip. A new outpost of the oldest restaurant in Florida (the original is in Tampa), **The Columbia** (649 Front St., 407/566-1505, 11:30 A.M.-10 P.M. daily, $4.95-22.95) purveys Spanish-Cuban cuisine in a lovely setting. None of the dishes, from the paella to the retro "1905 salad," are scintillating, but there's a nice selection of tapas and a fun cigar bar. **Café D'Antonio** (691 Front St., 407/566-2233, 11:30 A.M.-3 P.M. and 5-10 P.M. Mon.-Fri., 11:30 A.M.-10 P.M. Sat., until 9 P.M. Sun., $4.95-26.95) wins kudos from local and national publications for its stylish Italian cuisine and excellent wine list. My favorite is **Seito Japanese Restaurant** (671 Front St., 407/566-1889, 11:30 A.M.-2:30 P.M. and 5-10 weekdays, noon-11 P.M. weekends, $9.50-19.95), well-executed classic rolls and *nigiri*, and enough of those goofy East-West rolls to satisfy the stunt sushi eaters. For a more casual bite, a deli sandwich or a maybe a little meatloaf, head to **Market Street Café** (701 Front St., 407/566-1144, 11 A.M.-10 P.M. daily, $3.95-14.95). For ice cream, it's **Herman's Ice Cream Shoppe** (671 Front St., 407/566-1300, 11 A.M.-9:30 P.M. Sun.-Thurs., until 10 P.M. Fri.-Sat.) and for pizza try the **Upper Crust** (606 Market St., 407/566-1221, 11 A.M.-9 P.M. Sun.-Thurs., until 10 P.M. Fri.-Sat.).

KISSIMMEE AND VICINITY

dren 3–5). It's worth spending an hour or so and is one of the few truly inexpensive attractions around. Housed in an inauspicious cinderblock house, the collection numbers around 50 species, from vibrant East African green mambas to deadly Australian taipans. The numerous venomous snakes are regularly "milked" of their venom by owner George Van Horn—a spectator sport not for the faint of heart that takes place at noon and 3 P.M. daily. The business end of the fangs is sunk through a membrane stretched over a collection glass, and droplet by droplet the venom is harvested (used, ostensibly, for the study of coagulation factors and maybe even to collect chemicals that might prevent heart attack and stroke in humans). The snakes don't always seem thrilled about the process and occasionally Van Horn has tasted their wrath.

◖ HISTORIC BOK SANCTUARY

The winner of the "what the heck is this doing way out here?" award goes to Historic Bok Sanctuary (1151 Tower Blvd., Lake Wales, 863/676-1408, www.boksanctuary.org, 8 A.M.–6 P.M. daily, $10 adults, $3 children, younger than five free, half-price 8–9 A.M. Sat. morning). The 205-foot-tall marble-and-coquina bell tower houses a world-renowned carillon and is a National Historic Landmark. But why is it here, perched on a hill in the middle of 250 acres of not much?

As with so many things, it all began with a man, his dream, and a pile of cash. Edward William Bok, longtime editor of *The Ladies' Home Journal* and Pulitzer Prize–winning author, fell in love with the highest hill of Florida's Lake Wales Ridge in 1921. By gum, he

KISSIMMEE AND VICINITY

COURTESY OF CENTRAL FLORIDA VISITORS & CONVENTION BUREAU

Bok Tower at Historic Bok Sanctuary

thought, this place ought to be preserved as a bird sanctuary. This was not the first time Bok had championed a cause, having been a pioneer in the fields of public sex education, prenatal education and child care, and public health, as well as an activist in the saving of Niagara Falls.

Unlike Niagara Falls, the sanctuary needed a vision and a little finessing. After buying the land, Bok hired famous landscape architect Frederick Law Olmsted Jr., of Central Park fame, to design this hilltop paradise as "a spot of beauty second to none in the country." Like Central Park, it's a generous, natural-looking landscape of elegant juxtapositions (bursts of azaleas and camellias here, shaded ferns and vine-covered arbors there). You'll see a little wooden nature observatory cabin with a glassed lookout onto a busy pond; a reflecting pool welcomes birds and wildlife to its edge; and native subtropical plants provide food and shade for countless species.

In the midst of this verdant tableau rises a tall Gothic and art deco carillon tower de-

signed by architect Milton Medary, its stone crafted by sculptor Lee Lawrie, its tilework by H. Dulles Allen, and its wrought iron by premier metalworker Samuel Yellin. The interior of the tower is not open to the public (Bok's private study is on the first floor, the curator's workshop is on level 4 and a carillon library, the largest in the world, is on level 5), but the public is invited daily to hear the live 60-bell carillon show. The carillonneur walks up 211 stairs to the bell tower (okay, there's an elevator, too, but that's less romantic), seats him- or herself at the clavier keyboard, plinks the tiny hammers against several octaves of bells arranged in chromatic series, and music pours out across the Lake Wales Ridge.

Regularly scheduled recitals are at 1 P.M. and 3 P.M., but one may be added here and there on a luscious spring evening. In addition, Historic Bok Sanctuary has a small museum devoted to Edward Bok and his achievements, a short video about his vision, and regular walking tours of the gardens and on-site 20-room **Pinewood Estate** (tour $5 adults, $3 children; it's especially wonderful at Christmas when the mansion is all dolled up for the holiday). The Mediterranean Revival mansion was once the home of C. Austin Buck, an early 20th-century industrialist, and has been meticulously restored to its 1930s grandeur.

A WORLD OF ORCHIDS

In *The Secret Garden,* Mary stumbles upon a garden that has been locked up for 10 years, once-regimented roses left to creep and spread with weeds in a Darwinian hootenanny. A World of Orchids (2501 Old Lake Wilson Rd., 407/396-1881, www.aworldoforchids .com, 9:30 A.M.–4:30 P.M. Mon.–Sat., free admission) is a bit like that. The huge greenhouse, battered by recent hurricane seasons and flapping with tarps and duct tape, contains hundreds of species of epiphytes, orchids, weird subtropical plants, exotic birds, little lizards, koi, and a fair number of uninvited bugs and creatures.

In the 22,500 feet of conservatory, there once was an attempt to tag each plant with identification markers. But the lush, supercharged climate of Central Florida has rendered this task Sisyphean—vines wind around, several plants commingle, the flowers brilliant jewels in a tangle of lush green.

At the front, a little shop sells *dendrobium, phalaenopsis,* and other familiar orchid species along with a wild array of the rare and peculiar. The folks behind the cash register are a wealth of knowledge, eager to talk orchid husbandry, but it's through the back doors that you enter this Floridian secret garden with delightfully little evidence of human intervention. Spend a worthwhile half hour of wandering and quiet contemplation to recharge your theme-park batteries.

OSCEOLA COUNTY HISTORICAL SOCIETY AND PIONEER MUSEUM

Often what separates a community's historical museum from a garage sale is the signage. It's the same fascinating array of flotsam and jetsam cast off from citizens of another era—a dinged-up phonograph, faded commemorative plates, some treasures too esoteric to identify—but carefully categorized and rendered intelligible with a little placard of text. In this way, these possessions come to stand in for the lives of our forebears, a window into simpler yet almost invariably harder times. Osceola County Historical Society and Pioneer Museum (750 N. Bass Rd., 407/396-8644, 10 A.M.–4 P.M. Thur.–Sat., noon–4 P.M. Sun., $2 adults, $1 children) could use a little attention to the signage. The museum has good raw material, but a little elbow grease would help to tidy up the 1890s-era Cracker house, Cracker cow camp, genealogy library, and pioneer artifacts. Kids might enjoy a little wander through the small museum's sugarcane mill, blacksmithing shop, and eight acres of nature preserve, especially as an antidote to several days of being herded through crowded theme parks. Gnarled old oaks on the property make a nice shady spot for a picnic.

Sports and Recreation

◖ BOGGY CREEK AIRBOAT AND SWAMP BUGGY TOURS

Florida alligators lurk patiently under moss-draped cypress; purple gallinules skitter to a landing on wide lily pads; great egrets and diamondback terrapins sit cheek to jowl, motionless in the Florida sun. It sounds like a serene brush with nature, only there are few things less serene than an airboat ride. An invention brought to the world by Alexander Graham Bell in Nova Scotia in 1905 (his prototype was called the *Ugly Duckling*), an airboat is propelled entirely with air thrust, usually provided by an aircraft engine or big-block Chevy engine. It's loud—so loud that everyone on board is equipped with a set of hearing protectors.

Kissimmee's seminal airboat ride is to be had at Boggy Creek Airboat and Swamp Buggy Tours (2001 E. Southport Rd., 407/344-9550, www.bcairboats.com, 9 A.M.–5 P.M. daily, half-hour tours $21.95 adults, $15.95 children 3–12, two and younger free; private 45-minute tours $45 per person; one-hour night safaris $29.95 adults, $24.95 children; swamp buggy tours $20.95 adults, $15.95 children; airboat/swamp buggy combo $36.81 adults, $28.71 children). On a big airboat that travels at speeds of 40 mph, up to 18 passengers shoot through the wetlands, pointing and gesturing at the bald eagles, wild turkeys, and other animals rustled up by the airboat's approach. There's no way to ask questions, so the 30-minute ride is plenty, especially if followed by a swamp buggy tour through a working cattle ranch. The 40-minute tour takes place in an open-sided, all-terrain vehicle that looks like a monster truck mated with a school bus. It's not nearly as loud, and you can chat with your guide and get fairly reliable information about the wealth of local flora and fauna. (A second

THE BASS-ICS

Terry Segraves grew up in southern Indiana and northern Kentucky, fishing for bass and enjoying the great outdoors. Eventually he got serious about his hobby and began fishing local and regional tournaments, going on to compete nationally in the Citgo Bassmaster and Wal-Mart FLW bass fishing tours. And all that time, he was developing a deep love for Kissimmee's Lake Tohopekaliga – a tough one to get your mouth around. (The locals just call it Lake Toho.) The Kissimmee Chain of Lakes is in fact legendary among bass fishermen.

Why Lake Toho?

"It's a phenomenal place, a great habitat, in the upper basin of the Chain of Lakes. We've got a 12-month growing season, which affects not just the number of fish, but their size – I've seen some 15-pounders, and the record is 17 pounds. Until recently we had the four-day weight record, and we still hold the one-day record of 45 pounds two ounces, and that's only five fish. It's a great destination for the whole family. You can go to the amusement parks, but then do some of the best bass fishing around. It's a win-win situation."

But what exactly explains the meteoric increase in bass fishing's popularity?

"I think the tournament trails and the TV exposure have done a good job of bringing to the forefront that it's a great recreational activity for everyone, the whole family."

What makes it different from other kinds of sportfishing?

"It's something everybody can do. The bodies of water are, in most cases, in people's backyards. You can do it in a flat-bottom john boat that doesn't cost you that much. It's not like saltwater fishing, where you have to have a big boat to go out and find the fish."

What qualities make a great bass angler?

"Dedication and getting good with the tools that you're using. A great angler does their homework. Number one – they go out and study the body of water, study the tournaments. A lot of guys specialize in different things – in a lot of cases, if a guy is strong in top water fishing or in sight fishing, they work those strengths and capitalize on what they know."

Boggy Creek Airboat outpost is to the east at 3702 Big Bass Road in Kissimmee.)

HOUSTON ASTROS SPRING TRAINING

The boys of summer get to work early each March at **Osceola County Stadium** (631 Heritage Park Way, off U.S. Hwy. 192, 321/697-3201, www.ticketmaster.com, Mar. 1–31, reserve seats $15, box seats $18, parking $5). The Houston Astros have done their spring training here since 1985 (the sixth-longest tenure in the majors), when they moved over from Cocoa Beach. But it was in 2003 that the little stadium got an $18.4 million overhaul, becom-

ing, in the eyes of the baseball cognoscenti, a jewel among spring training facilities. With a capacity of 5,200, a party deck for private functions, and "Autograph Alley" down the third baseline (the best time to get autographs, though, is during workouts 9 A.M.–2 P.M. Feb. 18–27), it's a great place to take in a game or two. No pets, folding chairs, coolers, or glass bottles are allowed inside.

HORSE AND "COW HUNTER" ATTRACTIONS

Cows, branded or earmarked for owner identification, used to roam free all over Kissimmee. To round them up, Florida cattle ranchers

Do you have any tips for someone coming to fish Lake Toho?

"Lake Toho is a natural lake with a lot of grass. A lot of people may look at all that grass as confusing – just break it down to simple things like voids in the grass; look at the smaller picture. There are contour lines and places that hold fish more than others; look out for lily pads or hydrilla grass and a fish may be nearby. As per bait, you can use about anything you want to in Florida, but I recommend a 7.5-inch Culprit ribbontail worm in the junebug color. You'll catch fish. But it's all catch-and-release – the last time I ate a bass was 20 years ago."

So how do you get in on this Lake Toho bass fishing? There are a slew of reputable bass-fishing charter companies that will take you out for a day of guided fishing: **Tom and Jerry's Pro Guide Service** (800/328-5686, half day for two people $250, full day $375, does not include fishing license, lunch, or live bait); **Bass Fishing with John Leech** (877/274-8433, half day for two people $225, full day $325, live bait extra $50); and **Champion Pro Guide Services** (407/738-7652, half day for two people $250, full day $350, does not include fishing license, lunch, or live bait). A number of other outfits are listed at www.floridakiss.com/rec/fishing. In general, the outfitter brings all the gear, usually ferrying you around on a 20-foot light tackle bass boat; a tip is expected.

The lake's recent "drawdown," whereby thousands of acres of lake bottom are scraped, served to firm the lake bottom and increase the water's oxygenation, making it a locus of fishing competitions. In November there's the Big Fish Open and the Lake Toho Pro-Am, both a part of Kissimmee's Great Outdoor Days. But the granddaddy of them all, the Super Bowl of bass-fishing events, comes in February. It's the **Bassmaster Classic** (espn.go.com for info and tickets), one of the stranger spectator sports I've ever witnessed. On the final day of the classic, 10,000 fans pile into the Orange County Convention Center to watch fish getting weighed.

World-class anglers arrive like rock stars in the arena, their own theme songs blaring and the fans apoplectic with joy, standing on their bass boats pulled by pickups. Looking a bit like NASCAR racers with their jumpsuits festooned with sponsorship decals, they walk up to the podium with baggies of bass. These get weighed amid hoots and much ESPN-commentator speculation. Then the fish are whisked by the Florida Fish and Game commission back to the lake, ostensibly even near where they were caught. What must these fish think?

would crack long whips to get them moving. (Some people say it is this that earned rural Floridians the nickname "Crackers.") Unlike their brethren to the West, these folks weren't called "cowboys" but rather "cow hunters." Despite ever more urban sprawl, there are still a few ways to get a taste of Florida cow-hunting life.

Forever Florida

Spanish cattle were introduced to Florida in 1521 by Juan Ponce de León, and again later by Hernando de Soto. Through the course of four centuries, these fancy Spanish imports commingled with feral cows and Indian cattle to produce scrappy little bovines with bad dispositions—hardy creatures able to endure Florida heat and humidity, poor nutrition, and countless predators. To see the largest herd of these "Cracker" cattle and horses in the world, venture to the Crescent J. Ranch and Forever Florida (4755 N. Kenansville Rd., St. Cloud, 888/957-9794, www.foreverflorida.com).

The 4,700-acre working cattle ranch and wildlife preserve was purchased by William Broussard in 1969 as a bull stock operation for Charolais cattle. Broussard's son, a wildlife ecologist and naturalist, begged his dad to do whatever was within his power to protect the area and today the property operates as a nonprofit preserve.

Explore it via guided ecosafari ($19.95 adults, $14.95 children 6–12, younger than six free) on an elevated safari coach (in common parlance, that's a swamp buggy). The tour is little longer than 1.5 hours, traversing nine different ecosystems around the ranch and preserve property. Or meander through these different ecosystems by horseback, with a one-, two-, or three-hour guided horseback tour (one hour $37.50, two hour $57, three hour $73), or even a special "rawhide roundup" ($89), which includes a guided trail ride out to the main pasture, where guests are given an opportunity to work with cattle before a trail ride back and lunch.

The ranch sits on more than four miles of the Florida Trail, so hikers are invited to explore the stretch of trail free of charge. In addition, there are two primitive campsites (no water or electricity). Forever Florida is in the process of developing another campsite with services, including a bunkhouse for groups.

Horse World Riding Stables

On 750 acres of gentle sandy trail, Horse World Riding Stables (3705 Poinciana Blvd., 12 miles south of U.S. Hwy. 192, 407/847-4343, www .horseworldstables.com, open from 9 A.M. daily, reservations recommended, with $3 off if you reserve online, nature trail ride $39, $16.95 children five and younger, intermediate trail ride $47, advanced private trail ride $69) takes folks out on three types of guided rides. The basic nature trail ride is an easy 45-minute walk on horseback (kids five and younger ride with a parent); the intermediate trail ride is an hour-long walk/trot; and the advanced trail ride is about 1.5 hours of walking, trotting, and cantering. Regardless of your skill level and speed, you'll see an array of local wildlife along the trail and some peaceful countryside that harkens back to Central Florida at the turn of the last century.

Guests are also invited to feed and pet farm animals, play volleyball, toss horseshoes, and bring their own picnic lunches to enjoy under a shady oak tree or picnic pavilion.

Green Meadows Farm

If you didn't get your fill of farm animals, not far away Green Meadows Farm (1368 S. Poinciana Blvd., 407/846-0770, 9 A.M.–4 P.M. daily, $19 adults, $16 seniors, children two and younger free) conducts two-hour farm tours. Visitors learn to milk a cow and do other chores around the farm before taking a pony ride and then hopping aboard a tractor-drawn hayride. There are more than 300 farm animals (pigs, chickens, turkeys, ducks, geese, donkeys) and the approach is very hands-on. Bring wipes.

◖ Silver Spurs Rodeo

Part of Osceola Heritage Park's 120-acre multipurpose complex, the **Silver Spurs Arena** (1875 Silver Spur La., 407/677-6336, www.silver spursrodeo.com, rodeo tickets $10–30) plays host to an eclectic array of spectator enthusiasms, from Taekwondo Nationals to what sounds like high school team Civil War reenactments. But the arena is named for its biggest draw—the Silver Spurs Rodeo, founded in 1944. It's one of the country's most successful rodeos, for which organizers strew 1,400 cubic yards of dirt around the state-of-the-art arena twice a year, one weekend in mid-February and another the beginning of October. In homage to the area's cattle ranching heritage, the event showcases traditional rodeo competitions such as bareback, saddle bronc and bull riding, calf roping, and barrel racing.

The minutiae of rodeo rules may seem somewhat Byzantine, although they are clearly intelligible to the taciturn Stetson-wearing folk who made up the bulk of the audience. Visitors might find the calf roping somewhat cruel, both rider and horse complicit in a scheme to humiliate and befuddle the innocent young cows, but the rodeo clowns—now called bullfighters and barrelmen—are enjoyable as they kibbitz with the rodeo announcer and entertain the audience with physical comedy and skits; they are actually the bull riders' first line of defense. Other unsung rodeo heroes include the "pickup men," the dudes who ride around the periphery and swoop in to give a lift to the bull riders after their eight seconds are up, and the "rodeo queens" who manage to make pageant sashes and 10-gallon hats seem not at all incongruous.

If your trip doesn't coincide with the big

rodeo, Kissimmee also has a smaller weekly rodeo that is popular with local families. At the **KSA Rodeo** (958 S. Hoagland Blvd., 407/933-0020, www.ksarodeo.com, 8 P.M. Fri., Florida residents $12, adults $18, children 12 and younger $9), you won't see the megastars of rodeo, but it's a sweet local tradition.

WARBIRD ADVENTURES

The 2004 hurricane season demolished one of Kissimmee's most distinctive attractions, the Flying Tigers Warbird Restoration Museum, where visitors could watch vintage aircrafts being lovingly restored by owner Tom Reilly and his crew. There's some talk that the museum will be rebuilt, but there's another way to commune with historic planes in Kissimmee. A vintage aircraft—flying school, Warbird Adventures (233 N. Hoagland Blvd., 407/870-7366, www.warbird adventures.com, 9 A.M.–5 P.M. Mon.–Sat., 15 minutes $190, 30 minutes $320, 60 minutes $560) takes rookies and seasoned fliers alike up in the premier fighter/trainer of World War II, the North American T-6 *Texan*. Guests actually pilot the plane, and for an extra $35, the real pilot will teach you aerobatic moves such as flipping this legendary "Pilot Maker" upside-down. Guest pilots must be a minimum of four feet tall (no age restriction) and a maximum weight of 254 pounds. M*A*S*H helicopter flight lessons are also available (15 minutes for $120, 30 minutes for $210, and one hour for $390).

ICE-SKATING

After enduring a spring or summer vacation crisscrossing theme parks, one thing will become abundantly clear: Central Florida is hot and humid, often in heady tandem. To cool off, spend a few hours on the ice at **Ice Factory** (2221 Partin Settlement Rd., 407/933-4259, sessions $6, skate rental $3, free skate rental for kids younger than 10), Kissimmee's Olympic-class ice-skating and hockey rink. Tuesday nights is the cheap public skate ($5 session, skate rental included, 5:30–7 P.M.), with open skate hours 8–11 P.M. Friday and Saturday evenings, 1–3 P.M. Saturday afternoons, and 10 A.M.–2 P.M. weekdays. There's a large main rink and a smaller rink used primarily for classes, as well as a children's soft play area, a video arcade, and a snack bar.

PARKS AND RESERVES

Polk County has lovely parks and reserves that provide the antidote to Orlando theme park overload. Enjoy a nature walk at **Circle B-Bar Reserve** (two miles east of U.S. Hwy. 98 on the south side of Hwy. 540, southeast of Lakeland, 863/534-7377, 5 A.M.–7 P.M. daily, free admission). Part of the Polk County Environmental Lands Program, this preserve offers visitors a view of an oak hammock, freshwater marsh, hardwood swamp, and lakeshore. There is a tremendous bird population here, including a variety of wading birds, water fowl, ospreys, and bald eagles.

The 5,930-acre **Lake Kissimmee State Park** (14248 Camp Mack Rd., Lake Wales, 863/696-1112, 8 A.M.–sunset daily, $4 per car, $19.04 camping fee) has 15 miles of hiking trails (six miles of which are open to equestrians), great fishing on the state's third-largest lake, and on the weekends there's a living-history demonstration in an 1876-era cow camp. The resident "cow hunter" chats with visitors about what it was like in the early Florida cattle days. You're likely to see white-tailed deer, bald eagles, sandhill cranes, turkeys, and even bobcats. There are also full-facility campsites and picnic areas.

To see 15 of the state's rarest species, explore the three hiking trails of 4,778-acre **Tiger Creek Preserve** (Pfundstein Rd., east of Hwy. 17 between Babson Park and Frostproof, 863/635-7506, open sunrise to sunset, free admission) at the edge of Florida's oldest—and highest, but that's not saying much—land mass, the Lake Wales Ridge. The pristine blackwater stream that gives the preserve its name is entirely protected, as are the hardwood swamps, hammocks, oak scrub, pine flatwoods, sandhill, and longleaf pine habitats that surround it. Very close by is the **Babson Park Audubon Center** (200 N. Crooked Lake, Babson Park, 863/638-1355, open sunrise to sunset, free admission), where guests can learn about the birds, wildlife, and habitats of the Lake Wales Ridge.

Entertainment and Shopping

OSCEOLA CENTER FOR THE ARTS

Osceola Center for the Arts (2411 E. Irlo Bronson Memorial Hwy./U.S. Hwy. 192, 407/846-6257, www.ocfta.com, times and ticket prices vary) is really the area's catchall for performing arts, staging community theater comedies, musicals, and dramas, occasional local and regional ballet and dance performances, as well as painting and pottery classes for kids and adults. The center hosts a weekend visual arts festival in November and a number of holiday concerts during December.

SHOPPING CENTERS

If your mission is Operation Swanky Shopping, your best bet is in Orlando. For more basic retail needs, head to Kissimmee's newest shopping center, called **The Loop** (3208 N. John Young Pkwy., 407/343-9223, 10 A.M.–9:30 P.M. Mon.–Sat., 11 A.M.–6 P.M. Sun.). It includes a 16-screen multiplex, Kohl's department store, Old Navy, a pharmacy, and a handful of chain restaurants such as the Macaroni Grill and Chipotle. There's also the **Osceola Square Mall** (3831 W. Vine St., 407/847-6941, 10 A.M.–9 P.M. Mon.–Sat., noon–6 P.M. Sun.), really the locals' aging workhorse indoor mall, anchored by Bealls. In 2007, the mall was undergoing a slight spruce-up under new ownership.

In a similar vein, **Kissimmee Value Outlet Shops** (4673 W. Irlo Bronson Memorial Hwy./U.S. Hwy. 192, 407/843-1723, 10 A.M.–9 P.M. Mon.–Sat., noon–5 P.M. Sun.) offer outlet versions of Bealls, Dress Barn, Nike, Samsonite, and a few others.

HISTORIC DISTRICT

For a more distinctive shopping experience, wander around Kissimmee's little historic district on Broadway, just off U.S. Hwy. 192. **Lanier's Antique Marketplace** (108 Broadway, 407/933-5679, 9 A.M.–5:30 P.M. Mon.–Sat.) is perhaps the most interesting find, with two stories of antiques and collectibles to explore. There's a constellation of similar stores clustered in this block, from **Ann Teek's "Used to Have" Shop** (109 Broadway, 407/944-4109) across the street to **Showcase Antique Mall** (111 Broadway, 407/343-9477) next to that. Specialty shops fill in the gaps, with small storefronts devoted to needlework, coins, comics, and music.

MARKETS

For a real locals' experience, head to the huge enclosed **Osceola Flea and Farmers Market** (2801 E. Irlo Bronson Memorial Hwy./U.S. Hwy. 192, 407/846-2811, 8 A.M.–5 P.M. Fri.–Sun.), in which 900 specialty booths sell everything from specialty license plates to puppies or fresh produce. It's an inexpensive place to pick up kitschy Florida souvenirs, too.

Accommodations

VACATION HOMES

Spend an hour driving on I-4 or U.S. Highway 192 and it becomes clear that the greater Orlando area is embroiled in a protracted real estate boom. Trucks hauling roofing material and rebar jockey with landscaping crews and cement mixers. Real estate speculation continues unabated, with timeshares, rental properties, and condos going up at breakneck speed in a swath of land once given over to oranges and cattle. As a consequence, there are fairly good deals to be had on vacation-home rentals in Kissimmee, just a couple of miles from Disney's front door, and it often makes more financial sense to go this route, especially for large groups. Many vacation homes are equipped with pools, game rooms, and other amenities to soothe the tired beasts, and fully equipped kitchens obviate the need to dine out every meal. One thing to think about, though, is that vacation homes seldom offer shuttle service to the parks, so you're stuck driving.

At last count there were approximately 26,000 vacation homes in the four-county area surrounding Walt Disney World. How to go about finding one to suit? **All Star Vacation Homes** (7822 W. Irlo Bronson Memorial Hwy., 407/997-0733, www.allstarvacationhomes .com) manages luxury condos, townhomes, estates, and resort offerings, and it maintains a certain aesthetic homogeneity and very high standards for service and cleanliness. Most of its properties are within four miles of Disney and all are equipped with the latest bells and whistles (those superhuge TVs, alarms that sound when anyone has slipped out the back door to the pool—maddening, but a safety precaution with kids). **Windsor Palms Resort** (888/306-1766, www.windsorpalmsresort. com) is another longtime Kissimmee favorite, offering houses, condos, and townhomes in a complex three miles from Disney (shuttle service to the parks is $9/person). For other reputable rental companies, consult the chart on Kissimmee's Convention and Visitors Bureau site (www.floridakiss.com/stay/index.php).

CAMPING

Bass fishermen congregate at **Lake Toho RV Resort** (4715 Kissimmee Park Rd., St. Cloud, 407/892-8795, $22–30) right on West Lake Toho, part of Kissimmee's legendary Chain of Lakes. There are 200 full hookups for RVs and mobile homes (no tent camping) and pets are accepted. There are an on-site boat ramp and bait shop. Nearby is another RV resort, **Canoe Creek Campground** (4101 Canoe Creek Rd., St. Cloud, 407/892-7010), with more than 200 sites with full hookups, a swimming pool, modern restrooms, and a coin laundry. For tent camping, the **Kissimmee KOA Kampground** (2644 Happy Camper Pl., 407/396-2400, seasonal rates $40–50) has supersize tent sites as well as RV "patio sites" with fireplaces, a heated pool, playground, convenience store, free WiFi, and bus service to the Magic Kingdom ($1.50 each way). **Tropical Palms Fun Resort** (2650 Holiday Tr., 407/396-4595, RV spots $25–51, cottages $89–109) seems to get the nod from families. With RV camping and a handful of adorable pastel-colored cabins, it's within walking distance of Kissimmee's Old Town midway rides. There are a pool, poolside café, business center, laundry facilities, and basketball courts.

UNDER $50

Because of Kissimmee's proximity to Walt Disney World Resort, it's a logical home base for visitors aiming to spend the bulk of their stay at Walt Disney World. The stretch of Irlo Bronson Memorial Highway (also called U.S. Hwy. 192) east of U.S. Highway 4 also happens to be where the bulk of the bargains are. The whole stretch is dotted with low-rise, low-frills motels, many of which offer free shuttle service to the theme parks. You can drive along Highway 192 and bargain shop —all of the motels post their room rates and special deals on their marquees, many with enticing theme-park packages as well.

My favorite of these is the **Gator Motel** (4576 W. Irlo Bronson Memorial Hwy., 407/396-0127, $25.95–45.95), mostly for the photo op. Out in the parking lot there's a huge concrete alligator with open jaws—if you position it right, you can have a photo of your whole family being consumed by the beast. Rooms are clean and pleasant and there is a nice lighted swimming pool, discount attraction tickets, morning coffee, a play area for children, and barbecue and picnic facilities. Then, not far away, across the street is the **Viking Motel** (4539 W. Irlo Bronson Memorial Hwy., 407/396-8860), a small Tudor castle set next door to River Adventure Mini Golf and across the street from a 24-hour Super Wal-Mart. (I especially like the vision of Vikings playing minigolf and doing late-night Wal-Mart runs.) The rooms are tidy, with tile floors, dataports, and cable TV. The hotel has shuffleboard, a playground, a grill area, and guest laundry.

These are just the tip of the iceberg. On East Irlo Bronson you'll find the affordable **Days Inn Kissimmee East** (2095 E Irlo Bronson Memorial Hwy., 407/401-8703, $36–56), the **Stadium Inn and Suites** (2039 E. Irlo Bronson Memorial Hwy., 877/477-5817, $45–62), **Holiday Inn Express Kissimmee East** (2145 East Irlo Bronson Memorial Hwy., 407/396-4222, $60–89), and **Quality Inn and Conference Center** (2050 E Irlo Bronson Hwy., 877/586-8080, $49–89). As a rule of thumb, these are less expensive than the equivalent motels closer to the theme parks; these are roughly 10–15 miles from the Walt Disney World main gate, which can take as long as 40 minutes to traverse in peak season.

$50-150

The **Radisson WorldGate Resort** (3011 Maingate La., 407/396-1400, www.worldgateresort.com, $99–119) is one of the heavy hitters just outside the Walt Disney World Resort. There are 566 fairly slick and contemporary guest rooms, with a variety of amenities in business-friendly surroundings. Rooms have those cool "Sleep Number" beds, garden tubs, two-line phones with dataports and voice mail, and a big work desk. In addition to Direct TV's 60 channels, there are in-room movies and Sony Playstation games.

Radisson has another entry in Kissimmee. Majorly remodeled in 2001, the **Radisson Resort Orlando Celebration** (2900 Parkway Blvd., 407/396-7000, www.radissonparkway.com, $99.95–149.95) has lots going for it. Just 1.5 miles from Disney, it's adjacent to the Robert Trent Jones–designed Celebration Golf Club, with a championship-caliber 18-hole course. Set on 20 acres of tropically landscaped grounds, it's a big hotel, with 718 attractive rooms, a giant free-form pool with waterslides, and shuttle service to the theme parks included. Kids are treated well, with a "kids eat free" program for those younger than 10 and lots of recreational activities.

OVER $150

Good for families, **Westgate Vacation Villas** (2770 N. Old Lake Wilson Rd., 407/396-8523, www.wgvacationvillas.com, $99–308) is just one mile from the main entrance to Walt Disney World, with accommodations varying from one- to three-bedroom villas. Units include large-screen TVs with VCR/DVD, fully equipped kitchens, sleeper sofas, whirlpool tubs, and screened terraces. There are 13 pools for adults and children, a fitness room, picnic areas, miniature golf, arcade, volleyball, tennis courts, and shuffleboard on the Westgate Vacation Villas grounds. The on-site Wes T. Gator program for kids features daily activities, swimming, and games.

A recent condo-to-hotel conversion, **The Palms Hotel and Villas** (3100 Parkway Blvd., 407/396-2229, www.thepalmshotelandvillas.com, $149–219), is just 1.5 miles from Walt Disney World, with 228 king and double suites, two pools, a gazebo with gas grills, an exercise room, game room, laundry, and a little on-site food shop all clustered around a central courtyard.

My favorite place to stay on a splurge is the Florida-fantasy **Gaylord Palms Resort and Convention Center** (6000 W. Osceola Pkwy., 407/586-0000, www.gaylordhotels.com/gaylordpalms, $199–359). Riffing on a turn-of-the-20th-century Florida mansion, it's got an enormous, central greenhouselike dome within which Florida-native subtropical plants are manicured to their utmost effulgence. Within all this blossoming lushness are sections of the resort devoted to the Spanish-inflected St. Augustine, or the festive island spirit of Key West, or the dense mystery of Florida's Everglades. Approximately 1,200 rooms and suites are settled within these three sections, making the Gaylord not only the largest property in Kissimmee but a logical choice for meetings and midsize conventions. There's also a wonderful pair of swimming pools (one for families, one adults-only), several expertly run restaurants, and a tremendously service-oriented staff; the on-site Canyon Ranch Spa sweetens the deal. At Christmastime, the resort puts on a crazy show: It hauls in snow and bring Chinese ice carvers (there's a famous ice- and snow-carving school in Harbin, China) to work their ephemeral craft for several weeks.

Reunion Resort and Club (1000 Reunion Way, Reunion, 407/662-1100, $295–450) is kind of its own place—like Celebration, maybe even swankier. It's a planned, golf-mania-themed resort and club smack-dab between Walt Disney World and Kissimmee, just along I-4. Two of the courses were listed on *Golfweek's* list of America's Top 40 New Courses for 2005 (the Arnold Palmer–designed course and the Tom Watson–designed course). A third course, called The Tradition and designed by Jack Nicklaus, opened in 2006. A golf academy is set for completion at the end of 2007. Greens fees are $205 weekdays and weekends, and include use of a golf cart. Accommodations include one-bedroom villas, three-bedroom townhouses, and private homes. A handful of little neighborhoods make up the resort; the main neighborhood, Linear Park, features a multilevel water and swimming pavilion, whirlpool baths, a cardio-fitness center, game rooms, and a bar and grille at one end, and a golf clubhouse at the other. Think pampered, think golf attire—a natural for business meetings in Orlando away from the hoi polloi.

Food

Let's just take a little drive up West Irlo Bronson Memorial Highway, also known as U.S. Highway 192, and see what's there. Oh, there's Ponderosa Steak House, and another one, and another one, and there's Olive Garden, and Ruby Tuesday, Macaroni Grill, Cracker Barrel, Red Lobster, Bennigan's, T.G.I. Friday's, Outback Steakhouse. Are you starting to get the idea? If you're unswervingly devoted to a particular American chain restaurant—for me I guess that's Chevy's—chances are you'll find it along this stretch of commercial sprawl. It's also a locus of much all-you-can-eat buffet activity, from Maine lobster to kung pao chicken.

For your breakfast needs, I counted at least three Waffle Houses on West Irlo, two International Houses of Pancakes, and another couple of Perkins Restaurant and Bakeries (it's just like IHOP, but with a pie case and a greater breadth of lunch food). There's also a Dunkin' Donuts and a Krispy Kreme. Meanwhile, many motels in Kissimmee include a perfectly adequate breakfast buffet.

And for lunch? What are you doing still trolling around in Kissimmee? Either you're at a theme park, or you're luxuriating in the antidote to theme parks with a day of fishing or tramping around in nature. If you do happen to find yourself driving the strip in town during the noon hours, every fast-food chain and convenience food beckons with its siren's song. Listen to the song that's sweetest to you.

Kissimmee's real culinary innovation is the dinner adventure (see the sidebar *Dinner and a Show*). They dominate the playing field, and unlike many restaurant experiences, the words "playing field" are not a metaphor. Additionally, there are some notable independent restaurants tucked between the chains.

CASUAL DINING

Locals have recently gotten excited about **Asia Bagus** (2923 Vineland Rd., 407/397-2205, 11:30 A.M.–3 P.M. Mon.–Fri., 5–10 P.M. nightly, $7.95–16.95), one of the area's first Indonesian restaurants. It's reminiscent of Thai food, with a little more of the smoldering spices of India. Dishes include a traditional *gado-gado,* a composed salad of greens studded with boiled potato, tofu cubes, green beans, bean sprouts, and hard-boiled egg all napped with a sweet and addictive peanut sauce. Sound too exotic? Then opt for the chicken satay or the eggroll-like *lumpia.*

For a solid Cuban sandwich (that's a Cuban loaf, piled high with roast pork and Genoa salami, Swiss cheese—some say Emanthaler—sour pickles, and spicy mustard, all warmed and flattened in a special hot press), **Havana's Cafe** (3628 W. Vine St., 407/846-6771, 11 A.M.–11 P.M. daily, $8–14) is the place. It's an intimate, casual joint, the staff is kind and the black beans and rice wholesome.

Browsing Kissimmee's Historic District

KISSIMMEE AND VICINITY

DINNER AND A SHOW

Kissimmee has a love/hate relationship with Orlando. Orlando is the big Kahuna, the main event, and Kissimmee seems fated to be the redheaded stepchild, an also-ran. Even the convention and visitors' bureau tagline subtly reinforces this: "Make *more* dreams come true." So, your main dream involves mouse ears, but if you're not done dreaming, we've got some others we'd like you to test-drive.

Well, there's one arena in which Kissimmee dominates, leaving Orlando quivering and chagrined. It's the phenomenon of the Dinner Adventure. This is not your father's murder-mystery dinner theater. We're talking pageantry, death-defying feats of agility and cunning, costumes, whooping-and-hollering, all witnessed while gnawing on regulation medieval turkey legs. Many of these shows draw 1,000 people at a time, two shows a night, every night of the year.

The granddaddy of them all is the **Medieval Times Dinner and Tournament** (4510 W. Irlo Bronson Memorial Hwy./U.S. Hwy. 192, 407/396-1518, www.medievaltimes.com, 6:30 and 8:30 P.M. nightly, adults, $33.95 children 12 and younger), which opened in 1983. It's a journey back to the 11th century that begins with a waitress in medieval garb who says, "Hi, I'm Heather and I'll be your wench tonight." That said, it's entirely a family event, the ta-

Arabian Nights Dinner Attraction

COURTESY OF ARABIAN NIGHTS

bles set up in long rows around an arena. As with many of the dinner adventures, you get a color marker (in this case a paper crown) that identifies you with a section of fellow diners

can work up a powerful hunger. Appeased it by stopping in at **Broadway Coffee and Art** (127 Broadway, 407/931-1205) or enjoying a sandwich at **Joanie's Diner** (120 Broadway, 407/933-0519).

Here's a uniquely Kissimmee experience: The **Magic Mining Company Steak and Seafood** (7763 W. U.S. Hwy. 192, 407/396-1950, 5–10:30 P.M. nightly, $10–30) serves prime rib, baby-back ribs, and grilled shrimp; meanwhile, people putt their way through two 18-hole minigolf courses on the roof. The mining theme is carried through to the exterior of the building, where Styrofoam rock formations loom above, creating the illusion that the res-

taurant is carved into the side of the mine—and through all these fake mountains winds an elaborate scale-model electric train. Oh, and there's also a waterfall. In total, it has a "more is more" aesthetic that seems utterly at home at the edge of Disney's theme parks.

FINE DINING

Many of the "fine-dining" options are nestled within Kissimmee's growing number of luxury hotels and resorts. The three restaurants at the Gaylord Palms Resort and Convention Center (6000 W. Osceola Pkwy./I-4, 407/586-0000) are among the nicest in the area. The most elegant of the three is the dinner-only ◖ **Old**

and a particular knight – it encourages tribal behavior, bonding, and robust catcalling.

King Alfonso and his daughter, Princess Esperanza, greet everyone and the drama unfolds in the Grand Ceremonial Arena. There's a story about a princess's love for a gallant knight and treachery in the king's inner circle, but the action sequences are more compelling. For those of you not from Maryland (where jousting is the state sport, go figure), the jousting is not two knights astride regal Andalusians impaling each other on long pointy sticks – it's really knights on horseback trying to hook a series of brass loops with their pointy sticks. It's still cool. For the bloodthirsty, there are plenty of duels involving sword, ax, mace, and bola.

Here may be the sticking point for some: Food is served medieval-style, sans utensils; it's roast chicken and potatoes and ribs and apple pie with only a napkin assist.

It, in your mind, food is the most important part of dinner, **Capone's Dinner and Show** (4740 W. Irlo Bronson Memorial Hwy.,/U.S. Highway 192, 407/397-2378, www.alcapones .com, 8 P.M. nightly, $45.99 adults, $27.99 children 4-12) usually gets top marks for its cuisine – unlike at many of the dinner shows, you get to choose between lasagna, spaghetti with meatballs, and other Italianate entrées,

in addition to all the draft beer, sangria, and sodas you care to quaff. The show brings 1930s Gangland Chicago back with a colorful cast of characters, from Bunny-June the ditzy blonde to the true-blue Detective Marvel and the scheming Harry the Lip. Dancing girls, mobsters, some fake guns – this show has been going strong since 1992.

Another real classic in Kissimmee is **Arabian Nights Dinner Attraction** (3081 Arabian Nights Blvd., 407/239-9223, www.arabiannights.com, 8:30 P.M. Mon.-Wed. and Fri. and Sat., 6 P.M. Thurs. and Sun., $45.90 adults, $20.33 children 3-11). Opened in 1988, it brings together world-class riders and trainers with some of the finest horses of all breeds. Arabian horses (from the owners' farm in Tucson, Arizona), along with Andalusians, big draft horses like Belgians or Percherons, Lipizzans, quarter horses, and a bunch of other equine superstars strut around in an enormous arena. You don't have to love horses to be smitten with this show – the riders do regimented dressage movements and acrobatic gypsy bareback, and there are square-dancing quarter horses and comedy sketches. There's no real coherent plot to the whole thing, nor does the food really fit into some kind exotic Arabian Nights theme (workhorse prime rib, chicken tenders for the kids, and unlimited beer, wine, and coke).

Hickory Steakhouse (5:30–10 P.M. nightly, $22–40), a familiar American steak house idiom set in the lush "Everglades Atrium." Real gators honk, fake tree frogs call, and all around the dense subtropical greenery lends an atmospheric setting for well-executed steaks and chops, a sophisticated wine list, and the most exceptional cheese cart in the state of Florida (overseen by über-cheesemonger Terrance Brennan of Artisanal in New York City). The Gaylord's buffet restaurant, **Villa de Flora** (6:30 A.M.–10:30 A.M., 11:30 A.M.–2:30 P.M., 5–10 P.M. daily, $17.50 breakfast, $19.25 lunch, $26.50 dinner), is within plain sight of a replica of the historic Castillo de San Marcos in St. Augustine. The

Spanish-inflected decor influences the cuisine, which draws from many of the sun-kissed countries of the Mediterranean. This can mean Moroccan couscous, or lemony Greek leg of lamb, or even creamy pasta Alfredo. Villa de Flora's brunch always wins top honors in Orlando's culinary pecking order. For a more casual meal, search out the ship docked in the fake lagoon in the atrium. Don't worry, the ship is fake too, composed of the difficult seafaring material concrete. It's called **Sunset Sam's Fish Camp** (11:30 A.M.–4 P.M. and 5–11 P.M. daily, $10–20) and it is where to go for a Jimmy Buffet–inspired cheeseburger, an order of fried calamari with Key lime tartar sauce, or a blended margarita.

Practicalities

INFORMATION AND SERVICES
Begin a visit with a stop for maps and literature at the Kissimmee Convention and Visitors Bureau information center (1925 E. Irlo Bronson Memorial Hwy./U.S. Hwy. 192, 407/847-5000, 8 A.M.–5 P.M. Mon.–Fri.). You can also call 800/333-KISS (800/333-5477) to order a free vacation-planning kit.

Laundry
Many of the budget hotels and motels along West U.S. Highway 192 have on-site laundry rooms. If yours doesn't, you can take a drive to Coin-a-Magic (1415 N. John Young Pkwy., 407/933-1828) for a classic launderette experience.

Police and Emergencies
In an emergency, dial 911; for nonemergencies, the Kissimmee Police Department can be reached at 407/846-3333. In case of a medical emergency, Osceola Regional Medical Center (700 W. Oak St., 407/846-2266) offers full emergency-room services.

GETTING THERE AND AROUND
By Car
Kissimmee is about 10 miles slightly south and east of Walt Disney World Resort. From Walt Disney World Resort, take Highway 535 south to U.S. Highway 192 east; U.S. Highway 192 is also called Vine and East or West Irlo Bronson Memorial Highway in sections. The Osceola Parkway (Toll Road 522) is also a direct route to the Walt Disney World complex from the Kissimmee area.

I-4 is the area's main tourist thoroughfare, running from southwest of Walt Disney World northeast up through Downtown Orlando. In Kissimmee, U.S. Highway 192 is the main east-west road; from west to east, John Young Parkway, Orange Blossom Trail, and Florida's Turnpike are the major north-south roads. There are bright-green guide markers all along the West U.S. Highway 192 tourist corridor, which many hotels and attractions use in their directions. West U.S. Highway 192 seems in a perpetual state of construction—so allow plenty of time to get anywhere.

More broadly, major interstates—I-95, I-75, and I-10—provide access into Florida from the north, with connections directly into the area via I-4, Florida's Turnpike, and U.S. Highway 192. Interstates 75 and 95 and Florida's Turnpike also provide access from South Florida.

Rental cars are most easily rented at the airport, but all of the major rental companies (Hertz, Avis, Budget) have outposts along U.S. Highway 192 for drop-offs and car pickups. Although many hotels and motels offer bus service to Walt Disney World Resort, it is fairly difficult to stay in Kissimmee without a car. Restaurants and secondary attractions are spread along the length of U.S. Highway 192, not a pedestrian-friendly route.

By Air
The area is serviced by major airlines and charter services at the **Orlando International Airport** (1 Airport Blvd., 407/825-2001), 20 minutes away; the **Orlando Executive Airport** (4001 E. Concord St., 407/894-9831), also about 20 minutes away; the **Orlando Sanford Airport** (1200 Red Cleveland Blvd., Sanford, 407/585-4000), less than one hour away; and **Kissimmee Gateway Airport** (301 N. Dyer Blvd., Ste. 101, 407/847-4600), which is the closest general aviation facility to the area's attractions and the Orange County Convention Center. All major rental-car companies are available from the airport. Most accommodations in Kissimmee provide shuttle service if prearranged.

By Train
Amtrak (111 Dakin St., 800/872-7245, 10 A.M.–6:30 P.M. daily) has a ticket office with an enclosed waiting area, public restrooms, free short- and long-term parking, intercity bus service, and public transit connection. Bus service in Kissimmee is not great, but many hotels offer shuttle service to the theme parks.

EXCURSIONS

We lived in Europe for a year when I was a child. With our cultural education firmly in mind, my parents would embark on small, focused trips. Invariably, after the third day of, say, Paris museums, my father would begin shooting us murderous glances and muttering what may have been profanities under his breath. He was a fatigued shepherd and we his willful, disorganized flock. But herding us proved more onerous than herding regular sheep, because we whined. And some of us always seemed in dire need of a cheeseburger or a Band-Aid.

This is what will happen to you if you plan several days, back to back, at Orlando's theme parks. The murderous rage, the near mutinies, the whining. And I don't mean only if you're visiting with your family. Even travel-ing by yourself, you're at risk. The Florida sun and humidity, navigating crowds, shuf-fling through lines—you need a break. Luck-ily, the long, skinny peninsula that is Florida offers something different to do within an hour's drive in any direction from Orlando.

An hour due west brings you to the Tampa Bay area, with its easy beaches on the Gulf side and its affordable half-day family attractions on the other. Travel 50 miles northeast and you'll reach Daytona Beach, the birthplace of speed. Or head east and spend the day in Cape Canaveral and Florida's Space Coast.

Whether it's for an afternoon or an addi-tional few days of a trip, pick a direction and drive. Mickey et al will still be in Orlando when you return, refreshed.

COURTESY OF KENNEDY SPACE CENTER

EXCURSIONS

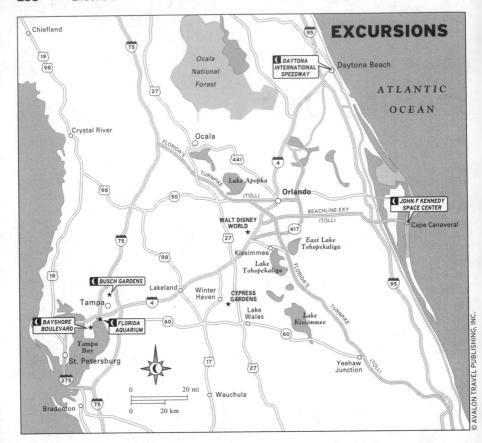

Tampa and Pinellas County

FlexTickets for SeaWorld Orlando and Universal Orlando Resort offer a tempting Tampa add-on. For not that much more money, you can head due west of Orlando an hour and hit the Gulf Coast Tampa Bay area, ostensibly to visit Busch Gardens. It's not an idiotic notion, really, but my question is: If you've spent three days at Disney, a day at Universal, and still another one at SeaWorld, do you want to get in the car and drive to another theme park? It's got animals like Animal Kingdom, monster coasters like Islands of Adventure, a handful of good shows like many of the Orlando theme parks, even an affiliated water park like a couple of the Orlando parks. But, to me, it's more of the same. Instead, visit the Tampa Bay area for its many other assets: Yes, it has Busch Gardens, but it also boasts a great zoo and aquarium, professional sports, affordable accommodations and restaurants, and a handful of truly spectacular beaches. Tack on a day to waggle your toes in the Gulf, watch the big cruise ships pull into town, or even take a soothing canoe trip down the Hillsborough River.

HIGHLIGHTS

◖ **Busch Gardens:** The park's inverted steel roller coaster called the Montu won ninth place in *Amusement Today* magazine's survey of top roller coasters worldwide; its Kumba took the 19th spot. The park is an unusual mix of thrill rides, animal attractions, and entertainment – a something-for-everyone approach that really works (page 263).

◖ **Florida Aquarium:** A marvelous Tampa attraction, this 152,000-square-foot aquarium focuses on Florida's relationship to the Gulf, estuaries, rivers, and other waterways, with a strong environmental message (page 263).

◖ **Bayshore Boulevard:** The five miles of sidewalk are bordered on one side by the wide open bay and on the other side by the fanciest historic homes on this stretch of Florida's Gulf Coast. Runners, walkers, bikers, and skaters take advantage of the amazing views and long expanse of carefully maintained walkway (page 264).

◖ **John F. Kennedy Space Center:** A visit to Florida's Space Coast is out of this world. Where else can you blast into orbit, walk on the moon, and land a space shuttle all without ever leaving Earth (page 269)?

◖ **Daytona International Speedway:** Ever since the historic timed trial in 1903, the Daytona Beach area has been, and continues to be, synonymous with speed. Plan your visit for February to watch famous race car drivers such as Jeff Gordon and Sterling Marlin compete in the Daytona 500 (page 275).

LOOK FOR ◖ TO FIND RECOMMENDED SIGHTS, ACTIVITIES, DINING, AND LODGING.

History

Despite a robust Native American population for a couple of centuries, it wasn't until Henry B. Plant extended his railroad into Tampa in 1884 and started a steamship line from Tampa to Key West to Havana, Cuba, that the area really began to lure people south. In 1891, Plant built the Tampa Bay Hotel, which launched the city as a winter resort for the northern elite. Around the same time, O. H. Platt bought 20 acres of land across the Hillsborough River to create Tampa's first residential suburb, Hyde Park (named after Platt's hometown in Illinois). Hyde Park was, and still is, the residential area of choice for many prominent citizens. Many of the 19th-century bungalows and Princess Anne–style cottages are still occupied today, and the Old Hyde Park Village collection of boutiques and restaurants is one of the city's biggest draws.

Don Vicente Martinez Ybor, an influential cigar manufacturer and Cuban exile, moved his cigar business from Key West to a scruffy stretch of land east of Tampa in 1885. His first cigar factory drew others, and the Spanish, Italian, German, and Cuban workers who settled here to work in the area's more than 200 cigar factories created a vivacious Latin community

EXCURSIONS

EXCURSIONS

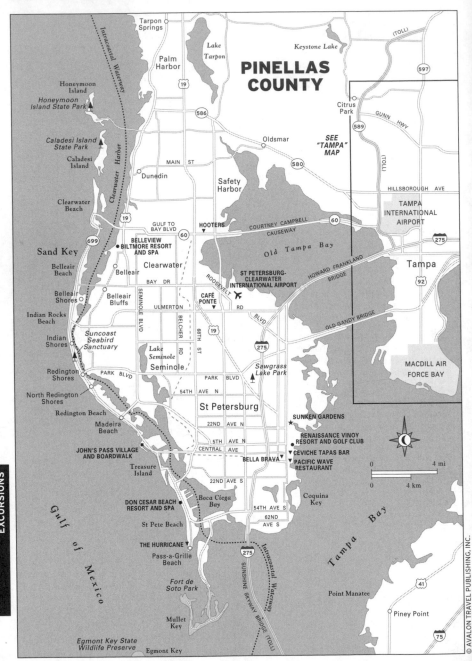

© AVALON TRAVEL PUBLISHING, INC.

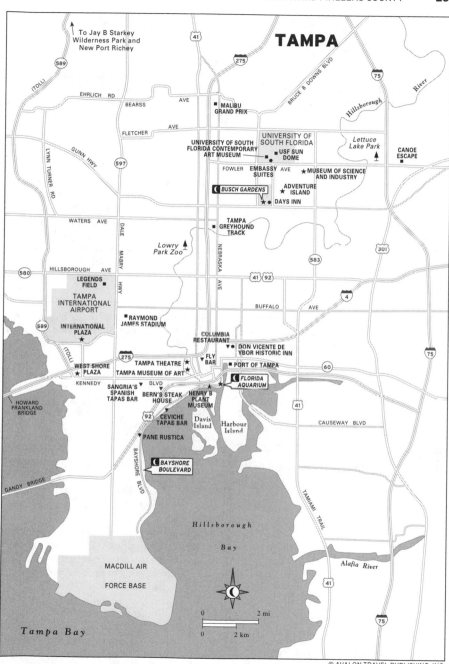

TAMPA

To Jay B Starkey Wilderness Park and New Port Richey

EHRLICH RD

BEARSS AVE

FLETCHER AVE

MALIBU GRAND PRIX

UNIVERSITY OF SOUTH FLORIDA CONTEMPORARY ART MUSEUM

UNIVERSITY OF SOUTH FLORIDA

USF SUN DOME

Lettuce Lake Park

CANOE ESCAPE

FOWLER AVE

EMBASSY SUITES

MUSEUM OF SCIENCE AND INDUSTRY

BUSCH GARDENS

ADVENTURE ISLAND

DAYS INN

WATERS AVE

TAMPA GREYHOUND TRACK

Lowry Park Zoo

HILLSBOROUGH AVE

LEGENDS FIELD

TAMPA INTERNATIONAL AIRPORT

BUFFALO AVE

INTERNATIONAL PLAZA

RAYMOND JAMES STADIUM

COLUMBIA RESTAURANT

DON VICENTE DE YBOR HISTORIC INN

WEST SHORE PLAZA

TAMPA THEATRE

FLY BAR

PORT OF TAMPA

TAMPA MUSEUM OF ART

KENNEDY

HOWARD FRANKLIN BRIDGE

SANGRIA'S SPANISH TAPAS BAR

BERN'S STEAK HOUSE

FLORIDA AQUARIUM

HENRY B PLANT MUSEUM

CEVICHE TAPAS BAR

Davis Island

Harbour Island

PANE RUSTICA

CAUSEWAY BLVD

BAYSHORE BOULEVARD

GANDY BRIDGE

Hillsborough Bay

MACDILL AIR FORCE BASE

Alafia River

Tampa Bay

0   2 mi

0   2 km

TAMIAMI TRAIL

EXCURSIONS

© AVALON TRAVEL PUBLISHING, INC.

known as Ybor City. The area is now a designated National Historic Landmark District, with a mix of historic buildings, artisan shops, restaurants, and nightclubs.

SIGHTS AND RECREATION
Spectator Sports

DirectTV has something called the Sports Fan Passion Index. Tampa Bay sports fans are at the top of it, fanatical for their professional sporting franchises. Why shouldn't they be at a constant fevered pitch of enthusiasm? There are the **Tampa Bay Buccaneers** (Raymond James Stadium, 4201 N. Dale Mabry Hwy., Tampa, 813/879-2827, www.buccaneers.com) for football; **Tampa Bay Lightning** for hockey (St. Pete Times Forum, 401 Channelside Dr., Tampa, 813/301-6600, www.tampabaylightning.com); **Tampa Bay Devil Rays** for baseball (1 Tropicana Dr., St. Petersburg, 888/326-7297, http://tampabay.devilrays.mlb.com), not to mention spring training for the New York Yankees, Philadelphia Phillies, Toronto Blue Jays, and their own Devil Rays spread around the Bay area; **Tampa Bay Storm** pro arena football (St. Pete Times Forum, 401 Channelside Dr., Tampa, 813/301-6600, www.tampabaystorm.com); and the gamut of **University of South Florida Bulls** athletics (Raymond James Stadium, 4201 N. Dale Mabry Hwy., Tampa, 800/462-8557, www.gousfbulls.com).

Beaches

Unlike in other urban centers along the Gulf, there are no beaches in the city of Tampa. For beaches, you need to drive west over the Howard Frankland Bridge (I-275) or the Courtney Campbell Causeway (Hwy. 60) to St. Pete or Clearwater (about 30 minutes from downtown Tampa) in Pinellas County. When you conjure in your mind a Florida Gulf Coast beach, it's Clearwater and St. Pete you're imagining. These are textbook stretches of white sand and warm Gulf water, with lots of comfy beachside hotels and waterside amenities for families. The area is home to a couple of world-class beach destinations, the kinds of places that often make Dr. Stephen Leatherman's ("Dr. Beach"

has been ranking America's beaches since 1991) annual top-10 list. **Clearwater Beach,** the only Pinellas County beach with year-round lifeguards, is a long, wide stretch offering showers, restrooms, concessions, cabanas, umbrella rentals, volleyball, and metered parking. **Pier 60,** where the beach meets the causeway, is the locus of lots of local revelry and activity.

South of St. Petersburg, **Fort De Soto Park** is an embarrassment of riches, with 1,136 unspoiled acres, seven miles of beaches, two fishing piers, picnic and camping areas, a small history museum, and a 2,000-foot barrier-free nature trail for guests with disabilities, set on five little, interconnected islands. Exploring the old fort is part of what makes this experience special, drawing more than 2.7 million visitors annually. After fondling the four 12-inch seacoast rifled mortars (the only ones of their kind in the United States), head on to one of the two swim centers, the better of which is the North Beach Swim Center (it has concessions).

Honeymoon Island (at the extreme west end of Hwy. 586, Dunedin) and **Caladesi Island** (accessible only by ferry service from Honeymoon) are more of a double whammy, perfectly suited to visiting back to back. In fact, the two islands were once part of a single larger barrier island split in half during a savage hurricane in 1921. Together, they offer nearly 1,000 acres of mostly undeveloped land, not too changed from how it looked when Spanish explorers surveyed the coast in the mid-1500s. Honeymoon Island offers visitors all kinds of fun activities, but especially good is the fishing—you're likely to catch flounder, snook, trout, redfish, snapper, whiting, sheepshead, and, occasionally, tarpon. The island is home to 208 species of plants and a wealth of shore and wading birds, including a few endangered bird species. Strong kayakers or sailors can find kayak and sailboat rentals on the causeway near Honeymoon Island. Once on Caladesi, there's a 3.5-mile canoe trail starting and ending at the south end of the marina that leads paddlers through mangrove canals and tunnels and along seagrass flats on the bay side of the island.

Busch Gardens

Now that I've dissed Busch Gardens (Busch Blvd. and 40th St., Tampa, 888/800-5447, single-day tickets from $51.95), I should note that it's a wonderful theme park, especially for thrill seekers. Major coasters are the biggest draw for those over 54 inches tall and with no serious health problems. The rides at Busch Gardens are either little-kiddie or wet-your-pants huge. The roller coasters, in descending order of excellence: The **Montu** at the far right of the park is one of the tallest and longest inverted roller coasters in the world. You are strapped in from above, so your feet dangle while you travel at 60 mph through 60-foot vertical loops. **Kumba** is second best, with a full three seconds of weightlessness, an initial 135-foot drop, some cool 360-degree spirals—good speed, long ride, one of the world's largest vertical loops. Launched in summer 2005, the nation's first dive coaster—the **SheiKra**—has a 138-foot drop through an underground tunnel at 70 mph, but it's a very short ride. In summer 2007, the ride went "floorless" for added drama. The **Python** has a double spiraling corkscrew and gut-lurching 70-foot plunge, but it's too short a ride, over in seconds. The **Scorpion** has some good 360s, fast speeds, but again it's too short. And the **Gwazi** is for purists—an old double wooden coaster, it's got that tooth-rattling charm as it barrels over the boards in 7,000 feet of track.

Beyond the coasters, the **Tidal Wave, Stanley Falls,** and **Congo River Rapids** boat ride are guaranteed to fully saturate you with water—so time them for the hottest part of the day and not right before you go see the modestly amusing 3-D movie called *R. L. Stine's Haunted Lighthouse.*

Busch Gardens also contains approximately 2,700 animals. Colorful lorikeets will land on your shoulder or flirt shamelessly with you in the aviary called **Lory Landing,** there's a **Birds of Prey** show, but the best animal attraction is the **Serengeti Plain,** which really takes up the whole right half of the park—you see it all by getting on the Serengeti Express Railway (or the Skyride or a Serengeti Safari). And the amusement park has a huge section of the park geared to children 2–7 years old, in a Dragoncentric part of the park to the far left when you're looking at the map, near Stanleyville.

Hours change seasonally: In winter, Busch Gardens is generally open 9:30 A.M.–6 P.M. daily; in summer, 9 A.M.–10 P.M. daily. Adjacent to Busch Gardens, but open only March–October, **Adventure Island** will wet your whistle and pretty much everything else. It's a 30-acre water park, with slides, corkscrews, waterfalls, a monstrous 17,000-square-foot wave pool, and a child's play area. There are 50 lifeguards on duty, but it's still appropriate only for the truly water-safe.

Florida Aquarium

Management has tried to gussy up this aquarium recently with outdoor water-play areas, but the Florida Aquarium (701 Channelside Dr., Tampa, 813/273-4000, www.flaquarium.org, 9:30 A.M.–5 P.M. daily, $17.95 adults, $14.95 seniors, $12.95 children under 12) doesn't want for anything, in my opinion. Opened in 1995, the 152,000-square foot aquarium is smart, focusing on the waters of Florida. It doesn't contain an exhaustive catalog of the world's aquatic creatures, but it tells a very compelling story about Florida's relationship to the Gulf, estuaries, rivers, and other waterways. There are some exotic exhibits (the otherworldly sea dragons, like seahorses mated with philodendrons), but the best parts are the open freshwater tanks of otters, spoonbills, gators, Florida softshell turtles, and snakes. The aquarium manages to have a very strong environmental message in its natives-versus-exotics exhibits, but it's all fun, never seeming pious or heavy-handed. There is also a wonderful big shark tank, a colorful coral grotto, and a sea-urchin touch tank. It's a small-enough aquarium that three hours is plenty of time, and not so crowded that kids can't do a little wandering on their own.

Museum of Science and Industry

Also a huge draw for families, Tampa's Museum of Science and Industry (MOSI, 4801 East Fowler Ave., Tampa, 813/987-6300, www .mosi.org, 9 A.M.–5 P.M. daily, $19.95 adults,

EXCURSIONS

$17.95 seniors, $15.95 children 2–12), is a wonderful resource for local schools, family vacationers, or local parents when they're just out of ammo (not literally). It's a sprawling modern structure that contains 450 hands-on activities grouped into learning areas. There are some goofy exhibits (the *Gulf Coast Hurricane Chamber,* which really just blows a bunch of loud air). Ignore that and head to the High Wire Bicycle, the longest high-wire bike in a museum, which allows visitors to pedal while balanced on a one-inch steel cable suspended 30 feet above ground, and exhibits such as *The Amazing You* that teaches all about the human body. The museum has an IMAX dome and hosts traveling exhibits as well.

Lowry Park Zoo

The Lowry Park Zoo (1101 W. Sligh Ave., 813/932-0245, www.lowryparkzoo.com, 9:30 A.M.–5 P.M. daily, $16.95 adults, $15.95 seniors, $12.50 children 3–11) is home to 1,500 native and exotic animals, organized into sensible housing developments ("Wallaroo Station," "African Veldt"). Lots of shade provided by big lush tropicals seems to keep all species fat and sassy, even in the fairly substantial summer heat. One of the zoo's highlights is its "Manatee and Aquatic Center," one of only three hospitals and rehabilitation facilities in the state of Florida for lugubrious sick sea cows.

Wilderness Park

You want to see big gators? Great blue herons the size of the Wright brothers' first plane? River otters, turtles, families of wild pigs? Paddle down the gently flowing Hillsborough River in a 16,000-acre wildlife preserve called Wilderness Park. You can rent canoes or kayaks and head out on your own, choosing from a variety of trails: Sargeant Park to Morris Bridge Park (4.5 miles); Morris Bridge Park to Trout Creek Park (4 miles); the sunny Trout Creek Park to Rotary Park (5 miles); and others—a trip can be as short as two hours and as long as all day. Or you can take a 3.5-hour interpreted guided tour with **Canoe Escape** (9335 E. Fowler Ave., 0.5 mile east of I-75, Tampa,

813/986-2067, self-guided tandem canoe or kayak rentals $19.50–27.50, which includes shuttle fee, paddles, and life vests; guided tours around $40). Whether you go on a guided tour or on your own, call ahead and then drive to Canoe Escape's building. It will equip you, give you maps and paddling pointers, and then take you over to your debarkation point and establish a pickup time.

◖ Bayshore Boulevard

Claimed as the world's longest continuous sidewalk, Bayshore Boulevard borders Tampa Bay for nearly five miles without a break in the gorgeousness. Joggers, walkers, skaters, and bikers dot its length, which runs from downtown through Hyde Park. Home to the fanciest addresses in Tampa, the boulevard was named one of AAA's "Top Roads" for its panoramic views. Even if you don't feel like walking, it's Tampa's most signature drive. The Tampa Preservation (813/248-5437) has an excellent driving tour of Hyde Park and a walking tour of part of the neighborhood geared for younger readers.

ENTERTAINMENT

Tampa has its share of multiplexes, but eschew the 20-screeners in favor of two hours in the dark at the **Tampa Theatre** (711 Franklin St., Tampa, 813/274-8981, www.tampatheatre .org). Built in 1926, it's a beloved downtown landmark with an acclaimed film series, concerts, special events, and backstage tours. The grand motion picture palace's decor is called "Florida Mediterranean," but to me it's vintage creepy rococo, with statues and gargoyles and intricately carved doors. Speaking of creepiness, many believe that the theater is haunted by the ghost of Foster Finley, who spent 20 years as the theater's projectionist. So if you feel a hand in your popcorn, it may not be your seatmate's.

SHOPPING

Tampa's downtown doesn't really have a retail center and even the outdoor shopping area along Hyde Park's West Swann, South Dakota, and Snow Avenues has experienced a decline in the past couple of years. The best shopping in the Tampa Bay area is clustered at a couple of indoor malls near the airport.

With anchor stores Neiman Marcus and Nordstrom, **International Plaza** (2223 N. West Shore Blvd., 813/342-3790, 10 A.M.–9 P.M. Mon.–Sat., noon–6 P.M. Sun.), gets the nod for fanciest shopping. A handful of usual mall stores (J. Crew, Banana Republic, Ann Taylor) are spiffed up by their proximity to 200 other specialty shops such as Tiffany and Co., Christian Dior, Louis Vuitton, Gucci, and Furla. Really, it's the poshest assembly of stores in any shopping center on the Gulf Coast, served by an open-air village of restaurants called Bay Street, all just minutes from the airport and downtown.

About a minute from International Plaza, **Westshore Plaza** (250 Westshore Plaza, 813/286-0790, 10 A.M.–9 P.M. Mon.–Sat., noon–6 P.M. Sun.) features more than 100 similarly fancy specialty shops and four major department stores, including a lovely Saks 5th Avenue. It contains a 14-screen AMC Theater and restaurants such as Maggiano's Little Italy, P. F. Chang's, and The Palm.

ACCOMMODATIONS

Tampa has a preponderance of pleasant, fairly priced accommodations, spread around the greater Bay area, from the Latin Quarter of Ybor City, to the Westshore business district or the Tampa Convention Center, to near Busch Gardens and the University of South Tampa.

Tampa

If you want to stay near USF or Busch Gardens and MOSI, there are a handful of reasonably priced chains. **Days Inn** (2901 E. Busch Blvd./I-275, Tampa, 813/933-6471, rates from $49.99) is right near the Busch Gardens entrance, with 130 nicely appointed rooms with roomy bathrooms, good lighting, large desks, and high-speed Internet access included. There's also a good-size pool and the hotel is pet friendly. The USF hotel of choice is **Embasssy Suites** (3705 Spectrum Blvd.,

813/977-7066, rates from $152) across the road. It's a tall, suites-only hotel with a soaring atrium. Rooms are pretty, with spacious living rooms and private bedrooms with either a king or two double beds.

Ybor City

To experience Ybor City, Tampa's Latin Quarter, head to the historic **Don Vicente de Ybor Historic Inn** (1915 Republica de Cuba, 813/241-4545, rates from $139), constructed in 1895 by Cuban patriot Vicente Martinez Ybor. The boutique hotel's 16 guest rooms contain genteel flourishes such as four-poster beds, but it also offers broadband, voice mail, and in-room desks. Even if you don't stay here, the opulent grand salon is worth peeking at.

Pinellas County

For a splurge, some of Pinellas County's greatest landmarks are grand old hotels. The huge, Pepto Bismol–pink **Don CeSar Beach Resort and Spa** (400 Gulf Blvd., St. Pete Beach, 727/363-1881, www.doncesar.com, rates from $194) is a landmark in St. Pete and a longtime point of reference on maritime navigation charts. Named after a character in the opera *Maritana*, the Don CeSar has hosted F. Scott Fitzgerald and his wife, Zelda, Clarence Darrow, Al Capone, Lou Gehrig, and countless other celebrities. Originally opened in 1928, the property was commandeered by the military during World War II and eventually abandoned. These days, it's a Loews hotel, with 340 lovely rooms, fishing, golfing, tennis, and the soothing Beach Club and Spa.

The **Renaissance Vinoy Resort and Golf Club** (501 5th Ave. NE, 727/894-1000, www.renaissancehotels.com, rates from $239) was built by Pennsylvania oilman Aymer Vinoy Laughner in 1925. At $3.5 million, the Mediterranean Revival–style hotel was the largest construction project in Florida's history. Exquisitely restored in 1992 at a cost of $93 million, the resort exudes the kind of rarefied glamour that helps put life's quotidian woes behind you. There are 360 guest rooms and 15 suites, many with views of the marina.

FOOD
Tampa

If you're in the mood for Spanish tapas, the historic, hip part of Tampa called Hyde Park has two laudable purveyors. **Sangria's Spanish Tapas Bar and Restaurant** (315 S. Howard Ave., 813/258-0393, 5 P.M.–midnight Mon.–Thurs., until 2 A.M. Fri.–Sat., entrées $6–25) is a sweet little place with pitchers of decent sangria, a good Spanish tortilla, and lots of messy shrimp in garlic. Not on the "Restaurant Row" but off on more posh waterside Bayshore, the suave late-night **Ceviche Tapas Bar and Restaurant** (2109 Bayshore Blvd., 813/250-0203, 5–11 P.M. Tues.–Thurs., until 3 A.M. Fri.–Sat., entrées $12–26) serves its namesake citrus-cured fish, sea scallops with manchego, and an array of little dishes with addictive olives and almonds, all in a sleek nightclub atmosphere.

    Fly Bar and Restaurant (1202 Franklin St., Tampa, 813/275-5000, 11:30 A.M.–3 A.M. Mon.–Fri., 5–11 P.M. Sat.–Sun., bar open until 3 A.M., entrées $8–14), launched in 2006, is the hottest thing to happen to Tampa's downtown in a while. It serves more small plates, this time "world-beat" and paired with suave cocktails, a little live music, and a minimalist-hip decor. Another Tampa hot spot isn't exactly new, but it opened fairly recently for dinner. **(Pane Rustica** (3225 S. Macdill Ave., 813/902-8828, 8 A.M.– 6 P.M. Tues.–Fri., 8 A.M.–5 P.M. Sat., 8 A.M.–3 P.M. Sun., entrées $12–20) used to be thronged every lunchtime for the stunning thin-crust pizzas, sophisticated *panini,* and glorious breads and cookies. Now it has added contemporary Cal-Ital dinners at moderate prices and is every bit as busy.

    The biggest gorilla of them all on the Tampa dining scene is undisputedly **Bern's Steak House** (1208 S. Howard Ave., 813/251-2421, 5–11 P.M. daily, entrées $17–59). A landmark that dates back to 1956, Bern's boasts a wine list that could break a toe and a menu that reaches new levels of hyperbole. Steaks are so lovingly described that it wouldn't be surprising to hear the eye color, hat size, or hobbies of the cows in question. So, it's big beef, rendered extra fancy by the bordello-like decor of gilded plaster columns, red wallpaper, Tiffany lamps, and murals of French vineyards. After dinner take the tour of the kitchen and wine cellar and head upstairs for dessert. Reservations are recommended.

Ybor City

Columbia Restaurant (2117 E. 7th Ave., 813/248-4961, 11 A.M.–10 P.M. Mon.–Thurs., until 11 P.M. Fri.–Sat., noon–9 P.M. Sun., entrées $21–30) bears the distinction of being the oldest restaurant in Florida (started in 1905) and the nation's largest Spanish/Cuban restaurant (13 rooms extending one city block). Frankly, the food's not spectacular these days, but the experience is worth picking through a ho-hum paella or sipping a pedestrian sangria. Some of these waiters have been here a lifetime, the many rooms manage to stay packed, and there are stirring flamenco shows Monday–Saturday nights.

Pinellas County

Pinellas County has had an amazing couple of years of restaurant openings. For when you're looking for something really gastronomically edifying, **(Cafe Ponte** (off Ulmerton Rd. in the Icot Center, 13505 Icot Blvd., Clearwater, 727/538-5768, www.cafeponte.com, 11:30 A.M.–2 P.M. Mon.–Fri., 5:30–10 P.M. Tues.–Thurs., until 11 P.M. Fri.–Sat., entrées $18–36) is the highly decorated place to be. Chef Christopher Ponte trained at Taillevent in Paris and turns out ultraluxe mushroom soup with a dollop of truffle cream; crispy whole snapper with mango, mint, and macadamia nuts over a ginger-vanilla rum sauce; and a supremely comforting yet vaguely exotic braised short-rib tagine.

    New on the scene in downtown St. Petersburg, **Ceviche Tapas Bar** (10 Beach Dr., St. Petersburg, 727/209-2302, 5–11:30 P.M. Tues.–Thurs., until 12:30 A.M. Fri.–Sat., 5–10 P.M. Sun., bar open till 2 A.M. Tues.–Sat., entrées $12–26) is a sister restaurant to the one in Tampa and is packed every night with well-dressed diners until the wee hours. Each of the 45 hot and cold tapas reflects the bold flavors, unfussy preparations, and affordable prices of the traditional small dishes of Spain, all served in a stylish setting at the bottom of the old Ponce de Leon Hotel. Another downtown newcomer, **Bella Brava** (515 Central Ave., St. Petersburg, 727/895-5515, 11 A.M.–11 P.M. Mon.–Fri., 5–11 P.M. Sat.–Sun., entrées $13–30) serves really stunning wood-fired pizzas and rustic Italian fare to a suitably stunning crowd.

And if you want a little Asian fusion, there's that, too. **Pacific Wave Restaurant** (211 2nd St. S., St. Petersburg, 727/822-5235, 5–10 P.M. Mon.–Thurs., until 11 P.M. Fri.–Sat., entrées $21–31) has a cool late-night crowd that comes for Hawaiian fish with chipotle grits or Laotian spring rolls sparked by Thai basil.

On the other hand, you may owe it to yourself and owl fans everywhere to go to the original **Hooters** (2800 Gulf-to-Bay Blvd., Clearwater, 727/797-4008, 11 A.M.–11 P.M. Sun.–Thurs., until midnight Fri.–Sat., entrées $7–16). The original Hooters, which opened in 1983, is a pleasant, ramshackle sports-oriented joint that is really a family restaurant with good chicken wings (order them not breaded, with the really hot sauce, but a little dry so they don't come all goopy). Except it's a family restaurant in which all waitresses are wildly pneumatic and wearing those flesh-colored pantyhose from the 1970s under orange nylon short-shorts.

Still, the Gulf Coast is all about grouper sandwiches, and the best in the area is to be had at **The Hurricane** (807 Gulf Way, Pass-a-Grille Beach, 727/360-9558, 11 A.M.–9:30 P.M. Sun.–Thurs., until 10 P.M. Fri.–Sat., entrées $8–24). I don't care if the place seems a little touristy, but give me that sweet white fish, amped with red and black pepper and lots of salt, add some tomato, lettuce, and a big swath of mayo, all on a pretty soft roll. A nice bar is adjacent to the restaurant and there's a rooftop sundeck up top for sunset scrutiny.

PRACTICALITIES
Information and Services
The area code in Tampa is 813 and in Pinellas County it's 727, but if you're trying to call the other side of the bay, you don't need to dial a "1" before it. The Tampa Bay Convention and Visitors Bureau's Visitor Information Center is in the waterfront Channelside entertainment complex (615 Channelside Dr., Ste. 108A, 813/223-2752, www.visittampabay.com) at the Port of Tampa. It provides lots of brochures and information on attractions, events, and accommodations. Tampa's daily newspaper is the *Tampa Tribune,* on the other side of the bay is the *St. Petersburg Times* (a much better paper), and the *Weekly Planet* is the city's free alternative weekly.

Getting There and Around
Both I-75 and I-275 travel north-south, but I-75 skirts the edge of Tampa while I-275 travels through the city and over Hillsborough Bay to St. Petersburg. Both connect to I-4, which travels east-west, connecting Tampa Bay to Orlando and the east coast of Florida.

In Tampa, from north to south, Bearrs, Fletcher, Fowler, and Busch Boulevard are the big east-west roads. Dale Mabry and Bruce B. Downs are the biggest north-south roads. This all sounds fairly simple, but once you get downtown in Tampa you really need a map to find your way out. There are lots of one-way streets and the highway on-ramps are a bit difficult to find. The Busch Gardens area and USF lie between I-75 and I-275 northeast of downtown. The airport is just southwest of downtown.

Once you're in Pinellas, Clearwater is in the north along the Gulf, St. Petersburg is in the south along the bay. To reach St. Petersburg from Clearwater, head south on U.S. Highway 19-A, a slow, densely trafficked mess. Farther to the east, the regular U.S. Highway 19 cuts down through the center of the peninsula to St. Petersburg.

In St. Petersburg, streets are set up in a grid pattern, with avenues running east-west and streets running north-south. Central Avenue divides north and south St. Petersburg, with the numbered avenues on either side—it's tricky, though, as to the left of Central there's 1st Avenue North and to the right it's

EXCURSIONS

1st Avenue South. There are some sections of town that are all one-way streets, so you may make a lot of little squares while driving.

From St. Pete Beach all the way up through Clearwater, all you need to know is that Gulf Boulevard (Hwy. 699) runs right up the coast and through each little town. The city of Clearwater is on the mainland, but Clearwater Beach is on a barrier island connected by Memorial Causeway.

The Space Coast

Here's a fun fact you get on the standard tour at Kennedy Space Center: The space shuttle reaches orbit in 8.5 minutes and orbits the earth at 17,500 miles per hour. If you were being transported from Orlando to Cape Canaveral in the shuttle, you would arrive in nine seconds. By more traditional conveyances, it takes about an hour from the theme park hubbub of Orlando. These days, the area around Cape Canaveral has a similar, tourist-friendly clamor to it. It wasn't always that way. The Kennedy Space Center Complex is an outgrowth of the 1960s practice of allowing space program workers' families to take a Sunday drive through the restricted government complex, so the kids had at least some idea of where Dad or Mom went every day. The public liked the sound of that, and thus a permanent visitor complex opened in 1967.

NASA doesn't run it these days. In 1995 the management and operation was farmed out to Delaware North Companies Parks and Resorts, which, like the slick machines that run in Orlando, maintains a steady aim at new attractions exhibiting cutting-edge technology. It's self-supported, with no government or taxpayer money, drawing in millions of visitors each year with the drama and mystery of space

EXCURSIONS

COURTESY OF KENNEDY SPACE CENTER

John F. Kennedy Space Center

THE SPACE COAST

Scottsmoor
Turnbull
Mims
Merritt Island National Wildlife Refuge
Titusville

Canaveral National Seashore

Mosquito Lagoon

JOHN F KENNEDY SPACE CENTER
(NASA)

Indian River

Banana River

Cocoa
Merritt Island
Rockledge
Cape Canaveral
Cocoa Beach
South Cocoa Beach

Lake Washington

ATLANTIC

OCEAN

Satellite Beach
Indian Harbour Beach

Melbourne
Palm Bay
Malabar

Indialantic
Melbourne Beach
Melbourne Shores

Indian River

0   3 mi
0   3 km

Micco

Sebastian Inlet

© AVALON TRAVEL PUBLISHING, INC.

exploration. Beyond the handful of Caribbean-bound cruise ships departing from Port Canaveral and the 72 miles of Atlantic beaches, space is the big draw in the greater Cape Canaveral area.

Some Semantics

Cape Canaveral or Cape Kennedy—which is it? The answer is a little confusing. After President Kennedy's assassination, the names of NASA and Air Force facilities were changed to Cape Kennedy in his honor. In 1973, Congress muddied things a bit, changing some of the names back. Today NASA launches the space shuttle from John F. Kennedy Space Center, while the U.S. Air Force operates Cape Canaveral Air Force Station on Cape Canaveral, the barrier island east of the Banana River from which military and commercial rockets are launched.

SIGHTS AND RECREATION
◖ John F. Kennedy Space Center

Forty-five minutes from Orlando's theme parks is a more focused, yet more infinite, world of thrills and chills. On an island refuge eight times the size of Manhattan, NASA has its launch headquarters and a theme park to the stars, or at least planets and smaller orbiting bodies. If you time your visit right, you can be on hand for the launch of one of NASA's space shuttle fleet, the *Discovery, Atlantis,* or *Endeavour;* or the unmanned launches of communication and surveillance satellites; or even history-making launches such as that of the 2003 rover to the planet Mars. But in the meantime, the vast complex holds a full day's entertainment on terra firma.

Because it's a working government facility employing 10,000 scientists, engineers, and technicians, visitors must begin any trip at the Kennedy Space Center Visitor Complex. From here you get to tour NASA's restricted areas by bus. With a standard tour, you view the space shuttle launch pads, visit the Apollo Saturn V Center with a simulated launch from mission control, and you see an authentic *Saturn V* moon rocket. Then you watch two IMAX

EXCURSIONS

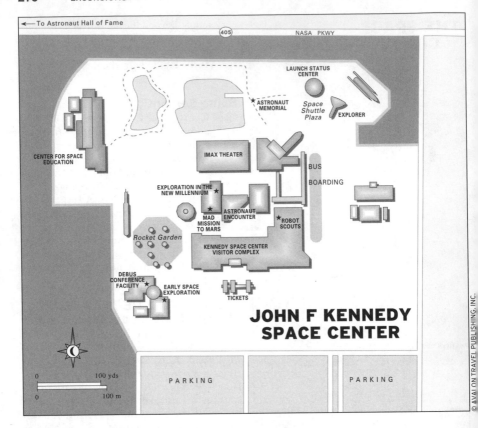

© AVALON TRAVEL PUBLISHING, INC.

movies back to back: **Magnificent Desolation: Walking on the Moon 3-D,** narrated by Tom Hanks, with rarely seen NASA footage and a simulated lunar landscape, followed by **Space Station 3-D,** narrated by Tom Cruise telling the tale of American astronauts and Russian cosmonauts meeting in orbit at the International Space Station.

A second "maximum access" admission adds to this a visit to the **Astronaut Hall of Fame,** with the world's largest collection of astronaut memorabilia and exhibits. You can also take a virtual walk on the moon, land a space shuttle, and experience four times the force of gravity in a simulator. (The day starts to get extremely long, so consider splitting it into two consecutive days.)

After the tour, the Visitor Complex contains a number of attractions you can peruse at your own pace. From clockwise around the complex from to the left of the entrance, the **Early Space Exploration** building houses exhibits on just that, a little staid and museumlike as a place to start, but it's a calm 20 minutes of wandering, with genuine consoles and components from Mercury Mission Control Room. Next to the small **Debus Conference Facility** is the outdoor **Rocket Garden,** which I suppose is technically a rocket graveyard, but that's just a semantic quibble. Historic rockets are bathed in moody light to simulate their blast-off glory: the early *Redstone, Atlas,* and *Titan* rockets; *Mercury, Gemini,* and *Apollo* capsules—free tours are given of this area at 10:30 A.M. and 4 P.M. each day.

The **SpaceWalk of Honor** is really a buy-a-brick-with-your-name-on-it fund-raiser, with the money going to America's space program. The walk is adjacent to the **Astronaut Memorial,** no big deal for kids but a stunning science-meets-art tribute to the 24 U.S. astronauts who gave their lives for space exploration. The memorial is composed of mirror-finished granite panels; sunlight illuminates the engraved names on the granite. After the two IMAX theaters, the **Exploration in the New Millennium** is a 12,000-square-foot attraction that takes visitors on a 2,000-year journey, A.D. 1000–3000, from Viking exploration to a spacecraft of the future. See Mars close up, then touch a piece of the red planet in a display. There are nice interactive exhibits for younger children in this area. At **Astronaut Encounter,** the Kennedy Space Center keeps a steady flow of real-life members of NASA's astronaut corps for visitors to meet and greet.

To me a tactical error, *Mad Mission to Mars* is yet another movie. Two IMAXes followed promptly by a "4-D" movie is just too much, even if this goofy animated flick with wind, water, and the other standard 3-D movie effects is appealing to young ones.

Adjacent to an information center and NASA-logo gift shop, the **Robot Scouts** is a funny look at unmanned space exploration, told from the point of view of a robotic planetary probe. And just outside in **Space Shuttle Plaza** you'll see a full-size replica of NASA space shuttle *Explorer.* Near that you'll find the **Launch Status Center,** where visitors get briefings on NASA launch and space flight activity.

The **Shuttle Launch Experience,** opened in May 2007, is one of the center's most technologically ambitious efforts yet, allowing people to experience the sensation of blasting into the Earth's orbit. The 44,000-square-foot, $60 million attraction uses a sophisticated motion-based platform, special effects seats, multiple-screen video, and high-fidelity audio to achieve an authentic simulation.

The center has a full-service, sit-down restaurant and a number of on-the-go space-themed eateries, offering a competent mix from burgers to sushi. Visitors can also take advantage of the **Lunch with an Astronaut** option each day at 12:30 P.M., in which guests dine while listening to a briefing from one of the space cowboys or girls.

The Kennedy Space Center Visitor Complex (Rt. 405 btwn. Range Rd. and E. Ave S.W., 321/449-4444, www.kennedyspacecenter.com) is open 9 A.M. to 5:30 P.M. daily. The Astronaut Hall of Fame is open until 6:30 P.M. "Maximum access" tickets are $38 adults, $28 children 3–11 for tour, IMAX movies, exhibits, simulators, shows, and Astronaut Hall of Fame. Admission for the Astronaut Hall of Fame only runs $17 adults, $13 children 3–11; an annual pass is $50 adults, $35 children 3–11. Bus tours run 2.5 hours, starting at 10 A.M. and run every 15 minutes; the last tour departs at 2:15 P.M.

Wildlife

NASA was a little overambitious with its initial land acquisition, so it turned over some of its property to the Merritt Island National Wildlife Refuge and Canaveral National Seashore. The refuge and seashore areas are usually closed during a launch at Kennedy Space Center. For recorded information on launch closures, call 321/867-0677.

Merritt Island National Wildlife Refuge (visitors center, Hwy. 402 five miles east of U.S. Hwy. 1, Titusville, 321/861-0667, www.fws.gov/merrittisland, 8 A.M.–4:30 P.M. Mon.–Sat., Sun. only Nov.–Mar., free admission), established in 1963, provides a safe haven for more endangered and threatened species than any other wildlife refuge in the country. Sure, it's a privacy buffer zone for NASA, but the 140,000 acres of brackish estuaries and marshes also provides habitat to bald eagles, ospreys, up to 400 manatees during spring, and an estimated 2,500 endangered Florida scrub jays. For visitors, there are five hiking trails varying 0.25–5 miles; trail maps are available at www.fws.gov/merrittisland. Of the hikes, Castle Windy and Turtle Mound trails have shell middens left by Timucuan Indians. There's also a seven-mile driving tour on Black Point Wildlife Drive that wanders through pine flatwoods and impounded marsh, guaranteeing at least a few wildlife sightings. Elsewhere in the refuge, observation towers let you watch birds and other creatures, and a separate manatee observation deck.

Canaveral National Seashore (321/267-1110, www.nps.gov/cana, 6 A.M.–6 P.M. daily, until 8 P.M. daily in summer, admission $3) is the longest swath of undeveloped coastline along the Florida Atlantic coast, where you may encounter bottlenose dolphins and manatees, giant sea turtles laying their eggs, and hundreds of species of shore and wading birds. It is accessible via U.S. Highway 1 and I-95, the southern access in Apollo Beach and the northernmost access in New Smyrna Beach.

Basically, this is mile after mile of underpopulated beach, with limited services and no designated picnic areas, phones, food, or drinking water. Lifeguards are on duty May 30–September 1 at Playalinda (one of Florida's loveliest beaches) and Apollo Beaches. While camping is not allowed in the refuge, limited backcountry camping is permitted on designated islands. Surfing is permitted, as is fishing (with a license), boating, and seasonal hunting of migratory waterfowl.

Beaches

For beaches with more traditional beachside amenities, head a bit south to **Cocoa Beach,** which has a number of appealing, family-friendly beaches in oceanfront parks: Alan Shepard Park (at the east end of Hwy. 520), Sidney Fischer Park (in the 2100 block of Hwy. A1A), Lori Wilson Park (1500 N. Atlantic Ave.), and Robert P. Murkshe Memorial Park (Hwy. A1A and 16th St. S). The whole city of Cocoa Beach has beach access really, with "stub-end" streets with a dune to cross over, parking spaces, and a litter barrel. No pets are allowed on the beaches.

Surfing

The area is fairly well known as an East Coast surf spot. With 72 miles of beach, you can choose between solitary adventure or more social surfing, somewhere along A1A from Sebastian Inlet to Cocoa Beach. A busy spot is the first peak at the inlet or second light at Patrick Air Force Base.

SHOPPING

Historic **Cocoa Village** is in restored downtown Cocoa between U.S. Highway 1 and the Indian River, near Highway 520. With some of the buildings on the National Historic Register, it has the kind of grace and charm that is lacking in so many of Florida's seaside towns. Wander the shops, grab an ice-cream cone, and watch artisans in their workshops. It's a nice place to browse through antiques, handcrafted jewelry, or casual clothing.

ACCOMMODATIONS

If you want to stay near Kennedy Space Center, **Radisson Resort at The Port** (8701 Astronaut Blvd., Cape Canaveral, 321/784-0000, rates from $129) is the very closest. A family favorite, it has nicely appointed, vaguely Carribbean-themed rooms, a huge pool surrounded by tropical gardens and waterfalls, a kiddie pool, and tennis court. There are also a fitness center, laundry services, and free shuttle service to the Port Canaveral cruise ships.

Also nearby is **Residence Inn Cape Canaveral Cocoa Beach** (8959 Astronaut Blvd., Cape Canaveral, 321/323-1100, rates from $179), but this one is all suites. Rooms are huge, with separate living, eating, and sleeping areas. Included are a full hot breakfast buffet and a nightly social hour with light dinner, beer, and wine.

If you'd prefer to stay within earshot of the lapping Atlantic waves, head to Cocoa Beach's **Doubletree Hotel Cocoa Beach Oceanfront** (2080 N. Atlantic Ave., Cocoa Beach, 321/783-9222, rates from $131), each of the 148 newly renovated guest rooms and suite with an ocean view. There is a private-access beach from which you can rent equipment for surfing or snorkeling, and from which deep-sea fishing trips can be arranged.

FOOD

The Space Coast is seriously chain restaurant central, and with a general overreliance upon the fry-o-lator there are not a ton of places to recommend. Kids enjoy the surfer-hip mayhem of ◖ **Ron Jon Surf Grill** (Ron Jon Cape Caribe Resort, 1000 Shorewood Dr., Cape Canaveral, 321/328-2830, 11 A.M.–10 P.M. daily, entrées $8–18) for burgers, straightforward steaks, and a lengthy kids' menu. The fish sandwich isn't bad.

Thai Thai III Restaurant and Sushi Bar (8660 Astronaut Blvd., Cape Canaveral, 321/784-1561, 11 A.M.–2:30 P.M., 5–10 P.M. daily, entrées $7–12) serves familiar but brightly flavored Thai standards along with middle-of-the-road sushi. Very nearby, **Ging-Seng Chinese Restaurant** (8501 Astronaut Blvd., Cape Canaveral, 321/868-3440, 11 A.M.–2:30 P.M., 5–10 P.M. daily, entrées $7–15) does the same with family-friendly Chinese. Be emphatic if you want something spicy.

In Cocoa Beach, the Cocoa Beach Pier is a casual place to grab a bite; try the **Oh, Shucks Seafood Bar** (11 A.M.–10:30 P.M. daily, entrées $6.99–24.99) for steamed shellfish. The more upscale **Mango Tree** (118 N. Atlantic Ave., Cocoa Beach, 321/799-0513, 6–10 P.M. Tues.–Sun., entrées $16–39) has waterfalls and koi ponds around the generous plantation-style house, with a menu that leans toward traditional continental.

PRACTICALITIES
Information and Services
The area code along the Space Coast is 321. The Florida Space Coast Office of Tourism/Brevard County Tourist Development Council (8810 Astronaut Blvd., Ste. 102, Cape Canaveral, 321/868-1126, www.space-coast.com) is open 8 A.M.–5 P.M. weekdays. It provides lots of brochures and information on attractions, events, and accommodations, and there's a separate Kennedy Space Center Visitor Complex information booth here.

Getting There and Around
To get to Kennedy Space Center from Orlando on Highway 528—the Beachline Expressway—travel east on Highway 528 until you reach the Highway 407 exit going to Kennedy Space Center and Titusville. Take Highway 407 until it dead-ends into Highway 405. Turn right (east) onto Highway 405 and follow the signs for Kennedy Space Center for about nine miles. The Visitor Complex will be on your right. From Highway 50, travel east on Highway 50 until you pass under the I-95 overpass. The next intersection is Highway 50 and Highway 405. Turn right (east) onto Highway 405 and follow the rest of the directions above.

Daytona Beach

The Daytona Beach area is one of the most popular vacation destinations in the country, with more than eight million visitors annually. It used to be a fair percentage of these were bikini-clad spring breakers, overrunning the eight little communities along this 23-mile stretch of Atlantic Coast beach every March and April. Volusia County has quietly gone about cordially disinviting these carousing hoards in recent years, focusing instead on other hoards that seem to bring in more money. The area essentially girds its loins for six weeks of special-event activities each spring.

There's the Daytona 500 in February, which draws more than 200,000 fans to the Daytona International Speedway and more than 300,000 to the area. The 10-day Bike Week in March is said to draw between 500,000 and 600,000. Then add in the remaining spring breakers and the nearly 100,000 visitors who come each spring for the three-day Black College Reunion (numbers that have surged in years when Black Entertainment Television has staged the filming of its "Spring Bling" concert here).

The rest of the year, people flock to the communities of Ormond Beach, Ormond-by-the-Sea, Daytona Beach, South Daytona, Daytona

Beach Shores, Holly Hill, Wilbur-by-the-Sea, and Ponce Inlet for other reasons. It's a mild year-round climate with an array of special sporting and cultural events, all within easy proximity of Orlando, the Space Coast, and other Florida Atlantic Coast destinations. One of its biggest draws may be that driving on the beach is permitted, a rarity in Florida. But this affection for all things automotive is certainly understandable given the area's history.

History

"The birthplace of speed" traces its racing roots back to Ormond Beach, a little seaside town just to the north, and to its most famous resident, billionaire John D. Rockefeller. At the turn of the last century, wintering industrialists and miscellaneous big shots would pit their sporty cars against each other, racing along a swath of beach at full throttle. The richest man in the world at that time, Rockefeller would lure his high-society buddies down for a bit of restorative sun, golf, and wheeled revelry. The upshot was the historic race in 1903 between Ransom Olds (of Oldsmobile) and Alexander Winton. Winton's "Bullet No. 1" beat out Olds's "Pirate" in the sport's first sanctioned timed trial, the Ormond Challenge Cup. Determined to save face, Winton set out the next year to set the land speed record at (hold onto your hats) 68 mph. After that, annual tournaments took place 1904–1935 along the beaches of Ormond and Daytona Beach, advancing that land speed record 15 times.

In the 1920s and '30s, Daytona Beach saw astounding increases in speed, far from industrialist W. K. Vanderbilt's impressive 92.3 mph in 1904—by 1927, Englishman Major Henry Segrave achieved the then-unbelievable speed of 200 mph, and in 1935, on his way to his eventual record of 300 mph, fellow Englishman Sir Malcolm Campbell hit the staggering speed of 276.82 mph.

Witness to much of the racing, avid fan William "Big Bill" Henry Getty France held the key to the next chapter of Daytona Beach racing. After buying an Amoco gas station, he became a devoted stock car racer in the mid-1930s. World War II saw little racing of any kind, but after the war France began promoting racing—motorcycles, stock cars, whatever. France and 18 other members of the racing industry formed the National Association for Stock Car Auto Racing (NASCAR) in 1947.

France opened a 4.1-mile stretch of beach track near Ponce Inlet, which also included a paved straightaway section of Highway A1A (today you can see the site of the original first turn at Racing's North Turn, a casual seafood restaurant). Though this track was an unmitigated success, drawing crowds from all over, France had a greater vision. In 1959, the high-banked, 2.5-mile, trioval track known as Daytona International Speedway was unveiled. There were 41,000 fans cheering on that first day's race—today that number

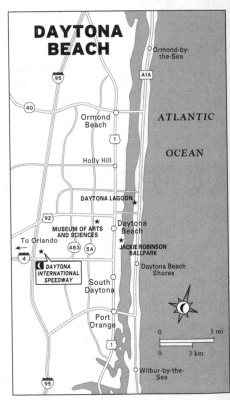

DAYTONA BEACH

PONCE INLET

Definitely worth a half-day trip, the double whammy of the Marine Science Center and the Ponce de Leon Inlet Lighthouse are adjacent to each other, about nine miles south of downtown Daytona Beach.

The **Marine Science Center** (100 Lighthouse Dr., Ponce Inlet, 386/304-5545, 10 A.M.-4 P.M. Tues.-Sat., noon-4 P.M. Sun., $3 adults, $1 children 5-12, younger than five free) packs a 5,000-gallon artificial reef aquarium, cool interactive exhibits on sharks' teeth and mangroves, a creepy-big mosquito, manatee models, and a great gift shop into a small structure. Beyond this, the center is primarily a sea turtle rehabilitation center, with a "turtle terrace" overlooking seven turtle hospital pools harboring injured turtles and hatchlings, all nursed back to health before being released to the wild. Also on-site, the Mary Keller Seabird Rehabilitation Sanctuary allows visitors to stroll a "birdwalk" and view pelicans, a variety of raptors, and other birds that are nonreleasable because of injury. There's also a bird observation tower along a short nature trail that provides a close-up view of avian activity.

The **Ponce de Leon Inlet Lighthouse** (4931 S. Peninsula Dr., Ponce Inlet, 386/761-1821, 10 A.M.-6 P.M. daily, until 9 P.M. in the summer, $5 adults, $1.50 children 11 and younger) is basically right across the street; it's the second-tallest lighthouse in the United States and the tallest in Florida. (The honor of Tallest Lighthouse goes to Cape Hatteras Lighthouse in North Carolina at 191 feet.) At 175 feet tall, it's a National Historic Landmark built in 1887, relit in 1982, and a working beacon today. To see the panoramic view from the top of the pristine red-and-black tower (you can see to Cape Canaveral and beyond), you've got to hoof it 203 steps around and around – not a task to be undertaken lightly. Even those who remain earthbound will be entertained by the maritime artifacts and educational exhibits in the little on-site nautical museum. The rotating lens used today at the top of the tower is a third-order Fresnel lens, but the first-order lens from the Cape Canaveral lighthouse was restored and placed on display in one of the Ponce Inlet lighthouse keepers' dwellings in 1995. The Ayres Davies Lens Exhibit Building is spectacular, its contents like some kind of futuristic jeweler's hallucination, like an elaborate crystal carousel of refracting light.

---

sometimes surges to 200,000 for the annual Daytona 500.

SIGHTS AND RECREATION
◖ Daytona International Speedway

In addition to the Daytona 500, held every February, the Daytona International Speedway (1801 W. International Speedway Blvd., 800/748-7467, ticket prices vary) has eight major weekends of racing activity. There's a month of car and stock-car testing in January, and then the Rolex 24 kicks off three weeks of NASCAR Nextel Cup, Busch Series, Craftsman Truck Series, Crown Royal IROC, and ARCA Re/Max Series racing that culminates with the Daytona 500. In March, coinciding with Bike Week, there are two weeks of intense motorcycle racing with Daytona 200 Week by Honda. During the Fourth of July weekend there's the Pepsi 400, and then in October the American Sportbike Racing Association and the Championship Cup Series features more motorcycle racing. And finally December brings go-carts' World Karting Association Finals. Even when the speedway is quiet, there's something to do at the 480-acre motorsports complex. There are 30-minute, wonderfully narrated tours of the speedway in open-air trams. Guests visit the garage area, pit road, Gatorade Victory Lane, and check out the famous 31-degree-high banks.

While at DIS, race fans can ride along with a specially trained instructor around the world-famous speedway via the **Richard Petty Driving Experience,** a program also offered at

EXCURSIONS

the Walt Disney World Speedway. The RPDE takes fans on "ride along," ($134, but there are discounts sometimes), in which you fly shotgun for three high-speed laps around the track in an authentic Winston Cup–styled stock car. There are loads of other driving experiences, most extremely expensive but a once-in-a-lifetime thrill for the racing enthusiast: the eight-lap Daytona High-Banks Eight Experience for $525, the 16-lap Super 16 for $1,999, and the 24-lap Daytona Driving Experience for $2,099.

In response to the mind-boggling popularity of NASCAR in recent years, the speedway opened **Daytona USA** (1801 W. International Speedway Blvd., 386/947-6800, 9 A.M.–7 P.M. daily, $24 adults, $19 seniors and children 6–12, younger than six free) in 1996, a motorsports attraction dedicated to auto racing and its rich history. Just outside the Speedway's fourth turn, it offers a combination of high-tech, hands-on excitement and a thoughtful historical perspective that makes it fun for visitors of all ages. Serious NASCAR fans will appreciate the "historic walk of fame" that chronicles milestones in racing with photos, memorabilia, and historic cars, but everyone will get a kick out of the racing simulator rides, Daytona Dream Laps and Acceleration Alley; an IMAX movie called *NASCAR 3-D*, narrated by Kiefer Sutherland with behind-the-scenes racing drama; and the interactive attractions such as changing a tire in a timed pit-stop competition, designing and video-testing your own cars, and getting to broadcast a famous race finish. Daytona USA is also where each year's Daytona 500 champion car resides.

If you arrive in Daytona Beach just jonesing to see racing and all is quiet at the speedway, every Saturday night you can catch racing at the nearby Volusia County Speedway in Barberville and the New Smyrna Speedway in New Smyrna Beach.

Museum of Arts and Sciences

The "birthplace of speed," former spring break *Girls Gone Wild* capital, and home of Harley-heavy Bike Week may not be widely lauded for its cultural allures, but the Museum of Arts and Sciences (352 S. Nova Rd., 386/255-0285, 9 A.M.–4 P.M. Tues.–Fri., noon–5 P.M. Sat. and Sun., $12.95 adults, $10.95 seniors, $6.95 children 6–17, five and younger free) is spectacular, reflecting the broad tastes and remarkable affluence and generosity of the local community. It's my favorite kind of museum, a something-for-everyone approach that is bound to spark interest at every age level. It's set on six acres in the Tuscawilla Nature Preserve, its Center for Florida History featuring a 130,000-year-old, 13-foot-tall giant ground sloth found near the museum in 1974. If that fails to thrill, take a walk through the numerous rooms of the Root Family Museum's collection of Americana—Chapman J. Root won the contest in 1916 to design a distinctive bottle for Coca-Cola. Not surprisingly, the Root collection, acquired in 2000, features an array of Coca-Cola-obilia, along with racing memorabilia (including three race cars and a 1948 green Lincoln Continental the Roots took on their honeymoon), quilts, an outrageous teddy bear collection, a couple of Pullman railroad cars, and, strangely, an old apothecary, perfectly re-created.

The museum goes on in this vein, with the area's only planetarium; a modern Cuban exhibit; a 2,000-square-foot African wing with 165 masks, ceremonial objects, and artifacts from numerous countries; Chinese decorative arts; and a huge hall of 17th- and 18th-century American art that includes furniture, painting, watercolors, and decorative arts. Then you add to that a dynamic array of traveling shows and community-oriented events (a New Year's Eve kids' disco sleepover, say), and it's a real locus of cultural activity in the greater Daytona Beach area.

Beaches

Daytona Beach's beaches are anomalous in Florida, in that 11 of the 24 miles of strand allow car access. You can drive right out on the packed sand near the water, park, and set up camp with beach umbrellas, sandcastle tools, boogie boards, fishing equipment, whatever. Beaches, 500 feet at their widest, are densely packed with humanity here, with concession stands, lifeguards, restrooms, and water-sports rentals at intervals. The Atlantic here varies from about 74–80°F, with a little bit of chop (watch for beach warning flags: Red flag means high hazard, yellow is medium hazard, green is low hazard, and blue flags indicate dangerous marine life), and sand is fairly fine-grained and white. Pets are not allowed on any beaches.

While beaches are always open, and free, to pedestrians, beach driving is allowed one hour after sunrise to one hour before sunset, and cost is $5 per car (the fee is waived during December and January). If you don't want to drive out to the beach, free parking is available along Ocean Avenue and most street-ends have beach access. Families with small children may prefer to stick to the safer, mile-long, vehicle-free area from International Speedway Boulevard to Seabreeze Boulevard, surrounding the **Daytona Beach Pier** (formerly known as the Main Street Pier, it's a historic relic, built by the Works Progress Administration in 1938). It includes a handful of pleasant, beachy restaurants and bars along with a skyway that runs the length of the pier and a 180-foot-tall Space Needle, which is no longer operational but provides a distinctive architectural landmark for the area.

Jackie Robinson Ballpark

Baseball fans will want to spend an hour or two touring Jackie Robinson Ballpark (105 E. Orange Ave., 386/257-3172), named such in 1990 because it was where Robinson made his first racially integrated plate appearance, playing in an exhibition game for the Brooklyn Dodgers Triple-A farm club against its parent club. The recently refurbished park honors the first African American player in the major leagues, along with players of all sports who broke the color barrier. It's also where the Daytona Cubs, a minor league affiliate of the Chicago Cubs, play ($6 general tickets). It's a gorgeous ballpark with a manually operated scoreboard, brand-new grass surfaces in the infield and outfield, and an old-fashioned, intimate scale. It's not often you get to eat peanuts and hot dogs in a site listed on the National Register of Historic Places.

ENTERTAINMENT

For something low on the culturally illuminating scale, but fun nonetheless, visit **Daytona Lagoon** (601 Earl St., 386/254-5020, www.daytonalagoon.com, 10 A.M.–10 P.M. Sun.–Thurs., until midnight Fri.–Sat., water park operates seasonally Mar.–Oct., go-karts, minigolf and laser tag $7, rock wall $6, one-hour unlimited activity $19.95), adjacent to the tourist-friendly Ocean Walk Village. High-speed go-carts, miniature golf, laser tag, 25-foot rock-wall climbing, Daytona's largest video arcade, and (in season) slide-intensive waterpark will tend to have attractions for everyone. The purist may be fine with a rigorous game of darts or air hockey, while others such as myself choose to spend an unknown fortune perfecting my Dance Dance Revolution, at least until my daughter stops rolling her eyes at me.

This was also the departure point of the TrolleyBoats tours, which has since shut down. There's some talk that the tour company may be reborn, but the next best thing is a tour on **The River Queen II** (125 Basin St., Ste. 131, 386/254-7560, www.riverqueenii.com). The old-fashioned river paddle wheeler offers narrated sightseeing tours along the Intracoastal Waterway (11:30 A.M. daily, $22 adults, $18 children) and has lunch and dinner cruises as well. The lunch cruise is offered Tuesday, Thursday, and Saturday noon–2 P.M. and costs $29.50 adults, $22.50 children. The Sunday brunch cruise is scheduled 11 A.M.–1:30 P.M., and costs $37.50 adults, $27.50 children. On Friday and Saturday, the dinner cruise runs 6–8:30 P.M., and costs $45 adults, $35 children.

SHOPPING

Regimented rows are extruded onto a refrigerated conveyor belt. They glide down the long, cold line until a mantle of molten chocolate pours down, swathing each creamy center. Before they are loaded manually into "packing

EXCURSIONS

ST. AUGUSTINE

Florida fourth-graders study the state's history which, if they're lucky, means a field trip to St. Augustine, the oldest continuously occupied European settlement in the United States. With world-class golf and tennis facilities, spas, scads of romantic bed-and-breakfasts, architecturally significant churches, it's in most ways more suited to a romantic weekend *a deux*. Regardless, the 60 historic sites draw busloads of scuffling, wound-up 10-year-olds each spring.

Due north of Daytona Beach 58 miles, St. Augustine is the historic area, while nearby Ponte Vedra Beach is the beachy, überluxury home to the PGA Tour and ATP Tour just a bit to the north. The area has 42 miles of unspoiled beaches, but the Old City is the central allure for many visitors.

For more information about St. Augustine, visit www.Getaway4Florida.com or call 904/829-1711.

ATTRACTIONS

The first stop for the fourth-graders is the **Castillo de San Marcos** (1 S. Castillo Dr., 904/829-6506, 8:45 A.M.-5:15 P.M. daily, $6 for those 16 and over, 15 and younger free), not a bad place for the rest of us to start. It took 23 years for the Spanish to build – begun in 1672 and completed in 1695 – and is made of coquina, a tough limestone comprising broken sea shells and corals. A double drawbridge is suspended over what is now a 40-foot dry moat, the whole imposing structure overlooking lovely Matanzas Bay. A self-guided tour brochure helps you navigate the fort's casements, gun deck, exhibits, and mostly outdoor park, but park rangers, some in period dress, give a variety of interpretive talks and weapons demonstrations throughout the day. There's also a 25-minute educational video

shown every hour that gives the history of the oldest extant 17th-century fort in North America (one that was never conquered). Nearby **Fort Matanzas** protected the inlet from pirates and British ships approaching from the south.

Next stop for the fourth-graders is within walking distance. **Old St. Augustine Village** (246 St. George St., entrance on Cordova St., 904/823-9722, 10 A.M.-4 P.M. Mon.-Sat., 11 A.M.-4 P.M. Sun., admission $5 adults, $2 children) is a small grouping of nine historic houses that date to as early as 1790 and as late as 1910. You'll see a blacksmithing shop, the Star General Store, formal gardens, and costumed living-history guides telling the tales of their designated inhabitants. Think historic Williamsburg, but even older. The most gruesome part is the re-creation of the original 16th-century hospital, in which guides gleefully tell you about early amputations and botched medical procedures sans anesthetic. Still, evidently the medical know-how of the early Spanish doctors was far superior to that of the British or other Western European settlers.

There are five worthwhile exhibit galleries tucked among the buildings' courtyards and gardens, as well as the site of the 1863 Emancipation Proclamation reading, freeing all slaves in Florida.

In a similar vein, you can wander through **St. Augustine's Oldest House** (Gonzalez-Alvarez House, 1704, 271 Charlotte St., 904/-824-2872, 9 A.M.-5 P.M. daily, admission $8 adults, $7 seniors, $4 students, younger than 6 free), which contains two museums, a changing exhibition gallery, an ornamental garden, and a museum store, or explore the 1740s living-history exhibits of the **Colonial Spanish Quarter Museum** (St. George St., 904/825-6830, 9 A.M.-5:30 P.M. daily, admission $6.50 adults,

$4 children), where you can learn about blacksmithing, carpentry, leatherworking, candlemaking, and other trades.

Right outside on **St. George Street,** though, is the central drama of 21st-century St. Augustine. It's 11 blocks of pedestrian-only shops, restaurants, and tourist-oriented attractions (the Government House Museum, The Lightner Museum, and others), great for an afternoon of wandering. If your aim is to pack in as much of the history as you can in a single day, the most efficient route is one of the narrated sightseeing tours of downtown conducted from charming trains (800/226-6545, $18.99 adults, $5.99 children, museum admission packages available), open-air trolleys ($24), horse-drawn carriages ($20), or by foot (these last three, all 904/827-0807). Walking tours are led by guides in period costumes, and there are loads of nighttime ghost tours of St. Augustine's purported haunted sites (walking ghost tours $10).

Beyond the gorgeous beaches, families may want to take advantage of St. Augustine's several half-day attractions: **St. Augustine Alligator Farm Zoological Park** (999 Anastasia Blvd., 904/824-3337, 9 A.M.–5 P.M. daily, admission $19.95 adults, $10.95 children 5–11), **Ripley's Believe It or Not!** (19 San Marco Ave., 904/824-1606, 9 A.M.–7 P.M. daily, until 8 P.M. Fri.–Sat., admission $14.99 adults, $11.99 seniors, $7.99 children 5–12), **Potter's Wax Museum** (17 King St., 904/829-9056, 9 A.M.–5 P.M. Sun.–Thurs., until 9:30 P.M. Fri.–Sat.,admission $8.99 adults, $7.99 seniors, $5.99 children 6–12), the **St. Augustine Lighthouse and Museum** (81 Lighthouse Ave., 904/829-0745, 9 A.M.–7 P.M. daily, admission $8 adults, $7 seniors, $6 children 6–11), and the go-carts and arcade at **Family Fun Factory** (2780 State Road 16, 904/827-9400, 10 A.M.–9 P.M. daily,

until midnight weekends, $7.50 go-carts, $7.50 mini golf).

SHOPPING

The **Prime Outlets St. Augustine** (I-95 Exit 318/Hwy. 16, 904/826-1311, 9 A.M.–9 P.M. Mon.–Sat., 10 A.M.–6 P.M. Sun.) features 150 factory outlet stores with the usual suspects. An exit north on I-95, the **World Golf Village** (1 World Golf Pl., 904/940-4123, 10 A.M.–6 P.M. Mon.–Sat., noon–6 P.M. Sun., admission $17 adults, $15 students, $8.50 children 4–12) has a huge array of golf-oriented clothing, toys, art, and sporting apparel stores clustered around a lake, including the **World Golf Hall of Fame** and the largest PGA Tour Stop shop.

ACCOMMODATIONS

St. Augustine has more than 30 romantic and historic Victorian and Spanish-style inns, many situated with views of Matanzas Bay or the historic district. In the historic district, **Casa Monica Hotel** (95 Cordova St., 904/827-1888, rates start at $199) dates to 1888 but has recently undergone a $17 million restoration to make it one of the fanciest offerings around. Guests staying in the 138 rooms and suites also have privileges at the Serenata Beach Club. For something on a more intimate scale, **Casa de Solana Bed and Breakfast** (21 Aviles St., 904/824-3555, from $149) has 10 sweet but recently renovated rooms, most with second-floor balconies from which one can listen to the soothing sound of horse-drawn carriages on the cobbled street below. If you'd rather stay right on the beach, **Castillo Real** (530 A1A Beach Blvd., 904/471-3505, from $119) is a newcomer, opened in 2005. This Mediterranean boutique hotel features multiple fountains, murals, and a three-story lobby atrium. There are 60 rooms, including six oceanfront suites and 28 whirlpool rooms and suites.

EXCURSIONS

off" boxes, a jiggling, mesh rack shakes off any excess chocolate. Not far away, a tumbler hums and rotates, coating plastic golf ball molds with a glossy layer of white chocolate.

Our tour guide at **Angell and Phelps Chocolate Factory** (154 S. Beach St., 386/252-6531, 10 A.M.–5:30 P.M. Mon.–Fri., Sat. until 5 P.M., free tours weekdays on the hour) has to raise her voice a little when describing how the chocolates begin life. And a lot of chocolates have begun life here since the company's inception in 1925 (it's been in this location only since 1994). It's tinkered with the lineup through the years, keeping the staff favorite chocolate-covered pecan brittle, adding sugar-free candies, maybe taking away the odd maple or orange cream that didn't sell. But it's still got more than 100 old-timey cordials and brittles and chews that commingle to create a heady scent that seeps into clothes and hair, reminding one of those rapturous moments at the threshold of the candy shops of youth. Around a corner from the bubbling kettles and molds, chocolate-smudged women hustle to fill Valentine's Day orders, the shop's old-fashioned glass cases displaying glorious heart-shaped boxes from a kinder and more hopeful era. It's a sweet hour of reverie, rendered all the sweeter by the free chocolate at the end of the factory tour.

Step outside onto **Beach Street** in the downtown Daytona Beach Historic District, and you're in the center of Daytona Beach's best shopping area. Along with the chocolate factory, the street is home to the **Halifax Historical Museum** (252 S. Beach St, 386/255-6976, http://halifaxhistorical.org, 10 A.M.–4 P.M. Tues.–Sat., admission $4), **Riverfront Park** (201 N. Beach St.), and a handful of charming antique shops and cafés.

For more tourist-oriented shopping and souvenir shops, **Ocean Walk Shoppes at Ocean Walk Village** (877/845-9255, www.oceanwalkvillage.com) is the place to explore. Adjacent to the historic oceanfront bandshell, the center includes a 10-cinema theater complex, Bubba Gump's Shrimp Company, Cold Stone Creamery, and plenty of apparel and gift stores.

ACCOMMODATIONS

◖ **Hilton Daytona Beach/Ocean Walk Village** (100 N. Atlantic Ave., Daytona Beach, 386/254-8200, rates starting at $143) is across from Ocean Center Convention Center and within easy reach of the speedway. The newly renovated guestrooms have some of the most comfortable beds ever (they're serious: A "Serenity Bed" has a supercush topper, down comforters, "Touch of Down" pillows, and soft, skajillion thread-count sheets), rendered even more delicious with a commanding view of the Atlantic or the Halifax River.

Really right down the street, the **Plaza Resort and Spa** (600 N. Atlantic Ave., Daytona Beach, 386/255-4471, rates starting at $139) has been a local tradition since 1876. It's a huge, high-rise property right on the beach, with 320 large guest rooms and the on-site, full-service Ocean Water Spa.

To stay in the same area but spend a lot less money, the **Super 8 Oceanfront** (133 S. Ocean Ave., Daytona Beach, 386/253-0666, rates from $89) offers 32 oceanfront rooms with efficiencies or microwave/refrigerators. Pets are welcome for an additional $10 per night. It's walking distance to the Boardwalk and Main Street.

If your interests lie more at the speedway, the **Ramada Inn Speedway** (1798 W. International Speedway Blvd., Daytona Beach, 386/255-2422, rates from $69) is about as close as you can get. The racetrack is close enough to hear from any of the clean, basic rooms. There's a big swimming pool and the hotel is just a mile from the airport and about five miles from the beach. A Pizzeria Uno is on the premises.

FOOD

For breakfast, you've got to drive 30 minutes west of Daytona Beach to the DeLeon Springs State Park. You're going to ◖ **Old Spanish Mill and Griddle House** (601 Ponce DeLeon Blvd., DeLeon Springs, 386/985-5644, 9 A.M.–4 P.M. Mon.–Fri., 8 A.M.–4 P.M. Sat.–Sun., entrées $8) where you actually make the breakfast yourself. You can do that at home anytime, you say? Not like this. Opened in 1961 by Peter and Marjorie Schwarze, the funky, wooden barnlike building has griddles built into the tables. The servers bring you two batters, a stone-ground wheat and a white flour version, you pour your pancakes on the hot griddle, add blueberries or chocolate chips, and have them accompanied by sausage or bacon. After breakfast, rent a canoe, kayak, or paddle boat and explore the state park and Woodruff Federal Wildlife Refuge area.

On the other hand, a great breakfast is on offer behind the Daytona Harley-Davidson dealership at the **Daytona Diner** (290½ N. Beach St., Daytona Beach, 386/258-8488, 7 A.M.–2:30 P.M. Mon.–Sat., entrées $4–8), and you can watch the array of Harleys revving up outside while you make a dent in your vast pancake (one pancake is more than formidable for most appetites). It's a classic retro diner, with burgers, omelets, meat loaf, and chili. It's open only for breakfast and lunch.

It's part of a chain, but **Bubba Gump Seafood Company** (250 N. Atlantic Ave., Ste. 120, 386/947-8433, 11 A.M.–10 P.M. Sun.–Thurs., until 11 P.M. Fri.–Sat., entrées $10–20) is in Ocean Walk Village. Shrimp comes several ways, mostly Southern, the drinks are tall and quenching, and the servers are always perky and ready with the Forrest Gump trivia. Turn your tabletop sign to "Run, Forrest, run" when you need service and then to "Stop, Forrest, stop" when all is well.

Inlet Harbor Marina and Restaurant (133 Inlet Harbor Rd., Ponce Inlet, 386/767-5590, 11 A.M.–9 P.M. daily, entrées $6–23) also features a shrimp- and seafood-heavy menu, but it's enjoyed alongside lovely Intracoastal Waterway views of boats, wading birds, and the nearby Ponce Inlet Lighthouse. Crab cakes and fried shrimp are the top offerings, with a very beloved Key lime pie for dessert. Right outside is a fishing pier (tackle shop on-site) and deep-sea fishing trips depart from here.

For dinner, **Stonewood Grill and Tavern** (100 S. Atlantic Ave., Ormond Beach, 386/671-1200, 4–10 P.M. Sun.–Thurs., until 11 P.M. Fri.–Sat., entrées $15–28) is a sophisticated but family-friendly Florida-based chain. The Ormond Beach outpost was the very first, opening in 1999, but the spins on steaks, chops, and simply prepared fish are contemporary American grill-house archetypes. It also serves a very good burger.

In Daytona Beach's Riverfront Marketplace, **Song Mongolian Grill** (132 N. Beach St., Daytona Beach, 386/253-1133, 5–10 P.M. Tues.–Sat., noon–10 P.M. Sun., entrées $21.95 adults, $8.95 kids) offers entertainment with your wholesome and brightly flavored dinner. It borders China, and Mongolia's flavors and ingredients have some overlap with that better-known Asian cuisine, but they're executed in an entirely different way. Bring your bowl to the food bar and select your beef, chicken, fish, seafood, or tofu. Then your veggies. Once your bowl is full, head to the grill and hand the chef your assembled ingredients. It will all be grilled together on a superhot griddle, and you can request whatever sauces or seasonings you like. The overall effect is healthful, with still-crisp vegetables and lively flavors of spicy Sriracha sauce or teriyaki.

Local publications keep slinging kudos at **Cancun Lagoon** (1735 W. International Speedway, Daytona Beach, 386/252-8159, 11 A.M.–10 P.M. Sun.–Wed., until 11 P.M. Thurs.–Sat., entrées $5.95–14.95) for its mahimahi tacos, tamales, frozen margaritas, and inspired margarita shrimp cocktail (chilled shrimp with avocado, cilantro, pico de gallo, and a big lemon squeeze). It's a fun, rowdy joint with a new palm-thatched bar on an outdoor patio and live music on the weekends.

PRACTICALITIES
Information and Services
Daytona Beach is the largest municipality within Volusia County. Its area code is 386. The Daytona Beach Convention and Visitors Bureau has an easy-to-use visitor-oriented website at www.daytonabeach.com, from which you can order a free visitors' guide. The *Daytona Beach News-Journal* (www.news-journal online.com) is the major local paper, with good local and regional coverage, as well as detailed coverage of racing at the speedway.

EXCURSIONS

Getting There and Around

Daytona Beach is 54 miles from Orlando, easy to reach via I-95 or I-4. Once you're in town, driving is fairly straightforward. North Atlantic Avenue is right at the Atlantic Ocean's edge, whereas South Beach Street fronts the Halifax River, which parallels the Atlantic. Daytona Beach International Airport is served by several major airlines, including Continental, Delta, Air Tran, and United, with service to more than 150 destinations worldwide.

BACKGROUND

The Land

GEOGRAPHY

Florida is bounded on the north by Alabama and Georgia, to the east by the Atlantic, to the south by the Straits of Florida, and to the west by the Gulf of Mexico. The state is young by geological standards, having been submerged for much of the geological history of the country. The peninsula rose above sea level perhaps a scant 20 million years ago. By and large, the entire state is a huge plateau right around sea level.

Central Florida is made up of Orange, Seminole, Osceola, and Lake Counties. Whereas much of the state is pancake-flat, this interior central spine features rolling hills, 100–250 feet high, and is dotted generously with lakes and springs. Sugarloaf Mountain in Lake County bears the distinction of being the tallest "peak" of peninsular Florida, a grand 312 feet. Some of these rolling hills, especially north of Orlando, are due to the "Ocala Uplift," one of the state's important geological features where the limestone bedrock has been pushed very close to the surface. It stretches all along West Central Florida from Brooksville in the south to Live Oak in the north, running parallel and west of I-75. Near Ocala, these rolling hills are the state's horse country.

Much of Central Florida is a vast tract of prairie land with large swamp areas. This was, and continues to be, where much of the cattle

COURTESY OF CENTRAL FLORIDA VISITOR'S & CONVENTION BUREAU

has been raised in the state. To the west, the coastal plain that runs along the length of the Gulf Coast is low-lying and sandy, skirted by a dense pine region and marshes in many parts.

Florida has more than 1,700 rivers, streams, and creeks as well as a wealth of lakes and other fascinating bodies of water. To the south of Orlando, Lake Okeechobee in south-central Florida is the largest of the state's approximately 30,000 lakes, ponds, and sinks. With a surface area of about 700 square miles, it is the fourth-largest natural lake lying entirely within the United States, and it is very shallow throughout. Farther south are the Everglades, about 4,000 square miles of flat prairie grass sloping southward at one-fifth of a foot per mile. The Seminoles called the park "grassy water," because it is essentially a wide, shallow river with no current, no falls or rapids, that flows very slowly southward along the subtle slope of the land, eventually meeting open water in Florida Bay 100 miles away. This river flows along sawgrass prairies, mangrove and cypress swamps, pinelands, and hardwood hammocks. Everywhere there are wading birds, alligators, and dense and exotic tropical plant life.

CLIMATE
Heat and Humidity
Florida is closer to the equator than any other continental American state—it's on the southeastern tip of North America with a humid subtropical climate and heavy rainfall April–November. Its humidity is attributed to the fact that no point in the state is more than 60 miles from saltwater and no more than 345 feet above sea level. If this thick steamy breath on the back of your neck is new to you, humidity is a measure of the amount of water vapor in the air. Most often you'll hear the percentage described in "relative humidity," which is the amount of water vapor actually in the air divided by the amount of water vapor the air can hold. The warmer the air becomes, the more moisture it can hold.

When heat and humidity combine to slow evaporation of sweat from the body, outdoor activity becomes dangerous even for those in good physical shape. Drink plenty of water to avoid dehydration and slow down if you feel fatigued or notice a headache, a high pulse rate, or shallow breathing. Overheating can cause serious and even life-threatening conditions such as heatstroke. The elderly, small children, the overweight, and those on some medications are particularly vulnerable to heat stress.

During the summer, expect temperatures to hover around 90°F and humidity to be somewhere near 100 percent. The most pleasant times of the year in Central Florida fall between December and April—not surprisingly, among the busiest times for tourism. Still, because summer vacations fall in, well, summer, many visitors flock to Orlando between June and August for a major family vacation. While you can count on everything indoors to be air-conditioned (sometimes overly so), be prepared for punishingly hot and humid conditions outdoors. Plan your days so there's some respite from the sun.

Rain
It rains nearly every day in the summer. And not just a sprinkle. Because of the abundance of warm, moist air from the Gulf of Mexico to the west and the Atlantic to the east, and the hot tropical sun, conditions are perfect for the formation of thunderstorms. There are 80–90 thunderstorms each summer, generally less than 15 miles in diameter—but vertically they can grow up to 10 miles high in the atmosphere. These are huge, localized thunderstorms that can drop four or more inches of rain in an hour, while just a few miles away it stays dry. The bulk of these tropical afternoon thunderstorms each summer are electrical storms.

Lightning
With these sudden thunderstorms comes lightning, a serious threat along the Gulf Coast. About 50 people are struck by lightning each year in the state. Most of them are hospitalized and recover, but there are about 10 fatalities annually. An hour to the west of Orlando, Tampa is the "Lightning Capital" of

the United States, with around 25 cloud-to-ground lightning bolt blasts on each square mile annually. The temperature of a single bolt can reach 50,000°F, about three times as hot as the sun's surface. There's not much you can do to ward off lightning except to avoid being in the wrong place at the wrong time. The months of June, July, August, and September have the highest number of lightning-related injuries and deaths. Usually lightning occurs during daylight hours, with the highest concentration between 3 P.M. and 4 P.M., when the afternoon storms peak. Lightning strikes usually occur either at the beginning or end of a storm and can strike up to 10 miles away from the center of the storm. Keep your eye on approaching storms and seek shelter when you see lightning.

Hurricanes

Hurricanes are violent tropical storms with sustained winds of at least 74 mph. Massive low-pressure systems, they blow counterclockwise around a relatively calm central area called the eye. They form over warm ocean waters, often starting as storms in the Caribbean or off the west coast of Africa. As they move westward, they are fueled by the warm waters of the tropics. Warm, moist air moves toward the center of the storm and spirals upward, releasing driving rains. Updrafts suck up more water vapor, which further strengthens the storm until it can be stopped only when it makes contact with land or cooler water. In the average hurricane just 1 percent of the energy released could meet the energy needs of the United States for a full year.

In Florida, the hurricane season is July–November. These storms have been named since 1953. It used to be just female names ("Hell hath no fury like a woman scorned," or some such nonsense), but now there's gender parity in the naming. The names of really powerful hurricanes are retired, kind of like the jerseys of sports greats.

Monitor radio and TV broadcasts closely for directions. Gas up the car, and make sure you have batteries, water supply, candles, and food that can be eaten without the use of electricity. Get cash, have your prescriptions filled, and put all essential documents in a large resealable bag. In case of an evacuation, find the closest shelter by listening to the radio or TV broadcasts (pets are not allowed in shelters).

Flora and Fauna

The abundance of sunlight and rain and the near absence of four traditional seasons allow for the successful growth of nearly 4,000 plant species and nearly that many animals in Florida. The state's plant life is richly diverse, providing a range of habitats. Even nonnative plants and animals flourish in these lush conditions, a fact that troubles Floridian scientists as more exotic species take hold. The trade in exotic pets and plants, as well as the movement of huge numbers of people and vehicles, can intentionally or unintentionally bring new species into Florida, devastating native species and invading natural areas. For avid horticulturalists and gardeners, **Epcot International Flower and Garden Festival,** from between the beginning of April to the beginning of June, is one-stop-shopping to learn about Florida plant life—the park is filled with plants and the festival sponsors celebrity guest speakers, seminars, and other gardening exhibits.

FLORA
Crops

The citrus fruit industry has been big business in Central Florida since the 1890s, when Chinese horticulturist Lue Gim Gong introduced a new variety of orange and a hardier grapefruit. Today, citrus is Florida's leading cash crop, producing 70 percent of the country's oranges and accounting for 89,000 jobs, many of them in Central Florida. Some reports place the value

COURTESY OF CENTRAL FLORIDA VISITOR'S & CONVENTION BUREAU

orange tree

at $1.6 billion—not surprisingly, the orange blossom is the state flower. Here's an interesting fact: 95 percent of the state's oranges are made into juice.

Beyond citrus, though, Central Florida is the "winter salad bowl," providing 80 percent of the fresh vegetables grown in the United States during January, February, and March. West of Orlando, Plant City near Tampa is the state's strawberry capital. The area around Sarasota and Bradenton is responsible for lots of tomatoes, peppers, and more strawberries. Roadside stands and U-pick farms abound southwest of Orlando—you won't regret pulling the car over for some sun-warmed berries or a quart of sweet-tart orange juice.

Trees

Palm trees are practically a Florida cliché. Also known as "cabbage palm" and "palmetto," the sabal palm is the source of hearts of palm. Sabal palm grows in all conditions in the state—wet, dry, coastal, swampy—and it is from the fronds of the sabal that

the Seminoles built watertight chickee roofs. You'll also regularly encounter royal palm, identified by its towering 80-foot pale gray trunk and bright, glossy crown shaft. Many of the other palm species usually associated with Florida are not native—the easily recognized coconut palm, the heavy-trunked Canary Island date palm, the slim, statuesque red latan palm. You'll see them all over Central Florida, but it's what they're in contrast to that gives this subtropical landscaping its own flavor.

Cypress is another oh-so-Florida tree. Forested wetlands in the state are often dominated by cypress trees, growing along stream banks and riverbanks or in ponds with slow-moving water. Bald cypresses (they aren't always bald; they just lose their leaves in winter) are the largest trees in North America east of the Rockies. They can live for hundreds of years, quietly ruminating with their roots in water, their "knees" protruding above the soil and waterline. The function of these knees, part of the root system that projects out of the water, isn't totally known, other than that they provide stability and more air for the base of these flood-tolerant trees.

Live oaks are certainly not the sole custody of Florida. In all of the South these huge semi-deciduous trees loom, gnarled and woebegone, draped with Spanish moss (which is neither Spanish, nor a moss). You'll see them all over Central Florida.

Mangroves are more distinctively Floridian, a species you'll see edging bodies of brackish water. Often called walking trees, they hover above the water, their arching prop roots resembling so many spindly legs. Seeds sprout on the parent tree and drop off, bobbing in the water until they lodge on an oyster bar or a snag in the shallows. There, the seed begins to grow to a tree, the foundation of a new, tiny island. Around its roots sediment and debris build up to create a thick layer of peat upon which other plant species begin to grow. This first tree drops more seed tubules, which get stuck in the mulch ground and create more trees, which in turn create a bigger island.

Epiphytes

"Epi" means "on" and "phyte" means "plant." Thus, an epiphyte is a plant that grows on another plant. They're sometimes called airplants because they grow above ground, in the air, roots wiggling in the breeze. Host plants support them high off the ground, where they don't need to compete for light and rainwater, where they don't have to cope with floodwater and marauding animals. Epiphytes generally do no harm to the host plant and get their nutrients from their own photosynthesis and their own water from runoff on their host. Cardinal airplant, resurrection fern—these are all wonderful plants to explore.

Within this category, orchids are probably the best known, with more genera than any other plant. **World of Orchids** in Kissimmee is a great clearinghouse for orchids and other cool kinds of epiphytes native to Florida.

FAUNA
Fish

No other state in the United States and few other countries boast a more varied marine environment. Florida has hundreds of species of fish teeming in its waters. It has the Atlantic and the fertile Gulf of Mexico with its hundreds of bays, sounds, inlets, and brackish marshes. But there are also freshwater rivers, lakes, estuaries, and a bazillion other marine environments.

Central Florida is legendary among anglers, with the Kissimmee Chain of Lakes and Lake Tohopekaliga (or just Lake Toho) known the world over as a bass-fishing destination. Headquartered in Orlando is ESPN, the parent company of B.A.S.S., the national bass-fishing organization and sponsor of events such as the Bassmaster Classic. And an hour in either direction brings you to the Gulf of Mexico or the Atlantic, both worthy of an angler's attentions for myriad saltwater species.

In much of this area, freshwater fishing is most productive in the spring while sportfishing is good all year. But you need a license. An annual nonresident saltwater fishing license is $31.50; a seven-day license is $16.50. The same prices apply to the freshwater licenses. You need to figure out what you're fishing for before you buy your license, but either way the revenue generated by the sale goes to the Florida Fish and Wildlife Conservation Commission.

Birds

With 500 bird species, both those native to the state and those that migrate here, Florida is a bird lover's paradise in a range of habitats. Mangrove estuaries are home to many species of **egrets, herons,** and numerous other **wading birds. Waterbirds** occupy interior wetlands, and countless **shorebirds, terns,** and **gulls** populate the white-sand beaches. Unique to the state, the **Florida scrub jay** lives in a small patch of scrub-oak habitat; **ospreys** and **bald eagles** make their gargantuan nests all over. The woods are aflutter with **red-shouldered hawks** and endangered **red cockaded woodpeckers.** In backyard ponds you'll spy the long, sinuous neck of the **anhinga**—what Native tribes called "snakebirds"—they sport rakish poses as they dry their wings after a deep dive for fish. You'll spot **white pelicans,** the second-largest flying bird in North America, sailing low over the water, while high above a

Egrets are among Florida's many bird species.

COURTESY OF CENTRAL FLORIDA VISITOR'S & CONVENTION BUREAU

frigate is barely a speck. You'll bristle at the shrewish nagging cry of a **little blue heron** and startle at the trilling bray of the enormous **sandhill cranes** that promenade gracefully in small family groups of three.

I could go on. It's serious birding country, with loads of expert birders to lead you through the prime birding spots. An hour northwest of the Orlando area is the 380,000-acre **Ocala National Forest** (from Highway 19 north of Eustis, take County Road 445 northeast five miles, and the entrance will be on left, $4 per person) in Marion County. Birders spot the endangered Florida scrub jay, bald eagles, wading birds, and migratory birds here. Fifteen miles south of Walt Disney World Resort, **Disney Wilderness Preserve** offers three miles of hiking and interpretive trails laid out over about 700 acres of the 12,000-acre property. The best bird-watching is in winter when the migratory species visit.

Avid birders also flock to **Lake Woodruff National Wildlife Refuge** in DeLeon Springs, about an hour north of Orlando. Its 19,500 acres of marsh, swamp, and upland are a refuge for migratory birds. **Lake County** is dotted with a wealth of notable birding spots: from the 7,089-acre **Emeralda Marsh Conservation Area** preserve, to **Bourlay Historic Nature Park** in Leesburg, to **Trout Lake Nature Center,** a 230-acre wildlife preserve on the north edge of Eustis.

The single best resource for Florida birding information can be found through the **Great Florida Birding Trail** (www.floridabirding-trail.com), a collection of 445 birding sites throughout Florida with maps by region.

Alligators

Alligators were first listed as an endangered species in 1967, their numbers threatened by hunting and habitat loss. Then the American alligator was removed from the endangered species list in 1987 after the U.S. Fish and Wildlife Service pronounced a complete recovery of the species. I'll say—conservative estimates put the population at around one million in Florida, Louisiana, Texas, and Georgia. Because they

Alligators are ubiquitous in Florida.

COURTESY OF CENTRAL FLORIDA VISITOR'S & CONVENTION BUREAU

can tolerate brackish water as well as freshwater, alligators can be found in rivers, swamps, bogs, lakes, ponds, creeks, canals, swimming pools, and lots of Florida golf courses.

The American alligator is the largest reptile in North America (distinguished from the American crocodile by its short, rounded snout and black color). They can live 35–50 years in the wild and 60–80 years in captivity. The average adult male is 13 feet long (half of the length is taken up by the tail), although they can grow up to 18 feet long. Bulls (males) are generally larger than females and weigh 450–600 pounds.

They're everywhere in Florida, and they eat just about anything. Usually that means lizards, fish, snakes, turtles, even little gators, but they'll also enjoy bologna sandwiches and schnauzer.

Florida residents have heretofore learned to be blasé about gators. They're an everyday part of living in this subtropical climate. But times are changing—some experts are even beginning to posit that alligators are "de-evolving" and becoming more dangerous to humans. Since 2000, several people have died in alligator attacks. It's hard to be as sanguine about gator-human relations when women are getting chomped while pruning their gardens. The problem is not just a function of large numbers—people feed the gators, thus alligators have gotten chummy and less fearful of humans and vice versa.

So now new policies are being put in place. In much of Florida, if gators get too large (longer than eight feet) they are taken away and "processed" (not a good euphemism); smaller ones are relocated. The jury is still out on this interspecies relationship.

History

While it was the first state to be settled by Europeans, Florida might be the last state to have entered fully into modernity. It remained more or less a frontier until the 20th century, with the first paved road not until 1920. It was really World War II that changed things in the state, prompting a period of sustained growth that lasted more than 50 years.

Still, it wasn't that long ago that Central Florida was cow pastures and some nominally useful swampland. The early economy, such as it was, could be summed up by the three Cs: first cattle, then cotton, and then citrus. The area was slow to be settled, with a few intrepid families wending their way here after the Seminole Wars in the mid-1800s, lured by cheap land and a paucity of rules and regulations. Ranchers allowed their Cracker cattle to roam the area's flat woods, rounding them up every year and driving them west, where they were shipped off to Cuba for beef. Orlando (population 85 in 1875) was Florida's version of the Old West, with rugged individuals wearing hats and spending the bulk of their days with ornery cows. A subsequent cotton boom in the area was wiped out by a hurricane in 1871, just as the area's farmers turned their sights on the lucrative citrus business.

Coastal parts of Florida saw a vogue in the early part of the 20th century as rich Northeasterners made an annual winter pilgrimage to the warmth, sun, and beaches of the 27th state. Central Florida received some of this migration, mostly centered around the charming town of Winter Park, but huge swaths of land remained largely unused.

That is, until Walt Disney had the idea of duplicating—or improving upon—the theme park he opened in California in 1955. He went about buying up 43 square miles of Florida swampland, upon which he began building Magic Kingdom in 1967. The park opened in 1971, followed by Epcot in 1982, Disney-MGM Studios in 1989, and Disney's Animal Kingdom in 1998. SeaWorld Orlando opened not far away in 1973, Universal Studios Florida opened in 1990, and its Universal's Islands of Adventure and Universal CityWalk opened

ORLANDO: GOLF CAPITAL OF THE WORLD

Certain pockets of America have always been magnets for golfers and the golf industry – Myrtle Beach, Palm Springs, Phoenix, and Scottsdale – but Orlando, with numerous golf courses, touring pros, national events, and a who's who of golf-industry leaders, is arguably the Golf Capital of the World.

Orlando might be more synonymous with Mickey and Goofy, but there's only one place that can lay claim to having Tiger and the King (that would be golf greats Tiger Woods and Arnold Palmer, of course). Today more than 100 touring golf professionals have made Orlando a popular place to live and play, including some of the game's biggest names. But it's more than just big-name golfers making a mark on Orlando; numerous world-class instructors are also based in the area.

As for the golf itself, 176 courses keep Orlando green – many designed by the biggest names in business – including top-notch public and semipublic courses such as Orange County National and Falcon's Fire, renowned resort layouts at Disney World and Grand Cypress, and ultraexclusive private facilities such as Isleworth Country Club and Lake Nona Golf and Country Club.

Moreover, Orlando regularly plays host to a handful of top professional events, including annual PGA Tour tournaments at Disney World and Palmer's Bay Hill Club, the nationally televised Father/Son Challenge at ChampionsGate, PGA Tour Qualifying School at Orange County National, and the newly formed Tavistock Cup, which pits Isleworth's high-profile members against Lake Nona's jet-setting clientele. All of these events are televised live, and the combined prize money is more than $12.5 million.

Through the years, as Orlando has grown in stature as a great golf destination, many golf-related businesses have set up headquarters in the City Beautiful, including the Golf Channel and *Golfweek* magazine, management company giant Meadowbrook Golf, and design company leader Palmer Course Design Company. Meanwhile, the PGA Merchandise Show annually draws 45,000 industry professionals to the Orange County Convention Center, making it the largest golf exhibition and show on the planet.

COURSES

In the spirit of golf, here's a look at eight of the Orlando area's must-visit golf courses:

Southern Dunes Golf Club: A unique layout, this award-winning course has been ranked by *Golfweek* magazine as one of the "Top 100 Courses in America" and awarded 4.5 stars by *Golf Digest*. The par-72, 7,227-yard Steve Smyers-designed course features imaginative bunkering and large sandy scrub areas that line dramatically rolling fairways. Unusual for Central Florida, the course has elevation changes of up to 100 feet and a series of enormous dunes that give it even more character. Fees and hours vary. (2888 Southern Dunes Blvd., Haines City, 863/421-4653, www.southern dunes.com)

Victoria Hills Golf Club: The home course to Stetson University's golf teams and site of the 2004 NCAA Men's Division II Championship, this relatively new layout preserves the natural flow of the environment in a unique Florida golf setting. Among the special characteristics of the par-72, 6,989-yard Ron Garl-designed course are generous fairways framed by mature oak and pine hammocks, elevated tough-to-hit greens, and a new Carolina-style Victorian clubhouse and tavern. Fees and hours vary. (300 Spalding Way, DeLand, 386/738-6000, www.joetowns.com/victoriapark/golf.asp)

MetroWest Golf Club: Open since 1987, this Robert Trent Jones Sr. masterpiece is one of Orlando's most solid mainstays and is considered by *Links Magazine* to be "the Southeast's finest example of the master's work." Set in a well-landscaped residential/commercial corridor minutes from Universal Studios, MetroWest has huge, undulating greens, expansive fairways bordered by mature trees, and rare elevation changes up to 100 feet. This lush par-72, 7,051-yard course is maintained in tournament playing conditions year-round. Fees and hours vary.

(2100 S. Hiawassee Rd., 407/299-1099, www.metrowestgolf.com)

Celebration Golf Club: In the critically acclaimed Disney-designed Celebration community, this par-72, 6,772-yard course is a rare collaboration of the father-and-son team of Robert Trent Jones Sr. and Jr. One of the final designs of the late Trent Jones Sr., this pristine core golf course is a challenging layout, to say the least, evident from the numerous state and national tournaments conducted at the upscale daily-fee track. Featuring strategic hazards and challenging greens, this championship-caliber course demands accurate approach shots and consistent putting. Fees and hours vary. (701 Golf Park Dr., Celebration, 888/275-918, www.celebrationgolf.com)

Falcon's Fire Golf Club: This Rees Jones signature design has a memorable back nine that wraps around two large, picturesque lakes with a run of holes (12-18) that will challenge the most skilled player. Boasting tournament playing conditions 12 months a year, the course is arguably one of the finest maintained in Central Florida, which explains why Falcon's Fire has often hosted such events as the Senior PGA Tour Qualifying School and the Oldsmobile Scramble National Finals. The pro shop is regarded as one of America's best. Fees and hours vary. (3200 Seralago Blvd., Kissimmee, 877/878-3473, www.falconsfire.com)

Bay Hill Club and Lodge: Best known for its beloved owner, Arnold Palmer, this private club and Palmer's winter home allows rare public access for guests staying at the on-site 70-room lodge. Besides the main par-72, 7,205-yard championship layout, Bay Hill also has the nine-hole, 3,409-yard Charger Course to test your best golf skills. A regular spring stop on the PGA Tour, Bay Hill is truly fit for the King himself, who can often be seen hitting balls on the course or relaxing at the club. Fees and hours vary. (9000 Bay Hill Blvd., 888/422-9445, www.bayhill.com)

Eagle Creek Golf Club: Opened in 2004, this 7,198-yard layout is Orlando's only par-73 course and lies within minutes of Orlando International Airport near prestigious Lake Nona Golf and Country Club. This Ron Garl/Howard Swan-designed layout features five fun par-5s, five sets of tees, and more than 90 bunkers and dramatic bulkheads that are reminiscent of those found in Scotland and England. The greens, featuring the rare Mini-verde variety of Bermuda grass, are some of the area's best. Fees and hours vary. (10350 Emerson Lake Blvd., 866/324-5342, www.eaglecreekgolf.info)

Marriott Grande Pines Golf Club: Recently renovated by the talented Steve Smyers and player consultant Nick Faldo, this par-72, 7,012-yard resort layout is adjacent to Sea-World in the heart of Orlando's tourist section known as International Drive. Bordered by tall natural pines, oaks, and palms, giving it a sense of escape, Grande Pines is one of the dozens of first-class properties managed by Marriott Golf. For a bonus, make sure to visit Marriott's nearby Faldo Golf Institute, which features a world-class practice facility and nine-hole executive course. Fees and hours vary. (5925 Avenida Vista, 407/239-6909, www.marriottgolf.com)

Shingle Creek Golf Club: Another top track in Orlando's tourist district, Shingle Creek has been one of the more decorated courses since the late David Harman opened the course in 2003. Bordered by dense oaks and pines in a backdrop along historic Shingle Creek, the course serves as headwaters to the Florida Everglades. Off the course, the par-72, 7,250-yard Shingle Creek features two award-winning amenities: the Brad Brewer Golf Academy and a pro shop ranked by *GolfWorld* as one of the top 100 shops in America in 2007. Fees and hours vary. (9939 Universal Blvd., 866/996-9933, www.shinglecreekgolf.com)

Contributed by **Scott Kauffman,** a former staff writer of *Golfweek*. Today, the Orlando-area resident is the country's leading writer on golf course development and real estate, and he regularly contributes to national magazines such as *Golf Connoisseur, Links, Luxury Living, Unique Homes,* and the *Robb Report*.

in 1999. Disney's Typhoon Lagoon opened in 1989 and Blizzard Beach in 1995, and then Downtown Disney in 1997.

This early critical mass of theme parks has ensured continued growth in the area. Every year new hotels and attractions are added, with an ever-widening maze of construction. By some estimates, there are more than 200 tourist attractions in the area, 4,000 restaurants, and 100,000 hotel rooms.

ECONOMY

It's easy to see why tourism has been central to much of the state's growth in modern times, with a yeoman's effort on the part of Walt Disney and his ever-expanding resort. In fact, Mickey Mouse and the empire that grew up around him in Central Florida are responsible for much of the state's economy. With more than 50 million people traveling annually to Orlando, nearly $30 billion is spent by visitors each year and about 25 percent of the area's total employment revolves around the tourism industry. Floridians tend to have a strong opinion about Walt Disney World Resort—some are not exuberantly positive, but most recognize that Mickey continues to give Florida a life-saving cash transfusion.

ESSENTIALS

Getting There

BY AIR

All of the online travel resources (Orbitz, Travelocity, Expedia) offer Orlando theme park/hotel/air packages as well as last-minute specials and weekend deals on travel. The way to get a good fare in advance on air travel or hotel rooms is by traveling off peak season (peak season includes December, March, and April, and the summer).

Orlando International Airport

Orlando International Airport (1 Airport Blvd., general information 407/825-2001, parking information 407/825-7275, www.orlandoairports.net) is nine miles southeast of downtown Orlando, at the junction of Highway 436 (Semoran Boulevard) and Highway 528 (Beachline Expressway, formerly the Bee Line Expressway). Serving more than 35 million passengers annually, with 898 commercial flights each day, it's a big, orderly, easy-to-use airport serving 51 airlines. On-site dining options include Carvel, Chick-Fil-A, Cinnabon, Macaroni Grill, McCoy's Bar and Grill, Nathan's, and Starbucks Coffee. Walt Disney World Resort, Universal Orlando Resort, and SeaWorld Orlando all have gift shops in the airport in case you forgot a little trinket for the folks back home.

Travelers get from their gates to one of two

COURTESY OF CENTRAL FLORIDA VISITOR'S & CONVENTION BUREAU

main terminals aboard an enclosed shuttle. From there, baggage claim, rental cars, hotel shuttles, taxis, and car services are well marked.

From Europe: Orlando International Airport has more flights, with more seats, to more U.S. destinations than any other airport in Florida. U.S. Immigration operates 44 checkpoints, clearing up to 2,600 passengers per hour (the average time for international passengers to exit the airport from a flight is 46 minutes). There is also a dedicated lounge on Airside 4 for international passengers in transit. The following airlines provide scheduled nonstop international service to and from Orlando International Airport: AeroMexico, Air Canada, Air Jamaica, Air Transat, Bahamas Air, British Airways, Cayman Airways, Condor, Continental Airlines, Copa Airlines, Delta, Martinair, US Airways, Virgin Atlantic, West Jet, and Zoom.

Airport Parking: A new cell phone parking lot, on the South Approach Road, about one mile south of the terminal building, is free for passenger pickup. Wait for passengers to call and then pick them up at curbside baggage claim. Terminal garage parking costs $1 per 20 minutes up to a maximum of $17 per day. Uncovered satellite parking costs $4 for the first three hours, after which the daily rate of $9 per 24-hour period applies. A free shuttle operates every 10 minutes between the three satellite parking lots and the Orlando International Airport main terminal. Parking fees for both terminal garage parking and satellite parking may be charged using American Express, MasterCard, or Visa credit cards.

Other Area Airports

Orlando Sanford International Airport (407/585-4000, www.orlandosanfordairport.com) is the area's second most popular entry point and accommodates most of the holiday charter services arriving in Central Florida. Its location off I-4 makes it convenient to the area's technology corridor and theme parks.

A third, smaller airport, **Greater Orlando Aviation Authority** (4001 E. Concord St., 407/894-9831) is three miles from downtown Orlando, 10 miles from Orlando International Airport, and 15 miles from the Orange County Convention Center. The airport provides 24-hour service, two paved runways, an FAA air traffic control tower, and full ILS capability.

Technically, Kissimmee's little airport is closest to Walt Disney World Resort. **Kissimmee Gateway Airport** (407/847-4600, www.kissimmeeairport.com) has two paved runways and accommodates general aviation air service 24 hours a day, with its air traffic control tower operating 7 A.M.–9 P.M. daily.

Tampa International Airport (five miles west of downtown Tampa, 813/870-8700) is the largest airport on the Gulf Coast and an hour west of the theme parks in Orlando. **Southwest Florida International Airport** (10 miles southeast of Fort Myers, 941/768-1000) has experienced enormous expansion recently and is approximately two hours southwest of Orlando. **Jacksonville International Airport** (14200 Pecan Park Rd., Jacksonville, 904/741-4902), about 160 miles from Walt Disney World Resort, is another option if you plan to spend time on Florida's Atlantic Coast.

Disney's Magical Express Transportation

Disney has launched a new service for visitors staying at the resort. Free round-trip airport transportation and baggage delivery service means you are whisked to your hotels and your luggage magically appears in your room. You can reserve this service online when booking a trip or by calling the **Disney Reservation Center** (407/939-7675). Then, attach the tags you receive in the mail to your luggage and bring the included vouchers with you to the airport. Upon landing, skip baggage claim and proceed to the Disney Welcome Center, in the main terminal building of Orlando International Airport on the B side on Level 1. Disney collects your luggage and delivers it directly to your hotel room. At the end of your trip, there's free transportation back to the airport, and domestic travelers can use the resort airline check-in service, which allows you to receive your return boarding pass and check your luggage from your Disney Resort hotel directly, bypassing airport check-in completely.

BY CAR

The main arteries into Florida include I-95, which crosses the Florida-Georgia border just north of Jacksonville and hugs the east coast of the state all the way down, and I-75, the huge north-south artery that runs down the center of the state before turning toward the Gulf Coast side of the Florida peninsula, stretching from where it enters the state at Valdosta, Georgia, all the way south to Naples, where it jogs across the state to the east along what is called Alligator Alley. I-4 extends southwest across the state from Daytona Beach in the east, through Orlando, and then connects to I-75 in Tampa on the state's Gulf Coast.

FLORIDA'S SCENIC HIGHWAYS

Maybe it reflects my own biases, but a vacation comprising day after day of theme parks is unavoidably monotonous, sure to prompt infighting and bad behavior, even when traveling alone. It's time for a road trip. Florida has 14 designated Scenic Highways, several of them in Central Florida within an easy drive of Orlando. This is a program developed whereby communities petition to preserve, maintain, protect, and enhance their cultural, historical, recreational, and natural resources. For the visitor, it means a well-marked, well-preserved slice of Old Florida, the antidote to all the theme park slickness.

About 20 miles to the west of downtown Orlando you'll actually encounter rolling hills in the 12.4-mile **Green Mountain Scenic Byway.** The lovely town of Montverde contains the town cemetery framed by moss-draped live oaks, and the Mediterranean Revival buildings of the 125-acre campus of the Montverde Academy, a fancy boarding school. It's among the state's most popular cycling routes, drawing serious cyclists for training, touring, and the occasional triathlon. To get in on a little of your own cycling, go to the County Line Station trailhead of the West Orange Trail, at the southern terminus of the Scenic Byway. It's a 19-mile paved bicycle/hiking trail through gorgeous countryside. To get on the Green Mountain Scenic Byway, take Florida's Turnpike to Exit 272 (Hwy. 50); go west on Highway 50 (Colonial Dr.) to Old Highway 50 north. Stay to the right at Montverde Junction and take Lake County Road 455 north, also called the Green Mountain Scenic Byway.

Up near Ocala, the **Old Florida Heritage Highway** is a 48-mile trail that winds through densely forested countryside and the communities of Micanopy (the oldest inland town in Florida), Rochelle, Evinston, and Cross Creek. It's Old Florida "Cracker" bungalows, ancient live oaks, little antique/hodgepodge shops, and plenty of hospitable cafés. The route also goes by two lovely state parks worth an afternoon hike: Paynes Prairie Preserve State Park is just a couple of miles north of Micanopy along U.S. Highway 441, and Marjorie Kinnan Rawlings Historic State Park, 10 miles east of U.S. 441 in Cross Creek. To reach Old Florida Heritage Highway, take I-75 north to Exit 374, Micanopy (Alachua County Road 234).

Due south of Orlando off I-4, **The Ridge Scenic Highway** is another lovely drive – one with a spooky tale associated with it. You'll see citrus groves, rolling hills, the sweet old-timey Haines City, Historic Bok Sanctuary (see the *Kissimmee and Vicinity* chapter), and Spook Hill.

The legend of Spook Hill goes like this: Many years ago an Indian village on Lake Wales (one of two lovely lakes in Haines City) was traumatized by a big, angry gator. The tribe chief fought the reptile and the ensuing battle created a small lake. Many years later, when the road was paved, cars miraculously coasted uphill. To try your own set of wheels on the hill, take Highway 27 to 17A (before Lake Wales), turn left (east), and follow signs for Spook Hill. To get to The Ridge Scenic Highway, take I-4 south to Exit 55 toward Haines City, then turn left on U.S. Highway 17/92 for about a mile, and then turn right on Highway 17, which is the Ridge Scenic Highway.

BY BOAT

Because Orlando is landlocked, it's tough to arrive under your own sail power, in a yacht, or aboard another kind of boat. However, Lake Tohopekaliga (called Lake Toho) and East Lake Toho are world-class bass-fishing lakes, worthy of pulling a bass boat behind your car. Fishing licenses are available at most bait shops, sporting goods stores, and the Osceola County Tax Collector's Office (360 N. Beaumont Ave., Kissimmee, 407/343-4000) or via phone with credit card at 888/347-4356. (The Disney Cruise Line is described in the *More Disney Attractions* chapter.)

Getting Around

BY CAR

Many visitors to Orlando choose to eschew renting a car, relying on free or cheap resort transportation to go between the airport and theme parks. Renting a car, however, gives visitors more flexibility to see some of the area's nature-based attractions and half-day destinations. In addition, during high season, public transportation from the theme parks can be very crowded, rendering it a hassle to go back to your room for a nap or some downtime.

Those who rent a car while in Orlando will find excellent signage that makes it easy to navigate throughout the area and around the various theme parks. I-4 is the main route to the theme parks and in the greater Orlando area, but it's tricky: It's an east-west highway, but it takes a north-south jog from Kissimmee up through Downtown Orlando to the north. It is also undergoing an interminable period of construction, rendering traffic fairly miserable. There are several other roads that provide alternate routes: International Drive parallels I-4 just to the east and is a long strip of hotels, shopping, restaurants, and other attractions. U.S. Highway 192 (known as Irlo Bronson Memorial Highway in parts) runs east-west, from Walt Disney World Resort in the west through Kissimmee and St. Cloud to the east. Several other local roads—Florida's Turnpike, Central Florida GreeneWay (Highway 417), and Osceola Parkway—are toll roads, so be sure to have cash in the car.

Florida law requires that all drivers carry a valid driver's license and proof of liability insurance. All passengers must wear a seatbelt and children five and younger must be in an approved restraint device/child seat in the back seat. Car headlights must be turned on at dusk; in the rain, headlights must be turned on day or night.

Car Rentals

It is said that Orlando is the world's largest rental-car market, with dozens of companies competing for visitors' dollars. Rental-car companies within Terminal A and Terminal B of Orlando International Airport, near Ground Transportation, Level 1, include Alamo (800/327-9633, www.goalamo.com), Avis (800/831-2847, www.avis.com), Budget (800/527-0700, www.budget.com), Dollar (800/800-4000, www.dollar.com), L&M Car Rental (800/277-5171), and National (800/227-7368, www.nationalcar.com).

Car rental companies off airport property, accessible by free shuttles, include Accessible Minivan Rental (800/308-2503), Anchor Auto Rental (407/438-8996), Bargain Car Rental (407/381-1055), Best Rate Car Rental (407/850-0340), Carl's Rent a Van (407/849-5211), Eagle (407/397-9799), Enterprise (800/325-8007, www.enterprise.com), E-Z Rent-a-Car (800/277-5171), Florida/Continental (800/327-3791), Hertz (800/654-3131, www.hertz.com), Orlando Rental Car (877/599-9227), Payless Car Rental (407/856-5539, www.paylesscarrental.com), Sunshine Rent a Car (407/857-8100), Thrifty (800/367-2277, www.thrifty.com), USA Car Rental (407/240-2323), and U-Save Auto Rental (800/272-8728).

You pay a small premium for the convenience of picking up and dropping off at the airport, and you pay an extra fee if you pick up a car in one city and drop it off in another. Most rental-car companies insist that the driver be at least 21 years old, some even older than that—be sure to have your driver's license and a major credit card (even if you aim to pay cash, they want a credit card for their own peace of mind) with you, or you'll be walking.

Whether to accept a rental agency's insurance coverage and waivers depends on your own car insurance—before leaving home, read your own car policy to determine if it covers you while you are renting a vehicle. Also, some credit cards cover damages to many basic types of rental cars, so it's worth checking into that as well. If you decline the insurance, rental-car companies hold you totally responsible for your rental vehicle if it's damaged or stolen. The rental agency's insurance may add $12–25 per day to your bill.

BY TAXI AND LIMO

The following companies provide car service from the airport, your hotel, or a theme park: Ace Metro/Luxury Cab (407/855-1111), Caesar's Transportation (407/850-1000), Diamond Cab Company (407/523-3333), Dixielimo (407/509-1710, www.dixielimo.com), Magic Touch Limousine (407/477-7724, www.limoorlando.com), Mears Transportation Group (407/423-5566, www.mearstransportation.com), Quicksilver Tours and Transportation (407/299-1434, www.quick-silvertours.com), Star Taxi (407/857-9999), Town and Country Transport (407/828-3035), Yellow Cab/ Checker Cab (407/699-9999).

BY BUS AND TROLLEY

Lynx (hot line 407/841-2279, www.golynx. com) is Orlando's public transportation system, offering stops at area attractions and hotels. Bus fare is $1.25 for adults and $0.50 for students with a valid ID and seniors. Children ages six and younger ride free. Lynx buses depart every 30 minutes from the Orlando International Airport to downtown Orlando and

International Drive between 5:30 A.M. and 11:30 P.M. (less frequently on Sundays and holidays). Bus stops are marked with a paw print of a lynx cat. The downtown Orlando **Lymmo** bus system provides free transit, reaching from the Amway Arena to City Hall. The 11 Lymmo stations are designated by kiosks and the eight Lymmo stops are indicated by a small sign.

Orlando's **Greyhound** (407/292-3440 or 800/231-2222, www.greyhound.com) bus terminal is at 555 North John Young Parkway. While service has gotten spottier in recent years, there are buses to and from Daytona Beach, Ocala, Tampa, and St. Petersburg. Call for schedules.

If traveling by Greyhound is new to you, here's some general information: There are no assigned seats (do not, under any circumstances, take the seats adjacent to the bathroom; it's olfactory suicide), no smoking, no pets, no meal service (but there are regular meal stops so you can jump out and buy something). There are no reservations, so you buy a ticket and show up. Stopovers at any point along the route are permitted if you've paid a regular fare. The driver gives you a notation on your ticket, or a coupon, and you can get back on whenever.

Along International Drive, the **I-Ride Trolley** (866/243-7483, www.iridetrolley.com) runs 8 A.M.–10:30 P.M. Trolley fare is $0.75 ($0.25 for seniors and free for children ages 12 and younger with a paying adult).

BY TRAIN

Amtrak (800/872-7245, www.amtrak.com) serves Orlando with two daily trains originating from New York and Miami with stops in downtown Orlando, Winter Park, Sanford, and Kissimmee, as well as with a triweekly train originating from Los Angeles. Amtrak also offers its popular Auto Train, which transports passengers and their vehicles and features the comfort of bilevel Superliner sleepers, a diner, and a lounge. The Auto Train runs daily between Lorton, Virginia, and Sanford, leaving each town at 4 P.M. and arriving at the destination at 8:30 A.M. the next morning.

Tips for Travelers

FOREIGN TRAVELERS
Visas
Unless you're coming from Canada, you need a valid passport and a tourist vista (a Non-Immigrant Visitors Visa B1, for business, or B2, for recreation). Keep your passport in a safe place, and make a copy of the passport number and other critical information and keep it elsewhere.

Time
The Orlando area is on eastern standard time. Daylight saving time takes place from the second Sunday in March (set clocks ahead one hour) through the first Sunday in November (set clocks back one hour).

Money
U.S. currency looks pretty fancy these days, with watermarks, lots of anticounterfeit devices, and huge heads (in the case of Ben Franklin, not a pretty turn of events), but working with dollars is fairly simple—there's the $1, the $5, the $10, the $20, and, less common, the $50. The $100 bill is very seldom used and very seldom accepted without a lot of scrutiny. (Don't worry; the old, small-head bills are still good.) In coins, one-cent pennies are practically good only for gumball machines and wishing wells, and then there's the five-cent nickel, the 10-cent dime, the 25-cent quarter, as well as the more rare 50-cent piece.

Money can be exchanged at the airport or before you arrive. You may also choose to work in U.S. travelers checks. For the most part, if you have a Visa or MasterCard, put all of your accommodations, restaurant meals, theme park tickets, and attractions expenditures on that—it's an easy way to keep track of how you spent your money on vacation.

Holidays
Banks, post offices, and most government offices are closed on these national holidays: Martin Luther King Jr. Day; President's Day; Memorial Day; Fourth of July; Labor Day; Columbus Day; Veteran's Day; Thanksgiving Day; Christmas Day; and New Year's Day.

Electricity
The United States uses 110–120 volts AC, as opposed to Europe's 220–240 volts. Almost all Orlando hotels will have hair dryers for your use, so leave yours at home. If you have other electrical devices for which you need a converter, bring one from home.

Tipping
Service-sector workers expect a tip—it's only in name a "gratuity," meaning an elective gift. It's how they make the bulk of their money. Fifteen percent is pretty much the minimum, whether it's at a restaurant, a hair salon, or in a taxi. Tip bellhops about $1 per bag; tip the valet parker $1–2 every time you get your car. Tip $3–5 per week for maid service in a hotel. Tip a good waiter or bartender 18–20 percent. But here's what's tricky: If the hairdresser or tour operator is the owner of the business, a tip can sometimes be seen as an insult. Keep lots of small bills at the ready for all these tips, but don't ever tip at a theme park, the movies, a retail shop, at the gas station, or at the theater, ballet, or opera.

Metric Conversions
The United States had a failed attempt at going metric in the 1970s. So, you need to know that one foot equals 0.305 meters; one mile equals 1.6 kilometers; and one pound equals 0.45 kilograms. Converting temperatures is a little trickier: To convert Fahrenheit to Centigrade temperatures, subtract 32 and then multiply by 0.555. Got it? Weights are measured in ounces, pounds, and tons; gas is measured in gallons (about 3.70 liters).

TRAVELERS WITH DISABILITIES
Parking
Out-of-state and foreign disabled parking per-

STAY GREEN

Spend a little time in Orlando and you can't help but notice the vast sprawl, the huge swaths of concrete and steel, the parks' use of electricity, the hundreds of thousands of cars gobbling up fossil fuel – it's a city in which eco-pigginess is unavoidable. The Department of Environmental Protection's **Florida Green Lodging Certification Program** has one easy way to assuage your conscience. In an effort to encourage the lodging industry to conserve and protect Florida's natural resources, it has launched www.FloridaGreenLodging.org. Those who like to patronize environmentally sound businesses can visit the site to see which Orlando properties have carried out waste reduction, energy and water conservation, and indoor air-quality improvement plans.

For instance, scroll through the Orlando properties and discover that Disney's Animal Kingdom Lodge features low-flush commodes and low-flow faucets and showerheads in guest rooms and automatic flush commodes in public areas; implements a linen-reuse program; uses reclaimed water for irrigation and uses xeriscape where possible; recycles office paper, cardboard, plastic, aluminum, steel, newspaper, food waste, toner cartridges, plastic six-pack rings, and glossy brochures; and more.

The site also gives tips for hotel guests interested in being environmentally conscious during a Florida stay:

- Report noisy, leaky faucets and toilets.

- Turn off the TV when leaving the room.

- Reduce the air-conditioning/heater when leaving the room.

- Turn off water while brushing your teeth.

- Take short showers.

- Fill the sink basin to shave.

- Participate in the linens and towels reuse program.

- Close the window drapes when leaving the room.

- Turn off the lights when leaving the room.

- Ask your hotel where to recycle newspaper, cans, and bottles, or use the website's Earth 911 locator for the area where you are visiting.

- If recycling is unavailable, consider taking your recyclable materials with you and recycle them at home.

- Leave unused amenities in the rooms for the next occupants' use.

- Provide feedback to the hotel about its environmental efforts.

mits are accepted as long as they are prominently displayed in the windshield of your vehicle. All major theme parks provide designated handicapped parking areas.

Wheelchair Rentals

Conventional and electric wheelchairs are available for rent at all major theme parks (prices and terms listed in each chapter). Park maps indicate which rides are accessible to wheelchairs and which require visitors to be reseated in a ride chair, and each park offers a booklet describing services and facilities for those with disabilities. All public buses in the Orlando area have a hydraulic lift and restraining belts for two wheelchairs.

In addition, the following companies rent wheelchairs and motorized scooters: AA Tourist Rentals (www.orlandoscooterrentals.com, 800/941-4662), Care Medical Wheelchairs Equipment (407/856-2273 or 800/741-2282, www.caremedicalequipment.com), and Walker Medical and Mobility Products (407/518-6000 or 888/726-6837, www.walkermobility.com).

Most major car-rental companies have hand-controlled cars in their fleets (give them 24- to 48 hours' notice to find one), but if you want to rent an accessible van, call one of the following companies: Accessible Vans of America (800/862-7475, www.vanconinc. com), Wheelchair Getaways (800/242-4990, www.wheelchairgetaways.com), Rainbow Wheels of Florida (800/910-8267, www.rainbowwheels.com), and Wheelchair Minivan Rentals (800/308-2503, www.discountmobilityusa.com).

Hearing-Impaired Travelers

Telecommunication Devices for the Deaf (TDD/TTY) are provided at all parks. At Walt Disney World Resort call 407/827-5141; at Universal Orlando Resort call 407/363-8265; at SeaWorld Orlando call 407/363-2617; and at Kennedy Space Center call 321/454-4198.

Vision-Impaired Travelers

Guest Relations at each theme park provides free audio guides to sight-impaired visitors (with a refundable deposit), and Braille guide maps are available at all parks. The **American Foundation for the Blind** (800/232-5463, www.afb.org) provides information on traveling with a seeing-eye dog, but each park has facilities for the care of seeing-eye dogs.

Access Guides

You may want to consider buying a copy of **Wheelchairs on the Go: Accessible Fun in Florida** (727/573-0434, www.wheelchairsonthego.com, $19.95 plus $3 shipping), Florida's only access guide for visitors who use canes, walkers, or wheelchairs. The 424-page paperback covers wheelchair-accessible and barrier-free accommodations, tourist attractions, and activities across the state.

Society for Accessible Travel and Hospitality (561/361-0017, www.sath.org) provides recommendations and resources to help travelers with disabilities plan their vacations, and **Able Trust** (888/838-2253, www.abletrust.org) offers helpful links to disability resources throughout Florida.

TRAVELING WITH CHILDREN

While Orlando is literally made for children, they nonetheless present certain challenges.

Accommodations

Many local on- and off-property hotels offer a kids-stay-free enticement, or a kids-eat-free deal, or both. Make sure to verify the age limits and particulars before booking. The benefits of staying on-property at a Disney hotel, a Universal hotel, or a theme park partner hotel are myriad for kids: With theme dinners, character decor, and kids' activities, your hotel stay becomes an extension of your theme park experience. In addition, they offer free transportation to the parks, along with perks such as Express Plus passes at Universal or getting to go an hour early or stay late at one of the Disney parks.

That said, the very inexpensive motels along U.S. Highway 192 in Kissimmee almost all have heated swimming pools and easy access to minigolf, fast food, and other inexpensive entertainment that may defray the cost of a multiday Orlando visit. Spend one day at Disney, the next day romping around Kissimmee, the next day at Universal, and so on—mix it up a little. A vacation-house rental makes good financial sense for large families, allowing for meals to be made at "home" while kids swim, watch a movie, or veg out. Downtime is that much more pleasant when you have a real living room, kitchen, patio, private pool, or game room to spread out in.

Driving

In high season, the free transportation to and from the park (shuttles, buses, monorails, whatever) is extremely busy. This can prolong your arrival and departure each day by hours—not ideal with small, tired children. Renting a car and parking in the theme park lots gives you the flexibility to leave early, park-hop, or accommodate a nap schedule.

If you're driving with children, remember that all children under 40 pounds (18 kilograms) must ride in an FAA-approved child restraint system. Visit www.buckleupflorida. com or call 877/KID-SEAT (877/543-7328) for more information on obtaining a car seat in Orlando.

For smaller kids, always take a change of

underpants or diapers in the car with you rather than in the trunk with the luggage. For older kids, encourage a layering approach to dressing—when one child is warm, peeling off another layer may be preferable to making everyone endure the car air conditioner.

Packing

If an ounce of prevention is worth a pound of cure, then travel light. Beyond the obvious notion of taking only what is essential (buy toiletries at your final destination, pack clothing that mixes and matches to perform double duty), there are more subtle ways to travel light—and smart. In an effort to cut a few ounces, don't pack your whole address book. Print out a single sheet of phone numbers and addresses you might need. In case your luggage is lost, this valuable book is tucked safely at home. In a similar vein, email yourself your travel itinerary, hotel confirmation numbers, and important telephone numbers for easy access in case your luggage or wallet is lost or stolen.

Then before you pack your bags, think about it: How many black carry-ons with wheels do you count spinning on the luggage carousel? Make sure your bags are personalized with big, colorful luggage tags or easily spotted bows. Think of giving each family member a tag or bow in the same pattern but in different colors, so you can distinguish between family members' bags at a glance. Because travelers liberally interpret what constitutes a "carry-on," consider checking all luggage through to Orlando, bringing to the cabin only the creature comforts that make for fun travel—a neck-rest ring (remember, most airlines have done away with blankets and pillows), a healthy snack, your iPod, and a special treat. Your local party goods and dollar stores are perfect places to find inexpensive new forms of amusement for traveling by plane, train, bus, or car. Wrap each new toy as a gift to make the excitement last. Caveat: Do not buy travel games with small pieces sure to get lost immediately under the seat. And for the sake of fellow travelers, veto choices that have wheels, anything that is easily made airborne, or anything that makes a noise or sings a song.

When traveling to Orlando with a baby, consider using the service **Babies Travel Lite** (888/450-5483, www.babiestravellite.com), which will deliver diapers, formula, food, and other baby gear and products to your hotel room door. It offers more than 1,000 name-brand baby products, including organic baby food and formula.

Safety

Families traveling internationally will certainly have their passports, but even families traveling domestically should have pictures of all family members. A picture is worth a thousand words when trying to describe a temporarily lost child to airport personnel or a theme park employee. Make sure each child has your cell phone number attached to him or her in some way (ballpoint pen on the inner arm is a tidy solution); bringing multiple cell phones or walkie-talkies assures groups will find each other during a day at the park. Dressing families alike, while sadistic, is an easy way to keep on eye on everyone at a crowded theme park.

SOLO TRAVELERS

Many of the attractions in Orlando are frankly more fun with a buddy—it's not nearly as satisfying to squeal and whoop on the rides by yourself—but there are advantages to traveling alone. Many of the theme parks have a "single rider" line, which saves you serious time in long lines. You may zip right in to fill an empty spot, even on the coveted first or last rows of major thrill rides. Otherwise, Orlando is a very safe, clean, and unintimidating place to be by oneself. Downtown Disney, CityWalk, and numerous other nightlife destinations make it an easy place to meet people, too. Because Orlando is the number two convention city in the country, packs of business travelers are often roaming the land looking for fun.

GAY AND LESBIAN TRAVELERS

Miami's South Beach and Key West are clearly the locus of lots of gay travel merriment and enthusiasm, but Orlando's no slouch. Every year since 1991, the weekend that includes the first Saturday in June has been designated **Gay Day** at Disney. It used to be held strictly at Magic Kingdom, but in recent years the venues around Orlando have included Islands of Adventure and other parks and attractions. The weekend tends to draw upward of 150,000 gays and lesbians to the city, with an official list of activities enumerated on the www.gayday.com website.

A gay landmark worth a visit, the historic **Parliament House** is the premiere all-gay resort in the entire Southeast, with 130 hotel rooms on Rock Lake in downtown Orlando. Having just undergone a major renovation and management change, the hotel's six clubs and bars, a notable female impersonation show, lakeside beach, and a full-service restaurant draw regular visitors from all over the world. The oldest gay-owned and operated bar in Orlando is the **Full Moon Saloon** (500 N. Orange Blossom Tr., 407/648-8725, noon–2 A.M. daily), right next to The Parliament House. **Southern Nights** (375 S. Bumby Ave., 407/898-0424) is another longtime local favorite, just north of the Orlando Executive Airport, while the **Karma Bar** (8723 International Dr., Orlando 407/903-9052) is the city's newest gay club.

For a list of gay and lesbian bars and nightclubs or other gay-friendly venues, or just to get oriented within your orientation, contact the **Gay, Lesbian and Bisexual Community Services of Central Florida** (407/425-4527, www.glbcc.org), for welcome packets and calendars of events, or the **International Gay and Lesbian Travel Association** (800/448-8550, www.iglta.org, to join is $150 annually) for a list of gay-friendly accommodations, tours, and attractions.

TRAVELING WITH PETS

More and more hotel chains are accepting people's canine companions (other pets, from potbellied pigs to naked mole rats, are a harder sell). Best Western, Motel 6, Holiday Inn, and even swishy chains such as Four Seasons often accept pet guests for an additional fee. To get good information, pick up a copy of *The Dog Lover's Companion to Florida* by Sally Deneen and Robert McClure or visit www.petswelcome.com.

Flying with your pet to and from Florida can be problematic, as most major airlines have an embargo against pets as checked baggage during the warmer months (any day in which the outdoor temperature might reach 90 degrees), and even for small pets that fit under an airplane seat, the airlines allow only one pet per cabin. The ASPCA strongly discourages pets as checked baggage. Many vets also discourage sedating pets during a flight. If you do choose to fly with a pet, always make reservations for the animal; have your leash and collar easily accessible (you must take the pet out of its travel container to pass through security); and make sure the pet kennel has your home address and phone number on it.

Dogs are prohibited on many walking trails, on beaches, and in many parks in Florida. All of the theme parks prohibit pets in the parks (except for service animals) but provide kennel services by the day for dogs and in some cases cats. See each chapter for specifics). Usually, pet owners must bring their own food and be willing to return to the kennel to walk the dog at a couple of points during the day. It is never permissible or advisable to leave a pet in a locked car in Florida. Daytime temperatures, even in the cooler months, can be fatal to animals. Also be aware that in much of Central Florida's wilderness areas, poisonous snakes and alligators pose more of a threat to your dog than to you.

Information and Services

HEALTH AND SAFETY

In a real emergency, always dial 911, and each of the theme parks has on-site first aid and emergency services. To be really prepared, before a trip call or log on to the Centers for Disease Control and Prevention (800/311-3435, www.cdc.gov) for information on health hazards by region. Should an unexpected illness or emergency arise, you'll find convenient medical services at several nearby 24-hour walk-in centers in one of several nationally ranked hospitals. Many hysterical travel articles suggest getting medical travel insurance. If you have insurance, though, that's probably all the coverage you'll need.

Hospitals

Florida Hospital Orlando has several locations, each with emergency services. Its main campus is at 601 East Rollins Street, 407/303-5600. Florida Hospital Kissimmee can be found at 2450 North Orange Blossom Trail, Kissimmee, 407/846-4343; and Florida Hospital/Celebration Health is at 400 Celebration Place, Celebration, 407/764-4000.

Orlando Regional Medical Center (1414 Kuhl Ave., 321/841-5111) is a 581-bed tertiary care center on the downtown Orlando Regional Healthcare campus. It's the only Level 1 Trauma Center in Central Florida and is one of the state's largest providers of intensive care.

Diabetic travelers can call the American Diabetes Association (800/342-2383) to get a list of hospitals that provide services to diabetics, or log onto Dialysis Finder at www.dialysis-finder.com.

Sunburn and Mosquitoes

Barring an unforeseen emergency, you want to do what you can to stay healthy during a visit here. The sun is probably the biggest underestimated foe. A full day of walking in a theme park means sunburn can be wicked, so be sure to slather on sunscreen with at least an SPF of 30. Because you'll be in and out of water,

and sweating in the steamy humidity, opt for waterproof or water-resistant cream such as Banana Boat Sport Sunblock Lotion (waterproof/sweatproof, SPF 30). Even better, one of my favorite finds, Avon, now makes an SPF 30 Skin So Soft cream with a DEET-free pesticide in it to cope with another big bully, the mosquitoes. DEET-based products are more effective in preventing mosquitoes from landing on you, but I hate to have that poison sitting on my skin all day. Lather up with the Avon product, and then apply a DEET-based spray only if the mosquitoes are bad. Mosquitoes aren't particularly fierce in Central Florida unless you're fishing or boating on a lake, especially near dusk.

COMMUNICATIONS AND MEDIA
Mail

Mail service within the United States generally takes 2–3 days, except during the Christmas holiday season when all bets are off. Within Florida post takes about two days to get anywhere (you speed things up if you use the full nine-digit zip code).

Telephone and Fax

Each urban area in Florida has its own area code of three numbers that must be dialed if calling from outside. For example, the area code in Orlando is 407 and in Tampa it's 813, but you needn't dial it if you're calling within the area code. If you're dialing another area code, you must first dial 1, then the three-digit area code, and then the seven-digit phone number. If calling from abroad, the international code for the United States is 1. Within the United States, the 800, 888, 877, and 866 area codes are toll free, meaning they cost you nothing to dial.

Since the telephone industry was deregulated, calling long distance from pay phones can be a total crapshoot, costing a different amount depending on the carrier. Public pay phone pricing is no longer regulated by the Florida Public Service Commission, but prices should be clearly marked, with local calls usually $0.35. If you don't have a cell phone that works in Florida, you're better off getting a prepaid international calling card. Hotels also charge by the call, so making calling-card calls is often more cost effective. Cell phone service in Orlando is generally very good.

Most hotels and motels will send/receive a fax for a fee, and multipage documents can be sent at any Kinko's shop.

Internet Access

This is changing so fast in Orlando that it's probably fruitless to weigh in. Even budget hotels offer free in-room wireless Internet now, and many low-tech coffee shops and cafés sport the "Wi-Fi Hotspots" sticker in the window for wireless Internet connections. Even if you're not packing a laptop on your trip, you can check web-based email from almost any hotel or motel, often for no fee.

Newspapers and Magazines

The big metro daily in the area is the *Orlando Sentinel,* widely available and with regional versions in different parts of the greater Orlando area. Its online version, www.orlandosentinel.com, is also a good resource for local information and restaurant reviews. The city's free alternative paper, the *Orlando Weekly* (407/377-0400) is published every Thursday and available at 1,300 locations across Orange, Osceola, and Seminole Counties. It has an online version at www.orlandoweekly.com, good for cultural events and evening activities. Also published every Thursday, the *Orlando Times* (407/841-3710) has published African American news since 1975. To get a feel for local business news, the *Orlando Business Journal* (407/649-8470) is one of 41 business newspapers owned by American City Business Journals, its online version (orlando.bizjournals.com/Orlando) providing daily business news updates.

Visitor magazines are myriad in Orlando, from the familiar *Where Magazine* to *Guest Informant* and other in-room publications. Locals turn to *Orlando Magazine,* a glossy lifestyle magazine that has covered arts, dining, travel, entertainment, shopping, health care, and real estate since it was founded in 1946. Visitors might also want to pick up a copy of the locally produced *Florida Monthly* (407/816-9596) or *Florida Travel and Life Magazine* (407/571-4794) at a local Barnes & Noble.

Radio and Television

Nearly every hotel, motel, and house rental in Orlando has cable TV with scores of channels to click your way through. On-property hotels at Disney broadcast a preponderance of Disney "infomercial" kinds of programming along with Disney Channel. To get you oriented with local TV, WESH Channel 2 is the NBC affiliate; WKMG Channel 6 is the CBS affiliate; WFTV Channel 9 is the ABC affiliate; WMFE Channel 24 is the PBS station; and WOFL Channel 35 is the FOX affiliate. Channel 21 is a local Spanish-language channel, and Channels 45, 52, and 55 are local religious stations.

A huge number of local radio stations means most of your programming tastes will be accommodated: WPYO 95.3 FM is Top 40; WPCV 97.5 FM is country music; head to WJRR 101.1 FM for rock; WLOQ 103.1 FM for smooth jazz; WTKS 104.1 FM for talk radio; and WOMX 105.1 FM for that ubiquitous mix of '80s and '90s pop. If you are an NPR junkie, you'll find two stations, WUCF 89.9 FM and WMFE 90.7 FM. On the local radio dial, the kids will point you to 990 AM for Radio Disney; for classic rock turn to WHTZ 96.5 FM; for a little sports radio head to WHOO 1080 AM; and for Central Florida's major country station, spin the dial to WWKA 92.3 FM.

MAPS AND TOURIST INFORMATION

Maps

Visit Florida (www.flausa.com) sends a great map of the whole state with its "Visit Florida" literature. (And, as always, AAA members should raid the free-map smorgasbord that is their divine right.) The state's tourism office also has several welcome stations near Florida's border (one north of Pensacola on I-10, one off Highway 231, one in Tallahassee, one in Jennings off I-75, and one on the state's east coast on I-95) that give out good state and regional maps.

The Orlando Travel and Visitors Bureau website (www.orlandoinfo.com) is an invaluable resource from which you can download local maps and order a free planning package that includes a Visitors Guide and a free Orlando Preferred Visitor Magicard, with up to $500 in savings at local attractions. (This package is sent only to addresses in the United States and Canada.) In addition, you can book hotels and theme park tickets through this site (or by calling 800/972-3304), sometimes with discounts on special packages.

Tourist Offices

The Orlando/Orange County Convention and Visitors Bureau also has an Official Visitor Center (8723 International Dr., Ste. 101, 407/363-5872), stocked with helpful personnel as well as literature and coupons. Kissimmee's visitor center (407/944-2427, info@floridakiss.com) is at 1925 East Irlo Bronson Memorial Highway, near Florida's Turnpike Exit 244 (from the north), Exit 242 (from the south).

Cameras and Photography

With regular 35mm film, developing film along the way is a snap—many of the theme parks even have film development services within the park. Otherwise, most big drugstores offer one-hour service. If you've gone digital, don't worry about photo development until you get home (uploading onto www.kodakgallery.com is a cheap way to get prints made and to digitally share your trip with everyone). That said, you need to bring an adequate amount of memory for the length of your trip. Digital memory cards are not affected by airport security X-rays, so bring extras. And don't forget extra batteries and your battery charger.

RESOURCES

Suggested Reading

DISNEY, THE MAN

Gabler, Neal. *Walt Disney: The Triumph of the American Imagination.* New York: Knopf, 2006. Written by the first writer to have complete access to the Disney archives, this is an unvarnished recounting of the man's life, pre- and post-Mouse. It's not one of the many glowing tributes to the man, but it's not a crafty smear campaign either. It's largely about the early days of the studio and less about the theme parks: "Even though Walt could neither animate, nor write, nor direct, he was the undisputed power at the studio." The book goes a long way to discrediting rumors of Disney's deep anti-Semitism, but it explores his anticommunist leanings. The writing is lively and there's lots of insider dirt about his disgruntled employees.

Selden, Bernice. *The Story of Walt Disney: Maker of Magical Worlds.* New York: Yearling, 1989. For kids in grades 4–7 (closer to fourth, if you ask me), this is a 96-page chapter book (a book with chapters for intermediate readers) biography of the man, with a section of black-and-white photographs. He's not breathlessly lionized, and the writing goes a long way to make him a living, breathing human being, equally split between his youth, the animation studio, and his theme parks and other work.

GUIDEBOOKS

More than 200 titles are in print that deal with vacationing in Orlando. Fodor's, Frommer's, Lonely Planet, Rand McNally, the Dummies series—every publisher wants a piece of the juicy pie that is the single greatest tourist destination in the world. What follows is a list of those that really stand out or offer special features.

Goldsbury, Cara. *The Luxury Guide to Walt Disney World Resort: How to Get the Most out of the Best Disney Has to Offer.* Guilford, CT: Globe Pequot, 2005. A few years ago this would have been a preposterous title, or just a very short book—more like a pamphlet. But, as the Hasidic rapper Matisyahu might remind us, things that seem oxymoronic might not be if you wait around long enough. A recent influx of luxury resort properties, celebrity chef–driven restaurants, spas, and legendary golf courses has made Orlando a luxury destination. Goldsbury's message gets watered down slightly by the inclusion of lots of less luxurious spots, but she shows real food knowledge.

Monaghan, Kelly. *The Other Orlando, 4th Edition: What to Do When You've Done Disney and Universal.* Branford, CT: The Intrepid Traveler, 2007. People come to Orlando again and again, for work or pleasure, and they need to know what *else* there is to do. The writing is lively in this book that explores the cultural allures as well as the natural treasures of Central Florida.

Safro, Jill, ed. *Birnbaum's Walt Disney World 2007.* New York: Disney Enterprises, 2007. This is the top-selling Disney guide. Why? Because it is produced by Disney and is the only guide sold inside the parks. That said, longtime editor Steve Birnbaum and his colleagues don't just parrot the Disney party line on everything. The book is descriptive about all four parks, hotels, water parks, restaurants, and shopping destinations, but it also recommends real standout attractions. The book's organization and aesthetic is meant to be appealing and useful for the whole family, with tips for teens and fun illustrations and photos. There's a second guide, *Birnbaum's Walt Disney World for Kids, By Kids 2007,* that has much of the same information but with goofier graphics.

Sehlinger, Bob, and Len Testa. *The Unofficial Guide to Walt Disney World 2007.* Hoboken, NJ: Jon Wiley and Sons, 2007. How many people need 800 pages on navigating Walt Disney World Resort and environs? Evidently quite a few. It's an exhaustively researched tome with zillions of foot soldiers in the trenches zapping emails to the editors. This is a great book if you aim to schedule every moment of your Orlando visit—if you plan your days a little more loosely, the military-like tactical charts and touring plans may give you a tension headache. Sehlinger and Katie Brandon also do a book called *Beyond Disney: The Unofficial Guide to Universal, SeaWorld, and the Best of Central Florida,* but it covers much of the same material as the Walt Disney World—focused book. *The Unofficial Guide* also hosts a website called www.touringplans.com, where visitors can use a variety of tools to help plan an Orlando trip.

Wills, Deb, and Debra Martin Koma. *Pass-Porter's Walt Disney World for Your Special Needs: The Take-Along Travel Guide and Planner.* Ann Arbor, MI: Passporter Travel Press, 2005. The woman responsible for Allearsnet. com (see *Internet Resources*) has written a book that is targeted at all the various special-needs visitors at the theme parks. And she means all the special needs: Keeping kosher? Mobility issues? In your last trimester of pregnancy? The book has 24 special-needs categories with very practical, forthright advice for navigating Walt Disney World. The same company does a book on "treasure hunts" at Walt Disney World Resort, with more that 100 different hunts that ferret out the Imagineers' most subtle additions to the parks.

THE NATURAL WORLD IN CENTRAL FLORIDA

Friend, Sandra, and Johnny Molloy. *The Hiking Trails of Florida's National Forests, Parks, and Preserves.* Gainesville, FL: University Press of Florida, 2007. These two nature authors have more than a dozen titles between them, many of them centered around hiking, canoeing, and kayaking in Florida. This particular volume covers Ocala National Forest, Canaveral National Seashore, and other destinations within an easy drive of Orlando's theme parks. A day of paddling or tramping about in nature is often the antidote to too much of the Mouse—this book rates trails and gives trailhead directions and other practical information. Sandra Friend also runs the www.floridatrail.org website, home of the Florida Trail Association and portal for information on the Florida Trail, one of eight National Scenic Trails in the United States.

Schultz, Ken. *Bass Madness: Bigmouths, Big Money, and Big Dreams at the Bassmaster Classic.* Hoboken, NJ: John Wiley and Sons, 2006. These days, the ESPN-owned organization B.A.S.S. has more than 500,000 members. Bass enthusiasm is at an absolute frenzy in Central Florida, focused around Lake Toho. This book is an entertaining inside look at the country's most prestigious fishing competition, the anglers who reel 'em in, and the media who amp up the drama of it all.

ORLANDO AND THEME PARK HISTORY

Imagineers. *Walt Disney Imagineering: A Behind the Dreams Look at Making the Magic Real.* New York: Disney Editions, 1998. It's just one among many of the books the Disney Imagineers have produced on the magic behind the scenes. This particular book features the work of these artists and engineers, broken up by department and projects, with sketches from Disney films and construction photographs. The Imagi-neers also have *The Imagineering Field Guide to Magic Kingdom at Walt Disney World,* another one for Epcot, and then a couple of how-to books on tapping into your creativity for the would-be Imagineers.

Rajtar, Steve. *A Guide to Historic Orlando.* Charleston, SC: The History Press, 2006. So much of the Orlando visitors see is slick and new. This slightly slow-paced guide by a local historian shows historic pictures and gives a bit of background to the area pretheme park. It lovingly describes Orlando's neighborhoods and districts with a street-by-street guide.

Internet Resources

GENERAL ORLANDO INFORMATION

International Drive
www.internationaldriveorlando.com

So many of the also-ran and half-day attractions are strewn along the commerce-heavy stretch of I-Drive that it's worth considering bunking down here. It's also a locus of much dining and nightlife activity in Orlando. This website is the official come-hither marketing effort, but it gives trolley service information along with an accommodation-search function.

Kissimmee-St. Cloud
Convention and Visitors Bureau
www.floridakiss.com

The town closest to Walt Disney World Resort and Lake Buena Vista, Kissimmee has lots of deals on hotels, motels, and house rentals. This site has an easy-to-use accommodations search function, a section on travel deals, and a free trip-planning kit.

Orlando/Orange County
Convention and Visitors Bureau
www.orlandoinfo.com

You'll get the scoop on nightlife, recreation, arts and culture, and shopping. The best thing about the site for Orlando visitors is the free Magicard you can download and print from the site or request online. The card offers savings on a variety of area attractions, accommodations, restaurants, and shops. Not Walt Disney World Resort, Universal, or SeaWorld, but a lot of the second-tier attractions offer two-for-one discounts that can really make a difference in your total vacation cost.

Orlando Sentinel, Destination Orlando
www.orlandosentinel.com/travel/ destinations/orlando

The local paper of record has a section of its website devoted to those vacationing in the area. It offers discount tickets (not a particularly good deal, as they are a mere $3–4 off gate prices—you'd do better going to the theme parks' websites and buying web-ticket deals directly from them online) and also a range of vacation-planning tools (budgeting, ride height charts, park hours). The main site of the *Orlando Sentinel,* www.orlandosentinel .com, will give you local news and sports coverage. The local alternative weekly offers better arts, music, and movie features at www .orlandoweekly.com.

Visit Florida
www.visitflorida.com

The tourism arm of the state of Florida adopts a very evenhanded approach to promoting Orlando. Walt Disney World Resort is just one among many options in the area, listed right alongside tiny Eatonville, one of the first communities in the United States to be incorporated by African Americans. The site has a bunch of smarmy podcasts, which you can quickly disable to enjoy the couple of dozen informative articles on attractions and destinations in the greater Orlando area. One of the best features is an easy-to-use access-at-a-glance element for travelers with disabilities visiting the theme parks.

OFFICIAL THEME PARK INFORMATION

Walt Disney World Resort
http://disneyworld.disney.go.com

This website drives me absolutely batty—every single page has its own theme song and video clip, making loading and navigating extremely frustrating. Also, the interactive maps don't function properly on many computers and there doesn't seem to be a way to print out the park maps so you can strategize at home. Still, it's got all the info on hours, operational rides, prices and special packages, the theme parks, hotels, restaurants, and more. Other elements of Walt Disney World have their own sites: www.disneycruise.com, www.disney honeymoons.com, www.disneyweddings .com, www.celebrationfl.com, and www.disney worldsports.com.

Universal Orlando
www.universalorlando.com

This is exactly what you'd expect—all the information and ticket prices (and a slight Internet-only discount) at the two Universal parks, the three hotels, and CityWalk.

SeaWorld Orlando
www.seaworld.com

Here you can also find all the information you'd expect about showtimes, ticket prices, and vacation packages at SeaWorld Orlando, with short video clips of the many shows. Discovery Cove has its own website at www.discovery cove.com, with short videos of all the main attractions. You can buy tickets on the site, but they are for a specific date, unlike tickets at SeaWorld, Universal, or Walt Disney World.

UNOFFICIAL THEME PARK INFORMATION

All Ears Net–Deb's Unofficial Walt Disney World Information Guide
www.allearsnet.com

One of the two best unofficial theme park sites out there, it's especially focused on Walt Disney World Resort, with very up-to-date information about rides and attractions, special events, and Disney news. The main force behind the site is a Disney enthusiast named Deb Wills, who started the project in 1996. At this point it has thousands of pages of archives and photos and a huge tips database, and she does a good job of keeping close tabs on openings and closures at the parks. The site also includes helpful information about non-Disney theme parks and other things to do in Orlando. There's a corresponding free weekly e-newsletter called "All Ears" that she puts out. It's also where to look for information on MouseFest, an annual gathering of maniacal Disney fans.

Hidden Mickeys
www.hiddenmickeys.org

This is a phenomenon that can best be explained as birding for Mouse fans. It started as an insider gag among the Imagineers—hiding Mickey's likeness somewhere in the design of an attraction or in its decorations. Diehard Disney fans scour the parks for these hidden Mickeys, keeping logs of all they've seen and trying to outdo each other with sightings of obscure ones. This website is devoted to sharing, crowing about, and otherwise discussing where people have seen the head-and-ears silhouette of Mickey (one big ball with two ear balls balanced on top). All Ears Net also keeps a running list of Hidden Mickeys in the theme parks and beyond.

Laughing Place
www.laughingplace.com

It's another unofficial resource for all things Disney. It's a little clunky to use, and I don't trust its opinions quite as much as the other two listed above, but it's a good clearinghouse for information with special-interest discussion boards.

Mousesavers
www.mousesavers.com

It's a hodgepodge of discounts on Disney—tickets, guidebooks, coupons for Disney merchandise, hotels, and vacation packages are all listed with click-throughs. Some of the deals are exclusive to this site; it also offers deals on Universal and SeaWorld.

Theme Park Insider
www.themeparkinsider.com

Robert Niles's Theme Park Insider is just about as good, with consumers themselves writing in about the various parks and attractions. The site has a wonderful discussion board where you can voice your questions or opinions, and it has a safety data section in which you can as-certain a particular attraction's accident record. Although it's not Orlando-specific, Disney's four parks, SeaWorld Orlando, and Universal Orlando Resort are exhaustively covered. This is the site to visit if you want to substantiate a rumor that Universal is going to install a Harry Potter attraction (the answer is February 6, 2007). Some people swear by the site jimhill-media.com for insider Disney information, but to me it seems so insider as to be unintelligible to the theme park rookie. He might have better contacts, though, because his take on the Harry Potter question as of February 6, 2007, was more emphatic than "it's now Universal that appears to have the Snitch."

Unofficial Imagineering Site
www.imagineering.org

If you get really into looking at the original sketches in the Imagineers books listed above, there are loads more good ones at this site, which is not in any way connected with Walt Disney World Resort. Nor is this one, but www.walt quest.com has lots of good information about Mr. Disney's ideas for the Experimental Prototype Community of Tomorrow (EPCOT). The same goes for www.waltopia.com, which has lots of fun historical documents.

Index

Acknowledgments

This book makes reference to various Disney copyrighted characters, trademarks, marks, and registered marks owned by The Walt Disney Company and Disney Enterprises, Inc. including:

The Boneyard®
Conservation Station®
Discovery Island Trails™
DisneyQuest®
Disney's Animal Kingdom® Theme Park
Disney's Wide World of Sports® Complex
Downtown Disney®
Epcot®
Expedition Everest™
Fantasyland®
FASTPASS
Frontierland
Indiana Jones™ Epic Stunt Spectacular
It's Tough to be a Bug!®
Kali River Rapids®
Kilimanjaro Safaris®
La Nouba™
Magic Kingdom® Park
Maharajah Jungle Trek®
Pangani Forest Exploration Trail®
Primeval Whirl®
Rock 'n Roller Coaster®
Soarin'™
Space Mountain®
Stitch's Great Escape! ™
Tomorrowland®
The Twilight Zone Tower of Terror™
Tree of Life® Attraction
Walt Disney
Walt Disney World® Resort

www.moon.com

For helpful advice on planning a trip, visit www.moon.com for the **TRAVEL PLANNER** and get access to useful travel strategies and valuable information about great places to visit. When you travel with Moon, expect an experience that is uncommon and truly unique.

HANDBOOKS | METRO | OUTDOORS | LIVING ABROAD

MAP SYMBOLS

▭▭▭	Expressway	**◖**	Highlight	✗	Airfield	⚲	Golf Course
▭▭▭	Primary Road	○	City/Town	✈	Airport	**P**	Parking Area
▭▭▭	Secondary Road	◉	State Capital	▲	Mountain	▰	Archaeological Site
▭▭▭	Unpaved Road	✪	National Capital	✦	Unique Natural Feature	▮	Church
- - - -	Trail	★	Point of Interest			▯	Gas Station
··········	Ferry	•	Accommodation	⋗	Waterfall	◌	Glacier
⊢—⊢—	Railroad	▼	Restaurant/Bar	▲	Park	▱	Mangrove
▭▭▭	Pedestrian Walkway	▪	Other Location	**T**	Trailhead	▱	Reef
▥▥▥	Stairs	⋀	Campground	✗	Skiing Area	▱	Swamp

CONVERSION TABLES

°C = (°F – 32) / 1.8
°F = (°C x 1.8) + 32
1 inch = 2.54 centimeters (cm)
1 foot = 0.304 meters (m)
1 yard = 0.914 meters
1 mile = 1.6093 kilometers (km)
1 km = 0.6214 miles
1 fathom = 1.8288 m
1 chain = 20.1168 m
1 furlong = 201.168 m
1 acre = 0.4047 hectares
1 sq km = 100 hectares
1 sq mile = 2.59 square km
1 ounce = 28.35 grams
1 pound = 0.4536 kilograms
1 short ton = 0.90718 metric ton
1 short ton = 2,000 pounds
1 long ton = 1.016 metric tons
1 long ton = 2,240 pounds
1 metric ton = 1,000 kilograms
1 quart = 0.94635 liters
1 US gallon = 3.7854 liters
1 Imperial gallon = 4.5459 liters
1 nautical mile = 1.852 km

°FAHRENHEIT   °CELSIUS

230 — 110
220 —
210 — 100 WATER BOILS
200 —
190 — 90
180 — 80
170 —
160 — 70
150 —
140 — 60
130 —
120 — 50
110 —
100 — 40
90 — 30
80 —
70 — 20
60 —
50 — 10
40 —
30 — 0 WATER FREEZES
20 —
10 — -10
0 —
-10 — -20
-20 — -30
-30 —
-40 — -40

MOON WALT DISNEY WORLD & ORLANDO

Avalon Travel Publishing
a member of the Perseus Book Group
1400 65th Street, Suite 250
Emeryville, CA 94608, USA
www.moon.com

Editor: Sabrina Young
Series Manager: Kathryn Ettinger
Acquisitions Manager: Rebecca K. Browning
Copy Editor: Karen Bleske
Graphics Coordinator: Stefano Boni
Cover Designer: Stefano Boni
Production Coordinator: Darren Alessi
Map Editor: Kevin Anglin
Cartographers: Kat Bennett, Suzanne Service
Cartography Director: Mike Morgenfeld
Indexer: Jean Mooney

ISBN-10: 1-59880-001-9
ISBN-13: 978-1-59880-001-2
ISSN: 1936-2978

Printing History
1st Edition – November 2007
5 4 3 2 1

Text © 2007 by Laura Reiley
Maps © 2007 by Avalon Travel Publishing, Inc.
All rights reserved.

Some photos and illustrations are used by permission
and are the property of the original copyright
owners.

Front cover photo: Cinderella's Castle at Night,
   © Disney
Title page photo: Spaceship Earth at Epcot, © Disney

Printed in the United States by Malloy, Inc.

Moon Handbooks and the Moon logo are the property
of Avalon Travel Publishing. All other marks and
logos depicted are the property of the original
owners. All rights reserved. No part of this book may
be translated or reproduced in any form, except brief
extracts by a reviewer for the purpose of a review,
without written permission of the copyright owner.

Although every effort was made to ensure that
the information was correct at the time of going
to press, the author and publisher do not assume
and hereby disclaim any liability to any party for any
loss or damage caused by errors, omissions, or any
potential travel disruption due to labor or financial
difficulty, whether such errors or omissions result
from negligence, accident, or any other cause.

KEEPING CURRENT

If you have a favorite gem you'd like to see included in the next edition, or see anything
that needs updating, clarification, or correction, please drop us a line. Send your
comments via email to feedback@moon.com, or use the address above.